Two week loan

Please return on or before the last
date stamped below.
Charges are made for late return.

IS 239/0799

INFORMATION SERVICES PO BOX 430, CARDIFF CF10 3XT

TRADE, FOREIGN POLICY AND DEFENCE IN EU CONSTITUTIONAL LAW

Trade, Foreign Policy and Defence in EU Constitutional Law

The Legal Regulation of sanctions, exports of dual-use goods and armaments

PANOS KOUTRAKOS

University of Durham

·HART·
PUBLISHING
OXFORD – PORTLAND
2001

Hart Publishing
Oxford and Portland, Oregon

Published in North America (US and Canada) by
Hart Publishing c/o
International Specialized Book Services
5804 NE Hassalo Street
Portland, Oregon
97213-3644
USA

Distributed in the Netherlands, Belgium and Luxembourg by
Intersentia, Churchillaan 108
B2900 Schoten
Antwerpen
Belgium

Hart Publishing is a specialist legal publisher based in Oxford, England.
To order further copies of this book or to request a list of other
publications please write to:

Hart Publishing, Salter's Boatyard,
Folly Bridge, Abingdon Road, Oxford OX1 4LB
Telephone: +44 (0)1865 245533 or Fax: +44 (0)1865 794882
e-mail: mail@hartpub.co.uk
WEBSITE: http//www.hartpub.co.uk

British Library Cataloguing in Publication Data
Data Available
ISBN 1–84113–166–0 (hardback)

Typeset by Hope Services (Abingdon) Ltd.
Printed and bound in Great Britain by
Biddles Ltd, www.biddles.co.uk

Στους γονείς μου

Acknowledgements

This book is based on a doctoral thesis submitted to the University of Birmingham in June 1999. I am grateful to my supervisor, Professor Anthony M. Arnull for his thoughtful supervision, guidance and encouragement.

I would also like to thank my examiners, Professor Alan Dashwood and Dr Julian Lonbay, for their comments.

The law is stated as at the end of June 2000.

Outline Table of Contents

Contents

Tables of Equivalences referred to in Article 12 of the Treaty of Amsterdam

Previous numbering	New numbering	Previous numbering	New numbering
Article A	Article 1	Article J. 17	Article 27
Article B	Article 2	Article J. 18	Article 28
Article C	Article 3	Article K. I	Article 29
Article D	Article 4	Article K.2	Article 30
Article E	Article 5	Article K.3	Article 31
Article F	Article 6	Article K.4	Article 32
Article F.1	Article 7	Article K.5	Article 33
Article G	Article 8	Article K.6	Article 34
Article H	Article 9	Article K.7	Article 35
		Article K. 8	Article 36
Article I	Article 10	Article K.9	Article 37
Article J.1	Article 11	Article K. 10	Article 38
Article J.2	Article 12	Article K. 11	Article 39
Article J.3	Article 13	Article K. 12	Article 40
Article JA	Article 14	Article K. 13	Article 41
Article J.5	Article 15	Article K. 14	Article 42
Article J.6	Article 16	Article K. 15	Article 43
Article J.7	Article 17	Article K. 16	Article 44
Article J.8	Article 18	Article K. 17	Article 45
Article J.9	Article 19	Article L	Article 46
Article J. 10	Article 20	Article M	Article 47
Article J. I I	Article 21	Article N	Article 48
Article J. 12	Article 22	Article O	Article 49
Article J. 13	Article 23	Article P	Article 50
Article J. 14	Article 24	Article Q	Article 51
Article J. 15	Article 25	Article R	Article 52
Article J. 16	Article 26	Article S	Article 53

B. TREATY ESTABLISHING THE EUROPEAN COMMUNITY

Previous numbering	*New numbering*	*Previous numbering*	*New numbering*
Article 1	Article I	Article 19 (repealed)	—
Article 2	Article 2	Article 20 (repealed)	—
Article 3	Article 3	Article 21 (repealed)	—
Article 3a	Article 4	Article 22 (repealed)	—
Article 3b	Article 5	Article 22 (repealed)	—
Article 3c	Article 6	Article 23 (repealed)	—
Article 4	Article 7	Article 24 (repeated)	—
Article 4a	Article 8	Article 25 (repealed)	—
Article 4b	Article 9	Article 26 (repealed)	—
Article 5	Article 10	Article 27 (repealed)	—
Article 5a	Article 11	Article 28	Article 26
Article 6	Article 12	Article 29	Article 27
Article 6a	Article 13	Article 30	Article 28
Article 7 (repealed)	—	Article 31 (repealed)	—
Article 7a	Article 14	Article 32 (repealed)	—
Article 7b (repealed)	—	Article 33 (repealed)	—
Article 7c	Article 15	Article 34	Article 29
Article 7d	Article 16	Article 35 (repealed)	—
Article 8	Article 17	Article 36	Article 30
Article 8a	Article 18	Article 37	Article 31
Article 8b	Article 19	Article 38	Article 32
Article 8c	Article 20	Article 39	Article 33
Article 8d	Article 21	Article 40	Article 34
Article 8e	Article 22	Article 41	Article 35
		Article 42	Article 36
PART THREE	PART THREE	Article 43	Article 37
Article 9	Article 23	Article 44 (repealed)	—
Article 10	Article 24	Article 45 (repealed)	—
Article 11 (repealed)	—	Article 46	Article 38
Section I (deleted)		Article 47 (repealed)	—
Article 12	Article 25	Article 48	Article 39
Article 13 (repealed)	—	Article 49	Article 40
Article 14 (repealed)	—	Article 50	Article 41
Article 15 (repealed)	—	Article 51	Article 42
Article 16 (repealed)	—	Article 52	Article 43
Article 17 (repealed)	—	Article 53 (repealed)	—
Section 2 (deleted)	—	Article 54	Article 44
Article 18 (repealed)	—	Article 55	Article 45

Previous numbering	*New numbering*	*Previous numbering*	*New numbering*
Article 56	Article 46	Article 79	Article 75
Article 57	Article 47	Article 80	Article 76
Article 58	Article 48	Article 81	Article 77
Article 59	Article 49	Article 82	Article 78
Article 60	Article 50	Article 83	Article 79
Article 61	Article 51	Article 84	Article 80
Article 62 (repealed)	—	Article 85	Article 81
Article 63	Article 52	Article 86	Article 82
Article 64	Article 53	Article 87	Article 83
Article 65	Article 54	Article 88	Article 84
Article 66	Article 55	Article 89	Article 85
Article 67 (repealed)	—	Article 90	Article 86
Article 68 (repealed)	—	Section 2 (deleted)	—
Article 69 (repealed)	—	Article 91 (repealed)	—
Article 70 (repealed)	—	Article 92	Article 87
Article 71 (repealed)	—	Article 93	Article 88
Article 72 (repealed)	—	Article 94	Article 89
Article 73 (repealed)	—	Article 95	Article 90
Article 73a (repealed)	—	Article 96	Article 91
Article 73b	Article 56	Article 97 (repealed)	—
Article 73c	Article 57	Article 98	Article 92
Article 73d	Article 58	Article 99	Article 93
Article 73e (repealed)	—	Article 100	Article 94
Article 73f	Article 59	Article 100a	Article 95
Article 73g	Article 60	Article 100b (repealed)	—
Article 73h (repealed)	—	Article 100c (repealed)	—
Article 73i	Article 61	Article 100d (repealed)	—
Article 73j	Article 62	Article 101	Article 96
Article 73k	Article 63	Article 102	Article 97
Article 731 (*)	Article 64	Article 102a	Article 98
Article 73m	Article 65	Article 103	Article 99
Article 73n	Article 66	Article 103a	Article 100
Article 73o	Article 67	Article 104	Article 101
Article 73p	Article 68	Article 104a	Article 102
Article 73q	Article 69	Article 104b	Article 103
Article 74	Article 70	Article 104c	Article 104
Article 75	Article 71	Article 105	Article 105
Article 76	Article 72	Article 105a	Article 106
Article 77	Article 73	Article 106	Article 107
Article 78	Article 74	Article 107	Article 108

Previous numbering	*New numbering*	*Previous numbering*	*New numbering*
Article 108	Article 109	Article 123	Article 146
Article 108a	Article 110	Article 124	Article 147
Article 109	Article 111	Article 125	Article 148
Article 109a	Article 112	Article 126	Article 149
Article 109b	Article 113	Article 127	Article 150
Article 109c	Article 114	Article 128	Article 151
Article 109d	Article 115	Article 129	Article 152
Article 109e	Article 116	Article 129a	Article 153
Article 109f	Article 117	Article 129b	Article 154
Article 109g	Article 118	Article 129c	Article 155
Article 109h	Article 119	Article 129d	Article 156
Article 109i	Article 120	Article 130	Article 157
Article 109j	Article 121		
Article 109k	Article 122	Article 130a	Article 158
Article 1091	Article 123	Article 130b	Article 159
Article 109m	Article 124	Article 130c	Article 160
Article 109n	Article 125	Article 130d	Article 161
Article 109o	Article 126	Article 130e	Article 162
Article 109p	Article 127	Article 130f	Article 163
Article 109q	Article 128	Article 130g	Article 164
Article 109r	Article 129	Article 130h	Article 165
Article 109s	Article 130	Article 130i	Article 166
Article 110	Article 131	Article 130j	Article 167
Article 111 (repealed)	—	Article 130k	Article 168
Article 112	Article 132	Article 1301	Article 169
Article 113	Article 133	Article 130m	Article 170
Article 114 (repealed)	—	Article 130n	Article 171
Article 115	Article 134	Article 130o	Article 172
Article 116 (repealed)	—	Article 130p	Article 173
Article 116	Article 135	Article 130q (repealed)	—
Article 117	Article 136	Article 130r	Article 174
Article 118	Article 137	Article 130s	Article 175
Article 118a	Article 138	Article 130t	Article 176
Article 118b	Article 139	Article 130u	Article 177
Article 118c	Article 140	Article 130v	Article 178
Article 119	Article 141	Article 130w	Article 179
Article 119a	Article 142	Article 130x	Article 180
Article 120	Article 143	Article 130y	Article 181
Article 121	Article 144	Article 131	Article 182
Article 122	Article 145	Article 132	Article 183

Previous numbering	New numbering	Previous numbering	New numbering
Article 133	Article 184	Article 168	Article 224
Article 134	Article 185	Article 168a	Article 225
Article 135	Article 186	Article 169	Article 226
Article 136	Article 187	Article 170	Article 227
Article 136a	Article 188	Article 171	Article 228
Article 137	Article 189	Article 172	Article 229
Article 138	Article 190	Article 173	Article 230
Article 138a	Article 191	Article 174	Article 231
Article 138b	Article 192	Article 175	Article 232
Article 138c	Article 193	Article 176	Article 233
Article 138d	Article 194	Article 177	Article 234,
Article 138e	Article 195	Article 178	Article 235
Article 139	Article 196	Article 179	Article 236
Article 140	Article 197	Article 180	Article 237
Article 141	Article 198	Article 181	Article 238
Article 142	Article 199	Article 182	Article 239
Article 143	Article 200	Article 183	Article 240
Article 144	Article 201	Article 184	Article 241
Article 145	Article 202	Article 185	Article 242
Article 146	Article 203	Article 186	Article 243
Article 147	Article 204	Article 187	Article 244
Article 148	Article 205	Article 188	Article 245
Article 149 (repealed)	—	Article 188a	Article 246
Article 150	Article 206	Article 188b	Article 247
Article 151	Article 207	Article 188c	Article 248
Article 152	Article 208	Article 189	Article 249
Article 153	Article 209	Article 189a	Article 250
Article 154	Article 2 10	Article 189b	Article 251
Article 155	Article 211	Article 189c	Article 252
Article 156	Article 212	Article 190	Article 253
Article 157	Article 213	Article 191	Article 254
Article 158	Article 214	Article 191a	Article 255
Article 159	Article 215	Article 192	Article 256
Article 160	Article 216	Article 193	Article 257
Article 161	Article 217	Article 194	Article 258
Article 162	Article 218	Article 195	Article 259
Article 163	Article 219	Article 196	Article 260
Article 164	Article 220	Article 197	Article 261
Article 165	Article 221	Article 198	Article 262
Article 166	Article 222	Article 198a	Article 263
Article 167	Article 223	Article 198b	Article 264

Previous numbering	New numbering	Previous numbering	New numbering
Article 198c	Article 265	Article 220	Article 293
Article 198d	Article 266	Article 221	Article 294
Article 198e	Article 267	Article 222	Article 295
Article 199	Article 268	Article 223	Article 296
Article 200 (repealed)	—	Article 224	Article 297
Article 201	Article 269	Article 225	Article 298
Article 201a	Article 270	Article 226 (repealed)	—
Article 202	Article 271	Article 227	Article 299
Article 203	Article 272	Article 228	Article 300
Article 204	Article 273	Article 228a	Article 301
Article 205	Article 274	Article 229	Article 302
Article 205a	Article 275	Article 230	Article 303
Article 206	Article 276	Article 231	Article 304
Article 206a (repealed)	—	Article 232	Article 305
Article 207	Article 277	Article 233	Article 306
Article 208	Article 278	Article 234	Article 307
Article 209	Article 279	Article 235	Article 308
Article 209a	Article 280	Article 236	Article 309
Article 2 10	Article 281	Article 237 (repealed)	
Article 211	Article 282	Article 238	Article 310
Article 212	Article 283	Article 239	Article 311
Article 213	Article 284	Article 240	Article 312
Article 213a	Article 285	Article 241 (repealed)	—
Article 213b	Article 286	Article 242 (repealed)	—
Article 214	Article 287	Article 243 (repealed)	—
Article 215	Article 288	Article 244 (repealed)	—
Article 216	Article 289	Article 245 (repealed)	—
Article 217	Article 290	Article 246 (repealed)	—
Article 218	Article 291	Article 247	Article 313
Article 219	Article 292	Article 248	Article 314

Table of Cases

1. INTERNATIONAL COURT OF JUSTICE

2. EUROPEAN COURT OF JUSTICE

Table of Legislation

1. INTERNATIONAL

2. EUROPEAN

EC Directives

EC Regulations

EC Decisions

1

Introduction

The role of international actors on the international scene is the outcome of a continuous and often implied interaction between factors as diverse as the regime of governance of the entity in question, the distribution of internal authorities, its economic power, its geographical position and the regional and international political circumstances. This is even more so in the case of the European Union, whose *sui generis* legal character renders the conduct of its external relations dependent upon a web of legal rules, political realities and economic conditions of both national and supranational nature whose influence cannot always be accurately ascertained.

The Treaty on European Union rendered the conduct of EU external relations subject to two legally distinct sets of rules, those contained in the EC Treaty and those laid down in Title V of the TEU on Common Foreign and Security Policy, which, under Article 3 TEU, are intended to operate within "a single institutional framework". This introductory chapter aims to outline the main characteristics of these frameworks, define the scope of this book and set out the problems to be addressed.

1. THE CANVAS: THE TWO PILLARS, EUROPEAN COMMUNITY AND COMMON FOREIGN AND SECURITY POLICY

The pillar structure of the European Union reflects the fact that the Community framework and the Common Foreign and Security Policy constitute two legal frameworks of distinct material scope and legal characteristics. As far as the European Community is concerned, the Treaty of Rome did not confine the establishment of the common market to the relations between the Member States. Instead, Article 281 attributed to the EC legal personality and hence enabled it to act autonomously in the international legal order. The Treaty expressly confers on the Community the power, within specific areas, to conclude international agreements,[1] foster co-operation at the international level[2]

---

[1] Namely regarding the Common Commercial Policy (CCP) (Art. 133), environmental policy (Art. 174(4)), development co-operation (Art. 181), matters related to monetary or foreign exchange regime (Art. 111(3)), research and technological development (Art. 170) and association agreements (Art. 310).

[2] In the areas of education (Art. 149(3)), vocational training (Art. 150(3)) and youth, culture (Art. 151(3)), public health (Art. 152(3)). The Community may also co-operate with third countries in relation to the trans-European networks (TENs) (Art. 155(3)).

and ensure the maintenance of all appropriate relations with international organisations.[3] In addition to its expressly established external activities, the Community is impliedly competent to conclude international agreements in various other areas. The legal foundation of this implied competence is the so-called "doctrine of parallelism" put forward by the European Court of Justice. According to this doctrine, the regulation of a specific matter by the Community entails the competence of the latter to engage in activities aimed at the external regulation of the same matter.[4] The role of the European Court of Justice in the development of the external relations of the Community has been pivotal. In accordance with its Article 220 EC duty to "ensure that the law is observed", it has defined the scope of the Community's express powers, the content of its implied powers, the extent to which it is exclusively competent and the conditions under which it is to share competence with the Member States. In doing so, the Court has been aware of the national political sensitivities underlying the conduct of external trade relations.

In contrast to the role of the Court in the development of the external relations of the Community, the CFSP constitutes the culmination of various influences of a non-legal character. The Member States started to co-operate in the area of foreign policy in 1970. In doing so, they gradually established the European Political Co-operation (EPC), a framework of objectives and procedures aiming at co-ordinating the foreign policies of the Member States and ultimately enhancing their influence on the international scene. The EPC acquired Treaty status when its rules were laid down in Title III of the Single European Act (SEA), whereby the commitment of the Member States to co-ordinate their foreign policies was given. Finally, the collective involvement of the Member States in international affairs was formalised in the second pillar of the EU by the TEU. The CFSP aims "to assert the identity [of the EU] on the international scene"[5] but, unlike the EC, the EU is not granted express legal personality. The scope of the CFSP is defined in very broad terms. Under Article 11 TEU, it is "to safeguard the common values, fundamental interests, independence and integrity of the Union", "to strengthen the security of the Union in all ways", "to preserve peace and strengthen international security", "to promote international co-operation" and to "develop and consolidate democracy and the rule of law, and respect for human rights and fundamental freedoms". It becomes clear that all matters of foreign policy are covered by the second pillar of the EU. They are to be pursued through, on the one hand, a clearly defined national obligation to participate in the formulation and implementation of a common stance on the international scene and, on the other hand, collective measures consisting mainly of common positions and joint actions.

---

[3] Art. 301.

[4] This principle was first elaborated in the landmark Case 22/70 *Commission* v. *Council* (ERTA) [1971] ECR 263, [1971] CMLR 355. The exact scope of this principle, along with the issue of the exclusivity of the Community competence, has been elaborated by the Court in its subsequent judgments and Opinions and become subject of wide academic analysis.

[5] Art. 2 TEU.

In addition to their material scope, the legal characteristics of the EC and the CFSP are also different. Both the Treaty and the Court's jurisprudence have developed a corpus of principles which underlie the operation of the Community framework. They can be generally typified by the extensive recourse to majority voting in the Council regarding external activities in general and the Common Commercial Policy under Article 133 in particular, the clearly defined control exercised by the European Parliament and legal supervision by the Court. In contrast to these supranational characteristics of the EC, the second pillar is broadly defined in intergovernmental terms: the Council of Ministers is the dominant institution,[6] unanimity prevails,[7] the role of the Parliament is significantly limited[8] and the jurisdiction of the Court is expressly excluded.[9]

2. THE SCOPE OF THE BOOK

This book will focus on the relationship between the Community pillar and CFSP in the light of the interactions between trade and foreign policy. The increasing recourse to trade measures in order to achieve foreign policy objectives raises various legal issues in the context of the European Union. These touch upon a series of interrelated questions of immense significance: the scope of the Community's exclusive competence over its Common Commercial Policy, the right of the Member States to conduct their foreign policy as fully sovereign subjects of international law and the extent to which the Court may exercise its jurisdiction over trade measures with fundamental foreign policy dimensions. Ultimately, the interaction between the EC and CFSP raises the question whether the interdependence between trade and foreign policy may be regulated in a legally sensible and effective way within the tripartite structure of the European Union.

However, one general point needs to be made. The distinction between trade and foreign policy is not as rigid as the establishment of the materially and legally distinct EC and CFSP may seem to imply. The link between the adoption of trade measures and the conduct of foreign policy may be ascertained at both political and legal level. At the political level, the establishment of the EPC and the development of the common foreign policy were due to a significant extent to the expectation, shared by both Member States and other international actors, of the Community's trade power to be accompanied by an equal political influence on the international scene. At the legal level, foreign policy considerations have influenced the Community's policies as a matter of practice for a long time. This is clearly illustrated by the human rights clauses inserted in

---

[6] Art. 13 TEU.
[7] Art. 23 TEU.
[8] Art. 21 TEU.
[9] Art. 46 TEU.

co-operation and association agreements between the Community and third countries. In general, as Advocate General Jacobs argued in *Centro-Com*,[10] many commercial measures may have a general foreign policy dimension in so far as they cannot be dissociated from the political context of the relations between the EU and other parties. It follows that a general study seeking to ascertain the precise extent to which trade measures serve foreign policy objectives would be fruitless for foreign policy objectives and commercial policy aims are to a great extent indistinguishable.

Therefore, by either influencing the adoption of commercial measures or instrumentalising trade measures for political objectives, it is accepted *a priori* that trade and foreign policy are to be linked and are, indeed, linked as a matter of practice under the existing EU order. However, there are cases with a more distinct foreign policy component which touches directly upon the relationship between the EC and CFSP. This book will focus on three such cases, namely (a) the imposition of sanctions on third countries, (b) the legal regulation of exports of dual-use goods and (c) that of armaments. The reason for this choice is the fact that the above aspects of the economic aspects of security are indicative of different ways in which an inter-pillar approach may be adopted. In the case of trade sanctions, Article 301 EC provides that they are imposed on the basis of both a Title V measure and a Council Regulation. The legal regime governing the exports of dual-use goods follows the same model, given that it is based on a Council Decision adopted under the second pillar and a Council Regulation adopted under the Common Commercial Policy; however, direct though this interaction may be, it is significantly distinct from that underlying the imposition of trade sanctions, for both the scope and the *modus operandi* of the Community measure are incorporated in the CFSP measure. Finally, the interaction between the EC and CFSP underlying the legal regulation of armaments is characterised by a paradox: on the one hand, it has long been perceived as non-existent, given the deeply entrenched view that the "sensitive character" of these products placed them at the margins of the Community legal order; on the other hand, and in the light of political and economic developments, the Commission has put forward comprehensive proposals towards the legal regulation of armaments on the basis of a variety of Community and CFSP measures, hence suggesting a direct interaction between the first two pillars.

While the above reasons explain why the legal regulation of sanctions, exports of dual-use goods and armaments were chosen as typical examples of how the interdependence between trade and foreign policy touches upon the relationship between the EC and CFSP, they also justify the title of this book. Indeed, the inter-pillar approach adopted under the Treaty, in the case of sanctions, and secondary legislation, in the case of exports of dual-use goods, makes clear that there is a set of legal rules established under both the first two pillars; the more

---

[10] Case C–124/96 *The Queen* v. *HM Treasury and Bank of England ex parte Centro-Com Srl* [1997] ECR I–81 at para. 41.

intrinsic their relationship, the more developed the system of EU law will become. Therefore, the argument, made in 1995, that "[t]here is no coherent corpus of law that deserves the name "EU law"[11] will need to be reconsidered.

3. THE STRUCTURE OF THE BOOK

Before addressing the legal problems posed by the direct interactions between Community law and CFSP, as typified by the legal regulation of trade sanctions, exports of dual-use goods and armaments, it is essential to analyse the legal characteristics of the second pillar. This task will be carried out in the second chapter of this book which will outline the genesis and development not only of the CFSP, but also of its precursor, namely European Political Co-operation. The analysis of the rules provided in the second pillar, most recently amended by the Amsterdam Treaty, will reveal three main characteristics of the legal framework within which the European Union has always conducted its foreign policy: its *sui generis* character, its incremental development and dynamic nature. Moreover, it will point out the extreme emphasis put by the Member States on procedural and institutional arrangements rather than the development of a political climate which would enable these arrangements to be fully used. These characteristics are directly relevant to the understanding of the main principle underlying the framework of the European Union, namely the provision for a single institutional framework ensuring the consistency and the continuity of the activities of the Union while respecting and building upon the *acquis communautaire*.

The third chapter will provide an overview of the legal issues raised by the imposition of trade sanctions against third countries prior to the Maastricht Treaty. Having, first, being imposed by means of national measures, sanctions were then implemented on the basis of the Common Commercial Policy following a non-Community measure. Analysis of this practice will indicate that the adoption of sanctions under Article 133 EC was based on practical considerations rather than a view that they genuinely fell within the Common Commercial Policy. In effect, trade sanctions, while being imposed under old Article 113 EC, had been dissociated in legal terms from the Common Commercial Policy, hence raising serious legal problems.

Viewed from this perspective, Article 301 EC introduced by the Maastricht Treaty is not a great leap towards ensuring the effectiveness of sanctions, for it formalised their adoption on the basis of an inter-pillar approach. The fourth chapter will analyse the legal problems raised by this approach and suggest that they are due to the inability of the institutional actors of the Union to agree upon questions of a substantive nature rather than the inherent limits of the inter-pillar approach underpinning Article 301 EC.

[11] S Weatherill, *Law and Integration in the European Union* (Oxford: Clarendon Press, 1995) at 32.

The fifth chapter will analyse a variation to the inter-pillar approach as adopted in the case of the common regime on exports of dual-use goods to third countries. The analysis of the relevant rules will indicate not only that the inter-pillar approach on which they are based is distinct from that underpinning Article 301 EC, but also that it is fundamentally flawed. Therefore, it will be argued that, consistently with the Commission proposals on its amendment, the Community regime on exports of dual-use goods should be based solely on Article 133 EC.

The question which then arises is whether the legal problems raised by the application of the inter-pillar approach to trade sanctions and the possible retention of that underpinning the common rules on exports of dual-use goods may be effectively addressed within the tripartite framework of the European Union. The sixth chapter will argue that the Court's approach to exports of dual-use goods is progressive and functional in nature: it ensures that neither is Community law undermined by non-Community instruments, nor is the competence of the Member States to conduct their foreign policy impinged.

This approach is part of a fully-fledged construction of the interactions between the EC and CFSP: the analysis of the case law on sanctions in the seventh chapter will indicate that the Court, on the one hand, construes the first two pillars as a functional whole whose consistency is fully based on the principles upon which the European Union is based, while, on the one hand, shows full awareness of the political reality amongst the Member States.

The eighth chapter will approach the problems that the legal regime of armaments raises in relation to delimitation of powers between the Community institutions and the Member States. It will refute the deeply entrenched perception of armaments as entirely beyond the Community legal order and will provide an interpretation of the relevant Treaty provision, namely Article 296(1)(b) EC consistently with both its wording and the spirit of the Treaty; furthermore, it will suggest the existence of an intrinsic link between this provision and the CFSP.

Drawing upon the above analysis, the ninth chapter will criticise the legal formula adopted by the Council in the case of the EU code of conduct on arms. On the other hand, it will outline how the Commission proposals on the adoption of a variety of Community and CFSP measures underline that an inter-pillar approach may transform the rhetoric of a "single institutional framework" serving the Union into a reality while ensuring the consistency between the pillars and respect for the *acquis communautaire*.

Finally, the tenth chapter will underline the thread that links the arguments put forward in this book together. It will argue that the establishment of the Union on distinct, albeit interdependent, legal frameworks does not in itself undermine the effectiveness of its activities; an inter-pillar approach viewing both the EC and CFSP as parts of a functional whole may contribute to the attainment of the objectives of the Union, build upon the *acquis communautaire* and respect the right of the Member States to conduct their foreign policy as fully sovereign subjects of international law.

2

The Common Foreign and Security Policy of the European Union

1. INTRODUCTION

The legal framework provided by Title V TEU is an essential component of the analysis of whether the legal regulation of the economic aspects of security, typified in the cases of sanctions against third countries, exports of dual-use goods and armaments can be achieved in a legally sensible and effective system within the constitutional order established under the Treaty on European Union. The aim of this chapter is not only to provide an overview of the legal rules of the second pillar and their application so far, but also to identify the main characteristics which have underpinned its development. This task is of central significance, for the main features of the second pillar have characterised not only the development of the precursor of the Common Foreign and Security Policy, namely European Political Co-operation, but also that of the European Union itself. It is for this reason that an analysis of the legal rules provided under the second pillar requires an understanding of the history of the foreign policy framework of the Union.

This chapter consists of four parts. The first outlines the genesis and development of European Political Co-operation and underlines the main characteristics of the foreign policy conducted under it. The second part deals with the provisions of Title V of the Maastricht Treaty and the activities carried out under it. The third outlines the amendments to Title V introduced by the Amsterdam Treaty and identifies the main characteristic of the foreign policy system of the Union. The fourth part examines the institutional, administrative and substantive interactions between the EC and CFSP in the light of the principles laid down in the TEU, namely a single institutional framework which ensures the consistency of the activities carried out by the Union and respects and builds upon the *acquis communautaire*.

2. THE PAST FRAMEWORK: GENESIS, DEVELOPMENT AND TREATY RECOGNITION OF EUROPEAN POLITICAL CO-OPERATION

The decision-making process, the institutional structure and the instruments of the Common Foreign and Security Policy were not established under Title V

TEU in a political and legal vacuum. Even before the inception of the EEC, attempts were made to enable Member States to present a common stance on the international scene. The aim of enabling the Member States to assume an important role in international relations was due to various factors,[1] the most important being the need for a political role equivalent to the combined economic role of the Member States and the high expectations of the Member States held by other international actors.

The development of the foreign policy framework under which the Member States would, prior to CFSP, formulate and put forward a common stance on the international scene can be divided into three phases. The first one (1950–70) is characterised by the genesis of a foreign affairs system for the Member States as a result of the failure of the European Defence Community. The second period (1970–86) consists of the establishment of European Political Co-operation and its development as a political framework without Treaty status. The third phase (1986–93) is characterised by the incorporation of EPC in the Single European Act.

This chapter does not aim to analyse either the organisation or the record of EPC.[2] Instead, it will suggest that the main principles underlying the institutional structure of EPC constitute early reflections of the principles underlying Title V TEU. In this respect, three points will be put forward. First, the framework under which the Member States attempted to co-ordinate their positions on the international scene was conceived as distinct from the Community framework. Secondly, the Member States realised very soon and well before the establishment of the pillar-based EU that foreign policy could not be conducted independently of trade policy and hence the Community legal framework. Thirdly, having acknowledged the previous point, the Member States, on the one hand, stated as frequently as they could and in the most unequivocal terms the distinction between the EPC and the then EEC and, on the other hand, sought to establish administrative measures in order to ensure consistency between the two frameworks.

2.1. Failure leading to genesis (1950–70): foreign policy prior to European Political Co-operation

The most significant event in the sphere of foreign policy in the first two decades of European integration is the formulation and rejection of the European

---

[1] See L Tsoukalis, "Looking into the Crystal Ball" in L Tsoukalis (ed.), *The European Community, Past, Present and Future* (Oxford: Blackwell, 1983) 229 at 235.

[2] For authoritative analyses of EPC, see D Allen, R Rummel, and W Wessels (eds.), *European Political Cooperation: Towards a Foreign Policy for Western Europe* (London: Butterworths, 1982); M Holland (ed.), *The Future of European Political Cooperation: Essays on Theory and Practice* (London: Macmillan, 1991); P Ifestos, *European Political Cooperation—Towards a Framework of Supranational Diplomacy?* (Aldershot: Avebery, 1987); S Nuttall, *European Political Cooperation* (Oxford: Clarendon Press, 1992); P de Schoutheete de Tervarent, *La Coopération Politique Européenne* (2nd edn., Brussels: Editions Labor, 1986).

Defence Community (EDC).[3] Based on a French proposal, the Treaty was signed by the original Member States of the European Coal and Steel Community in May 1952[4] and required the Parliamentary Assembly of the ECSC, which, after the addition of nine deputies, was named "*Ad Hoc Assembly*", to formulate a proposal for a Political Community.[5] This proposal suggested the creation of a European army organised and supervised by a single institution answerable to a European Assembly. This project, supranational *par excellence*, was rejected by the French Parliament in 1954.[6]

2.2. The informal phase of EPC (1970–86)

Before acquiring Treaty status by incorporation into the Single European Act, EPC had been developed on the basis of Reports presented by the Ministers of Foreign Affairs of the Member States to the Heads of State and Government.[7] These Reports set out, with varying degrees of clarity and precision, the objectives and the institutional framework under which the Member States attempted to formulate their stance on the international scene. In many cases, they simply formalised existing procedures.

The Luxembourg Report[8] was the first formal attempt of the Member States to set out a mechanism of co-operation in foreign affairs. The need for the international presence of the then EEC to be equivalent to its economic role was stressed as the main reason for the establishment of a common foreign policy mechanism. Hence, a link, albeit loose and implied, between foreign policy and trade was acknowledged. EPC was conceived as being of potentially unlimited scope,[9] whereas its modest objectives were confined to co-ordination of national views. These objectives were to be achieved through equally modest consultation mechanisms confined to meetings between Foreign Affairs Ministers and

---

[3] See R Aron and D Lerner (eds.), *France Defeats EDC* (London: Thames and Hudson, 1957) and E Furdson, *The European Defence Community: A History* (London: Macmillan, 1980).

[4] For the text of the Treaty, see European Parliament, *Selection of texts concerning institutional matters of the Community from 1950 to 1982* (Luxembourg: Office for Official Publications of the European Communities, 1983).

[5] See J Mischo, "Les efforts en vue d'organiser sur le plan juridique la coopération des Etats membres de la Communauté en matière de politique étrangère" in F Capotorti (ed.), *Du droit international de l'intégration: liber amicorum Pierre Pescatore* (Baden-Baden: Nomos, 1987) 441 at 442.

[6] After this setback, the most important event in this period consisted of the "*plan Fouchet*", named after the French ambassador presiding over an intergovernmental commission charged to prepare the plan of a Union of States; in contrast to the European Defence Community, the *plan Fouchet* was based on an intergovernmental conception of the Union.

[7] See D Allen and W Wallace, "European Political Cooperation: The Historical and Contemporary Background" in Allen, Rummel and Wessels (eds), *supra* note 2 at 21 *et seq.*

[8] It was adopted on 27 Oct. 1970; see *European Political Co-operation (EPC)* (5th edn., Bonn: Press and Information Office of the Federal Government, 1988) at 24 *et seq.*

[9] According to Art. IV, "Member States may propose any question of their choice for political consultation".

the then established Political Committee.[10] The establishment of EPC as distinct from the EC is reflected by the significantly limited role of the Commission, according to which it "will be invited to make known its views should the work of the Ministers affect the activities of the European Communities".[11]

The subsequent Copenhagen Report[12] reaffirmed the modest and vague objectives of EPC,[13] confirmed procedural improvements of the consultation mechanism which had already been applied[14] and construed the role of the Member States under EPC in the broadest terms.[15] The important feature of the Copenhagen Report, for the purposes of this study, is the express recognition of the principles which would underlie all subsequent foreign policy mechanisms among the Member States. On the one hand, it was made clear that EPC was of a different legal and organisational nature from the Community; under Article 10 of the Copenhagen Report, EPC "is distinct from and additional to the activities of the institutions of the Community which are based on the juridical commitments undertaken by the Member States in the Treaty of Rome. Both sets of machinery have the aim of contributing to the development of European unification." On the other hand, it was implied that, in the light of "the widening scope of the European Communities and the intensification of political co-operation at all levels",[16] the one framework could not operate in total isolation from the other; hence, the development of EPC should "keep in mind . . . the implications for and the effects of, in the field of international politics, Community policies under construction."[17] This provision seems to constitute an embryonic form of the consistency requirement provided in Title V TEU. The distinction between the two frameworks is reflected in procedural terms in

[10] The Political Committee is composed of the directors of political affairs of the Member States. Apart from the mechanism which would achieve co-ordination of national views, the Luxembourg Report provided for the involvement of the EP in order to meet the need for democratic legitimacy. Therefore, on the one hand, informal biannual meetings between the Council and the Political Commission of the EP were provided for and, on the other hand, the chairman of the Council was required to address a communication on progress achieved under EPC: see Art. VI and Part III(4).

[11] Art. V.

[12] It was adopted on 23 July 1973; see *supra* note 8 at 34 *et seq.*

[13] Namely "promoting the harmonisation of . . . views and the alignment of . . . positions and, wherever it appears possible and desirable, joint action": *ibid.* at 35.

[14] Namely, more frequent meetings of the Council and the Political Committee, establishment of a Group of Correspondents set to study problems of organisation and general nature, working groups comprised by national officials, a communication system establishing direct contact between national foreign ministries, more frequent meetings with the Political Committee of the EP. In addition, the Copenhagen Report attempted to clarify the priorities of EPC by stating that "the purpose of consultation is to seek common policies on practical problems" and "the subject dealt must concern European interests whether in Europe itself or elsewhere where the adoption of a common position is necessary or desirable": see *supra* note 8 at 41–2.

[15] Under Art. 11, "each State undertakes as a general rule not to take up final positions without prior consultation with its partners within the framework of the political co-operation".

[16] Art. 10.

[17] Art. 12(b). A practical consequence of administrative nature was the right of the Ministers, presumably operating under the EPC framework rather than in their capacity as the Council of the EEC, may instruct the EPC machinery to prepare studies on political aspects of problems under examination within the EEC framework: see Art. 12(c).

the provision requiring the Presidency to inform the Council through the President of COREPER of conclusions reached under EPC. This administrative measure indicates the Member States' concern to avoid any suggestion that the relation between the two frameworks might be seen as impinging upon the purely intergovernmental nature of EPC. In practical terms, this often led to absurd situations. A striking example is a meeting of the Foreign Ministers in 1973 which took place in Copenhagen in the morning, the agenda being EPC issues; the Foreign Ministers were not allowed, by their French colleague, to discuss Community issues in that meeting and, instead, were forced to move to Brussels in the afternoon of the same day in order to discuss those issues as the Council of the European Communities.[18]

The third phase of the development of EPC beyond the Treaty is characterised by the London Report[19] which sets out the objectives of EPC in grander terms than the previous two Reports.[20] The London Report further underlined the duties of the Member States under EPC,[21] stated that joint action should be formulated more often and introduced or formalised various procedural improvements.[22] In relation to the present study, three points need to be made. The first one is to note the increasing realisation of the significance of the relationship between EPC and the Community. While the Copenhagen Report acknowledged the political dimension of Community policies, the London Report implied the use of Community instruments for foreign policy objectives. In its preamble, it was stated that "the maintenance and development of Community policies in accordance with the Treaties will be beneficial to a more effective co-ordination in the field of foreign policy and will expand the range of instruments at the disposal of the [then] Ten".[23] Secondly, the consistency requirement, already implied in the Copenhagen Report, was repeated and its application was entrusted to the Presidency.[24] In procedural terms, EPC

[18] R Stein, "European Political Cooperation (EPC) as a Component of the European Foreign Affairs System" (1983) 43 *ZaoRV* 49 at n. 14.

[19] Adopted on 13 Oct. 1981: see *supra* note 8 at 61 *et seq.*

[20] Member States must "play a role in the world appropriate to their combined influence", "increasingly seek to shape events and not merely to react to them" and "speak with one voice in international affairs": *ibid*. at 62–3.

[21] Member States were under a duty not to undertake national positions before recourse is had to the EPC consultation mechanism.

[22] Informal meetings between the Foreign Ministers, the so-called Gymnich meetings, were introduced, the role of the working groups was described in further detail, procedures for contacts with third countries were introduced, meetings between the heads of the diplomatic missions of Member States and the political director of the host Member State in capitals of the EC were formalised, officials from the Member States comprising the Troika were provided to assist the Presidency, the contacts between the Foreign Affairs Ministers and the EP were intensified at both formal and informal level. Finally, a crisis procedure was introduced, whereby the Political Committee or the Foreign Ministers and the Heads of Missions of the Member States in third countries could convene within 48 hours at the request of three Member States.

[23] *Supra* note 8 at 62–3.

[24] Under Art. 11, "[t]he Presidency will ensure that the discussion of the Community and the political Co-operation aspects of certain questions is co-ordinated if the subject matter requires this".

meetings were to be held on the occasion of Foreign Affairs Councils and, hence, the absurd results mentioned above were to be avoided. A clear indication that the Member States acknowledged the increasing interaction between EPC and the Community was provided in the upgrading of the role of the Commission.[25] Thirdly, the increasing contacts at all levels between the Member States under EPC produced a "consultation culture" which allowed the political and economic aspects of security to fall within the scope of EPC for the first time.[26]

The Solemn Declaration on European Union[27] recognised the need for common principles, objectives and interests of Member States to be defined, envisaged various procedural improvements[28] and acknowledged "the contribution [of] the EP . . . to the development of a co-ordinated foreign policy".[29] The distinction between EPC and the EC could have not been clarified more: "[w]ith a view to bringing the institutional apparatus of the Community and that of Political Co-operation closer together, the Council deals with matters for which it is competent under the Treaties in accordance with the procedures laid down by the latter, and its members will deal also, in accordance with the appropriate procedures, with all other areas of European Union, particularly matters coming within the scope of Political Co-operation".[30] The requirement of coherence between the two frameworks was repeated in the final provisions.[31] Finally, the co-ordination of national positions on the political and economic aspects of security of the Member States was put forward twice as a priority influencing the strengthening and development of EPC.

2.3. EPC under the Single European Act

Under Article 30 of the Single European Act, EPC became a Treaty-based mechanism.[32] In general terms, the commitment of the Member States was phrased

---

[25] Under Art. 11, "within the framework of the established rules and procedures the Ten attach importance to the Commission . . . being fully associated with Political Co-operation at all levels".

[26] Under Art. 11, they could be discussed subject to a "flexible and pragmatic approach".

[27] For the text of the Declaration, which was signed on 19 June 1983 see *supra* note 8 at 70 *et seq.*

[28] Closer co-operation between the missions of the Member States in third countries in relation to diplomatic and administrative matters. However, most importantly, the Solemn Declaration formalised the role of the European Council which, in relation to EPC, was to issue general political guidelines and ensure the consistency between different aspects of maters concerning EU.

[29] Art. 3.2.

[30] Art. 2.2.1.

[31] According to Art. 4.2, "European Union is being achieved by deepening and broadening the scope of European activities so that they coherently cover, albeit on a variety of legal bases, a growing proportion of Member States' mutual relations and of their external relations".

[32] For a commentary on Title III SEA see S Nuttall, "European Political Co-operation and the Single European Act" (1985) 5 *YEL* 203; S Perrakis, "L'incidence de l'Acte Unique Européen sur la Coopération des Douze en Matière de Politique Etrangère" (1988) XXXIV *AFDI* 807. For the various positions taken by the Member States under EPC between 1985 and 1993, see *European Political Co-operation Bulletin* (Luxembourg: Office for Official Publications of the European Communities).

in vague and ambiguous terms,[33] the main mechanism remained that of consultation and administrative improvements, the creation of a Secretariat in Brussels being the most significant, were introduced.[34]

With regard to its relationship with the Community legal framework, the principles which defined the character of EPC through its informal phase underlie Article 30 itself. Thus, its intergovernmental character, as opposed to that of the Community's, could not have been stressed more. Under the Preamble to the SEA, the European Union is to be implemented "on the basis, firstly, of the Communities operating in accordance with their own rules and, secondly, of European Political Co-operation among the Signatory States in the sphere of foreign policy".[35] Moreover, Article 1 stated that "[t]he European Communities and European Political Co-operation shall have as their objective to contribute together to making concrete progress towards European unity" and distinguishes the former, which "shall be founded on the Treaties . . . and on the subsequent Treaties and Acts modifying or supplementing them", from the latter which "shall be governed by Title III [of SEA]". In addition, Title III SEA made reference to "the High Contracting Parties" as opposed to "the Member States", wording similar to that of traditional international agreements and not to the unique character of the Treaty.[36] Hence, the exclusion of Article 30 from the Court's jurisdiction.[37]

The requirement of consistency, already a familiar theme in relation to the management of materially interdependent issues between EPC and EC, was reiterated and entrusted to the Presidency and the Commission "each within its own sphere of competence".[38] Finally, the High Contracting Parties were meant to have been "ready to co-ordinate their positions more closely on the political and economic aspects of security".[39]

[33] Under Art. 30(1), the High Contracting Parties were not obliged to "jointly formulate and implement a European foreign policy" but mainly to "endeavour" to do so; Art. 30(2)(c) also provided that they "shall ensure that common principles and objectives are gradually developed and defined". Moreover, "the determination of common policies shall constitute a point of reference for the policies of the High Contracting Parties" which "shall endeavour to avoid any action or position which impairs their effectiveness as a cohesive force in international relations or within international organizations" (Art. 30(2)(d)). In procedural terms, this commitment meant that they "shall, as far as possible, refrain from impeding the formation of a consensus and the joint action which this could produce" (Art. 30(3)(c)). Another facet of national commitments under EPC focused on international institutions and conferences in which "the High Contracting Parties shall endeavour to adapt" under Art. 30(7)(a).
[34] Under Art. 30(10)(g), its role was to assist the presidency in its duties under EPC. It is interesting that a British proposal to define its role as "assisting the Presidency in ensuring . . . the consistency [of EPC] with EC positions" was rejected as potentially undermining the role of the Commission: see Nuttall, *supra* note 2 at 255.
[35] Second recital.
[36] See R Dehousse, and JHH Weiler, 'The Legal Dimension" in W Wallace, (ed.), *The Dynamics of European Integration* (London: Pinter, 1990) 242 at 244; D Freestone and S Davidson, "Community Competence and Part III of the Single European Act" (1986) 23 *CMLRev.* 993 at 796.
[37] See Art. 31 SEA.
[38] Art. 30(5).
[39] Art. 30(6)(a); in addition, rhetorical mention to the role of closer co-operation on European security issues was made.

In relation to the nature of the obligations undertaken by the Member States, it was argued that their vague wording, the purely intergovernmental structure of EPC and the exclusion of the Court's jurisdiction indicated that they were of symbolic rather than legal significance.[40] In a noteworthy coda, the Irish Supreme Court held that Article 30 SEA was binding under international law on Member States "to engage actively" in the procedures laid down therein.[41] It is suggested that the legally binding nature of the obligation to consult under Title III SEA is not a moot point any more.[42] It is recognised under international law that the way an obligation is phrased cannot be regarded as a hindrance to the acknowledgement of its legal content; the general and loose wording of an obligation may undermine its effective application but not its legal significance.[43]

2.4. The paradox: the dynamic, incremental and *sui generis* foreign policy under EPC and the limits of procedural requirements

The process which led to the development of the foreign affairs system before the Treaty on European Union was defined by the following three characteristics. First, it was of a dynamic nature, that is formulated subject to various pressures and influenced by distinct but interdependent developments. The pressures which culminated in the formulation and development of the EPC were of a multiple nature. Third parties did not perceive the influence of the Member States as confined to the objectives of the EC Treaty; instead, they considered the Member States as a collective actor on the international scene and welcomed the role they could play as such in international politics. Moreover, the development of the then European Economic Community fostered a culture of co-operation amongst the Member States whose influence by far exceeded the boundaries set by the specific powers attributed to the Community. A symbolic illustration of this, along with a tacit acknowledgement of the relationship

---

[40] See C Bosco, "Commentaire de l'Acte Unique Européen des 17–28 Fevrier 1987" (1987) XXIII *CDE* 355 at 381; J-P Jacqué, "L'Acte unique européen" (1986) 22 *RTDE* 575 at 611.

[41] *Crotty* v. *An Taoiseach and Others* [1987] 2 CMLR 666 at para. 37. This action was brought by an Irish citizen against the Irish Government on the basis of the latter's refusal to include Title III SEA in the European Communities Bill 1986 ratifying the SEA. For analyses of the judgment of the Supreme Court, see JP McCutcheon, "The Irish Supreme Court, European Political Co-operation and the Single European Act" (1988) 2 *LIEI* 93; F Murphy and A Gras, "L'Affaire *Crotty*: La Cour Supreme d'Irlande Rejette l'Acte Unique Européen" (1988) 24 *CDE* 276; J Temple Lang, "The Irish Court Case which Delayed the Single European Act: *Crotty* v. *An Taoiseach and Others*" (1987) 24 *CMLRev.* 709; A Passas, "On the Ratification of the Single European Act: A Dialogue which Did Not Take Place" (1988) 23–24 *Theseis* 99 (in Greek).

[42] See Freestone and Davidson, *supra* note 36 at 793.

[43] See the arbitral award issued by the Arbitral Tribunal for the Agreement on German External Debts, established under the London Agreement on German External Debts, in *Kingdom of Greece* v. *Federal Republic of Germany*, [1974] 47 *ILR* 418 *et seq.*

between foreign policy and trade, was the incorporation of the EPC mechanism in the SEA itself.[44]

Secondly, it was based on the pattern which has defined the development of the Community itself, namely incrementalism. There was no specific model against which a common foreign policy was structured. Instead, it consisted of *ad hoc* arrangements, each one based on and further developing those already in operation. It is noteworthy that the Luxembourg, Copenhagen and London Reports formalised to an important extent pre-existing practice. Therefore, the development and accumulation of these arrangements constituted the core of what was to become a foreign affairs system of the Union. This character of the EPC was acknowledged by the European Council itself, when it referred to the "vocation of the Union to deal with aspects of foreign and security policy, in accordance with a sustained evolutive process and in a unitary manner".[45]

Thirdly, the dynamic and incremental process described above led to the development of a *sui generis* foreign policy. Both the genesis of the core of EPC beyond any treaty framework and the absence of a clear model against which it would be fashioned resulted in a foreign policy framework distinct from both national models and international mechanisms of conduct of foreign policy.[46] The Member States failed accurately to define their common interests which would give rise to EPC procedures or instruments sufficient to indicate the role of EPC on the international scene. It was for this reason that the core of the structure of EPC throughout its development was confined to procedural provisions and measures of an administrative character.[47] This focus on issues of procedure rather than on substance determined the model of foreign policy envisaged by EPC, that is co-operation between the Member States through consultations on the basis of the minimum duties imposed.

This *sui generis*, dynamic and incrementally developed model of foreign policy is inherently paradoxical. On the one hand, its focus on procedural issues enabled the Member States to reject claims that their involvement in EPC entailed in any way erosion of national sovereignty over the conduct of foreign policy.[48] On the other hand, it was fashioned against the model of foreign

---

[44] See Nuttall, *supra* note 2 at 252. The implied recognition of the interaction between trade and foreign policy was also reflected in the upgrading of the Commission's role and its supervision, along with the Presidency, of the requirement of consistency.

[45] Conclusions of the Rome European Council of Dec. 1990, *Bull. EC* 12–1990 at 7.

[46] On the unique character of EPC, see JHH Weiler and W Wessels, "EPC and the Challenge of Theory" in A Pijpers, E Regelsberger and W Wessels (eds.), *European Political Co-operation in the 1980s: A Common Foreign Policy for Western Europe?* (Dordrecht: Nijhoff, 1988) 229.

[47] In this respect, EPC was characterised as "a procedure as substitute for policy" by W Wallace and D Allen, "Political Cooperation: Procedure as Substitute for Policy" in W Wallace, C Webb and H Wallace (eds.), *Policy Making in the European Communities* (Chichester: John Wiley and Sons, 1977) 227.

[48] This argument is illustrated in a Greek declaration in the minutes of the Solemn Declaration, according to which "in signing this declaration, Greece states that nothing may restrain its right to determine its foreign policy in accordance with its national interests": see Ifestos, *supra* note 2 at 305. The inclusion of such a declaration in the minutes of a non-legally binding document can be useful only in order to demonstrate a nationally proud stance in the international arena; on the other

policy traditionally adopted by sovereign states. The scope of EPC was very broad, covering all aspects of foreign policy,[49] and its practice mainly consisted of declaratory interventions in relation to events all over the world. In other words, the common foreign policy of the Member States was conceived on the basis of the national model, albeit with neither the intention nor the means to be implemented as such.

This paradox, which underpinned the development of the collective position of the Member States on the international scene, was clearly illustrated in the war in ex-Yugoslavia.[50] On the one hand, it indicated that, despite the *sui generis* character of EPC, it was traditional instruments of diplomacy that defined the stance of the Member States. On the other hand, it underlined the demand for a distinctive European role.[51] The use of traditional tools of international law as a political means of influencing events was indicative of a traditional state foreign-policy model. The most characteristic, albeit controversial, example was the recognition of new entities on the international scene. While, initially, the Member States concentrated all their efforts on preserving the territorial and political integrity of Yugoslavia,[52] they changed their view when it became clear that the continued tensions and the declaration of independence by Croatia and Slovenia rendered the protection of the *status quo* impossible. It was then that the Member States decided, within the EPC framework, to use recognition as an instrument to avoid both further conflicts and any alteration of the internal frontiers of the so far federated entities. This policy was illustrated in the "Declaration on Yugoslavia"[53] which set out specific conditions

hand, it revealed in the most manifest way the national inhibitions and restraints that the process of a European foreign policy would meet. On national debates regarding sovereignty over foreign policy in the light of EPC see A Pijpers, E Regelsberger and W Wessels, W., "A Common Foreign policy for Western Europe?" in Pijpers, Regelsberger and Wessels (eds.), *supra* note 46, 259 at 261–2. On the Member States as individual factors influencing the record of EPC see S Stavridis and C Hill (eds), *Domestic Sources of Foreign Policy* (Oxford: Berg Publishers, 1996).

[49] For an indication of the broad scope of EPC activities, see the diagrams in W Wessels, "EC–Europe: An Actor *Sui Generis* in the International System" in B Nelson, D Roberts and W Weit (eds.), *The European Community in the 1990s: Economics, Politics, Defence* (Oxford: Berg Publishers, 1992) 161.

[50] On the Union's role in relation to the war in ex-Yugoslavia see E Remacle, *La politique étrangère européenne: de Maastricht à la Yugoslavie* (Brssels: GRIP dossier, 1992); CJ Smith, "Conflict in the Balkans and the Possibility of a European Union Common Foreign and Security Policy" (1996) XIII/2 *International Relations* 1; and PN Stangos, "La Communauté et les Etats membres face à la crise yougoslave" in M Telò (ed.), *Vers une nouvelle Europe?* (Brussels: ULB, 1992) 177.

[51] In this respect, the statement of the Secretary of Foreign Affairs of Luxembourg, Jacques Poos, is noteworthy: "[t]his is the hour of Europe"; see *Financial Times*, 1 July 1991 at 1.

[52] TC Salmon, "Testing Times for European Political Cooperation: The Gulf and Yugoslavia, 1990–1992" [1992] 68 *International Affairs* 233.

[53] This declaration made reference to the Declaration on the Guidelines on the Recognition of New States in Eastern Europe and in the Soviet Union, adopted on 16 Dec. 1991 and in which the Community and the Member States expressed their intention to recognise "subject to the normal standards of international practice and the political realities in each case" those states which "have constituted themselves on a democratic basis, have accepted the appropriate international obligations and have committed themselves in good faith to a peaceful process and to negotiations". In particular, they set out certain conditions which the new entities must fulfil in order to be

subject to which the "Community and the Member States" would recognise new entities.[54] Furthermore, it set out the process for the recognition to be made, according to which the entity seeking recognition had to provide a written application to the Community which was to be examined by the Arbitration Committee.[55]

The war on the doorstep of the Community determined to a great extent the public perception that the Member States were unable to adopt a common stance, let alone implement it and consistently stand by it. However, the approach of the Member States in relation to the war in ex-Yugoslavia may be understood on the basis of the following argument: the dynamics which enabled the external relations system of the Member States to develop from the modest informal arrangements of the 1960s to the institutionalised framework of the SEA also determined its shortcomings. The Member States sought first to preserve and then restore peace and security on their doorstep within a framework which was based on consultation amongst them but lacked clear objectives, offered procedures instead of policies, provided for declarations instead of means of action. In other words, the Member States sought to organise their approach on the basis of a set of rules which was not only ill-equipped but also not designed to respond to the challenge raised by the war in ex-Yugoslavia.[56]

---

recognised, namely to (i) respect the Charter of the United Nations and the Final Act of Helsinki and the Charter of Paris, (ii) guarantee the rights of ethnic and national groups and minorities on the basis of obligations under CSCE, (iii) ensure that the frontiers are inviolable and would only be changed "by peaceful means and by common agreement", (iv) accept all commitments concerning disarmament and nuclear non-proliferation and (v) commit to settle by agreement any issue which might arise concerning state succession and regional disputes. Finally, the Member States declared that they would not recognise entities resulting from acts of aggression.

[54] These conditions included acceptance of the provisions set out in the draft convention under consideration by the conference on Yugoslavia and support for any efforts for a peaceful settlement of the disputes in the area made by both the Secretary General and the Security Council of United Nations and the Conference on Yugoslavia. The Conference on Yugoslavia was the institutional umbrella covering efforts undertaken first by the EC and then a number of international organisations in order to bring an end to the war. The official documents produced thereunder are included in BG Ramcharan (ed.), *The International Conference on the Former Yugoslavia* (The Hague: Kluwer Law International, 1997) i and ii. On these and other inititatives see D McGoldrick, "Yugoslavia—The Responses of the International Community and of International Law" (1996) 49 *Current Legal Problems* 375.

[55] The Arbitration Committee was a body specifically established in relation to the Yugoslavian crisis. Widely known as Badinter Committee, after its French President, it operated under the auspices of the EC and its members were drawn from national constitutional courts. Opinions 1–3 of the Committee were published in (1992) 3 *EJIL* 182 and Opinions 4–10 in (1993) 4 *EJIL* 74. See MCR Craven, "The European Community Arbitration Commission on Yugoslavia" (1995) LXVI *BYIL* 333. For a detailed analysis of the recognition of new entities in ex-Yugoslavia by the Member States see R Kherad, "La Reconnaissance des Etats Issus de la Dissolution de la Republique Socialiste de Yugoslavie par les Membres de l'Union Européenne" (1997) 101 *RGDIP* 663; R Rich, "Recognition of States: The Collapse of Yugoslavia and the Soviet Union" (1993) 4 *EJIL* 36.

[56] In this respect, Nuttall rightly points out that "[t]he question is not whether the Communiy succeeded or failed [in former Yugoslavia], but whether it had the means of fulfilling its ambitions, and if not, whether it prefers to give itself the means or abandon its ambitions" in "The EC and Yugoslavia—Deus ex Machina or Machina sine Deo" (1994) 32 *JCMS* 25.

It was this paradox which led to the genesis of the much-quoted term "capabilities-expectations gap" in an attempt to understand the approach of the Member States in the Balkan crisis.[57] Indeed, this approach relied upon three main types of instruments, namely economic sanctions, recognition and mediation. While aiming to, first, deter and then bring about an end to the war, these instruments did not form a part of the institutional machinery of the foreign affairs system of the Member States developed so far. Therefore, their application proved itself highly problematic. In the absence of a clear provision regarding the extent to and the conditions under which recourse should have been had to Community law, the imposition of sanctions against third countries raised serious legal problems. As for the recognition of governments by the Member States, their inability to agree on the use of this public international law instrument reserved to traditionally sovereign states[58] resulted in confusion and was criticised as seriously undermining the effort of the Union to bring an end to the war. Finally, in assuming a mediating role, the European Union relied more heavily upon the personality of the European statesmen who intervened at various stages and quite less on the procedures provided for under SEA.

3. COMMON FOREIGN AND SECURITY POLICY UNDER THE MAASTRICHT TREATY

The problems outlined above gave rise to a debate over enabling the Member States to adopt and implement a fully-fledged common foreign policy. The focus of this debate is formulated in the following question: how can the Member States establish an institutionalised framework which, on the one hand, would enable them to adopt and effectively implement a common stance without, on the other hand, undermining their national sovereignty over the exercise of foreign policy? This question was addressed in the 1992 Intergovernmental Conference by establishing the second pillar of the European Union. At this stage, a methodological point must be made: Title V rules of the Maastricht Treaty will be analysed in detail despite the entry into force of the Amsterdam Treaty. The reason for this is not confined to the fact that the latter draws significantly upon the former; in addition, since the new Treaty entered into force quite recently, the general character and scope of the CFSP record can only be assessed on the basis of the activities undertaken under the Maastricht Treaty. In order to avoid confusion, the following part, contrary to the remainder of this book, will refer to Title V provisions as numbered in the Maastricht Treaty.

---

[57] C Hill, "The Capabilities-Expectations Gap, or Conceptualising the European International Role", (1993) 31 *JCMS* 305.

[58] See the comment by Judge Higgins of the International Court of Justice on the use of recognition by the Member States as "an unfortunate exemplar for a common EC [sic] foreign policy" quoted in N Winn, "The Proof of the Pudding Is In the Eating: the European Union "Joint Action" As an Effective Foreign Policy Instrument?" (1997) XIII/6 *International Relations* 19 at 29.

3.1. The CFSP provisions of the Maastricht Treaty

The Common Foreign and Security Policy, set out in Title V TEU, was defined by the principles which underlie the development of the foreign policy framework since the establishment of EPC. In other words, the second pillar of EU is characterised by very distinct intergovernmental features.[59]

The scope of CFSP was construed in very broad terms, analogous to those of national foreign policy, consistently with the pre-Maastricht period. However, a qualification should be made. Article J.8(5) defines the material scope of the role of the Political Committee as "the areas covered by common foreign and security policy". This provision must be read in conjunction with the exclusion from the scope of the CFSP of those areas which give rise to the Community's competence.

Under Article J.2.(1), "Member States shall inform and consult one another within the Council on any matter of foreign and security policy of general interest in order to ensure that their combined influence is exerted as effectively as possible by means of concerted and convergent action". The objectives of CFSP are set out in equally broad terms, namely to "safeguard the common values, fundamental interests and independence of the Union, strengthen the security of the Union and its Member States in all ways, preserve peace and strengthen international security",[60] to "promote international co-operation, to develop and consolidate democracy and the rule of law, and respect for human rights and fundamental freedoms". An indicative list of criteria defining the Union's important common interests which would give rise to the adoption of joint actions under Article J.3 is provided in the Conclusions of the Lisbon European Council in June 1992. According to this list, in defining the areas and issues for joint action account should be taken, among other factors, of the geographical proximity of a region or country, an important interest in the political and economic stability of a region or a country and the existence of threats to the security interests of the Union.[61]

The intergovernmental character of CFSP is reflected in both the role of the institutions and the decision-making procedure.[62] Under Article J.8(1), "the

---

[59] On the negotiations which led to the adoption of Title V TEU see J Cloos, G Reinesch, D Vignes and J Weyland, *Le Traité de Maastricht. Genèse, Analyse, Commentaires* (Brussels: Bruyland, 1993) at 463 *et seq*; P de Schoutheete de Tervarent, "The Creation of the Common Foreign and Security Policy" in E Regelsberger, P de Schoutheete de Tervarent and W Wessels (eds.), *Foreign Policy of the European Union. From EPC to CFSP and Beyond* (London: Lynne Rienner Publishers, 1997) 41.

[60] Under Art. J.1(2) TEU, this objective is to be served "in accordance with the principles of the United Nations Charter as well as the principles of the Helsinki Final Act and the objectives of the Paris Charter".

[61] *Bull.* EC 6–1992 at 19.

[62] For a concise analysis of the decision-making and institutional framework of Title V see F Fink-Hooijer, "The Common Foreign and Security Policy of the European Union" (1994) 5 *EJIL* 173; D McGoldrick, *International Relations Law of the European Union* (London: Longman, 1997) at ch. 8; I MacLeod, ID Hendry and S Hyett, *The External Relations of the European Communities*

principles and general guidelines" of CFSP are to be defined by the European Council.[63] The instruments are adopted by the Council unanimously. Under Article J.3(2), Council decisions can be adopted under qualified majority voting. However, this is itself subject to a unanimous Council decision.[64]

The instruments through which the above aims are to be served consist of common positions and joint actions. The Maastricht Treaty did not clarify what their distinction would be. The former were to be adopted by the Council "whenever it deems it necessary".[65] The obligations of Member States consist of ensuring that their national policies conform with the common positions[66] and upholding them in international organisations and at international fora.[67]

Joint actions are adopted by the Council unanimously[68] on the basis of general guidelines from the European Council. The Council must define the specific scope, the Union's general and specific objectives in carrying out such action, if necessary its duration, the means, procedures and conditions for its implementation.[69] In relation to joint actions, Title V sets out a number of obligations of the Member States of varying degree. Under Article J.3(4), they are committed in the positions that they adopt and in the conduct of their activity, whereas in cases of national positions or actions pursuant to a joint action, they shall provide information "in time to allow, if necessary, for prior consultations within the Council".[70] However, Member States are allowed "in cases of imperative need arising from changes in the situation and failing a Council decision . . . [to] take the necessary measures as a matter of urgency having regard to the general objectives of the joint action" provided that they "inform the Council immediately".[71] Moreover, the Council is to seek solutions to "major difficulties" that a Member State may have in implementing a joint action.[72]

(Oxford: Clarendon Press, 1996) at ch. 24; DT Murphy, "The European Union's Common Foreign and Security Policy: It is Not Far From Maastricht to Amsterdam" (1998) 31 *Vanderbilt Journal of Transnational Law* 871.

[63] See H-J Glaesner, "The European Council" in D Curtin and T Heukels (eds.), *Institutional Dynamics of European Integration. Essays in Honour of Henry G. Schermers* (Dordrecht, London: Nijhoff, 1994) ii, 101.

[64] Under Art. J.3(2) para. 2, in cases of Council decisions adopted under qualified majority under this provision, the votes are to be weighted in accordance with Art. 148(2) of the EC Treaty and, for their adoption, acts of the Council shall require at least 62 votes in favour, cast by at least 10 members.

[65] Art. J.2(1) TEU.

[66] Art. J.2(2) TEU.

[67] Art. J.2(3) TEU. Under the second para. of this provision, Member States participating in international organisations and at international fora where not all the Member States participate "shall uphold the common positions".

[68] Art. J.8(2) TEU.

[69] Art. J.3(1) para. 2 TEU. In cases of "changes in circumstances having a substantial effect on a question subject to joint action", a review mechanism is established under Art. J.3(3) TEU.

[70] Art. J.3(5) TEU. This obligation does not apply regarding measures which merely transpose Council decisions at national level.

[71] Art. J.3(6) TEU.

[72] Provided that these solutions "shall not run counter to the objectives of the joint action or impair its effectiveness": see Art. J.3(7) TEU.

3.2. The CFSP record under the Maastricht Treaty

An analysis of all CFSP measures in terms of both their substance and effectiveness is outside the scope of this book.[73] However, no specific aspect of the interactions between the Community legal framework and CFSP can be examined unless the general character and scope of the measures adopted under the latter rules are highlighted. In this respect, the CFSP record will be outlined and divided into four categories, namely declaratory, preventive, constructive and coercive diplomacy.[74]

The bulk of the activity undertaken under Title V consists of statements, that is a traditional and not too ambitious foreign policy instrument. It is noteworthy that during 1995 106 statements were issued by the EU Presidency regarding various issues around the world.[75] The subject matter of these statements covers all areas within the scope of traditional national foreign policy. In the absence of clearly defined CFSP objectives, these statements fall within the broad scope of objectives set out in Article J.1(2). Their aim is to define the Union's position regarding an international event but not to set out a specific response, an aim to be fulfilled by common positions. However, the distinction between declarations and common positions is not always easy to draw, especially when the latter are phrased in very general terms.[76]

The second category of measures adopted under the second pillar focuses on preventive diplomacy, that is measures aiming to consolidate international peace and security. Such measures are not adopted in order to respond to a specific crisis and may be characterised by institutional features of permanent or semi-permanent existence. The most prominent such measure is the Stability Pact. Establishing a pan-European negotiating process, the Stability Pact aims to ensure good neighbourly relations between the participating states through various diplomatic, political, economic and cultural measures.[77] A joint action incorporated the conclusion of the Pact, hence making reference to areas which

---

[73] For an analysis of specific activities undertaken under Title V see M Holland (ed.), *Common Foreign and Security Policy. The Record and Reforms* (London: Pinter, 1997).

[74] This categorisation, suggested in T de Wilde d'Estmael, "La politique Etrangère et de Sécurité Commune de l'Union européenne. Essai d'évaluation au-délà du syndrome yougoslave" (1996) 11/3 *Revue politique* 17, is by no means exhaustive. There are developments in the CFSP area which cannot easily be included in any of these categories. An example is given by the Council decision, defining neither a common position nor a joint action, to establish a liaison bureau in New York: see RH Ginsberg, "The EU's CFSP: the Politics of Procedure" in Holland, *supra* note 73, 12 at 30.

[75] See *43rd review of the Council's work. The Secretary-General's Report. 1 January–31 December 1995* (Luxembourg: Office for Official Publications of the European Communities, 1995) at 150–4.

[76] P Willaert and C Marqués-Ruiz, "Vers une politique étrangère et de securité commune: état des lieux" (1995) 3 *Révue du Marché Unique Européen* 35 at 71.

[77] The idea of launching this initiative was of the then French Prime Minister Balladur and was agreed upon by the Member States in the Brussels European Council. It was adopted by the Council as a joint action in Dec. 93/728/CFSP, [1993] OJ L 339/1 and was formally inaugurated in Paris on 26–27 May 1994.

would promote the Pact's objectives, namely regional transborder co-operation, issues regarding minorities, cultural co-operation, economic co-operation and administrative training and environmental issues.[78] In addition to the establishment of the Stability Pact, other preventive diplomacy measures adopted by the EU consist of a joint action regarding the preparation of the 1995 Conference on the Non-Proliferation Treaty[79] and another one setting up common rules on export restrictions of dual-use goods.[80]

A third category of activities undertaken by the Union under Title V TEU may be defined as constructive diplomacy. Most of these activities consist of the EU's participation in various international initiatives. The various efforts undertaken by the EU towards a solution in the Yugoslav civil war constitute a characteristic example of such initiatives. The International Conference on Yugoslavia was launched in The Hague on 7 September 1991, but was also operating after the TEU. In addition to this longstanding process, various initiatives were taken in co-operation with the UN Secretary General, United States and Russia, such as inviting the fighting parties to Geneva for talks.[81] After the Dayton agreement was signed, a joint action was adopted regarding its implementation.[82] Another component of the CFSP is the Union's participation in international initiatives, such as the Korean Peninsula Energy Development Organisation (KEDO).[83] In order to raise its status as a significant international actor, the EU sought to establish its presence in areas of constant crisis. Therefore, it adopted joint actions defining its support for the Middle East peace process,[84] on the establishment of an assistance programme to support the Palestinian authority in its efforts to counter terrorist activities emanating from the territories under its control.[85] There was also a joint action in support of the Bosnian Peace Process which aimed to provide rapid short-term assistance to

---

[78] Council Dec. 94/367/CFSP, [1994] OJ L165/1 which prolonged the application of Dec. 93/728/CFSP. For a detailed analysis see T Ueta, "The Stability Pact: from the Balladur Initiative to the EU Joint Action" in Holland (ed.), *supra* note 73 at 92.

[79] Council Dec. 94/509/CFSP [1994] OJ L205/1. For a detailed analysis, see H Mueller and L van Dassen, "From Cacophony to Joint Action: Successes and Shortcomings of the European Nuclear Non-Proliferation Policy" in Holland (ed.), *supra* note 73 at 52.

[80] The rules were first set up by Council Dec. 94/942/CFSP [1994] OJ L367/8 and Council Reg. 3381/94 [1994] OJ L367/1.

[81] See AG Kintis, "The EU's Foreign Policy and the War in Former Yugoslavia" in Holland (ed.), *supra* note 73 at 148 *et seq*.

[82] Council Dec. 95/545/CFSP [1995] OJ L309/2.

[83] Council Dec. 96/195/CFSP [1996] OJ L63/1.

[84] Council Decs. 94/276/CFSP [1994] OJ L119/1; 95/205/CFSP [1995] OJ L130/1; 95/403/CFSP [1995] OJ L238/4; 96/676/ CFSP [1996] OJ L315/1. On the Union's role in the peace process see COM(97)715 final, "The Role of the European Union in the Peace Process and its Future Assistance to the Middle East", published in *Europe Documents*, 23 Jan. 1998 at 1 *et seq*. Also see F Perroni, "Le processus de paix au Proche-Orient et l'Union européenne" [1997] *Revue du Marché Commun et de l'Union Européenne* 318.

[85] Council Dec. 97/289/CFSP [1997] OJ L120/2.

the new Government of the Republic Srpska[86] and nominated a Special Envoy for the African Great Lakes Region.[87]

A significant number of the constructive diplomacy measures adopted by the Union under Title V focus on humanitarian aid to regions in crisis, ex-Yugoslavia being just one of them.[88] However, this type of activity is not a novelty under the second pillar, for it constitutes the aim specifically served by the European Community Humanitarian Office (ECHO).[89] An important feature of CFSP was the administration of the city of Mostar, whereby a European Union-appointed administrator was for two years in charge[90] of providing the administrative and material means which would enable the city to overcome the divisions between its Bosnian and Serb population.[91] This activity was mainly of an administrative character and seems to fall short of the grand objectives that the Treaty sets. However, it suggests an innovative approach which contributed to the stabilisation of the situation in Mostar and overcame the fundamental differences of Member States' approach to the Yugoslavian crisis.[92] Administrative assistance was offered in various cases by the EU under Title V, namely support for the electoral process in Bosnia-Herzegovina,[93] dispatch of observers to Russian Parliamentary elections,[94] support for transition towards a democratic and multiracial South Africa,[95] support for the democratic transition process in Congo.[96]

Finally, the EU adopted various measures of coercive diplomacy, that is measures arising from the outbreak of hostilities and aiming to respond to a specific crisis. The most important measures in this category consist of trade and

---

[86] Council Dec. 98/117/CFSP [1998] OJ L35/1 which provided for 6 million ECUs to be allocated for this purpose, charged to the general budget of the Communities and managed in accordance with the Community procedures applicable to the budget.

[87] Council Dec. 96/250/CFSP [1996] OJ L87/1; 96/441/CFSP [1996] OJ L185/1; 97/448/CFSP [1997] OJ L197/1.

[88] Council Decs. 93/603/CFSP [1993] OJ L286/1; 93/729/CFSP [1993] OJ L339/3; 94/158/CFSP [1994] OJ L70/1; 94/308/CFSP [1994] OJ L134/1; 94/501/CFSP [1994] OJ L205/3; 95/516/CFSP [1995] OJ L298/3.

[89] For an account of the significant volume of aid dispatched by ECHO see the Annual Report published since 1992 by the Commission under the title *Humanitarian Aid from the European Community* (Luxembourg: Office for Official Publications of the European Communities).

[90] The EU administration of the city of Mostar was set up on 16 May 1994 and ended on 22 July 1996.

[91] Council Decs. 94/790/CFSP [1994] OJ L326/2; 95/23/CFSP [1995] OJ L33/1; 95/517/CFSP [1995] OJ L298/4; 95/552/CFSP [1995] OJ L313/1; 96/442/CFSP [1996] OJ L185/2; 95/476/CFSP [1996] OJ L195/1; 96/508/CFSP [1996] OJ L212/1.

[92] For a general comment on the initial joint actions see J Monar, "Mostar: Three Lessons for the European Union" (1997) 2 *EFA Review* 1.

[93] Council Dec. 96/406/CFSP [1996] OJ L168/1.

[94] Council Dec. 94/604/CFSP [1994] OJ L286/3.

[95] Council Dec. 93/678/CFSP [1993] OJ L316/45. For a detailed account of the EU approach towards South Africa see M Holland, *European Union Foreign Policy: from EPC to CFSP Joint Action and South Africa* (Basingstoke: MacMillan, 1995).

[96] Council Decs. 96/656/CFSP [1996] OJ L300/1; 97/875/CFSP [1997] OJ L357/1; 97/817/CFS, [1997] OJ L338/1.

economic sanctions; an analysis of the legal problems raised by their imposition under the Maastricht Treaty will be provided in a later chapter.

3.3. The character of the Union's foreign policy confirmed

The analysis of both the CFSP rules of the Maastricht Treaty and the activities carried out thereunder confirms the two main arguments put forward in this chapter. On the one hand, the wide variety of ways, often not confined to the Treaty provisions, in which the Union engaged in a wide variety of activities supports the character of its foreign policy as *sui generis*, incremental and dynamic. On the other hand, the rather modest, in the light of its aim to "assert its identity on the international scene", reactive and often declaratory nature of the Union's record confirm the inherent limits of a framework mainly focused on procedural provisions.

It is a truism that the performance of the Union under Title V is bound to be dependent upon the limits set by the institutional framework within which it operates. Therefore, the dominant role of unanimous decision-making constitutes an inherent constraint in the formulation of a common stance on the international arena, even more so in relation to urgent events and crises. As such, not only does it slow down the adoption of the Union's position, but it also determines the substance of this position on the basis of a compromise subject to a great extent to internal politics of the Member States.

However, it does not follow by any means that all the shortcomings of the Union foreign policy are to be attributed to the decision-making process. The institutional framework established under the TEU illustrates the model of policy that the Member States envisage or, more accurately, do not envisage. On the one hand, they clearly do not intend to build a foreign policy structure which would follow the Community framework, that is providing for the adoption, often under majority voting and with the participation of supranational institutions, of measures justiciable before an independent judicial body and supreme over national rules.[97] On the other hand, they tacitly acknowledge that the effectiveness of a common foreign policy system relies, to a considerable extent, upon Community policies. This conclusion may be explained on three grounds. The first one is the substantive diversity and depth of Community policies and the institutional sophistication through which these are pursued. The second reason relates to the post-Cold War international environment which, in the absence of an on-going conflict of universal dimensions, places trade and economic policies in the very centre of inter-state relations. The third reason focuses on the peculiarities of the Union's attributes and ambitions, namely the Member States' continuous refusal to create a defence mechanism within the

---

[97] For an illustration of this approach see D Hurd, "Developing the Common Foreign and Security Policy" (1994) 70 *International Affairs* 421.

structure of the European Union in addition to their ambition to assert the Union's identity on the international scene.

The *sui generis* character of the system of rules established under the second pillar of the Maastricht Treaty is apparent in the semiotics of the Treaty. Article A refers to "the High Contracting Parties", whereas the rest of both the Common Provisions and Title V refer to "the Member States". As for the activities carried out within the second pillar, the model they follow, consistently with European Political Co-operation, defies traditional categorisation: it owes its existence and development to the integration attained within the Community but renounces the latter's normative characteristics; it occasionally relies upon Community instruments, yet it implements them under a distinct legal framework; it is fashioned in the model of national foreign policy while negating any features of the traditionally sovereign state and fully respecting national competence over the conduct of foreign policy. The *sui generis* character of the Union's foreign policy and the inherent limitations of the procedural rules within which this policy is to operate are so closely interconnected that it is not apparent which is due to what. This is also demonstrated by the extent to which groups of Member States co-operate closely in foreign affairs activities beyond the Treaty framework and in addition to actions undertaken within it. The Contact Group in ex-Yugoslavia and the bi-annual meetings of the UK, France, Spain, Italy and Germany with the Turkish Prime Minister may seem to deviate from the framework established by Title V, yet they illustrate the incomplete, dynamic and *sui generis* nature of CFSP.

The combined consideration of the inherent limits set by procedural rules and the ambivalent conceptual relationship between the European Community and CFSP indicate that the effectiveness of the CFSP activities is not entirely dependent on procedural provisions or their absence. It is not the requirement of unanimity, for instance, which prevents the Union from formulating a common policy in relation to how violations of human rights should affect its relations with China.[98] Had the Treaty provided for qualified-majority voting, the Union's position would not necessarily have been more credible and influential on the international scene. As Monar points out, "[a] majority decision on a foreign policy matter is totally different in character from a majority decision on an EC legal act: adopted against the will of some Member States it would lose much or even most of its international credibility and could be easily subverted by signals from the opposing Member States through its national diplomatic

---

[98] The Union's approach to violations of human rights by the Chinese authorities has been an issue of controversy. In 1997 it created a crisis, when Denmark and the Netherlands, supported by 8 other Member States and the United States, proposed a resolution in the United Nations Commission on Human Rights condemning China, whereas Germany, France, Italy, Spain and Greece opposed; see *Financial Times*, 7 Apr. 1997 at 2. In 1998, the General Affairs Council decided not to support any condemnation of the Chinese government but, instead, to engage in a general dialogue with it: see *Agence Europe*, 7166 23–24 Feb. 1998 at 2–3. For an argument against the lack of a clear and unequivocal condemnation of the violations of human rights in China by the Union see C Flinterman, "Editorial: The European Union and China" (1997) 4 *MJ* 217.

channels".[99] Hence, the actual effectiveness of the formulation and implementation of the CFSP are dependent only to a limited extent on the dynamics of procedural provisions.

4. THE CURRENT FRAMEWORK: CFSP UNDER THE AMSTERDAM TREATY

It was suggested above that the Member States' political choice to conduct their foreign policy under a set of rules distinct from but interdependent with the Community legal framework sets the very limits of this policy and indicates the relative effect of procedural rules. This argument raises the question whether the Member States themselves are prepared to modify or even abandon their national stance in order to contribute to the formulation of a single, instead of a common, foreign policy. The answer given by the Member States as recently as three years ago tacitly reaffirmed their determination for the Union's foreign policy to be conducted under a multipolar legal structure, on the basis of a framework distinct from, yet closely interconnected with, the Community set of rules.

4.1. The CFSP provisions under the Amsterdam Treaty

The Amsterdam Treaty[100] amended Title V to a significant extent.[101] At a general level, it is important to note that Article 11(1) provides that the objectives of the CFSP include the safeguard of not only the common values, fundamental interests and independence of the Union, but also its "integrity". It is suggested that this inclusion refers to the territorial integrity of the Union.[102] As such, it

---

[99] J Monar, "The European Union's Foreign Affairs System after the Treaty of Amsterdam: A 'Strengthened Capacity for External Action?'" (1997) 2 *EFA Review* 413 at 418. See also P VerLoren van Themaat, "The Internal Powers of the Community and the Union" in JA Winter, DM Curtin, AE Kellermann and B de Witte (eds.), *Reforming the Treaty on European Union—The Legal Debate* (The Hague; London: Kluwer Law International, 1996) 249 at 262. In any case, the suggestion that the removal of the unanimity requirement is essential is in stark contrast to the prevailing role of unanimity in areas of Community's external relations, namely emergency aid, balance of payments aid, co-operation with countries other than developing countries. Community acts in these areas are adopted under Art. 308 and, hence, unanimously.

[100] For an assessment of the Amsterdam Treaty see T Heukels and MB Blokker (eds.), *The European Union after Amsterdam: A Legal Analysis* (The Hague: Kluwer Law International, 1998); R Barents, "Some Observations on the Treaty of Amsterdam" (1997) 4 *MJ* 332; F Dehousse, "Le Traité d'Amsterdam, Reflet de la Nouvelle Europe" (1997) XXXIII *CDE* 265; J-M Favret, "Le Traité d'Amsterdam: Une Revision *A Minima* de la "Charte Constitutionnelle" de l'Union Européenne—De l'intégration a l'incantation?" (1997) XXXIII *CDE* 555; S Langrish, "The Treaty of Amsterdam: Selected Highlights" (1998) 23 *ELRev.* 3; M Nentwich and G Falkner, "The Treaty of Amsterdam: Towards a New Institutional Balance" (1997) 1 *EIoP* No 15; M Petite, "The Treaty of Amsterdam", Harvard Jean Monnet Paper 98/2; JHH Weiler, "Editorial: Amsterdam, Amsterdam" (1997) 3 *EJIL* 309.

[101] For an analysis of the new Title , see Monar, *supra* note 99.

[102] *Ibid.* at 415.

would put an end to such absurdities as, on the one hand, the Union's tendency to issue declarations on most events around the globe but, on the other hand, its inability to react when the territorial integrity of a Member State is challenged.[103] The absence of a military capacity of the Union to intervene in such situations reduces neither the symbolic significance of this objective nor its potential to facilitate the Union's adoption of a common stance. In the light of this new objective, the removal of the reference to strengthening the Member States' security from Article 11.1 cannot be read as denying the significance of national concerns within the Union's system of foreign policy.[104] However, the extent to which these concerns determine the content of the Union's response is directly relevant to various political and economic circumstances often unrelated to the institutional structure of Title V.

As far as the decision-making process is concerned, the Amsterdam amendment maintained unanimity as the central voting method. However, this rule is qualified in three ways. First, the *ratio* of Article 148(3) EC is extended to Title V. In other words, under Article 23(1) abstentions are not to prevent the adoption of decisions requiring unanimity. Secondly, the principle of constructive abstention is introduced, whereby a Member State may abstain and make a formal declaration which would absolve it from being bound by the decision in question while accepting its binding effect on the Union. In such a case, the abstaining Member State must refrain, under the principle of solidarity, from any action which is likely to conflict with or impede the Union's actions under the decision in question. Thirdly, under Article 23(2) TEU qualified majority voting is provided for in two cases, namely when joint actions, common positions or other decisions are adopted on the basis of a common strategy and when decisions are adopted in order to implement joint actions or common positions. However, this qualification to the unanimity rule is further qualified in a twofold way: on the one hand, it does not apply to decisions with military or defence implications; on the other hand, any Member State may declare its intention to oppose the adoption of a decision by qualified majority voting "for important and stated reasons of national policy", in which case a vote is not to be taken and the Council may request by qualified majority that the European Council decide unanimously.

Under Article 12 TEU, the CFSP objectives are to be pursued by the Union by defining the principles and general guidelines for the CFSP, deciding on common strategies, adopting joint actions and common positions, strengthening systematic co-operation between Member States in the conduct of policy. The principles of and general guidelines for the CFSP are to be decided by the European Council and are expected to follow the pattern of the general guidelines which

---

[103] Indeed, the Union's inability to intervene in the escalation of Greek–Turkish tensions caused by Turkish claims that Greek islets in the Aegean Sea were of disputed sovereignty allowed Richard Holbrooke, the then Under-Secretary of the State Department, to comment that it was "sleeping through the night": *Financial Times*, 1 Apr. 1998 at 18.

[104] *Cf. supra* note 99.

the European Council has produced so far and hence provide general political guidance. As far as common strategies are concerned, Article 13(2) provides that they are to be adopted by the European Council in areas where the Member States have important interests in common.[105] Moreover, under Article 12(3) the Council shall recommend common strategies and implement them on the basis of the main CFSP instruments, namely joint actions and common positions. In contrast to the Maastricht amendment of the Treaty, the Treaty of Amsterdam provides a definition of both instruments. Under Article 14(1), joint actions "shall address specific situations where operational action by the Union is deemed to be required" and "shall lay down their objectives, scope, the means to be made available to the Union, if necessary their duration and the conditions for their implementation". It is suggested that in the light of CFSP instruments relying heavily upon Community measures, the coherence of the Union's action is enhanced by the new Article 14(4), whereby the Council may request the Commission to submit proposals regarding the implementation of a joint action. Finally, under Article 15 common positions "shall define the approach of the Union to a particular matter of a geographical or thematic nature". It is noteworthy that, in defining the effect that CFSP instruments are to exert on Member States, the Treaty of Amsterdam follows the pattern of the Maastricht amendments. In other words, only in relation to joint actions is specific reference made to their "commit[ing] the Member States in the positions they adopt and in the conduct of their activity".[106] However, this cannot deny the binding effect of the other CFSP instruments. In this respect, two points need to be made. First, the absence of a specific reference to their binding effect is due to their general character. Secondly, to deny such an effect would contravene the general provisions of Title V regarding the obligations of Member States, namely to support the Union's external policy actively and unreservedly in a spirit of loyalty and mutual solidarity and to refrain from any action likely to impair the Union's effectiveness as a cohesive force in international relations.[107]

Under Article 18(3) TEU, the Secretary-General of the Council is to assist the Presidency by exercising the function of the High Representative for the Common Foreign and Security Policy.[108] In the light of Article 18 *in toto*, it is assumed that the above role of the High Representative consists of representing the Union on the international scene. In addition, under Article 26 TEU, the High Representative shall assist the Council in its Title V role by contributing to the formulation, preparation and implementation of policy decisions. Moreover, he/she shall conduct political dialogue with third parties "when appropriate and on behalf of the Council at the request of the Presidency".

---

[105] The first Common Strategy was on Russia [1999] OJ L157/1 and was adopted on 4 June 1999.

[106] Art. 14(3) TEU.

[107] Art. 11(2) TEU.

[108] The functions currently exercised by the Secretary-General of the Council are to be exercised by his/her Deputy. Javier Solana was appointed as the first High Representative.

A final issue that deserves some analysis is the absence of a closer co-operation clause from Title V in contrast to both the Community framework and Title VI.[109] The absence of such clause is all the more impressive in the light of the fact that the introduction of a flexibility clause stemmed from the debate over the effectiveness of Title V TEU. The question which may arise is whether the general closer co-operation clause, provided in the new Title VII of the Treaty on European Union as amended by the Amsterdam Treaty may be applicable to Title V.[110] The application of this general closer co-operation clause in the CFSP area may seem in principle desirable; in practical terms, it would impose the specific conditions and guarantees provided thereunder to the anomalies of *ad hoc* groups of big Member States acting in various issues of foreign policy beyond Title V. It is noteworthy that the pathological role that such coalitions may play in relation to the effectiveness of CFSP has recently become a concern amongst various Member States.[111] However, the extension of this clause to Title V seems highly problematic on two grounds. First, its express application to Title V, proposed by the Dutch Presidency, was deliberately rejected at the last minute of the Intergovernmental Conference by the European Council.[112] Therefore, its application would run counter to the express intention of the drafters. Secondly, under Article 43(h) TEU, co-operation between Member States is envisaged "provided that [it] complies with the specific additional criteria laid down in [EC Treaty and Title VI]", thus indicating that the absence of any such provision in Title V rules out the applicability of the clause altogether.[113]

4.2. The *sui-generis* character of the Union's foreign policy confirmed: the issue of international legal personality

The Treaty of Amsterdam does not expressly confer legal personality on the Union. However, not only the European Community[114] but also the other two

---

[109] A closer co-operation clause is introduced in the Community framework under the new Art. 11 EC and in Title VI under the new Art. K.12.

[110] On the concept of closer co-operation under the Amsterdam Treaty see F Tuytschaever, *Differentiation in European Union Law* (Oxford: Hart Publishing, 1999) and G Edwards and E Phillippart, *Flexibility and the Treaty of Amsterdam: Europe's New Byzantium* (CELS Occasional Paper No. 3, 1997); CD Ehlermann, *Differentiation, Flexibility, Closer Cooperation: the New Provisions of the Amsterdam Treaty* (Florence: Robert Schuman Centre, European University Institute, 1998); and J Shaw, "The Treaty of Amsterdam: Challenges of Flexibility and Legitimacy" (1998) 4 *ELJ* 63.

[111] In the General Affairs Council of 17 Apr. 1998, the Foreign Secretaries of Belgium, The Netherlands and Luxembourg presented a letter raising this issue and undertaking to present a working paper: see *Agence Europe*, 7210 29 Apr. 1998 at 3.

[112] Ehlermann, *supra* note 110 at 9.

[113] See G Gaja, "How Flexible Is Flexibility under the Amsterdam Treaty?" (1998) 35 *CMLRev.* 855 at 857–8.

[114] Under Art. 281 EC, the European Community has legal personality. See P Lachmann, "International Legal Personality of the EC: Capacity and Competence" (1984) 1 *LIEI* 3. On its

Communities,[115] are endowed with legal personality. Under public international law, legal personality in general entails treaty-making capacity, capacity to present international claims by diplomatic procedures or in other available forms, a liability for the consequences of breaches of international law and privileges and immunities in relation to the national jurisdiction of states.[116] The fact that, in its relations with third countries and international organisations under the second pillar, the Union must act through its Presidency, whereas the legal relations stemming from or leading to the conclusion of international agreements give rise to the role of Community institutions, often along with that of Member States, has created practical problems acknowledged by the Council itself.[117] Not only the Commission[118] and the European Parliament[119] but also the majority of the Member States suggested that legal personality should be given to the Union for, according to the Report of the Reflection Group, this would "enable it to conclude international agreements in the areas of Titles V and VI".[120] This suggestion was also made by the High Level Group of Experts on the CFSP, set up by Commissioner van den Broek in the context of the preparation from the 1996 Intergovernmental Conference. [121]

relations with international organisations see R Frid, *The Relations Between the EC and International Organizations. Legal Theory and Practice* (The Hague: Kluwer Law International, 1995) and V Réseau, *L'Union européenne et les organisations internationales* (Brussels: Bruylant et Editions de l'Université de Bruxelles, 1997); see also E Denza, "The Community as a Member of International Organizations" in N Emiliou and D O'Keeffe (eds.), *The European Union and World Trade Law After the GATT Uruguay Round*, (Chichester: Wiley, 1996) 3; J Sack, "The European Community's Membership of International Organizations" (1995) 32 *CMLRev.* 1227. For the relations of the Community with specifically the Council of Europe see T Ouchterlony, "The European Communities and the Council of Europe" (1984) 1 *LIEI* 59.

[115] ECSC under Art. 6 and Euratom under Art. 184 of their constituent Treaties have legal personality.

[116] I Brownlie, "International Law at the Fiftieth Anniversary of the United Nations. General Course on Public International Law" (1995) 25 *RdC* 9 at 52 and 63–5. In the Advisory Opinion of the International Court of Justice on *Reparation for Injuries suffered in the Service of the United Nations* [1949] ICJ Reports 194, the international legal personality of international organisations has been understood as entailing "a permanent association of states, with lawful objects, equipped with organs; a distinction, in terms of legal powers and purposes, between the organization and its member states; the existence of legal powers exercisable on the international plane and not solely within the national systems of one or more states": I Brownlie, *Principles of Public International Law* (5th edn., Oxford: Clarendon Press, 1999).

[117] See its *Report on the Functioning of the Treaty on European Union* of 10 Apr. 1995, Doc. 5082/95 at para. 69.

[118] See its *Report on the Operation of the Treaty on European Union* (Brussels, 10 May 1995), SEC(95)731 fin.

[119] See its *Report on the Functioning of the Treaty on European Union with a View to the 1996 Inter-Governmental Conference—Implementation and Development of the Union* of 19 May 1995, EP Doc. A4-102/95 at para. 14(ii).

[120] Report of 5 Dec. 1995, Brussels, SEC(95)2163. The majority of the Group's members "consider the fact that the Union has no existence as a legal entity to be a source of confusion in the outside world which diminishes its external profile". However, "other members took the view that the creation of an international legal personality for the Union could give rise to confusion with the legal prerogatives of the Member States"; see at 40. For national positions on this matter, see the Briefing No 20 on the 1996 IGC prepared by the European Parliament.

[121] See its second report entitled *European Foreign and Security Policy in the Run-up to the year 2000: Ways and Means of Establishing Genuine Credibility* of 28 Feb. 1996.

In addressing the issue of the international legal personality of the European Union, the Member States focused on a specific aspect of it, namely the conclusion of international agreements; this was due to the latter's direct relevance to the conduct of the Union's foreign policy. The Member States had already acknowledged this fact, as the case of the administration of Mostar clearly illustrates, whereby a Memorandum of Understanding was signed between "the Member States of the European Union acting within the framework of the Union in full association with the European Commission" and "the Member States of the Western European Union"[122]; this agreement was ratified by all the Member States. Hence, in addressing the problem that the European Union, in relation to its actions on the international scene, was capable of engaging in policy making but not treaty making,[123] the Amsterdam Treaty, instead of conferring express legal personality, introduced a rather ingenious arrangement. Under Article 24, the Council may unanimously authorise the Presidency to negotiate agreements with States or international organisations when this is deemed necessary for the implementation of Title V. The Presidency, which in negotiating the agreement may be assisted by the Commission "as appropriate", will make a recommendation to the Council which then may conclude the agreement by unanimity. Such agreements will not be binding on Member States which, according to their representative in the Council, have to comply with requirements of their national constitutional procedures.[124]

The new procedure introduced by Article 24 TEU illustrates the reluctance of the Member States to have recourse to legal solutions requiring Community procedures and instruments when the conclusion of agreements in the area of CFSP is required. Indeed, in other areas where recourse to Community instruments was deemed necessary, an inter-pillar approach involving both the Community legal order and the CFSP has been adopted either explicitly under Article 301 EC, in the case of sanctions against third countries, or by means of secondary legislation, in the case of common rules on exports of dual-use goods.[125] This approach is based upon the adoption of a Community instrument implementing a Title V measure. In the case of agreements in the CFSP area, this pattern would consist of a Title V instrument referring to the legal

---

[122] See RA Wessel, "The International Legal Status of the European Union" (1997) 2 *EFA Review* 109 at 127–8. On the basis of this document, the Member States requested the WEU to assist the Union administrator to restore public order and security in Mostar. Hence, police officers from WEU countries are directly responsible to him. Wessel argues that claims on the basis of this agreement would be addressed to the Union and not the Member States. However, the legal formula followed by the Member States seems to question this conclusion without providing an answer to the practical problems arising in relation to claims against the Member States under the Memorandum.

[123] M Cremona, "The European Union as an International Actor: The Issues of Flexibility and Linkage" (1998) 3 *EFA Review* 67 at 67–8.

[124] Under the second limb of Art. 24 TEU, the procedure set out therein is also applicable to the third pillar.

[125] In this area, common rules were established on the basis of an inter-pillar approach; these rules were originally set out in Council Reg. 3381/94, adopted under Art. 133 EC, and Decision 94/942/CFSP, adopted under Art. J.4 TEU: see *supra* note 80. For an analysis of these rules, see *infra* at ch. 5.

personality of the Community and relying upon the procedures established under the EC Treaty regarding the negotiation and conclusion of international agreements. The example of the memorandum of Mostar indicates the link between the CFSP action and the Community framework which would justify their interaction, namely the financing of the former from the budget of the latter. However, the introduction of the new Article 24 procedure illustrates the reluctance of the Member States to follow this pattern of instrumentalisation of Community measures and procedures to serve CFSP objectives. This approach may be understood as underlining their concern over the potential dilution of the intergovernmental integrity of the second pillar.

However, while enhancing the effective implementation of CFSP measures, the procedural novelty provided under Article 24 is of yet unclear implications. Academic opinion differs on whether it will be the Union or the Member States that will become parties to an agreement negotiated and concluded under the new Article 24.[126] The "assistance" that the Commission may provide in the negotiation of agreements to the Presidency, along with their conclusion by the Council, may seem to suggest that it will be the Union which will become a contracting party to the relevant agreement. On the other hand, the reference to national ratification procedures indicates that it will be the Member States that will be parties to an agreement negotiated and concluded thereunder.

As regards to the related issue whether the European Union possesses international legal personality, Declaration No 4 annexed to the Amsterdam Treaty may seem to provide a negative response; it states that the establishment of the Article 24 procedure and any agreements resulting from it "shall not imply any transfer of competence from the Member States to the European Union".[127] This approach is consistent with the Member States' refusal to endow the Union with legal personality when it was first established under the Maastricht Treaty.[128] This attitude may be explained, on the one hand, by their concern that to confer express legal personality on the Union may risk the intergovernmental character underpinning Title V and, on the other hand, by their reluc-

---

[126] Monar argues, *supra* note 99 at 427, that only the Member States will be contracting parties, whereas Langrish, *supra* note 100 at 14, supports the opposite view, namely that the agreement will be concluded on behalf of the Union. Cremona argues that it is the Member States that will engage in the international obligation stemming from an agreement concluded under Art. 24: see "External Relations and External Competence: The Emergence of an Integrated Policy" in P Craig and G de Búrca (eds.), *The Evolution of EU Law* (Oxford: OUP, 1999) 137 at 168.

[127] Art. 24 TEU is also to be applied to matters falling within Title VI. Declaration No 4 refers, in addition to Art. 24 , to Title VI.

[128] See the reference to the yet unpublished *travaux préparatoires* of TEU in MR Eaton, "Common Foreign and Security Policy" in D O'Keeffe and P Twomey (eds.), *Legal Issues of the Maastricht Treaty* (London: Chancery Law, 1994) 215 at 224. His thesis that the Union lacks legal personality is shared by D Curtin, "The Constitutional Structure of the Union: A Europe of Bits and Pieces" (1993) 30 *CMLRev.* 17 at 27; U Everling, "Reflections on the Structure of the European Union" (1992) 29 *CMLRev.* 1053; T Heukels and JW De Zwaan, "The Configuration of the European Union: Community Dimensions of Institutional Interactions" in Curtin and Heukels, *supra* note 63, 195 at 202; Willaert and Marqués-Ruiz, *supra* note 76 at 28.

tance to deprive the Community of its legal personality, since that of the Union's would render it redundant.

However, the agreement of the Member States not to endow the European Union with international legal personality leaves open the question whether the Treaty on European Union does indeed have the intended effect. The definition of international legal personality put forward by the International Court of Justice in its *Reparations for Injuries* Advisory Opinion has been accepted as referring not only to subjective but also to objective legal personality.[129] In other words, the question which arises is not so much why the Member States did not confer express legal personality on the Union but rather whether the latter's attributes, along with its capacity to conclude international agreements, indicate its objective legal personality.

The difficulty in providing a definite answer to whether the European Union possesses objective international legal personality relies to a certain extent on the fact that the notion of international legal personality and the legal capacities it entails are understood in the context of sovereign states or international organisations. Given that the European Union may not be characterised as either,[130] to address the issue of its legal personality would require an examination of its whole constitutional structure and an elaborate analysis of the delimitation of power both between the Member States and the institutional actors of the Union and amongst the institutional actors themselves. There are strong arguments suggesting the European Union does possess international legal personality.[131] However, a definite answer would require close examination of how the treaty-making procedure set out in Article 24 TEU is to be applied. In other words, the answer to the question of the European Union's legal personality would be dependent upon how the existing institutional machinery is relied upon and the treaty-making procedure utilised.

For the purpose of this book, suffice it to conclude that the approach adopted by the Member States to the issue of the international legal personality of the European Union has been consistent with that underpinning the development of the CFSP. The latter has evolved incrementally and on the basis of a dynamic process; furthermore, instead of following a coherent conceptual model, its development sought to respond to specific problems that the Member States

---

[129] [1949] ICJ Rep. 174. According to the definition of legal personality given therein, "the rights and duties of an entity . . . must depend upon its purposes and functions as specified or implied in its constituent documents and developed in practice. . . . Under international law, the [United Nations] Organization must be deemed to have those powers which, though not expressly provided in the Charter, are conferred upon it by necessary implication as being essential to its duties. . . . [I]t could not carry out the intentions of its founders if it was devoid of international personality."

[130] On the Union's legal nature as alien to that of international organisations see AD Pliakos, "La nature juridique de l'Union européenne" (1993) 29 *RTDE* 187 at 211–13, where the argument that the Union may possess objective legal personality under the Maastricht Treaty is rejected. For the conclusion that the European Union defies any traditional legal classification see CA Stephanou, "The Legal Nature of the European Union" in N Emiliou and D O'Keeffe (eds.), *Legal Aspects of Integration in the European Union* (London: Kluwer Law International, 1997) 171.

[131] For an elaborate analysis reaching this conclusion, see Wessel, *supra* note 119.

deemed necessary to address collectively. This is the approach adopted by the Member States regarding the question of the legal personality of the Union: the Member States' focus on the latter's treaty-making action clearly illustrates that it was issues of practical significance and relevance to its international action that were sought to be accommodated, while the more general legal issue was avoided.[132] In so far as the foreign policy of the Union relies effectively upon the arrangements introduced in the Amsterdam Treaty, the question of the legal personality of the Union will be the subject of only academic interest[133]; it will become of direct concern to the Member States when a specific issue stemming from it will raise specific practical problems that will have to be addressed.

5. THE PRINCIPLES UNDERPINNING THE CFSP OF THE EUROPEAN UNION

The above analysis indicated that the inception and implementation of the Union's foreign policy has been subject to various legal developments and political circumstances: it has purported to be common but not single, effective but with only indirect and limited recourse to military force and only for very specific aims, of a different character from national models of foreign policy yet instrumentalising public international law tools traditionally available to sovereign states. In short, the Union's foreign policy is of a *sui generis* character. The legal framework under which this policy is pursued has been of an equally unique character, combining sets of rules of a different normative quality, providing for institutions to act in varying roles depending on the subject matter under consideration and relying heavily upon procedures of ambiguous implications. Finally, it was argued that the establishment of this multipolar framework is due, on the one hand, to the refusal of Member States to surrender their dominant role in the conduct of foreign policy and, on the other hand, to their tacit acknowledgement of the interdependence between trade and foreign policy.

These characteristics of the CFSP raise the following question: does the framework established by the Treaty on European Union provide the legal guarantees which would ensure that its *sui generis* character is not an ill-conceived effort to accommodate conflicting models of integration? In other words, is the merger of legally distinct but interdependent sets of rules capable of operating as a functional system, relying upon the synergy between the relevant rules while preventing the dilution of their legal characteristics?

Any answer to this question requires an analysis of the principles underlying the relationship between EC and CFSP which are spelled out in Article 3 TEU;

---

[132] It is in the light of this feature that the Union has been characterised as "mov[ing] from one package-deal compromise to the next with a good deal of inertia, with determined efforts to defend entrenched advantages and a built-in reluctance to address strategic issues" by H Wallace and W Wallace, quoted in Edwards and Phillippart, *supra* note 110 at 35.

[133] See A von Bogdandy and M Nettesheim, "Ex Pluribus Unum: Fusion of the European Communities into the European Union" (1996) 2 *ELJ* 267 at 286.

under this provision, "[t]he Union shall be served by a single institutional framework which shall ensure the consistency and the continuity of the activities carried out in order to attain its objectives while respecting and building upon the *acquis communautaire*". Therefore, three concepts are identified as the foundation of the constitutional link between the first and second pillars, namely a single institutional framework, the requirement of consistency and that of respect for the *acquis communautaire*.

It must be stressed at the outset that the above three concepts essentially flesh out the idea that the Community legal framework and the CFSP operate on the basis of a symbiotic relationship. It is this idea that Article 3 TEU refers to when providing that the activities carried out by the Union are not only to "respect" but also "build upon" the *acquis communautaire*. Therefore, it is not entirely accurate to argue that the establishment of the second pillar reflects in principle a rigid distinction between the Community legal framework and the CFSP. The question, then, is whether it establishes a fully-fledged set of legal guarantees to implement the Article 3 TEU principles and hence bring about a symbiotic relationship between the first and second pillars.

5.1. "A single institutional framework": institutional interactions between EC and CFSP

The provision of "a single institutional framework" in Article 3 TEU has been described "a mere lip service to an ideal".[134] In order to ascertain the accuracy of this statement, it is necessary to examine, first, the Treaty provisions establishing the institutional interactions between EC and CFSP and, secondly, the practice of the institutions so far. It must be pointed out at the outset that the "single institutional framework" does not provide merely for interactions between various institutions but essentially for interactions between functions of a legally distinct character performed by the existing institutions.

The Treaty does not establish distinct institutions to operate under the second pillar; instead, Community institutions are to apply the Title V rules. However, they do not enjoy the same powers that the EC Treaty confers on them.[135] The Commission's right of initiative, exclusive under EC Treaty, is shared with the Member States under Article 22 TEU. It is interesting that there are two provisions regarding the participation of the Commission in activities carried out within the CFSP: it "shall be fully associated with the work carried out in the common foreign and security policy field" in general[136] and the

---

[134] Curtin, *supra* note 128 at 28.

[135] For an analysis of practical issues regarding the institutional interactions under EPC see S Nuttall, "The Institutional Network and the Instruments of Actions" in R Rummel (ed.), *Toward Political Union: Planning a Common Foreign and Security Policy in the European Community* (Baden-Baden: Nomos, 1992) 55.

[136] Art. 27 TEU.

Presidency's task to represent the Union and ensure the implementation of common measures in particular.[137] Its delegations in third countries and international organisations co-operate with the diplomatic and consular missions of the Member States in order to ensure that the measures adopted under Title V are complied with and implemented.[138] Most significantly, it has the duty under Article 3(2) TEU to ensure, along with the Council, the consistency of the Union's external activities as a whole.

The role of the Commission under Title V, albeit not equal to that established in the Community legal framework, is not to be underestimated.[139] Having recourse to the full potential of its right of initiative, it can significantly contribute to the development of the common foreign policy. The Commission's claim to an exclusive right of initiative is unrealistic[140] on both legal and political grounds. As far as the former is concerned, it is contrary to the very nature of the system of foreign policy put forward by the Treaty on European Union which consists of a common rather than single foreign policy. Regarding the latter ground, the consensus of all Member States on the central role they are to play in the development of the Union's international presence leaves no doubt about their unwillingness to surrender their right of initiative. It is quite a different point whether the Commission's exclusive right of initiative would enhance the effectiveness of CFSP. However, it is not immediately apparent why the abolition of the right of Member States to put forward initiatives would render the second pillar more effective. A counter-argument in this direction may be based, on the one hand, on the objective of coherence of the external activities of the Union and, on the other hand, on the duty of the Commission as a guardian of the EC Treaty which the relevance of EC measures to CFSP activities renders all the more pertinent. However, the Commission already enjoys a pivotal role in achieving this objective. Under the Treaty, it is, on the one hand, to ensure the consistency of the external actions of the Union and, on the other hand, to safeguard the *acquis communautaire* as the guardian of the Treaty. The extent to which this role is of rhetorical significance greatly depends upon whether the Commission will make full use of these powers. The Amsterdam Treaty points towards this direction. It does not bestow on the Commission an exclusive right of initiative, but gives it the right to make proposals to the newly set-up Policy Planning and Early Warning Unit, a body established within the

---

[137] Art. 18(3) TEU.

[138] Art. 20 TEU. Moreover, under the second para., they must "step up co-operation by exchanging information, carrying out joint assessment and contributing to the implementation of the provisions referred to in Article 20 [EC]", that is providing protection to EU citizens in the territory of a third country.

[139] For the Commission's role in the development of the Union's foreign policy framework see S Nuttall, "The Commission and foreign policy-making" in G Edwards and D Spence (eds.), *The European Commission* (London: Cartermill, 1995) 287.

[140] See CWA Timmermans, "General Institutional Questions: the Effectiveness and Simplification of Decision-Making" in Winter, Curtin, Kellerman and de Witte (eds.), *supra* note 99, 133 at 138.

structure of the Council Secretariat[141] in order to enhance the effectiveness of CFSP by analysing international developments, following up the Union's policy, identifying areas and events of significance for the Union's policy and producing policy papers.

The European Parliament shall be consulted "on the main aspects and the basic choices of [CFSP] activities" by the Presidency, which "shall ensure that the views of the European Parliament are duly taken into consideration".[142] In addition, the Presidency and the Commission "shall regularly inform [it] of discussions in [CFSP] areas".[143] Moreover, the Parliament enjoys the right to submit questions and make recommendations to the Council and hold a debate on the progress made in the implementation of CFSP.[144]

The attribution of the above powers to the Parliament has been criticised as minimal and of rhetorical significance.[145] However, it must be pointed out that even in a national context parliaments do not enjoy considerably greater powers in the area of foreign affairs,[146] for the latter are considered to be a matter for the executive. It is rather the power of national parliaments to sanction ministers and/or governments for failures in the area of foreign affairs that renders them of central significance. This is due to the direct link between national parliaments and governments which is manifestly alien to the relationship between the Council and the European Parliament. Therefore, the unique legal character of the European Union being taken into account, the European Parliament does not have an apparently justified claim to a more active involvement in the conduct of foreign policy.[147] This is even more so in the light of its inability to exploit the full potential of its current powers. Because of internal problems regarding the interpretation of its Rules of Procedure, the Parliament has yet to

---

[141] The Policy Planning and Early Warning Unit is established under a Declaration to the Final Act. For the interim report on the role and size of the Unit drawn up by the British Presidency, see *Agence Europe*, 7193 2 Apr. 1998 at 2.

[142] Art. 21 TEU.

[143] *Ibid.*

[144] *Ibid.* at para. 2.

[145] See R Bieber, "Democratic Control of European Foreign Policy" (1990) 1 *EJII* 148; T Grunert, "The Association of the European Parliament: No Longer the Underdog in EPC?" in Regelsberger, de Scoutheete de Tervarent and Wessels (eds.), *supra* note 59 at 109; P Dankert, "Pressure from the European Parliament" in G Edwards and A Pijpers (eds.), *The Politics of European Treaty Reform. The 1996 Intergovernmental Conference and Beyond* (London: Pinter, 1997) 212; B Kaleagasi, "A New European Order, the EC, Foreign Policy and Democracy" in Telo (ed.), *supra* note 50 at 185; K-H Neunreither, "The European Parliament: An Emerging Political Role?" in G Edwards and E Regelsberger (eds.), *Europe's Global Links. The European Community and Inter-Regional Cooperation* (London: St.Martin's, 1990) 169; S Stavridis, "The Democratic Control of the CFSP" in Holland (ed.), *supra* note 73 at 136. For an early account of the role of EP in the external relations of the Community see JHH Weiler, "The European Parliament and Foreign Affairs: External Relations of the European Economic Community" in A Cassese, (ed.), *Parliamentary Control over Foreign Policy* (Alphen an der Rijn: Sijthoff & Noordhoff, 1980) 151.

[146] This is also mentioned in the Reflection Group's Report, SEC(95)2163 at 44.

[147] It is noteworthy that even regarding Community measures adopted under Art. 133 within the Common Commercial Policy, the Parliament does not enjoy any formally established power, even though it is consulted as a matter of practice when the adoption of the measure in question is not of urgency.

make recommendations and has submitted only a handful of resolutions under Article 21 TEU.[148] In this respect, its demand to be consulted in advance regarding the adoption of common positions and joint actions[149] seems premature, unnecessary and contrary to basic principles underlying the conduct of foreign policy, namely efficiency and speediness. Indeed, the role of the Parliament can be enhanced without modification of the Treaty, provided that its present powers are fully used. Thus, it could play a significant political role in the development of CFSP.

It is not only the functions of the Community institutions which are central to the operation of the "single institutional framework"; it is also the role undertaken by various administrative bodies which can be of significance. In addition to the dual role attributed to the primary Community institutions with varied characteristics, administrative bodies originally conceived in the Community framework are to play a role under the second pillar. The principal administrative body since the inception of Political Co-operation has been the Political Committee, that is the Political Directors of the Foreign Ministries of Member States. Under Article 25 TEU, the Political Committee monitors the international situation and the implementation of the agreed policies[150] and delivers opinions to the Council either at the request of the latter or on its own initiative. However, the central role of the Council under Title V entails the extension of the preparatory role of COREPER which, under Article 207 EC, shall be responsible for preparing the Council's work and for carrying out the tasks assigned by it; in order to avoid tensions stemming from overlapping functions, Article 25 TEU states that the role of the Political Committee must be carried out without prejudice to Article 207 EC. In addition to COREPER, the role of the Council's Secretariat was also expanded in the area of the foreign policy of the Union. This becomes all the more evident in the light of the incorporation of the Political Co-operation's Secretariat into the Council's Secretariat as an autonomous division.[151] The same applies to the Political Co-operation Working Groups.[152]

There is one objection which may be raised to the above administrative interactions. The involvement of various administrative bodies set up and operating under different legal frameworks in the preparation and implementation of foreign policy leads to unnecessary confusion about the allocation of tasks and responsibilities. This confusion undermines the effectiveness of the policies to

---

[148] See *Report of Committee on Foreign Affairs, Security and Defence Policy on Progress in Implementing the Common Foreign and Security Policy* (Jan. to Dec. 1996), A4–0193/97.

[149] See Grunert, *supra* note 145 at 113.

[150] Under the second limb of Art. 25 TEU, the Political Committee is to fulfil this role without prejudice to the responsibility of the Presidency and the Commission.

[151] See Declaration on practical arrangements in the field of the common foreign and security policy (No. 28) to the TEU.

[152] By means of a ministerial decision: see E Regelsberger and W Wessels, "The CFSP Institutions and Procedures: A Third Way for the Second Pillar" (1996) 1 *EFA Review* 29 at 36–7 for further details on problems resulting from this development.

be adopted. This criticism is justified to a certain extent. The effectiveness of the policies adopted may be weakened by undue emphasis on the procedural side of the policy-making rather than its substance. This is in line with the general characteristic of the foreign policy system of the Union since its inception. However, it is a moot point whether the interaction of COREPER and the Political Committee constitutes *per se* a pathological characteristic of the CFSP. The relationship between Community and CFSP administrative bodies can only be viewed as a secondary component of the overall structure of the Union, that is different legal contexts operating within a single institutional framework. Arguments against this structure may be based on a different perception of the development of the Union but they cannot have their foundation on administrative difficulties of secondary bodies. In this respect, the practical arrangements established by the Council seem adequately to address the problem.[153] Indeed, the administrative problems regarding the interactions between Community and CFSP bodies are not so complex as to defy regulation by the Union institutions on the basis of the Treaty principles, that is co-operation within a single institutional framework.

5.2. The requirement of consistency and substantive interactions between EC and CFSP

5.2.1. The definition of "consistency"

The requirement of consistency is introduced under Article 1 TEU, which provides that the task of the Union "shall be to organize, in a manner demonstrating consistency and solidarity, relations between the Member States and between their peoples". The Article 3 provision is further elaborated upon in its second paragraph, according to which "[t]he Union shall in particular ensure the consistency of its external activities as a whole in the context of its external relations, security, economic and development policies". In relation specifically to Title V, under Article 13(3) TEU, the Council "shall ensure the unity, consistency and effectiveness of action by the Union".

The definition of the requirement of consistency is not without problems. Contrary to the English version of the Treaty, the French one refers to "*cohérence*". The same term is used in the German version.[154] This terminological discrepancy may be of significance, for "consistency" and "coherence" are not identical concepts. The former denotes lack of contradictions, whereas the latter the construction of a united whole; in this respect, consistency seems to be

---

[153] A Council report of 21 Oct. 1993 provides that the opinion of the Political Committee addressed to the Council would be part of the agenda of COREPER and forwarded to the Council as quickly as possible on the basis that COREPER would not normally intervene: see G Edwards, "Common Foreign and Security Policy" (1993) 13 *YEL* 497 at 499.

[154] "*Cohaerentz*". The same term is used in the Italian, Spanish and Portuguese versions.

a precondition, albeit not a sufficient one, of coherence.[155] It is suggested that it would be too narrow an interpretation of Articles 1 and 3 in general and 13(3) TEU in particular to deduce merely a requirement for the various components of the Union's external activities not to contradict one another. The argument that the relationship between the first and second pillars is envisaged as not merely a non-contradictory one is supported by the provisions for direct inter-actions between the two frameworks. Article 301 EC, for instance, provides for the imposition of sanctions on third countries under a system combining a common position or a joint action adopted under Title V TEU and a Council Regulation adopted under Article 301 itself. Leaving the legal problems that such a formula may give rise to aside,[156] the *ratio* of this provision indicates that in principle Title V and the Community legal framework are to operate in synergy.

It follows from the above that the notion of consistency under the Treaty must be construed in broader terms than merely connoting the absence of con-tradictions between the pillars. The requirement of consistency is to be applied to the activities undertaken on the basis of Title V, the relationship between the CFSP and national foreign policies and that between the Community and the CFSP. It is the latter application of the requirement of consistency that is rele-vant to the subject of this book.

5.2.2. *Substantive interactions*

The study of the activities undertaken within Title V indicates that the substan-tive interactions between Title V and the EC may be either direct or indirect. A direct substantive interaction consists of a system of rules adopted under both frameworks. The imposition of trade sanctions on third countries is a case in point, for it is based on a common position under Article 15 TEU and a Community regulation under Article 301 EC. The establishment of common rules on export controls of dual-use goods also seeks to follow this pattern.[157] Alternatively, an indirect interaction consists of a reference in the measure adopted under Title V to Community activities. The wording of this reference and, hence, its legal repercussions vary and may take two forms.

---

[155] C Tietje, "The Concept of Coherence in the Treaty on European Union and the Common Foreign and Security Policy" (1997) 2 *EFA Review* 211 at 212–13 where further references are pro-vided on the definition of consistency and coherence in law. In the light of the reference to "coher-ence" in various versions of the Treaty, Tietje analyses the Treaty requirement of consistency under the name of coherence and regard being taken of the definition given above. The role of consistency as a requirement of coherence and that of both of them as prerequisites of effectiveness indicate the limits and complexities of an attempt to provide an accurate legal definition. For the purpose of this book, it is the notion of consistency under TEU that will be analysed in the light of the broad defin-ition given below.

[156] See *infra* ch. 4.

[157] Trade sanctions to third countries and exports of dual-use goods are discussed in detail in chs. 3–4 and 5 respectively.

First, CFSP measures make reference to activities already undertaken within the Community legal framework. An example of this is Decision 97/817/CFSP on anti-personnel landmines[158] which makes express reference to the Community's action in this area in the context of its humanitarian aid, reconstruction and development co-operation. It also provides that "the Commission will continue to support these activities" and "to pursue research activities relevant to mine clearance".[159] Moreover, Article 7 reiterates the responsibility of the Council and the Commission under Article 3 TEU to ensure consistency of the Union's activities in the specific context of mine clearance, including relief for victims. It is interesting that the wording of Article 3 is adopted almost *verbatim*.[160]

Secondly, Title V measures make reference to measures to be taken within the Community legal framework in order to assist the CFSP activity in question. An example is offered by Council Decision 98/117/CFSP adopting a joint action in support of the Bosnian Peace Process[161] which provides in its preamble that Community measures are to be taken in support of the new Government in the Entity of the Republic Srpska and in addition to those adopted in the action itself, the aim being "the consistency of the Union's external activities". In the common position on Angola adopted by Council Decision 95/413/CFSP,[162] Article C provides that "[t]he Council and the Commission, acting within the framework of their respective competences, shall take the measures necessary for the implementation of th[at] common position". Council Decision 94/779/CFSP on the Union's objectives and priorities towards Ukraine[163] constitutes another example of a CFSP measure falling within this category. It makes reference to the measures and programmes undertaken by the Community. Moreover, Article A.3 notes the importance of the early entry into force of the Partnership and Co-operation Agreement between the Union and Ukraine in the context of the former's support of the latter's economic stabilisation. Finally the standard provision for the Commission's adoption of Community measures in support of the common position is included. Furthermore, in Council Decision 96/656/CFSP on the Union's support of the democratic transition process in Zaire[164] Article 5 makes reference to the Commission's intention to propose measures to help achieve the objectives of the joint action *inter alia* under the European Development Fund. Under Council Decision 97/289/CFSP on the establishment of a Union's assistance

---

[158] [1997] OJ L338/1.

[159] Art. 5. The same provision was inserted into Decision 95/170/CFSP [1995] OJ L115/1 as well as in Dec. 96/251/CFSP [1996] OJ L87/3, Art. 3 of which notes that "the Commission intends to support other mine clearance operations within the framework of Community cooperation".

[160] Under Art. 5, the Council and the Commission "shall ensure implementation of their respective action, each in accordance with its powers".

[161] *Supra* note 86.

[162] [1995] OJ L245/1.

[163] [1994] OJ L313/1.

[164] *Supra* note 96.

programme to support the Palestinian Authority in its efforts to counter terrorist activities emanating from the territories under its control, a Union adviser is
appointed to oversee the implementation of the programme set up thereby.[165]
Article 2 provides that both he/she and the Commission "within the scope of
their respective competences, shall ensure appropriate coordination between
the programme, Community assistance and the bilateral assistance provided by
the Member states and shall cooperate to this end". Moreover, under Article
3(6) the Council "takes note of the measures which the Commission intends to
propose as Community action in support of the objectives of th[at] Joint Action,
in particular in the fields of human rights training, procurement of equipment
and services, information technology, secure communications and explosive
ordnance disposal". In the Joint Action nominating a Special Envoy of the
Union for the African Great Lakes Region adopted by Council Decision
96/250/CFSP,[166] the Council notes in Article 4(4) the Commission's intention to
provide logistical support in the region.

Decision 98/108/CFSP adopting a common position on Afghanistan[167] sets
out the objectives of the Union in the light of the conflict in that country. Among
objectives arguably falling within the scope of CFSP, namely sustainable peace,
termination of foreign intervention and encouragement of dialogue between
national parties, Article 1 refers to the provision of effective humanitarian aid
which falls within the competence, albeit non exclusive,[168] of the Community
under Articles 177–181 of the EC Treaty. In this respect, Article 4 stressed that
the Union "shall continue to provide humanitarian aid to Afghanistan" and
Article 5 "notes the importance of implementation of the Community's project
in support of the Union's Central Asia Drugs Initiative". Finally, in Article 6
"the Council notes that the Commission will direct its action towards achieving
the objectives and priorities of this common position by appropriate
Community measures". Another example of a CFSP measure falling within this
category is Council Decision 94/697/CFSP on the Union's objectives and priorities *vis-à-vis* Rwanda.[169] This measure makes elaborate reference in the preamble not only to the measures and programmes undertaken by the Community in
the context of the existing ACP/EEC Conventions but also to the Commission's
intention to continue actions contributing to the Union's objectives and priorities towards Rwanda and to take appropriate steps in the context of the fourth

---

[165] See *supra* note 85.
[166] [1996] OJ L87/1.
[167] [1998] OJ L32/14.
[168] See Cases C–181 and C–284/91 *European Parliament* v. *Council and Commission (Bangladesh Cases)* [1993] ECR I–3685 according to which the result of the non-exclusive competence of the Community in the area of humanitarian aid is the right of the Member States to exercise their con-current competence collectively, within or outside the Council. The non-exclusive nature of the Community's competence was extended to development policy in general in Case C–316/91 *European Parliament* v. *Council (European Development Fund Case)* [1994] ECR I–625.
[169] [1994] OJ L283/1.

ACP/EEC Convention.[170] The annex to the Decision which sets out the objectives and priorities of the Union towards Rwanda includes various Community policies, such as humanitarian aid to refugees, development co-operation, measures for the repair of economic, ecological and social damages in those countries bordering Rwanda, which have been particularly struck by the refugee crisis. It is remarkable that these objectives coexist with statements of purely political character which could not be adopted under Community rules, namely the importance attributed by the Union to the rapid total deployment of United Nations troops in order to assure protection against acts of revenge and persecution and the consideration given to the establishment of an international tribunal.

5.2.3. Administrative interactions

A particular form of interaction between the Community legal framework and the CFSP consists of the arrangements in relation to the financing of actions undertaken under the latter. In relation to administrative expenditure, consistently with the Maastricht Treaty, the Amsterdam Treaty[171] provides that it is to be charged to the Community budget. In relation to operational expenditure, however, under the Maastricht Treaty a choice was left to the Council to charge either the Community budget or the Member States. If the latter was the case, it was provided that the procedures laid down in the relevant EC Treaty were to be applied. This provision led to a twofold result. On the one hand, when the Council unanimously agreed to charge the Community budget, the European Parliament sought to use its relevant powers under Community law to influence the substance of the CFSP measure in question. It is interesting to note that, in its first reading of the 1993 budget, it inserted one million ECUs in the Commission's operational reserves and made it clear that it could be transferred to the operational costs of the CFSP, in which case its approval was necessary under the Community budgetary rules.[172] The problems between the Council and the Parliament stemming from the implications of Article J.11(2) are demonstrated by the fact that an inter-institutional agreement was signed as late as 16 July 1997, that is more than three and half years after the entry into force of the Treaty.[173] On the other hand, the Council found it very difficult to agree on charging operational expenditure to national budgets. This problem was illustrated in the case of the Bosnia-Herzegovina operation, where agreement was reached six months after the adoption of the joint action and hence, in the

---

[170] In the recent Council Dec. 98/252/CFSP [1998] OJ L108/1, which updates Dec. 94/697/CFSP, Art. 3 notes that "the Commission intends to direct its action towards achieving the objectives and the priorities of th[at] common position, where appropriate, by pertinent Community measures".

[171] Art. 28(2) TEU. This was provided under Art. J.11(2) of the Maastricht Treaty.

[172] See J Monar, "The Finances of the Union's Intergovernmental Pillars: Tortuous Experiments with the Community Budget" (1997) 35 *JCMS* 57 at 63–4.

[173] Interinstitutional Agreement on the financing of the common foreign and security policy: *Bull. EU* 7/8-1997, point 2.3.1.

absence of any action to be implemented, the relevant funds were transferred to the budget of the administration of Mostar.

These problems and their repercussions on the effectiveness of the Union's common foreign policy[174] led to the amendment of the Article J.11(2) provision by the Treaty of Amsterdam. Under the new Article 28(3), the standard procedure for financing CFSP activities consists of charging the Community budget.[175] This rule, in addition to the Interinstitutional Agreement signed by the Council, the Commission and the Parliament, seems adequate to establish a system which, albeit based on two distinct frameworks, may enhance the effectiveness of the CFSP actions.

5.3. Respect for the *acquis communautaire*

The substantive interactions between Community policies and the CFSP outlined above put forward a rather self-evident fact: trade and foreign policy can neither be pursued nor implemented in isolation. They are intrinsically linked and their effectiveness relies, in practical terms, to a great extent upon their consistency and coherence. However, when this conclusion is to be given substance, legal problems arise because the relevant legal frameworks are characterised by different features. The same institutions are to perform various functions under different rules, the decision-making processes vary depending on the subject of the measure to be adopted and Article 46 TEU excludes Title V from the jurisdiction of the Court. Therefore, the following question arises: does the TEU ensure a symbiotic relationship between EC and CFSP as a consistent and effective system whose operation would not undermine the *acquis communautaire*?

This question has been answered in two ways, illustrated in the Reflection Group's Report.[176] According to one view, the substantive interactions outlined above threaten to dilute the supranational character of both Community procedures and institutions by the intergovernmental structures prevailing under Title V. According to this argument, if measures adopted unanimously under Title V refer to intended Community action which would normally be adopted under majority voting, then the *acquis communautaire* would be undermined in various ways: the Commission's sole right of initiative would not be respected, the participation of the European Parliament would be sidelined and the voting method under the EC Treaty ignored. This approach seems to be based on the binding character of the Title V instruments. It is pointed out that the binding character of foreign policy measures ceased to be a moot point since the adoption of the Single European Act.[177] Title V does not leave much room for dis-

---

[174] See J Monar, "The Financial Dimension of the CFSP" in Holland, *supra* note 73 at 34.
[175] This rule is qualified in cases of decisions with military or defence implications and those where the Council unanimously decides to charge national budgets.
[176] See *supra* note 120 at 39.
[177] See *supra* under 2.4.

pute[178]; under Article 14, "joint actions shall commit the Member States in the positions they adopt and in the conduct of their activity",[179] under Article 15, "Member States shall ensure that their national policies conform to the common positions", under Article 19, they "shall co-ordinate their action in international organizations".

The exactly opposite view of the substantive interactions between the EC and CFSP causes equal concern. This view holds that, the more Title V measures deal with Community issues, the more its intergovernmental character would be undermined: the Commission would have grounds to argue for its sole right of initiative, the Parliament would seek to exercise pressure and hence influence the substance of CFSP measures and the Court would be likely to be asked to rule upon the ensuing controversies.

Both the above contentions stem from the conclusion that the relationship between the Community legal framework and CFSP is not a static one. As was argued above, its dynamic and incomplete character reflects both the legal character of the Union itself and the model of foreign policy envisaged by the Member States. In this respect and in the light of the interdependence between trade and foreign policy, the principle of measures referring to activities under both legal frameworks does not seem *per se* objectionable. However, any such conclusion must be examined against two criteria: the interaction must respect both the *acquis communautaire* and the constitutional arrangements reflected in the structure of the Union.

The two categories of indirect interactions between the CFSP and EC must be examined against the first requirement, that is respect for the *acquis communautaire*. It is suggested that the first category consisting of measures making reference to existing Community activities meets this requirement. Not only would it be unduly formalistic to deny the possibility of reference being made in a Title V measure to Community activity, but it would also undermine the coherence of the external action of the Union. In this respect, Title V measures referring not only to existing but also to intended action seem to give rise to legal problems. Disagreement amongst Member States, the Council and the Commission over the legality of this practice led to the elaboration of a *mode d'emploi* on the scope of common positions under Article J.2.[180] This document provides for the possibility of a Title V measure covering the Union's external actions *in toto* in so far as the competences of each institution are respected. It

---

[178] See CWA Timmermans, "The Uneasy Relationship between the Communities and the Second Union Pillar: Back to the 'Plan Fouchet'"? (1996) 1 *LIEI* 61 at 66 and Wessel, *supra* note 121 at 118.

[179] However, Heukels and de Zwaan, *supra* note 128 at 210, argue that joint actions "will have a predominantly political character" and "their nature of the [Council] decision [adopting them] will be similar to those laid down in declarations in the framework of European Political Co-operation". This conclusion seems to run counter not only the wording of the Treaty but also its legal character and that of the system it establishes.

[180] See Timmermans, *supra* note 178 at 63 who notes that this *mode d'emploi* has not been adopted but was taken note of by the Council as late as 6 Mar. 1995. It has also never been published. See also the Commission's Report on the functioning of the TEU, *supra* note 117 at point 156.

is suggested that this formula is consistent with both the underlying Treaty principle of pursuing Community activities and conducting foreign policy as a consistent, coherent and effective whole and the constitutional concept of the EC and CFSP as legally distinct frameworks. In this respect, it is pointed out that Title V measures referring to Community institutions specifically mention the fact that they are confined to the exercise of their competences.

It has been argued that any reference to Community activities, even confined to the definition of objectives and priorities, in the operative part of a Title V measure encroaches upon the allocation of powers within and the institutional structure of the Community.[181] According to this view, it is legally unacceptable for the Community to be legally bound to conform to objectives and priorities defined in a common position adopted under Title V. However, this view underestimates the following two points. First, Article 15 TEU provides for the Member States' duty to conform with the common positions. No such duty is established regarding the Community and its institutions.[182] Therefore, the question raised above may be of theoretical interest but of rather "theological character".[183] Secondly, the provision of Article 3(2) TEU, under which the consistency of the Union's activities is to be ensured by the Council and the Commission and the scheme of the Treaty providing the Union with a single institutional framework point towards a duty on both institutions to co-operate in good faith in order to ensure the consistency, coherence and effectiveness of the Union's action. An express provision of this duty may be helpful in clarifying their relationship, but it is mainly for the institutions themselves to develop a culture of co-operation in the area of external affairs *in toto*. This may, in turn, result in a *modus vivendi* which undermines neither the *acquis communautaire* nor the effectiveness of the external action of the Union. The *mode d'emploi* referred to above is a clear indication that such a development is feasible, as it is also demonstrated by the Interinstitutional Agreement regarding the financing of CFSP actions.

Alternative suggestions have been put forward, according to which reference to Community activities should only be made in the preamble of a Title V instrument. If, however, it is deemed necessary for policy objectives and priorities to be defined regarding the whole external relations of the Union, then a *sui generis* instrument such as a resolution or conclusions may perform this function and operate as the umbrella for two distinct measures covering Community and Union activities respectively.[184] However, both these suggestions may give rise to the legal problems they purport to solve. Given that no direct legal oblig-

---

[181] *Supra* note 178 at 67. Timmermans bases his objections on Arts. 1 TEU, according to which the Union "is founded on the European Communities, supplemented by the policies and forms of cooperation established by this Treaty", notably Arts. 3 and 47 TEU according to which "nothing in this Treaty shall affect the Treaties establishing the European Communities".

[182] See H-G Krenzler and HC Schneider, "The Question of Consistency" in Regelsberger, de Schoutheete de Tervarent and Wessels, *supra* note 59, 133 at 145.

[183] Justus Lipsius, "The 1996 Intergovernmental Conference" (1995) 20 *ELRev*. 235 at 251.

[184] Timmermans, *supra* note 177 at 69.

ation may be imposed by a Title V instrument on Community institutions, the benefits of a reference to the latter in the preamble as opposed to the operative part of the former are hardly apparent. As far as the second suggestion is concerned, it raises questions regarding the legal nature of the instrument in question, the procedure leading to its adoption, its relationship with the subsequent specific EC and CFSP measures, the degree of precision it may adopt in defining the scope of the subsequent measures and the relationship between the measures themselves in the light of their legal source. These questions are not only as complex as those arising from the current practice, but also duplicate the problem, for they apply to an additional instrument which is to operate as an alternative connecting element between the pillars.

6. CONCLUSION

This chapter sought to establish that the model of the foreign policy conducted by the Union since the inception of EPC and indeed under CFSP has been of a dynamic character, incrementally developed and implemented within a *sui generis* legal framework. Furthermore, it highlighted that the implementation of CFSP within the single institutional framework provided under the Treaty entailed, in practical terms, reference to Community activities and measures in instruments adopted under Title V. This chapter pointed out that various problems raised by the institutional, substantive and administrative interactions between the EC and CFSP have been addressed as a matter of practice by the Union itself. The practical arrangements prior and in addition to the amendments introduced in the Amsterdam Treaty aim at enhancing the effectiveness of the activities undertaken within the second pillar. This pattern of incremental improvement on the basis of specific practical needs is consistent with the incremental development of the Union's foreign policy in general. Viewed from this perspective, the concerns outlined above regarding the diluting effect of the institutional, substantive and administrative interactions between the EC and CFSP on the *acquis communautaire* or the intergovernmental character of the second pillar are overstated. In the light of this argument, the concerns raised over either the subordination of the Community legal framework to the intergovernmental Title V or the dilution of the character of the latter by supranational features of the former put forward an impossible dilemma. The reason for this is that these contrasting views effectively imply that the foreign affairs of the Union should be served by either a communitarised framework or one based on a rigid distinction from Community activities. The first option is politically unrealistic for it requires procedural and substantive means to serve the aim of a single foreign policy, a prospect clearly lacking in the current political landscape, as the 1996–7 Intergovernmental Conference arguably confirmed.[185] The

---

[185] Accordingly, French Prime Minister Lionel Jospin argued that the implementation of the CFSP must fully accept "the autonomy of each partner"; see *Financial Times*, 24 July 1998 at 2. The

second option is not only unrealistic in an increasingly interdependent and globalised international environment, but also runs counter to a substantial *corpus* of *acquis politique* accumulated since the inception of the EPC.[186]

In the light of the above arguments, the debate over the interactions between the Community legal order and the CFSP should focus on the principles set out in Article 3 TEU, namely the provision for a single institutional framework ensuring the consistency of the Union's activities and respecting and building upon the *acquis communautaire*. In particular, there are two separate but interrelated issues that need to be addressed: first, how do Member States adhere to these principles when adopting and applying rules based on both the first and second pillars; secondly, how and to what extent is the Court prepared to ensure that no measure adopted under Title V undermines either the powers of institutions within the Community legal order or the procedural rules regarding the adoption of Community measures or the latter's substantive content. Given the practical arrangements that, consistently with the *sui generis* character of the CFSP, have been incrementally applied, the above two questions are more relevant in the case of more direct and express interactions between the first two pillars. These are illustrated in the case of legal regimes based on both the EC Treaty and Title V TEU, which are likely to give rise to specific legal disputes touching upon not only the delimitation of competence between the Union, Community and the Member States but also the limits of the jurisdiction of the European Court of Justice. These direct interactions between the first two pillars are typified in the case of sanctions regimes imposed on third countries under Article 301 EC and Title V TEU and exports of dual-use goods currently regulated under Article 113 TEU and a Title V instrument. It is the legal problems stemming from these sets of rules that the following chapters will analyse.

political realities within which the CFSP framework is set and operated are described very succinctly by the deputy Irish Representative to 1996 IGC: "one cannot simply ignore the continued political reality of the pursuit of perceived national interests. One cannot wish a Political Union into existence. One cannot act as if one already exists. The simple fact is that, at the present stage of the Union's development, there is a limit to the extent to which any Member State is prepared to submerge a perceived important foreign policy interest within a single European position"; and he adds that "[t]he CFSP is thus also delicate because it is the process through which a national perspective and a European perspective on foreign policy issues can, painstakingly and sometimes imperceptibly, move closer together. The development of the CFSP has to be based on reality. It has to be gradual. To act as if the perception of national interests could suddenly be dismissed, as if we had reached the promised land of a brave new world, far from representing a leap forward for the CFSP, could undermine it fatally": B McDonagh, *Original Sin in a Brave New World: The Paradox of Europe* (Dublin: Institute of European Affairs, 1998) at 113–14.

[186] These arguments are also valid regarding the suggestion to introduce a global instrument to incorporate objectives, priorities and measures covering the external relations of the Union under both the Community legal framework and Title V: *cf.* A Dashwood, *Reviewing Maastricht. Issues for the 1996 IGC* (Cambridge: LBE, 1996) at 222–3.

3

Economic Sanctions by the Member States: Definition, General Issues and Past Practice

1. INTRODUCTION

The imposition of economic sanctions on third countries constitutes a trade measure aimed at achieving political objectives. As such, it has always played a central role in the exercise of foreign policy. In the context of the European Union, the ability of the Member States to impose and implement sanctions in a uniform way has been instrumental in the fulfilment of one of the main objectives laid down in Article 2 TEU, namely "to assert [the] identity [of the European Union] on the international scene". Being directly relevant to the highly integrated trade policy of the Union, whose regulation is subject to Community law, the imposition of sanctions on third countries has been considered a means of indirectly adding leverage to a policy of the Union which is still under development, namely the Common Foreign and Security Policy. However, even prior to the establishment of the CFSP, the imposition and implementation of sanctions raised important legal issues regarding the relationship between the Member States and the Community the crux of which is the following: to what extent, if at all, is the right of the Member States to impose and implement sanctions on third countries affected by their membership of Community and the duties this entails?

The Member States' effort to address this question has followed two patterns. The first one was followed in the 1970s and was focused on the question of legality, namely whether the Member States were justified in not involving the Community at all. The answer they provided to this question was affirmative: sanctions on third countries were implemented under national law and Member States relied upon new Article 297 EC in order to justify the deviation from the Common Commercial Policy this necessarily entailed. The second pattern underpinning the imposition of sanctions by the Member States was evident in the 1980s and until the entry into force of the TEU, and focused on the question of effectiveness, namely whether the sanctions the Member States sought to impose would be more effective if implemented through a Community instrument. This question was also answered in the affirmative: sanctions were imposed under a regulation adopted on the basis of new Article

133 EC pursuant to a decision adopted in the framework of European Political Co-operation.

An analysis of both the above patterns followed by the Member States in imposing sanctions on third countries and the legal issues they gave rise to is essential to an understanding of the autonomous legal basis for sanctions provided under the TEU, that is new Article 301 EC. In order to carry out such an analysis, this chapter will be structured as follows. The first part will seek to define economic sanctions, outline the various forms they may take on the international scene and provide an overview of the on-going debate regarding their effectiveness as a foreign policy instrument. Due to the central role of the Common Commercial Policy in the determination of the appropriate legal framework regulating the imposition of sanctions on third countries, the second part of this chapter will highlight its general principles and outline the debate regarding its scope. The third part will examine the pattern underpinning the implementation of sanctions in the 1970s, namely under national measures sought to be justified on the basis of new Article 297 EC. The fourth part will outline the pattern whereby sanctions were imposed under new Article 133 EC. Finally, the fifth part will question whether recourse to Article 133 EC formed a genuine link between sanctions against third countries and the CCP.

2. DEFINITION AND PROBLEMS REGARDING THE EFFECTIVENESS OF ECONOMIC SANCTIONS

Economic sanctions connote the exercise of pressure by one state or coalition of states to produce a change in the political behaviour of another state or group of states. This term is often confused with "boycott", "embargo" and "blockade". The strict definition of these terms is not identical: a boycott is usually initiated and conducted by groups of private individuals acting on their own initiative, an embargo is imposed by state authorities and a blockade connotes an act of sea warfare aimed at cutting off access to the target state's coasts by means of warships, thereby permitting the blockading state(s) to control the shipment of goods outside its/their own territorial waters. Despite these distinctions, all the above terms are commonly used interchangeably and are deemed to be encompassed by the general notion of economic sanctions. Therefore, for the purposes of the following analysis, reference will be made to the term "economic sanctions", further distinctions being made whenever necessary.

There is an on-going debate amongst political scientists and international relations theorists about how effective economic sanctions actually are. According to the prevailing view, despite the increasing recourse to them as an instrument of conduct of foreign policy, they are ineffective in terms of both the objectives they seek to achieve and the cost their imposition entails.[1] It is note-

---

[1] For a review of the academic literature supporting this view see D Baldwin, *Economic Statecraft* (Princeton: Princeton University Press, 1985) 51–8.

worthy that even the European Parliament has subscribed to this view. In a Resolution on the significance of economic sanctions, particularly trade embargoes and boycotts, and their consequences for the then EEC's relations with third countries adopted in 1982,[2] the Parliament argued that "economic sanctions have a history of failure".[3] However, it is interesting to note that the Parliament did not follow the considerably stronger wording of the Report of the Committee on External Economic Relations on the basis of which it was adopted.[4] Indeed, in its motion for a Resolution the latter went as far as to urge "the Commission and the Council not to impose or associate themselves with any general and hence, in practice, unenforceable economic sanctions"[5]; however, the Resolution actually adopted by the Parliament "urges the Commission and the Council not to associate themselves with any general sanctions which are manifestly unenforceable."[6] In addition, the Parliament, contrary to the Seeler Report, acknowledged that sanctions "may be appropriate to complement other forms of action".[7] Finally, it set out certain principles by which Community institutions should adhere in cases whereby sanctions directed at specific areas of economy would be considered necessary.[8]

It must be acknowledged that to determine the effectiveness of economic sanctions is a task fraught with methodological problems.[9] Economic sanctions may be imposed to serve a variety of objectives; these may be directly relevant to the conduct of the sender state's foreign policy, namely to persuade the target state to change its behaviour, to weaken the target, thereby leaving it less able to disrupt international relations, to punish the target, thereby deterring it and others from disrupting international relations in the future, to reassure the sender state's allies that it will actively support them in future crises, to inflict

[2] [1982] OJ C292/13.

[3] *Ibid.* at 13.

[4] EP Working Document 1-83/82 of 8 Apr.1982 drawn up on behalf of the Committee by HJ Seeler, MEP. On the discrepancy of the wording between the two documents see J-V Louis, "L' efficacité des Moyens de Pressions" (1984–1985) XVIII *RBDI* 122 at 129.

[5] *Ibid.* at 6.

[6] *Supra* note 2 at 14.

[7] *Ibid.* at 13.

[8] *Ibid.* at 14–15. These principles include the following: Community sanctions should be focused on precisely defined economic areas and products in which the Community and its allies have a strong market position; financial measures should be organised in conjunction with financial and monetary centres beyond the Community; the vigorous and swift implementation of the necessary measures should be ensured; any exceptions must be ruled out for maximum effectiveness of the sanctions to be achieved; the unconditional support and full co-operation of all Member States and other countries involved must be established before the imposition of the sanctions and ensured for as long as the latter are in force by the prompt and detailed exchange of information; economic losses and damage incurred as a result of the sanctions should be borne equally by all Member States and national economies involved; finally, contracts concluded before the imposition of sanctions should be respected as a matter of principle.

[9] For the problems regarding the assessment of the effectiveness of economic sanctions from the viewpoint of an economist see PAG van Bergeijk, *Economic Diplomacy, Trade and Commercial Policy. Positive and Negative Sanctions in a New World Order* (Aldershot: Edward Elgar, 1995) at ch. 3.

punishment as vengeance and to raise an issue to prominence on the international agenda.[10] Furthermore, the imposition of economic sanctions may be decided in the light of military action, that is either to operate as a consensus-building tool for military action, should it later become necessary, or as an alternative solution lacking the risk of human lives that the latter entails.[11]

It becomes apparent that it is against the specific objectives served by the imposition of sanctions in a given case that their effectiveness must be assessed. However, not only are these specific objectives very difficult to determine, but also the criteria upon which the effectiveness of sanctions is to be assessed may vary considerably depending on how the success of sanctions is defined.[12] In this respect, it is interesting to note that, according to certain analysts the success of sanctions must be determined by whether their imposition compels the target state to change its behaviour, whereas others argue that it is whether their threat can deter the target state from taking a certain action that must be taken into account.[13] In addition to different approaches regarding the evaluation of economic sanctions, a moral argument, whereby sanctions condemn innocent civilians and, hence, states must refrain from their use, is sometimes also put forward.[14]

---

[10] ES Rogers, "Using Economic Sanctions to Control Regional Conflicts" (1996) 5 _Security Studies_ 43 at 49.

[11] Finally, economic sanctions may be imposed for reasons related to domestic policy, that is to bolster the sender state government's public image domestically as decisive.

[12] Amongst political scientists and international relations theorists, the most authoritative study on economic sanctions is that by GC Hufbauer, JS Schott and KA Elliott, _Economic Sanctions Reconsidered_ (2nd edn., Washington, DC: Institute for International Economics, 1992) i and ii, which assesses the effectiveness of 116 economic sanctions regimes imposed between 1914 and 1990, mainly by the USA. This research examines, on the one hand, whether the sender state achieved the policy goals which the imposition of sanctions purported to support and, on the other hand, the extent to which the sanctions contributed to the policy outcome. Accordingly, every sanctions regime was scored on a four-point scale in relation to the first question, i.e. whether its outcome was failed, unclear but possibly positive, positive or successful, and a four-point scale in relation to the second question, i.e. whether its contribution was zero or negative, minor, modest or significant. The aggregate score given to each sanction by multiplying its scores on these two scales resulted in a ranking of all sanctions under examination on a scale running from 1 to 16. The authors of this research define economic sanctions as successful when they are given a score of at least nine and they reached the conclusion that 34% of the sanctions they examined were successful in this respect. Furthermore, the authors of this study elaborated certain principles adherence to which may be deemed to ensure the effectiveness of sanctions as a foreign policy instrument; this task is commonly carried out by political scientists and led the authors of the abovementioned study to produce three rules of surprisingly pristine clarity, namely "don't bite off more than you can chew", "big fish eat little fish" or "don't pick on someone your own size" and "the weakest go to the wall" or "do pick on the weak and helpless". See _ibid._ i, at 76–9 and 85.

[13] See Rogers, _supra_ note 10 at 50.

[14] For a counter-argument, albeit leading to the same conclusion, see R McGee, "Trade Embargoes, Sanctions and Blockades. Some Overlooked Human Rights Issues", (1998) 32 _JWT_ 139, where it is argued that it is inherently impossible to measure the gains and losses suffered by civilians as a result of economic sanctions. Therefore, McGee suggests that the criterion upon which the imposition of sanctions must be assessed focuses on whether it violates individual rights of property, contract or association; the fact that sanctions do violate those rights leads to the conclusion that states must not have recourse to them as an instrument of foreign policy.

Determining the effectiveness of economic sanctions as an instrument of foreign policy exceeds the bounds of this book. In this respect, the starting point for the following analysis is that economic sanctions constitute an important instrument of foreign policy, as states have increasing recourse to them in the post-Cold War era.[15] Therefore, the question focuses on the problems that recourse to these trade measures serving foreign policy objectives may raise regarding the allocation of powers between the Member States and the Community within the constitutional order of the European Union.

3. THE COMMON COMMERCIAL POLICY OF THE EUROPEAN COMMUNITY

The very nature of sanctions against third countries as trade measures raised at an early stage the question whether their imposition should be regulated within the framework of the Common Commercial Policy of the European Community. The central role that the CCP has played in the debate regarding the appropriate legal framework for the imposition of sanctions on third countries requires that its main provision, the principles underpinning it and the debate about its scope be presented.

The main provision on the Common Commercial Policy is Article 133 EC which reads as follows:

> The common commercial policy shall be based on uniform principles, particularly in regard to changes in tariff rates, the conclusion of tariff and trade agreements, the achievement of uniformity in measures of liberalisation, export policy and measures to protect trade such as those to be taken in cases of dumping or subsidies.

Within the scope of the CCP, the Council acts by qualified majority on a proposal by the Commission. As for the aim, the CCP has been viewed by the Court "in the context of the operation of the Common Market, for the defence of the common interests of the Community, within which the particular interests of the Member States must endeavour to adapt to each other".[16]

3.1. The main principles of the CCP

The Court has consistently held that CCP should be interpreted broadly. This principle relies upon the following three interlinked propositions. First, the

---

[15] It was argued in J Kirshner, "The Microfoundations of Economic Sanctions" (1997) 6 *Security Studies* 32 that the considerable use of economic sanctions by states as a foreign policy instrument renders the analysis of their effectiveness in general terms by political theorists and international relations analysts largely irrelevant. Instead, the question which should be asked is how and why different sanctions work in different settings, account being taken of contextual variables, namely the comparative cost of other options, the full set of purposes for which sanctions are introduced and an understanding of the magnitude of the value the target places on resistance, and identity variables, including the relative size of the target, its exposure to different possible forms of influence and the prospects for international co-operation.

[16] *Opinion 1/75* [1975] ECR 1355 at 1363.

enumeration provided for in new Article 133 is indicative rather than exhaustive.[17] Secondly, the content of the CCP must be the same as that of the external trade policy of a state.[18] Thirdly, the CCP must not be viewed as confined to traditional aspects of external trade, for "a commercial policy understood in that sense would be destined to become nugatory in the course of time"[19]; instead, the Court held that it must be understood as encompassing measures which aim to adapt to the changing nature of world trade,[20] hence requiring, in general, that "the question of external trade must be governed from a wide point of view"[21] and in particular that an interpretation of the CCP "the effect of which would be to restrict the common commercial policy to the use of instruments intended to have an effect only on the traditional aspects of external trade" should be rejected.[22] Correlative of this premise is what the Court has expressly and consistently referred to as "the open nature of the common commercial policy".[23]

The CCP has been consistently held by the Court to give rise to the Community's exclusive competence,[24] for otherwise "Member States may adopt positions which differ from those which the Community intends to adopt, and which would thereby distort the institutional framework, call into question the mutual trust within the Community and prevent the latter from fulfilling its task in the defence of the common interest".[25] The corollary of the Community's exclusive competence is that the Member States can only act unilaterally in areas covered by the CCP on the basis of a specific Community authorisation.[26]

[17] *Opinion 1/78* [1979] ECR 2871; [1979] 3 CMLR 639 at para. 45.

[18] See *Opinion 1/75, supra* note 16 at 1362, where, in applying this principle, the Court held that "systems of aid for exports and particularly measures concerning credits for the financing of local costs linked to market operations" fall within the scope of CCP.

[19] *Opinion 1/78, supra* note 17 at para. 44.

[20] *Ibid.*; in *Opinion 1/78*, the Court, in applying this principle, held that the conclusion of the International Agreement on Natural Rubber under the aegis of the United Nations Conference on Trade and Development (UNCTAD) fell within the scope of the CCP.

[21] *Opinion 1/78, supra* note 17, para. 44.

[22] *Ibid.* Furthermore, the Court opined, at para. 45, that "[a] restrictive interpretation of the concept of common commercial policy would risk causing disturbances in intra-Community trade by reason of the disparities which would then exist in certain sectors of economic relations with non-member countries".

[23] Most recently in *Opinion 1/94 on International Agreements Concerning Services and the Protection of Intellectual Property* [1994] ECR I–5267, [1995] 1 CMLR 205 at para. 41; for the effect of *Opinion 1/94* on the scope of CCP see *infra* at 3.2. of this ch.

[24] See *Opinion 1/75, supra* note 16, Case 41/76 *Suzanne Criel, née Donckerwolcke and Henri Schou* v. *Provureur de la République au Tribunal de Grande Instance, Lille and Director General of Customs* [1976] ECR 1921; [1977] CMLR 535; *Opinion 2/91 on ILO Convention 170 on Chemicals at Work,* [1993] ECR I–1061, [1993] 3 CMLR 800; *Opinion 1/94, supra* note 23.

[25] *Opinion 1/75, supra* note 16 at 1364. In relation to, specifically, the agreement under consideration, the Court held that "any unilateral action on the part of the Member States would lead to disparities in the conditions for the grant of export credits, calculated to distort competition between undertakings of the various Member States in external markets. Such distortion can be eliminated only by means of a strict uniformity of credit conditions granted to undertakings in the Community whatever their nationality".

[26] See *Donckerwolcke, supra* note 24; however, the Court's approach to how specific the Community authorisation should be has not been entirely consistent. In Case 174/84 *Bulk Oil* v. *Sun International* [1986] ECR 559, [1986] 2 CMLR 732, the Court adopted a rather broad approach and

3.2. The scope of the CCP

The absence of an express definition of the scope of the CCP has given rise to controversy. A specific aspect of the debate which has ensued is focused on whether international agreements on intellectual property rights and services fall within the ambit of Article 133.[27] This question was answered in *Opinion 1/94*, whereby, to the Commission's claims to exclusive competence in these areas due to their direct or indirect effect on the volume and structure of trade,[28] the Court gave a dual response: on the one hand, it held that trade in services cannot be viewed *a priori* as either excluded from or covered by the CCP[29] and, on the other hand, it ascertained that the link between the intellectual property rights covered by the agreement under consideration and trade in goods under Article 133 was rather tenuous.[30] The Court's conclusions in *Opinion 1/94* are endorsed by the amendment introduced by the Treaty of Amsterdam.[31]

A more general aspect of the debate over the definition of the scope of CCP which has always been directly relevant to the choice of legal basis for economic sanctions against third countries is whether trade measures adopted for political purposes fall within the ambit of Article 133 EC and hence are covered by the Community's exclusive competence. Two main theories have been put forward regarding this issue.

held that Art. 10 of and the Annex to Reg. 2603/69, [1969] OJ L324/25 on common rules on exports to third countries constituted sufficiently specific an authorisation to Member States to impose quantitative restrictions on exports of oil. An equally broad approach was adopted in Case 242/84 *Tezi BV* v. *Minister for Economic Affairs* [1986] ECR 933, [1987] 3 CMLR 64, as opposed to that in Case 51/87 *Commission* v. *Council* [1988] ECR 5459.

[27] See P Gilsdorf, "Portée et Délimitation des Competences Communautaires En matière de Politique Commerciale" (1989) RMC 195 and P Mengozzi, "Trade in Services and Commercial Policy" in M Maresceau, (ed.), *The European Community's Commercial Policy after 1992: The Legal Dimension* (Dordrecht: Martinus Nijhoff, 1993) 223.

[28] The Commission's contention that the Community enjoys exclusive competence under Art. 133 to conclude international agreements on intellectual property rights and services was criticised as "extravagant", "maximalistic" and "extreme": see A Dashwood, "The Limits of European Community Powers" (1996) 21 *ELRev.* 113 at 119; N Emiliou, "The Death of Exclusive Competence?" (1996) 21 *ELRev.* 294 at 302; and M Hilf, "Unwritten EC Authority in Foreign Trade Law" (1997) 2 *EFA Review* 437 at 447 respectively.

[29] *Opinion 1/94*, *supra* note 23 at paras. 41–7; instead, the Court held that the specific modes of supply of services covered by the agreement in question should be examined against those which, under Art. 3 EC, are understood as covered by Art. 133.

[30] For a critique of *Opinion 1/94*, see JHJ Bourgeois, "The EC in the WTO and Advisory Opinion 1/94: an Echternach Procession" (1995) 32 *CMLRev.* 763; D Chalmers, "Legal Base and the External Relations of the European Community" in N Emiliou and D O'Keeffe (eds.), *The European Union and World Trade Law after the GATT Uruguay Round* (Chichester: Willey, 1996) 46 at 59–60 and M Hilf, "The ECJ's Opinion 1/94 on the WTO—No Surprise, but Wise?" (1995) 6 *EJIL* 245.

[31] The new Art. 133(5) reads as follows: "[t]he Council, acting unanimously on a proposal from the Commission and after consulting the European Parliament, may extend the application of paragraphs 1 to 4 to international negotiations and agreements on services and intellectual property insofar as they are not covered by these paragraphs". For an analysis of this new provision see O Blin, "L'Article 113 CE Après Amsterdam" (1998) 420 *Revue du Marché Commun et de l'Union Européenne* 447.

According to the teleological approach, it is the objective of the measure in question which determines whether it must be adopted under the CCP rules. Hence, if this objective is alien to the aims of the CCP, then it falls outside its scope and hence it does not give rise to the Community's exclusive competence. This approach was put forward by the Council in relation to the conclusion of the International Agreement on Natural Rubber.[32] The Council argued that the objectives of this agreement were not confined to those of commercial policy and included various others, namely general political objectives, economic policy factors, development aid factors, establishment of fair labour standards in the rubber industry, technological assistance, research activities and tax policies[33]; given that these objectives are not covered by the scope of Article 133, the thrust of the Council's argument was that the conclusion of the agreement in question could not give rise to the Community's exclusive competence, and hence Member States were to remain competent to participate in the agreement along with the Community under the formula of a mixed agreement.[34]

According to the instrumentalist approach, it is the nature of the measure in question that determines the appropriate legal framework. In other words, if the measure in question constitutes an instrument regulating international trade, then it is covered by the CCP and gives rise to the Community's exclusive competence irrespective of its objective.[35] In relation to the measures specifically mentioned in Article 133, this theory entails that they fall *ipso facto* within the Community's exclusive competence along with any other measures which, albeit not specifically mentioned in the non-exhaustive list provided therein, are closely linked with it, namely ancillary measures or measures having an effect

---

[32] See *Opinion 1/78, supra* note 17.

[33] *Ibid.* at 2889–91.

[34] This line of reasoning was also supported by the British Government. On mixed agreements in general see JHJ Bourgeois, J-L Dewost and M-A Gaiffe (eds.), *La Communauté européenne et les accords mixtes. Quelles perspectives?* (Brussels: Presses Interuniversitaires Européennes, 1997) and D O'Keeffe and HG Schermers (eds.), *Mixed Agreements* (Deventer: Kluwer, 1983). Consistently with this approach, the Council argued in Case 45/86 *Commission* v. *Council (Generalized Tariff Preferences)* [1987] ECR. 1493 at 1499–1500 that the Regs. implementing a Community system of generalised tariff preferences served essentially a development policy objective and hence should not be adopted under Art. 133; it is interesting to note that Council Regs. 3599/85 [1985] OJ L352/1 and 3600/85 [1985] OJ L352/107 which were the subject of the annulment action brought by the Commission cited as their legal basis "the Treaty establishing the European Economic Community" instead of a specific Treaty provision. It has not been only the Council that supports this line of reasoning. In Case C–120/94 *Commission* v. *Greece (F.Y.R.O.M.)* [1996] ECR I–1513, Greece argued that the scope of CCP must be construed as covering measures whose genuine and main objective is to influence the volume or flow of trade: see *The European Commission's Action before the ECJ Following the Counter-measures Adopted by the Hellenic Republic against F.Y.R.O.M.* (in Greek) (Athens-Komotini: A.N.Sakkoulas, 1996) at 78–83.

[35] This argument essentially relies upon, on the one hand, the construction of the CCP by the Court in *Opinion 1/75* as being of the same content as that of the external commercial policy of a state and, on the other hand, the indeterminate nature of the definition of a commercial policy objective. According to the Commission, to render the aim of a measure to influence the volume or pattern of trade the decisive criterion for its inclusion in the scope of Art. 133 would, in certain cases, result in either too narrow or too broad an area to be covered by the CCP: see *ibid.* at 2885.

equivalent to restrictions or taxes on imports or exports.[36] Put forward in *Opinion 1/78*, this approach argued that the conclusion of the International Agreement on Natural Rubber, aiming at the stabilisation of prices for natural rubber, was a characteristic measure for regulating external trade and, hence, as an instrument of commercial policy, should be concluded by the Community under Article 133.[37]

The Court has endorsed neither of the above theories.[38] Instead, it seems to have adjudicated upon the issues before it by following a two-fold approach. On the one hand, it has put forward a broad construction of the CCP and, hence, viewed it as an "open-ended and evolutionary concept".[39] On the other hand, it has applied the principles stemming from this approach in a rather restrictive way to the facts of the cases before it. This approach has been characterised as "pragmatic",[40] for it indicates that national concerns over too broad a construction of the Community's exclusive competence are seriously taken into account by the Court.[41] However, the application of this approach has given rise to judgments of questionable consistency. Whereas in *Opinion 1/75* the Court pointed out that the role of the Member States regarding the financial execution of an international trade agreement was "of little importance",[42] in *Opinion 1/78* it held that the Community was not exclusively competent to conclude the International Agreement on Natural Rubber in so far as the Member States were to contribute under the agreement in question to the financing of the operations provided therein. Finally, in relation to the WTO Agreement, the Court held that "the fact that the Member States will bear some of its expenses cannot, on any view, of itself justify [their] participation in the conclusion [of the Agreement]".[43]

---

[36] See the arguments put forward by the Commission in Case 45/86, *supra* note 34 at 1498–9. According to the Commission, the exceptions to this rule consist of special regimes laid down, in particular, by Arts. 26 and 37 EC, the scope of which, in relation to that of Art. 133, should be defined by reference to their main objective pursued.

[37] *Ibid.* at 2880–7. In the *Generalized Tariff Preferences* cases, the Commission argued that the measures in question should have been adopted "solely [under] Article [133] because they overtly and specifically govern[ed] external trade in so far as they relate[d] to changes in tariff rates within the meaning of that article" in *supra* note 34 at 1499.

[38] An alternative approach has been suggested by Professor Ehlermann, according to which measures explicitly mentioned in Art. 133 EC are covered by the scope of the CCP and give rise to exclusive Community competence. All other measures give rise to exclusive Community competence only if their objective is identical to those of the CCP: see "Communautés européennes et sanctions internationales—Une Réponse à J. Verhoeven" [1984–85] *RBDI* 96 at 108–9.

[39] FG Jacobs, "The Completion of the Internal Market v the Incomplete Common Commercial Policy" in SV Konstadinidis. (ed.), *The Legal Regulation of the European Community's External Relations after the Completion of the Internal Market* (Aldershot: Dartmouth, 1996) 3.

[40] See T Tridimas and P Eeckhout, "The External Competence of the Community and the Case-Law of the Court of Justice: Principle versus Pragmatism" (1995) 14 *YEL* 143.

[41] As Tridimas and Eeckhout put it in *ibid.*, "[t]hrough pragmatism, the case-law seems to have reached a golden balance: in effect, it is as difficult to establish that the Community has no competence on a given area as it is to establish that the Community's competence is truly exclusive".

[42] *Supra* note 16 at 1364.

[43] *Supra* note 23 at para. 21.

4. THE FIRST PHASE OF THE IMPOSITION OF SANCTIONS PRIOR TO TEU: NATIONAL MEASURES AND THE RELEVANCE OF ARTICLE 297 EC

When the imposition of sanctions first raised the issue of the relevance of the CCP, the Member States strongly rejected any such claim by relying upon the so-called "Rhodesia doctrine".[44] Under this principle, Member States were deemed to be free to implement economic sanctions serving political aims against a third country under national rules justified on the basis of Article 297 EC.[45] The rationale underpinning this approach lay upon the conception of economic sanctions as beyond the scope of the Common Commercial Policy and, hence, not covered by the Community's exclusive competence.

4.1. The "Rhodesia" doctrine: sanctions under Article 297 EC

This approach was put into practice when the Member States decided for the first time since the establishment of the Community to impose sanctions against a third country. When the United Nations Security Council adopted Resolutions between 1965 and 1968 calling for economic sanctions to be imposed against Rhodesia,[46] the Member States faced the dilemma of how to combine compliance with their Article 48 UN Charter obligations with respect for their Community obligations. It was in this context that the "Rhodesia doctrine" was put forward. However, its application gave rise to insurmountable practical problems. The Member States implemented the Resolutions in question with national measures of differing content and at different times.[47] These material discrepancies rendered the whole embargo, because of the rules of the common market, ineffective.[48]

4.2. Comment on the implementation of sanctions under national measures

The reasons which led to the adoption of the "Rhodesia doctrine" may be summarised as follows. First, at the time of its application, the principles underlying

---

[44] See P Sturma, "La participation de la Communauté Européenne à des "sanctions" internationales" [1993] *RMC* 250 at 252.

[45] Written Question No 526/75 [1976] OJ C89/6 at 7.

[46] Under Security Council Resolutions 216 (1965) and 217 (1965), the international community was asked to cut off its trade relations with Rhodesia, including oil and petroleum products. Under Security Council Resolution 232 (1966), the UN members were asked to impose a trade embargo on a variety of products, whereas under Security Council Resolution 253 (1968) a complete embargo was asked to be imposed.

[47] See PJ Kuyper, "Sanctions against Rhodesia the EEC and the Implementation of General International Legal Rules" (1975) 12 *CMLRev.* 231.

[48] On the problems that the implementation of the relevant Security Council Resolutions encountered internationally and its questionable effectiveness see P Willaert., "Les sanctions économiques contre la Rhodésie (1965–1979)" (1985–1985) XVIII *RBDI* 216.

the CCP had not been fully realised. Indeed, the Court's case law illustrating the broad scope of the CCP and clarifying the implications of the Community's exclusive competence continued to develop well into the 1970s. Secondly, the formalisation of the EPC, that is a political framework within which the Member States consulted with each other in order to maintain a common stance on the international arena, started only in 1970 with the Luxembourg Report.[49] It follows that notions such as "co-operation", "common stance" and "solidarity" had yet to be introduced as the determining parameters of a new institutional framework regarding foreign policy and involving all Member States, albeit beyond the Community legal order. In this respect, the prevailing position amongst them was of extreme concern not to jeopardise their absolute freedom to determine individually their foreign policy. In the case of economic sanctions, this position led to their implementation by the Member States individually, by varying measures and at various times. Thirdly, the unanimous agreement of commentators indicates that the third ground of Article 297 EC, namely the "obligations [the Member State in question] has accepted for the purpose of maintaining peace and international security", refers to decisions binding on Member States under Articles 41 and 42 of the UN Charter.[50] On this basis, the Member States argued that, in so far as the "wholly exceptional clause"[51] of Article 297 provides for deviation from Community law, the Member States are under no obligation to implement Security Council Resolutions on the basis of Community law principles and procedures. Otherwise, this ground for deviation from the Treaty would be of no practical significance.

The historical context into which the above sanctions were adopted explains their implementation by national measures. It is noteworthy that even the Commission at that time supported the view that sanctions imposed by the UN Security Council were totally distinct from the Community legal order in general and the CCP in particular.[52] However, the extreme concern of the Member States not to associate economic sanctions with Community law and their reluctance to make full use of the evolving EPC framework resulted in their implementing the Article 297 consultation process incompletely and inadequately.[53]

---

[49] On the development of the EPC see the overview provided *supra* in ch. 2.

[50] See S Bohr, "Sanctions by the United Nations Security Council and the European Community" (1993) 4 *EJIL* 256 at 265; J-L Dewost, "Article 224" in *Commentaire Mégret* (Brussels: Presses Universitaires de Bruxelles, 1987), xv at 437; J Verhoeven, "Article 224" in V Constantinesco, R Kovar and D Simon (eds.), *Traité sur l'Union européenne: (signé le 7 février 1992): commentaire article par article* (Paris: Economica, 1996) at 1402; Kuyper in *supra* note 47; H Smit and PR Herzog, *The Law of the European Community—A Commentary on the EEC Treaty* (New York: Matthew Bender 1996) at 6–216.85.

[51] Case 222/84 *Marguerite Johnston* v. *Chief Constable of the Royal Ulster Constabulary* [1986] ECR 1651, [1986] 3 CMLR 240 at para. 27.

[52] See Written Question No 527/75 [1976] OJ C89/8 at 9. The same point was put forward by the Council in its Answer to Written Question No 526/75 [1976] OJ C89/6 at 7.

[53] On the interpretation of Art. 297 and the duties imposed on the deviating Member States thereunder see *infra* at ch. 7, 6.2.

5. THE SECOND PHASE OF THE IMPOSITION OF SANCTIONS PRIOR TO TEU:
RECOURSE TO COMMUNITY LAW UNDER ARTICLE 133 EC

The "Rhodesia doctrine" did not underpin the imposition of sanctions for a long period of time. In the early 1980s a second pattern regarding the legal formula followed by the Member States emerged. This consisted of the adoption of a Council Regulation under Article 133 EC prior to a decision reached in the framework of European Political Co-operation. It is apparent that the very foundation of this pattern is directly contrary to that of the first phase outlined above, for economic sanctions are now considered as within the CCP of the Community. The reasons behind this shift and the underlying motives of the Member States are highlighted below.

The imposition of sanctions by the Member States on the basis of a regulation under Article 133 EC was characterised by considerable confusion about the exact implications of the legal formula chosen. This is illustrated in the very first sanctions regime imposed under Article 133 EC, namely on the USSR by Council Regulation 596/82[54] after the declaration of martial law in Poland in December 1981. This Regulation provided no reference to the political motive behind the imposition of sanctions beyond the very vague phrase that "the interests of the Community require that imports from the USSR be reduced".[55] To argue that the interest of the *Community* require the imposition of sanctions without any further explanations of how this is so is in marked contrast with past practice, whereby the political motive of sanctions was deemed to render them beyond the scope of the Treaty altogether. The political side of the measures against Soviet Union was provided for only in a *communiqué* issued after a Foreign Ministers' meeting. In addition to the expression of "utter disapproval" and "concern" and the issuing of "a solemn warning against any . . . intervention [by the Warsaw Pact]", the Member States declared that "[o]ther measures will be considered . . . in particular . . . measures concerning the Community's commercial policy with regard to the USSR".[56]

Furthermore, the lack of uniformity in the implementation of the sanctions against the Soviet Union was not entirely justified under the sanctions regime itself. On the one hand, Greece was exempted from the application of the above measures on the basis of a Council Regulation adopted under Article 133 EC; this exemption was justified "in view of the stage reached . . . in [its] progressive integration into the customs union on which the Community was based" and "in order to avoid particular difficulties for [its] trade and economy".[57] On the other hand, Denmark, without formally being exempted, ceased to apply the measures imposed under Regulation 596/82 against the Soviet Union; instead, it

---

[54] [1982] OJ L72/15.
[55] *Ibid.* at recital 6 of the preamble.
[56] *Bull. EC* 12–1981, point 1.4.2.
[57] Council Reg. 597/82 [1982] OJ L72/19.

prohibited products imported from the USSR from being exported to the other Member States except for Greece.[58]

The incoherence which characterised the imposition of sanctions on the Soviet Union under Article 133 EC was further illustrated in the case of the sanctions against Argentina imposed by Council Regulation 877/82.[59] Contrary to the measures against the USSR, the political side of the measures against Argentina could not have been highlighted more: the very first paragraph of the preamble made reference to "discussions in the context of European political cooperation which have led in particular to the decision that economic measures will be taken with regard to Argentina in accordance with the relevant provisions of the Community Treaties"; in addition, it was stated that the imposition of unilateral measures by the United Kingdom led the Member States to hold consultations under Article 297 EC[60] and that "in the context of these consultations it has proved important to take urgent and uniform measures".[61] These provisions seem to refer to the statement of the Presidency issued six days earlier which made clear the decision for economic sanctions to be imposed.[62] Finally, it is only at the last paragraph of the preamble that Article 133 is mentioned as the Regulation's legal basis.

The adoption of all the above measures against Argentina under Article 133 EC was not without problems. Denmark argued that, as a matter of principle, sanctions should be imposed under Article 297 rather than Article 133. Moreover, despite the express reference in the initial Regulation to the negotiations held under Article 297, it declared that it would not apply it and adopted national measures imposing identical national sanctions. In addition, both Ireland and Italy did not apply the Regulations extending the embargo for political reasons. In order to prevent trade-diversion as a result of this position, they engaged in consultations with the Commission. It is noteworthy that both the Regulations which extended the initial one contained the standard provision according to which they "shall be . . . directly applicable in all Member States" and neither exempted Italy and Ireland from its scope.

The express and elaborate references to the political framework which enabled the adoption of sanctions on the basis of Article 133 EC, already evident in the case of the measures against Argentina, were also made in the case of the sanctions regime against Iraq. When the latter invaded Kuwait, the United Nations Security Council adopted Resolutions 660(1990) and 661(1990); the former demanded the immediate and unconditional withdrawal of Iraqi troops from Kuwait, whereas the latter, because of Iraq's refusal to conform with the

[58] J Verhoeven, "Sanctions internationales et Communautés Européennes—A propos de l'affair des iles Falkland (Malvinas)" [1984] *CDE* 259 at 263.

[59] [1982] OJ L102/1. For an account of the Falklands affair and the international law aspects of the measures adopted see E David, "Les sanctions économiques proses contre l' Argentine dans l'affaire des Malouines" (1984–1985) XVIII *RBDI* 150.

[60] Recital 2 of the preamble.

[61] Recital 3 of the preamble.

[62] See *Bull. EC* 4–1982, point 1.1.5.

above demands, required that a comprehensive sanctions regime be imposed, comprising an economic, trade, finance and arms embargo. The Member States implemented this sanctions regime by adopting Council Regulation 2340/90,[63] the preamble to which made reference to both the above Security Council Resolutions in its first two recitals. Furthermore, reference was made to developments under the umbrella of the EPC, namely a declaration "by the Community and its Member States" adopting the reaction and demands of Resolution 660(1990) and a "decision that economic measures will be taken against Iraq".[64] Finally, after the conclusion that "in these conditions, the Community's trade as regards Iraq and Kuwait must be prevented",[65] it is stated that "the Community and its Member States have agreed to have recourse to a Community instrument in order to ensure uniform implementation, throughout the Community, of the measures concerning trade with Iraq and Kuwait decided upon by the United Nations Security Council".[66] Finally, at the end of the preamble reference is made to the Regulation's legal basis, that is Article 133 EC.

The same formula was followed in all four measures which amended Regulation 2340/90, namely Council Regulations 3155/90,[67] 542/91,[68] 811/91[69] and 1194/91.[70] In all but the first of these instruments, reference is made to "the Community and its Member States meeting in the framework of political cooperation". This formula is employed to denote developments with foreign policy implications going beyond the scope of the then EEC Treaty, such as the conclusions that "there is no reason to maintain the embargo measures imposed by the Community with regard to Kuwait",[71] "it [was] desirable to facilitate humanitarian action in Iraq and, therefore, appropriate to enlarge . . . the possibility for supplies of products intended strictly for medical purposes within the scope and conditions laid down in the relevant Resolutions of the United Nations Security Council"[72] and that "it [was] necessary to amend Regulations 2340/90 and 3155/90 so as to incorporate the changes made by the United Nations Security Council to the prohibitions against the sale or supply to Iraq of commodities or products and the prohibitions against the import of commodities and products originating in Iraq".[73] Instead, Regulation 3155/90, that is the first of the amending Community measures, makes reference to "the Community and its Member States" as the source "confirm[ing] the necessity of

---

[63] [1990] OJ L213/1.
[64] First recital of the preamble.
[65] Third recital of the preamble.
[66] Fourth recital of the preamble.
[67] [1990] OJ L304/1.
[68] [1991] OJ L60/5.
[69] [1991] OJ L82/50.
[70] [1991] OJ L115/37.
[71] Fourth recital of the preamble of Reg. 542/91, *supra* n. 68.
[72] Third recital of the preamble of Reg. 811/91, *supra* n. 69.
[73] Third recital of the preamble of Reg. 1194/91, *supra* n. 70.

implementing [the relevant] Resolutions and express[ing] their determination to take effective action".[74]

6. COMMENT ON THE IMPOSITION OF SANCTIONS PRIOR TO THE ADOPTION OF TEU

The lack of co-ordination and the consequent ineffectiveness of the sanctions against Rhodesia was one of the factors that led the Member States to implement sanctions by means of a Community instrument. In addition, they realised that new Article 297 EC could only be invoked under very specific conditions. These conditions were not met in the case of sanctions against the USSR, which was the first time sanctions were imposed under new Article 133 EC. Of the circumstances required thereunder, it was only "serious international tension constituting a threat of war" which might have seemed relevant. However, the large gas delivery contracts which had just been concluded by some Member States seemed to constitute evidence to the contrary.[75]

Another reason which made the adoption of a Community instrument possible was the development of the CCP; its broad definition had already been established along with the implications stemming from the exclusive competence of the Community in this area.[76] This development could not be ignored by the Member States. In addition, another, no less important, development had taken place beyond the Community framework, namely the evolution of the EPC. This mechanism, despite its development beyond the Community legal framework and its lack of Treaty status until the Single European Act came into force, provided a political framework which enabled the Member States to consult with each other and co-operate for the achievement of a common goal, that is a co-ordinated position in the area of high politics. The significance of the development of the EPC is indicated by the Regulations adopted under Article 133 themselves. Regulation 877/82 imposing sanctions against Argentina makes reference to the political consultation between the Member States under Article 297 EC, whereas all subsequent measures imposing sanctions under Article 133 EC made no reference to Article 297[77]; instead, they referred to consultations and decisions taking place in the EPC framework. In other words, the EPC provided the basic institutional preconditions which, while not threatening

---

[74] Third recital of the preamble. Finally, Art. 133 was also the legal basis for sanctions against certain areas of Angola. Because of the continuing conflict, the UN Security Council adopted Resolution 864(1993) which imposed an embargo on petroleum and petroleum products in specific areas of Angola. Following this Resolution and the Member States' agreement within the EPC, Reg. 2967/93 was adopted, [1993] OJ L268/1.

[75] PJ Kuyper, "International Legal Aspects of Economic Sanctions" in P Sarcevic. and H Van Houtte (eds.), *Legal Issues in International Trade* (London: Kluwer Law International, 1990) 145 at 167–8.

[76] See *supra* section 3 of this ch.

[77] PJ Kuyper, "Trade Sanctions, Security and Human Rights and Commercial Policy" in Maresceau, *supra* note 27 at 395.

national sovereignty in the conduct of foreign policy, enabled a culture of consultation to become the norm in this highly sensitive area. The influence of this culture and the commonality of purpose it presupposed cannot be overstated. They relaxed state-centred national reflexes, impaired the excuse of eroding national sovereignty and rendered the role of the Community in the interaction of foreign policy and trade acceptable.

It is suggested that it was on the basis of the above practical considerations that Article 133 EC was chosen as the legal basis for economic sanctions against third countries. However, a paradox seems to emerge. Economic sanctions were implemented by a Community measure adopted under Article 133 EC while the Member States were arguing that economic sanctions did not form part of the CCP. This paradox is illustrated in the wording of the sanctions regulations themselves, for a standard formula is repeated in their preamble according to which ". . . the Community and its Member States have agreed to have recourse to a Community instrument in order to ensure uniform implementation throughout the Community [of prior UN Security Council measures]". This is the case in Regulation 2340/90, the so-called "mother regulation" of all those imposing sanctions against Iraq and Kuwait.[78] It also appears in Regulation 1432/92 imposing a trade embargo on Serbia and Montenegro,[79] whereas in the subsequent Regulation 2656/92 it is further stressed that "it is of utmost importance to ensure effective application of the embargo".[80] The need for uniform implementation is further underlined in Regulation 990/93 which amended the previous two.[81] It also appeared in Regulation 945/92 imposing sanctions on Libya. This standard formula indicated that the main reason for the adoption of economic sanctions under Article 133 was not the conception of the implementing Community measures as part of the CCP. Effectiveness through uniformity was the main concern of the Member States, and this was the factor which determined Article 133 EC as the appropriate legal basis.

Another indication that the choice of Article 133 EC was underpinned by reasons of practical consideration and political expediency rather than a coherent conception of the ambit of the Common Commercial Policy is offered by the scope of the relevant regulations. The case of sanctions against Iraq is indicative of this approach. Both Regulations 2340/90 and 3155/90 covered services and transport. The Court, in *Opinion 1/94*, declined to include the services *in toto* within the CCP and hence denied that the Community was exclusively competent.[82] It is also noteworthy that the Member States unequivocally refused to accept at the 1996 Intergovernmental Conference the Commission's proposal to include international agreements on services in old Article 113 (now 133).[83]

---

[78] Fourth recital; see also Reg. 1432/92 at the tenth recital of the preamble.

[79] [1992] OJ L151/4 at the tenth recital of the preamble.

[80] [1992] OJ L266/27 at the third recital of the preamble.

[81] [1993] OJ L102/14 at the twelfth recital of the preamble.

[82] See Tridimas and Eeckhout, *supra* note 40 at 162.

[83] See ch. 11 of the Irish Presidency proposal (CONF 2500/96) which was rejected by the Member States. On the new Art. 133(5), see *supra* note 31.

Moreover, the Council issued a declaration according to which the above Regulations, by covering trade in services, did not prejudice the debate about the applicability of Article 133 in that area.[84] As far as transport matters were concerned, the Court had already established in *ERTA*[85] that the Community's exclusive external competence was not express under Article 133; instead, it was implied by Title V EC which provided for the common transport policy.[86] It is beyond doubt that such material discrepancy cannot be perceived as the Member States' intention indirectly to expand the scope of the CCP. Instead, it may be explained in the light of the Member States' political agreement, that is the decision adopted beyond the Community framework and prior to adoption of the Community measure. It is the political genesis of the Community measure which points towards the decisive factor, namely the effectiveness of the sanctions. It is in the light of this argument that the very first measure imposing sanctions under Article 133 EC, namely Regulation 596/82, must be viewed; even though it does not make any reference to the political agreement over the use of a Community instrument, it would not be plausible to argue that it implied the Member States' consensus over the Community's exclusive competence in this area.[87]

7. CONCLUSION

It was argued above that the Member States' reliance upon Article 133 EC regarding the imposition of sanctions on third countries was based on pragmatic considerations, that is the effectiveness of the sanctions regime, rather than a coherent conception of sanctions as falling within the Common Commercial Policy. This is illustrated in the pattern underpinning the implementation of sanction regimes under Article 133 EC, based on the conditionality of recourse to Article 133 EC upon prior agreement beyond the Community legal framework, the inconsistency between the scope of the Article 133 EC measures with that of the CCP and the non-authorised divergence of application of the sanctions Regulations.

The argument that trade sanctions were imposed under Article 133 EC for pragmatic rather than legal reasons illustrates in the most express way the political parameters which enabled the adoption of a Community measure. Therefore, it demonstrates the extent to which political considerations can bypass legal controversies and determine the legal basis of a Community measure. Viewed from this angle, trade sanctions against third countries were treated as a *sui generis* category of measures based on their "sensitive" nature as foreign

---

[84] Kuyper in *supra* note 77 at 396.
[85] [1971] ECR 263.
[86] This position was reaffirmed in *Opinion 1/94*, *supra* note 23 at para. 48.
[87] See J Verhoeven, "Communautés Européennes et sanctions internationales" (1984–1985) XVIII *RBDI* 79 at 89.

policy instruments. As a consequence, their legal regulation gave rise to the following paradox: sanctions were actually imposed under a Community law instrument on the basis of Article 133 EC while, in effect, being dissociated from the Common Commercial Policy.

This paradox was problematic in two respects: first, the non-formalised institutionalisation of the political input the above arrangement entailed was inconsistent with the role of the legal basis in the Community legal order; indeed, it has been stressed by the Court that the legal basis is directly relevant to the content and the aim of the measure and subject to judicial control rather than political compromises;[88] secondly, in effect the arrangement under consideration negated the Community's exclusive competence over the Common Commercial Policy as far as the imposition of sanctions was concerned.

The argument that trade sanctions against third countries, although adopted under Article 133 EC, were actually construed as legally distinct from the CCP raises the following question: can the introduction of an autonomous legal basis, on the one hand, ensure the effective application of sanctions and, on the other hand, be consistent with both the principles underpinning the Community legal order and the powers reserved to the Member States within the current constitutional structure of the European Union?

---

[88] See Case 300/89 *Commission* v. *Council (Titanium Dioxide)*, [1991] ECR I–2867, [1993] 3 CMLR 359 at para. 19 *et seq*. For a general analysis see D Chalmers, "Legal Base and the External Relations of the European Community" in Emiliou and O'Keeffe, *supra* note 30 at 46 *et seq*.

4

Economic Sanctions under the Law of the European Union

1. INTRODUCTION

Article 301, inserted into the EC Treaty by the Maastricht Treaty, constitutes an autonomous legal basis for the imposition of economic sanctions on third countries. It reads as follows:

> Where it is provided, in a common position or in a joint action adopted according to the provisions of the Treaty on European Union relating to the common foreign and security policy, for an action by the Community to interrupt or to reduce, in part or completely, economic relations with one or more third countries, the Council shall take the necessary urgent measures. The Council shall act by a qualified majority on a proposal from the Commission.[1]

The distinctive feature of this provision lies in the inter-pillar procedure it sets out. This is hardly a novelty; as the previous chapter illustrated, even prior to the establishment of the Union upon three legally distinct frameworks, sanctions had been imposed as a matter of practice pursuant to a combination of Community and non-Community measures, namely a Community Regulation based on new Article 133 EC and a decision adopted in the framework of European Political Co-operation. However, although the inclusion of new Article 301 EC signified the formalisation of this procedure, it gives rise to problems of its own. One is that the formalisation of the inter-pillar approach confines the power of the Community to impose sanctions to cases where agreement has already been reached beyond the Community legal framework. In this respect, the reliance of the adoption of the Community Regulation under Article 301 EC upon a Title V measure may question the extent to which Community law rules and guarantees are applied to the sanctions regime. This concern would apply to the extent to which the Court's control would be exercised over the application and interpretation of the sanctions regime; it would also raise the issue of whether the unanimity required under Title V regarding the adoption of a common position or a joint action would render the majority voting requirement for the adoption of a

---

[1] In addition to Art. 301 EC, the Treaty of Maastricht inserted the new provision of Art. 60 which reads as follows: "If, in the case envisaged in Article 301, action by the Community is deemed necessary, the Council may, in accordance with the procedure provided for in Article 301, take the necessary urgent measures on the movement of capital and on payments as regards the third countries concerned".

subsequent regulation under Article 301 EC redundant. In effect, in light of the legally distinct features of the Community legal framework and the CFSP, the legal problems arising from the dependence of the Article 301 EC Regulation upon a Title V instrument may suggest that the former measure is of questionable legal character within the Community legal order.

The second problem raised by the formalisation of the inter-pillar procedure applied to the imposition of economic sanctions is the effect that it may have on the power of the Member States to have recourse to the essentially intergovernmental procedures of the CFSP. Again, this view raises both substantive and procedural issues. The former focus on whether this new legal basis may be construed as enabling the Community to impose sanctions independently of a Title V decision. In addition, and irrespective of the answer given to the previous question, the provision of an inter-pillar procedure under Community law questions whether the Court is enabled to extend its supervision over Title V.

It thus becomes clear that the inter-pillar procedure established under Article 301 EC raises important issues regarding the scope of this new provision and its implications for the delimitation of competence between the Community and the Member States under Title V. The analysis of these issues will be structured as follows. First, a typology of the sanctions regimes imposed under Article 301 EC will be outlined and, secondly, the main common features underpinning their application highlighted. The third part will analyse the scope of Article 301 EC, while the fourth will examine the relationship between Article 301 EC and the Common Commercial Policy and the fifth the relationship with the wholly exceptional provision of Article 297 EC. Finally, the sixth part will highlight the main problems raised by the imposition of sanctions under that provision.

2. TYPOLOGY OF SANCTIONS IMPOSED UNDER ARTICLE 301 EC

The Maastricht Treaty rendered irrelevant the debate about whether the imposition of trade sanctions on third countries falls within the scope of the Common Commercial Policy; under Articles 301 and 60 EC, sanctions on third countries are to be imposed by means of a Council Regulation adopted by qualified majority and pursuant to a common position or joint action already adopted under Title V TEU.

An exhaustive account of all the sanctions imposed under Article 301 EC would be out of place here, for this book aims at examining the substantive and institutional problems arising from the inter-pillar procedure expressly provided for under Article 301 EC.[2] What the following analysis does require is an overview of the sanctions regimes adopted pursuant to the inter-pillar proce-

---

[2] For an enumeration of the sanctions regimes imposed under Arts. 301 and 60 EC see the *General Report on the Activities of the European Union*, produced annually by the Commission and the *Review of the Council's Work—The Secretary-General's Report*, produced annually by the Council.

dure in question which will serve two purposes: on the one hand, it will provide a typology of the measures adopted under Article 301 EC, hence indicating the scope of the latter provision; on the other hand, it will highlight the common substantive and procedural characteristics of these regimes. This overview will provide the canvas against which the legal problems posed by the adoption and implementation of sanction regimes under Article 301 EC will be analysed.

Economic sanctions may be broadly divided into the following three categories: trade sanctions, which involve the imposition of restrictions on imports from the target country and/or exports to the target state; financial sanctions, aiming to interrupt the flow of resources to the target state by banning lending and/or investment; finally, sanctions on transport services, aiming at cutting off any transport communication between the sender state and the target state and, hence, depriving the latter of any benefit that communications with the former would normally bring.[3]

2.1. Trade sanctions under Article 301 EC

One of the most common features of sanctions imposed under Article 301 EC has been the prohibition of imports to and exports from the target country. This is illustrated in Council Regulation 2465/96 following Common Position 96/741/CFSP[4] which imposed a comprehensive embargo on Iraq. Imports of all commodities and products originating in or coming from Iraq and the export to Iraq of all commodities and products originating in, coming from or in transit through the Community were covered by Regulation 2465/96. In addition, a number of other activities were also prohibited, namely the provision of non-financial services which promote the Iraqi economy, taking off from, landing in, or overflying the territory of the Community by aircraft carrying any cargo to or from Iraq or is destined to land in, or take off from Iraq and any activity the object or effect of which would be to promote the above activities.[5]

---

[3] This typology seeks to serve as a tool aiming to facilitate the analysis to follow. As such, it is by no means exhaustive. A far more detailed categorisation has been suggested in J Kirshner, "The Microfoundations of Economic Sanctions" (1997) 6 *Security Studies* 32 at 36–7, whereby the following three more specific types of sanctions are identified: aid sanctions, which cease to supply aid to the target state; monetary sanctions, which aim to destabilise the value and upset the stability of the target state's currency, mainly through increasing inflation and debt burdens and upsetting public and private economic planning; finally, seizure of the target's assets, that is physical property, securities and bank accounts, which may consist of freezing them, thereby preventing the target state from having access to them, or transferring ownership of them from the target state to the sender. Kirshner further proceeds to determine the characteristics of these forms of sanctions. He argues, for instance, that the imposition of trade sanctions normally offers private market actors incentives to undermine them by directing trade to the target state through third parties, whereas supervision of adherence by national legislation imposing financial sanctions is easier. For the characteristics of the above types of sanctions, see *ibid*. at 38–41.

[4] [1996] OJ L337/1 and /5 respectively.

[5] Art. 1 of Reg. 2465/96. Consistently with all Council Regs. imposing sanctions on third countries, the abovementioned measure provides for various exceptions subject to authorisation by

The scope of trade sanctions imposed by the Union under Article 301 EC may vary. Whereas Regulation 2465/96 imposed a comprehensive embargo, the Union has often deemed it necessary to restrict the scope of its action to very specific products. This is clearly illustrated in Regulation 2465/97 adopted by the Council under Article 301 EC pursuant to Common Position 97/826/CFSP[6] concerning the interruption of certain economic relations with Sierra Leone. This measure prohibited the sale or supply of petroleum and petroleum products, whether or not originating in the Community, in the territory of Sierra Leone, along with any activity of whatever nature the object or effect of which was, directly or indirectly, to promote the selling or supply of petroleum or petroleum products.[7]

2.2. Financial sanctions under Articles 60 and 301 EC

The imposition of financial sanctions has been a measure frequently used by the European Union. Council Regulation 1607/98 adopted under Articles 60 and 301 EC pursuant to Common Position 98/374/CFSP[8] concerning the prohibition of new investment in Serbia provides an example. Having stated in the preamble that the measure in question is covered by the EC Treaty, this measure prohibits the "transfer of funds or other financial assets". It is noteworthy that not only the personal,[9] but also the material scope, of the Regulation in question is set out in quite broad terms; Article 1 prohibits the transfer of "cash, liquid assets, dividends, interest or other income on shares, bonds, debt obligations and any other securities, or amounts derived from an interest in, or the sale or other disposal of, or any other dealing with tangible and intangible assets, including property rights".

The imposition of financial sanctions is an instrument often used by the Union. Other examples include Council Regulation 1705/98 adopted under

---

either the competent authority of the Member State in question or the Sanctions Committee set up by the UN Security Council, depending on the nature of the goods under consideration.

⁶ [1997] OJ L344/1 and 6 respectively. This embargo on Sierra Leone was repealed by Council Reg. 941/98 [1998] OJ L136/1, adopted under Art. 301 EC and pursuant to Common Position 98/300/CFSP [1998] OJ L136/2.

⁷ As in most cases of sanctions against third countries, a number of exceptions is provided for, in that specific case regarding the democratically elected Government of Sierra Leone, for verified humanitarian purposes or the needs of the Military Observer Group stationed in that country. These transactions are to be permitted in so far as no objection is raised by the Sanctions Committee already set up under UN Security Council Resolution 1132 (1997).

⁸ [1998] OJ L209/16 and L165/1 respectively.

⁹ Under Art. 1(1) of Reg. 1607/98, the prohibition of new investment applies to the State or Government of the Federal Republic of Yugoslavia and the Republic of Serbia; any person in, or resident in, Serbia; any body carrying out business in, incorporated or constituted under Serbian law; any body owned or controlled by and any person acting on behalf of any of the above governments, persons or bodies, in so far as the funds in question are transferred "for the purposes of establishing a lasting economic link with the Republic of Serbia, including the acquisition of real estate there".

Articles 60 and 301 EC and pursuant to Common Position 98/425/CFSP[10] concerning the interruption of certain economic relations with Angola in order to induce the National Union for the Total Independence of Angola to fulfil its obligations in the peace process. This instrument imposes, in addition to financial sanctions, a ban on trade and provision of services.

A specific example of sanctions imposed on a third state consists of freezing the target state's assets. An example of this type of sanctions is illustrated in Regulation 1295/98 which the Council adopted pursuant to Common Position 98/326/CFSP.[11] This Regulation provided for all funds held outside the Federal Republic of Yugoslavia and belonging to its Government or/and that of the Republic of Serbia to be frozen; in addition it prohibited any funds to be made available, directly or indirectly, to or for the benefit of, either or both, those Governments.[12] Both the terms "funds" and their "freezing" were defined broadly: the former covered funds of any kind, including interest, dividends or other value accruing to or from any such funds, whereas the latter was defined as preventing any change in volume, amount, location, ownership, possession, character, destination or other change that would enable the use of the funds concerned.[13]

This model of sanction consisting of freezing the funds of the target state was followed in other cases where Article 301 EC was invoked. What is interesting in Regulation 1295/98 in particular is the fact that its adoption had already been envisaged even prior to the adoption of its accompanying Common Position 98/326/CFSP; indeed, Common Position 98/240/CFSP,[14] adopted more than three months prior to Regulation 1295/98 and less than two months prior to Common Position 98/326/CFSP, provided in its preamble that "the Union will move to further international measures, and specifically to pursue a freezing of the funds held abroad by the Federal Republic of Yugoslavia and the Serbian Governments, should the . . . steps [demanded by the above Governments in order to stop the violence and engage in a commitment to find a political solution to the issue of Kosovo elaborated in the preamble to that Common Position] not be implemented".

2.3. Sanctions on transport services under Article 301 EC

A specific sanction often imposed by the Union on a third country consists of the prohibition of flights between the target state and the Community. This is illustrated in Regulation 3274/93 adopted by the Council under Article 301 pursuant to Common Position 93/614/CFSP[15] preventing the supply of certain goods and

[10] [1998] OJ L215/1 and L190/1 respectively.
[11] [1998] OJ L178/33 and L143/1 respectively.
[12] Art. 2 of Reg. 1295/98.
[13] *Ibid*. Art. 1.
[14] [1998] OJ L95/1.
[15] [1993] OJ L295/1 and /7 respectively.

services to Libya. The scope of the ban on flights between the Community and Libya was quite broad, for it applied to permission to any aircraft to take off, land in or overfly the territory of the Community if it was destined to land in or had taken off from Libya.[16] Furthermore, this embargo was accompanied by various other secondary measures: all commercial transactions with the national air carrier of Libya and the activities and operation of all its offices were prohibited, whereas the latter were closed completely and the supply or provision, directly or indirectly, of specifically listed goods and services related to flights were prohibited.[17]

The scope of a ban on flights between the Community and the target state may vary. This is illustrated in the case of Regulation 1901/98 adopted by the Council under Article 301 EC pursuant to Common Position 98/426/CFSP[18] concerning a ban on flights of Yugoslav carriers between the Federal Republic of Yugoslavia and the European Community. The scope of this measure is limited to any aircraft "operated directly or indirectly by a Yugoslav carrier, that is a carrier having its principal place of business or its registered office in the Federal Republic of Yugoslavia".[19]

3. COMMON FEATURES OF SANCTION REGIMES IMPOSED UNDER ARTICLE 301 EC

The variable scope of sanctions imposed by the Union under the procedure set out in Article 301 has not prevented the measures undertaken thereunder from sharing certain characteristics. Their identification is essential to the understanding of the pattern which underlies the Union's practice under Article 301 EC.

3.1. Reference in the common position to the political background and the main thrust of the sanctions regime

The common position pursuant to which the Council Regulation is adopted under Article 301 EC sets out in its preamble the political background that led to the adoption of the sanctions in question. Common Position 98/240/CFSP, for instance, on restrictive measures against the Federal Republic of Yugoslavia refers to "recent events in the Federal Republic of Yugoslavia, and in particular the use of force against the Kosovar Albanian Community in Kosovo, [which] represent an unacceptable violation of human rights and put the security of the

---

[16] Art. 1 of Reg. 3274/93. Under Art. 1(2), an exception is provided for regarding particular flights approved on grounds of significant humanitarian need by the Sanctions Committee already set up under UN Security Council Resolution 748 (1992).

[17] See Art. 3 of and Annex to Reg. 3274/93.

[18] [1998] OJ L248/1 and L190/3 respectively.

[19] Art. 1 of Reg. 1901/98, *supra* note 18. Under Art. 2, an exception is provided for in relation to emergency landings on the territory of the Community and ensuing take-offs, as well as authorisations for charter series flights between Leipzig and Tivat by Montenegro Airlines.

region at risk"; it then goes on to state that "the European Union strongly condemns the violent repression of the non-violent expression of political views . . . [and] demands that the Government of the FRY take effective steps to stop the violence and engage in a commitment to give a political solution to the issue of Kosovo through a peaceful dialogue with the Kosovar Albanian Community".[20] It is noteworthy that the above reference to the political background is in marked contrast to the first sanctions regime imposed by the Member States by means of a Community measure. That was the case of Council Regulation 596/82 imposing sanctions on the Soviet Union after the declaration of martial law in Poland; there was no reference to the political motive behind the imposition of sanctions either in the Community measure or in a measure adopted within the European Political Co-operation framework.[21]

3.2. Provision for exceptions

It is characteristic that even in cases of total embargoes on third countries, the relevant regulations provide for certain exceptions. One of the most commonly set out is that for humanitarian reasons. In the case of the trade embargo on Iraq under Regulation 2465/96, for example, the general prohibition of exports from or transit through the Community did not apply to, amongst others, products intended strictly for medical purposes, foodstuffs, materials and supplies for essential civilian needs.[22] Exceptions following this pattern are also provided for in cases of financial sanctions: under Regulation 1607/98, the release of funds or other financial assets may be authorised on a case-by-case basis, provided that they are to be used "solely for projects in support of democratisation, humanitarian and educational activities and independent media".[23]

3.3. Scope for independent action left to the Member States

The sanctions regime established under regulations adopted pursuant to Article 301 EC leaves considerable scope for action to the Member States. This is mainly illustrated in the clause inserted in most sanctions regulations enabling the competent authorities of the Member States to authorise, under certain

---

[20] The preamble to Common Position 98/240/CFSP further specifies these measures by demanding that the Yugoslav Government "withdraw the special police units and cease action by the security forces affecting the civilian population, allow access to Kosovo for the International Committee of the Red Cross and other humanitarian organisations as well as the representatives of the Union and other Embassies, commit itself publicly to begin a process of dialogue with the leadership of the Kosovar Albanian Community, cooperate in a constructive manner in order to implement the action set out in . . . the Contact Group statement".

[21] See *supra* ch. 3, section 5.

[22] See Art. 2(3)(a), (b) and (c) in *supra* note 4.

[23] Art. 2 in *supra* note 8.

conditions, activities which deviate from the sanctions regime. This constitutes a common feature of the sanctions regime imposed on the basis of Article 301 EC; in the case of Regulation 2472/94, for instance,[24] which leaves intact the prohibition on flights and ferry services carrying cargo between the Community and the Federal Republic of Yugoslavia, the competent authorities of the Member States may authorise otherwise. In cases where the sanctions regulations implement an embargo provided under a United Nations Security Council Resolution, the right of the Member States to authorise deviation from the sanctions regime may be conditional upon the approval of the Sanctions Committee, that is a Committee established by the UN Security Council in order to facilitate the implementation of sanctions.[25]

However, there are various cases where the competent authorities of the Member States may authorise deviation from the sanctions regime without the approval of the Sanctions Committee being required. In these cases, the sanctions regulations impose certain substantive conditions which need to be met by the national authorities. Under Regulation 2471/94, for instance, the Member States may authorise economic activities, hence deviating from the comprehensive trade and financial embargo imposed thereunder on the areas of Bosnia-Herzegovina under the control of Bosnian Serb forces, only "having satisfied themselves on a case-by-case basis that the activities do not result in the transfer of property or interests in property to any person or body [covered by the personal scope of the Regulation in question]".[26]

3.4. Establishment of a co-operation procedure amongst the Member States and between them and the Commission

In the light of the scope left under the sanctions regulations to Member States for independent action, it is hardly surprising that all sanctions regulations under Article 301 EC establish a co-operation procedure involving, on the one hand, the Commission and the Member States and, on the other hand, the Member States themselves. This procedure covers both the exchange of information regarding specifically the measures taken under the relevant regulations and any information generally in connection with these regulations[27]; as Regulation 2465/97 specifies, the latter may refer to breaches and other enforce-

[24] [1994] OJ L266/8. This Reg. was adopted pursuant to Common Position 94/673/CFSP [1994] OJ L266/11.
[25] See Art. 3 of Reg. 2472/94, *supra* note 24; Arts 5 and 9 of Reg. 2471/94 introducing a further discontinuation of the economic and financial relations between the European Community and the areas of Bosnia-Herzegovina under the control of Bosnian Serb forces [1994] OJ L266/1 pursuant to Common Position 94/672/CFSP [1994] OJ L266/10. On the Sanctions Committee and its role in the implementation of sanctions, see *infra* at 3.6.
[26] Art. 3. Furthermore, see Art. 2(3)(a) of Reg. 2465/96, *supra* note 4.
[27] See, for instance, Art. 7 of Reg. 1295/98, *supra* note 11.

ment problems, judgments handed down by national courts or decisions of relevant international *fora*.[28]

This procedure performs a two-fold function: on the one hand, it aims at ensuring uniformity of application and, ultimately, the effectiveness of sanctions; on the other hand, in the light of the exceptional clauses that all sanctions regulations under Article 301 EC, even the most comprehensive ones, provide, it also aims at ensuring that no deviation from the embargo takes place except in accordance with the conditions set out in the relevant regulations.[29] This is illustrated by cases where the right of the Member States to authorise any deviations from the sanctions regime and its co-operation duty become subject to further conditions, such as a deadline; under Regulation 3274/93, for instance, a Member State authorising the supply to Libya of goods generally covered by the embargo imposed therein must inform the other Member States and the Commission within 30 days of the exports allowed.[30]

3.5. The right of the Member States to determine the penalties for breach of Article 301 EC regulations

In addition to the scope left for the Member States to authorise certain deviations from the sanctions regime in accordance with certain conditions, the sanctions regulations leave them free to determine the penalties for any breach.[31] Furthermore, certain regulations require such penalties to be "effective, proportionate and dissuasive".[32]

3.6. The Sanctions Committee in cases of regulations adopted under Article 301 EC pursuant to United Nations Security Council Resolutions

When the Council adopts regulations under Article 301 EC in order to implement sanctions imposed under a United Nations Security Council Resolution, special reference is made to the Sanctions Committee. This is a quasi-judicial body established by the United Nations Security Council when the latter requires that the international community impose sanctions on the target state. It is the United Nations Resolution which sets out a sanctions regime that establishes a Sanctions Committee, thereby confining the latter's mandate to that

---

[28] Art. 6 of Reg. 1901/98, *supra* note 18; see also Art. 5 of Reg. 2465/97 [1997] OJ L344/1; Art. 7(2) of Reg. 2465/96, *supra* note 4; Art. 8 of Reg. 1705/98, *supra* note 10; Art. 6 of Reg. 926/98 [1998] OJ L130/1; Art. 5 of Reg. 1607/98, *supra* note 8.

[29] See, for instance, Art. 4(2) of Reg. 3274/93, *supra* note 15.

[30] See *ibid.* at Art. 3(3).

[31] See, for instance, Art. 13(1) of Reg. 2471/94, *supra* note 25; Art. 7(3) of Reg. 2465/96, *supra* note 4; Art. 5 of Reg. 926/98, *supra* note 28; Art. 7 of Reg. 1705/98, *supra* note 10.

[32] See, for instance, Art. 6 of Reg. 1295/98, *supra* note 11; Art. 3 of Reg. 1607/98, *supra* note 8; Art. 5 of Reg. 1901/98, *supra* note 18.

specific sanctions regime, hence the Yugoslavia Sanctions Committee[33] or the Iraq Sanctions Committee.[34] The role of the Sanctions Committee consists of facilitating the implementation of sanctions imposed under the United Nations Security Council Resolution in accordance with the functions assigned thereunder. These functions may vary depending on the intensity of the sanctions regime under the relevant United Nations Security Council Resolutions. A task commonly assigned to a Sanctions Committee consists of ensuring that the exceptions provided under the relevant Sanctions United Nations Security Council Resolutions are applied by the international community in accordance with the provisions set out therein. In the case of trade sanctions, for instance, the "non-objection" of the Sanctions Committee to national authorisations of supplies of foodstuffs of products for humanitarian purposes is required.[35] The Committee can perform this task on the basis of a procedure established under the relevant United Nations Security Council Resolutions, whereby all states bound by the latter are required to notify to the former any authorisation they grant pursuant to exceptional clauses under the sanctions regime. Another function performed by a Sanctions Committee consists of interpreting the United Nations Sanctions Resolutions by issuing communications in cases where a clarification is sought by a state. The lack of an express mandate to this effect notwithstanding, the communications issued by a Sanctions Committee are considered to be as authoritative an interpretation of the relevant United Nations Sanctions Resolution as can possibly exist in the current system of sanctions under the aegis of the United Nations.[36]

4. THE SCOPE OF ARTICLE 301 EC

Article 301 EC formalised the political genesis of a Community measure. The Member States' agreement beyond the Community legal order to have recourse to a Community legal instrument constitutes the political genesis of a

---

[33] See MP Scharf and JL Dorosin, "Interpreting UN Sanctions: the Rulings and Role of the Yugoslavia Sanctions Committee" (1993) 19 *Brooklyn Journal of International Law* 771.

[34] See P Conlon, "Lessons From Iraq: The Functions of the Iraq Sanctions Committee as a Source of Sanctions Implementation Authority and Practice" (1995) 35 *Va. J Int'l L.* 669.

[35] See, e.g., Art. 2(3) of Reg. 2465/96, *supra* note 4; Art. 4 of Reg. 1705/98, *supra* note 10.

[36] In this respect, see the Opinion of Jacobs AG in Case C–84/95 *Bosphorus Hava Turizm* v. *Ticaret AS ve Minister for Transport, Energy and Communications, Ireland and the Attorney General* [1996] ECR I–3953, [1996] CMLR 257 at para. 46, where he argues that "[c]learly, due regard should be given to the opinion of the [Sanctions] Committee; it consists of representatives of States which are members of the Security Council, and their views must carry considerable weight. The Committee has developed into an important standing body for the day-to-day supervision of the enforcement of the sanctions and can promote the consistent interpretation and application of the resolutions by the international community". However, he adds that "it seems questionable whether in the present case the Committee's opinion could be regarded as binding if only because such an effect is not provided for by the relevant provisions of the resolutions". It is noteworthy that, in its judgment, the Court does not make reference to the relevant communications of the Sanctions Committee. For an analysis of both the Opinion of Jacobs AG and the *Bosphorus* judgment, see *infra*, ch. 5.

Community measure. As such, it attributes a quality to the measure adopted under Article 301 EC that distinguishes it from all other Community instruments. It is true that political reasons are not alien to the adoption of most Community measures. However, the procedure established by Article 301 EC expressly renders the adoption of a Community measure dependent on prior political agreement, which would otherwise only be implied. This is the new element that Article 301 EC introduces in the Community legal order, namely the formalisation of the political input which underlies the adoption of a Community act.

This feature of Article 301 EC is linked to the argument put forward in the previous chapter, namely that prior to the TEU and despite the imposition of sanctions under Article 133 EC, the drafting of the relevant regulations and their implementation by the Member States amounted to the construction of sanctions as a *sui generis* genre of measures within the framework of the CCP; therefore, instead of assimilating the sanctions regimes to the rules applicable to the CCP, the above practice in effect dissociated sanctions from the CCP. The scope of Article 301 EC confirms this conclusion; indeed, its wording suggests that its material scope is considerably broader than that of Article 133 EC. Under Article 301, "an action by the Community to interrupt or to reduce, in part or completely, economic relations with one or more third countries" is envisaged. Such a measure is not to be covered by the CCP in so far as the latter does not operate as a common policy on external economic relations.[37] In this respect, it has been argued that it covers transport, development aid and financial relations.[38] Therefore, it enables the adoption of measures whose scope would be at odds if adopted under Article 133.

The discrepancy between the scope of Article 133 and that of Article 301, in addition to the formalised political genesis of the measures adopted under the latter, indicates that measures imposing economic sanctions on third countries are not meant to be similar to those adopted under the CCP. It follows that, with regard to measures adopted under Article 301 EC, the debate over their nature and status within the Community legal order must transcend the limits set by the instrumentalist/teleological debate over the CCP. Any debate regarding economic sanctions under these terms has become *de facto* irrelevant.

The above development may have some positive effects. The express provision of the inter-pillar procedure under which sanctions are to be adopted may reduce inter-institutional tensions within the Community. The instrumentalism/teleology debate having become largely irrelevant in the case of sanctions, the Commission and the Council may not have any grounds for legal

---

[37] A Arnull, "The Scope of the Common Commercial Policy: A Coda on Opinion 1/94" in N Emiliou and D O'Keeffe (eds.), *The European Union and World Trade Law after the GATT Uruguay Round* (Chichester: Willey, 1996) 343 at 359.

[38] See C Schmitter, "Article 228a" in V Constantinesco, R Kovar and D Simon (eds.), *Traité sur l'Union européenne: (signé le 7 février 1992): commentaire article par article* (Paris: Economica, 1996) at 763.

controversy over the appropriate legal basis of the implementing Community measure. Moreover, this inter-institutional consensus may contribute to a great extent to the effectiveness of the sanctions. It may ensure the less time-consuming and cumbersome adoption of the embargo. Moreover, it may focus the whole process on the crucial element of sanctions, that is their exact nature and content. Finally, it indicates that the European Union is, in principle, in a position to impose more comprehensive and far-reaching sanctions in the post-Maastricht era. However, whether these results have actually come about is dependent upon, on the one hand, the relationship between Article 301 EC and other potential Treaty bases for sanctions and, on the other hand, the way in which the institutions of the Union have recourse to the inter-pillar procedure of Article 301 EC.

5. THE RELATIONSHIP BETWEEN ARTICLES 301 AND 133 EC

It was argued above that the introduction of Article 301 EC, consistently with pre-existing practice, dissociates sanctions from the CCP. However, it has not provided a definite answer to whether and under which circumstances sanctions may be imposed pursuant to Article 133 EC.

In the *FYROM* case, where the Commission challenged the legality of Greek measures restricting trade with FYROM under Article 298 EC, the starting point of the Opinion delivered by Advocate General Jacobs after the Maastricht Treaty came into force was the inclusion of embargoes, in principle, within the CCP. He argued that "[a] measure which has the effect of directly preventing or restricting trade with a non-member country comes within the scope of [CCP], regardless of its purpose" and therefore "the decisive element is not the purpose of the embargo but its effects".[39] Having established that such economic measures are covered by the exclusive competence of the Community, he concluded that "the Member States have surrendered the power to adopt unilateral measures restricting trade with the outside world". It follows that an embargo for which justification is claimed under Article 297 EC is to be understood as a Community law exception to the Common Commercial Policy. Indeed, as Advocate General Jacobs pointed out, "[a]lthough Greece argues that the embargo on trade with F.Y.R.O.M. lies outside the scope of [CCP], it is important to note that Greece has none the less accepted from the outset the need to rely on Article 297 of the Treaty in order to establish the compatibility of the embargo with Community law".[40]

It is not immediately apparent how this conclusion is consistent with the dissociation of economic sanctions from Article 133 EC achieved under Article 301 EC. An answer to this question may rely upon the construction of the latter as

---

[39] Case C–120/94 *Commission* v. *Greece* [1996] ECR I–1513, para. 42.
[40] Para. 43.

an exception to the former. In other words, if the application of Article 301 EC is to be confined to cases where agreement has been reached in the form of a common position or a joint action under Title V TEU, in cases where no agreement has been reached under Title V TEU the Member States would be free to rely upon Article 133 EC in order to impose sanctions. If this is the case, then the sanctions adopted under Article 133 EC would be confined to the scope of the Common Commercial Policy.[41] It is suggested that the above construction of Article 133 EC would not lead to the problems encountered prior to the TEU, namely the adoption of measures whose scope was at odds with that of CCP and the non-authorised divergence of application of the sanctions regimes; the ensuing marginalisation of sanctions as a *sui generis* category within the CCP was due to the dependence of the sanctions regulations entirely upon prior political agreement, whereas in the scenario envisaged above recourse to Article 133 EC would be due to the lack of political agreement.

However, reliance upon Article 133 EC for the imposition of sanctions on third countries raises two issues. The first is of a practical nature; it is very unlikely that the absence of political agreement beyond the Community legal framework will trigger the submergence of sanctions into the Common Commercial Policy through the Commission's exercise of its exclusive right of initiative. This would be too drastic a response to a foreign policy problem of the Union and would defy more than three decades of careful construction of sanctions as a *sui generis* case of trade measures. The second issue deals with Article 301 EC itself. The construction of Article 133 EC as an alternative legal basis for the imposition of sanctions in cases where no political agreement is reached under Title V would eventually marginalise reliance upon Article 301 EC. The guarantees of effectiveness and uniform application enjoyed by CCP measures would be too important and apparent to ignore. On the other hand, were such a development to take place, the more limited scope of Article 133 EC in relation to that of Article 301 EC would inevitably undermine the effectiveness of the sanctions regime; this remark is valid in so far as the scope of the sanctions regulations under Article 133 EC would correspond to that of the CCP so as to avoid the legal confusion characterising the implementation of sanctions in the pre-TEU era.

6. THE RELATIONSHIP BETWEEN ARTICLES 301 AND 297 EC

The broad scope of Article 301 EC raises the question whether the Member States may impose sanctions on occasions and under procedures other than those envisaged in Article 301 EC. This question becomes all the more

---

[41] See SV Konstadinidis, "The New Face of the Community's External Relations: Recent Developments on Certain Controversial Issues" in SV Konstadinidis (ed.), *The Legal Regulation of the European Community's External Relations after the Completion of the Internal Market* (Aldershot: Dartmouth, 1996) 19 at 30 and P Willaert and C Marcués-Ruiz, "Vers une politique étrangère et de sécurité commune: état des lieux" (1995) no 3 *Revue du Marché Unique européen* 35 at 40.

significant in the light of the absence of any relevant indication in the provision under consideration. This is contrary to Article 60 EC regarding the application "in the case envisaged in Article 301" of the inter-pillar procedure set out therein to the movement of capital and to payments to third countries; under Article 60 EC, in the absence of measures by the Council pursuant to Article 60 EC, unilateral measures may be taken "for serious political reasons and on grounds of urgency". This right of the Member States is granted "without prejudice to Article 297", while both the Commission and the other Member States "shall be informed of such measures by the date of their entry into force at the latest".[42]

In the absence of a similar provision, the Treaty provision which seems particularly relevant is Article 297 EC, that is the same one under which sanctions were implemented collectively by the Member States prior to recourse being had to a Community instrument.

Article 297 EC reads as follows: "Member States shall consult each other with a view to taking together the steps needed to prevent the functioning of the common market being affected by measures which a Member State may be called upon to take in the event of serious internal disturbances affecting the maintenance of law and order, in the event of war or serious international tension constituting a threat of war, or in order to carry out obligations it has accepted for the purpose of maintaining peace and international security".

6.1. The interpretation of Article 297 EC

Close examination of Article 297 EC makes it clear that the scope of national action envisaged therein is unlimited. Furthermore, the scope of Community rules from which deviation is justified under Article 297 EC is equally unlimited. In this respect, Article 297 EC is not similar to other public security Treaty provisos, such as Articles 30, 39(3) and 46(1), for the latter enable Member States to deviate from Community rules regarding the freedom of movement of goods, persons and establishment respectively in order to protect, amongst other interests, their public security; in doing so, these exceptional clauses "deal with exceptional cases which are clearly defined and which do not lend themselves to any wide interpretation".[43] However, the derogation introduced by Article 297

---

[42] Art. 60(2) EC provides that "[t]he Council may, acting by a qualified majority on a proposal from the Commission, decide that the Member State concerned shall amend or abolish such measures. The President of the Council shall inform the European Parliament of any such decision taken by the Council". It is interesting that the above provision envisages the involvement, albeit limited, of the European Parliament in the case of financial sanctions imposed unilaterally, whereas no such right is granted in relation to sanctions imposed by the Union. Furthermore, this provision raises the following paradox: it gives the Council the power to intervene by a qualified majority in relation to a unilateral imposition of financial sanctions in a case where these sanctions are adopted precisely because of the Council's failure to act by a qualified majority voting.

[43] Case 13/68 *Salgoil SpA* v. *Italian Ministry for Foreign Trade*, [1968] ECR 453 at 463 and Case 222/84 *Marguerite Johnston* v. *Chief Constable of the Royal Ulster Constabulary* [1986] ECR 1651, [1986] 3 CMLR 240 at paras. 26–7.

EC authorises the Member States to deviate from all the rules relating to the common market. In this respect, its effect is significantly different from that of the above exceptional clauses.[44] This special feature of Article 297 justifies its status as of a "wholly exceptional character".[45]

The strict interpretation of the exceptional Treaty provisos aims at ensuring the maximum protection of the *acquis communautaire* and the attainment of the Treaty objectives by allowing the minimum deviation from Community law within limits set under Community law and interpreted by the Court. These considerations are also relevant to the interpretation of Article 297 EC. Indeed, the unlimited scope of national measures and the deviation from Community law *in toto* may render Article 297 EC subject to abuse from the Member States which may seek to invoke it to an extent not envisaged by the Treaty. It is for this reason that three safeguards are provided by the Treaty. The first one consists of the consultation procedure amongst the Member States in relation to the measures that are to be taken under Article 297 EC. The second guarantee that the Treaty has provided in order to confine the invocation of Article 297 EC to measures that are absolutely essential is the consultation procedure that Article 298 has established; under this provision, "[i]f measures taken in the circumstances referred to in Article 297 have the effect of distorting the conditions of competition in the common market, the Commission shall, together with the State concerned, examine how these measures can be adjusted to the rules laid down in the Treaty". Finally, the Treaty, in order to prevent Article 297 EC from being unduly invoked, has introduced the exceptional procedure of Article 298(2) EC which provides for judicial control in cases of "improper use of the powers provided for in Articles 296 and 297".[46]

Various issues regarding the interpretation of Article 297 EC remain unclear. Is the consultation amongst the Member States provided under Article 297 EC to take place prior to or following the adoption of the measures which a Member State may be called upon to take? What is the form that this consultation must take? What is the extent to which national actions under Article 297 EC are subject to the Court's exceptional jurisdiction under Article 298 EC? These issues and the interpretation of Article 297 EC in general have recently

---

[44] See the Opinion of AG Jacobs in Case C–120/94 *Commission* v. *Greece, supra* note 39 at para 46, where he argues that "the analogy between Articles [30] and [297] should not be taken too far. . . . Certainly it is correct to say that Articles [30] and [297] must both be construed strictly since they derogate from the ordinary rules of the Treaty. That much the two provisions have in common. There are, however, important differences. In the first place, whereas the situations covered by Article [30] (and [39(3) and 46(1)] may be described as exceptional, those covered by Article [297] are, as the Court recognised in paragraph 27 of the *Johnston* judgment, *wholly* exceptional [emphasis in the original]. That is confirmed by the fact that Article [297] has so rarely been invoked, while recourse to Article [30] is relatively common. A second difference relates to the breadth of the possible derogations permitted by the two articles. Article [30] permits derogations from one aspect of the common market (admittedly a fundamental one); Article [297], on the other hand, permits derogations from the rules of the common market in general"; see also the comment on Art. 296 by J Verhoeven in Constantinesco et al. in *supra* note 38 at 1393.

[45] *Johnston* judgment, *supra* note 43 at para. 27.

[46] For an analysis of Art. 298(2) EC, see *infra* at ch. 6.

been the subject of academic interest.[47] The Court has never delivered a judgment under Article 298 EC. The *Commission* v. *Greece (FYROM)* case, regarding an action brought by the Commission before the Court under Article 298 EC in relation to the Greek embargo against Former Yugoslavian Republic of Macedonia, was resolved after Advocate General Jacobs delivered his Opinion.[48]

A detailed analysis of Article 297 in the light of its "wholly exceptional character" is beyond the scope of this book. What is of direct relevance, however, is the extent to which Article 297 EC may be invoked in order to justify the imposition of sanctions on third countries. In order to answer this question, the following three separate issues must be addressed: first, whether the Member States can rely upon Article 297 EC in order to impose collective sanctions on a third country; secondly, whether the Member States may rely upon Article 297 EC in order to implement United Nations Security Council Resolutions imposing sanctions on a third country; thirdly, whether a Member State may rely upon Article 297 EC in order to impose unilateral sanctions on a third country.

6.2. Article 297 EC as the legal basis for collective sanctions against a third country

There are two possibilities regarding the role of Article 297 EC as justifying the imposition of collective sanctions against a third state that need to be distinguished. The first one deals with all the Member States relying upon Article 297 EC following consultations within the CFSP framework. Remote though this scenario may be, it would enable the Member States to impose sanctions collectively without recourse being had to a Community instrument and, hence, claim that the sanctions regime in question is not subject to the ordinary jurisdiction of the Court. This would be clearly against the Treaty, for the latter, in introducing Article 301 EC, provides that the "measures which a Member State may be called upon to take" in relation to collective sanctions be taken within the Community legal framework. It follows that to invoke Article 297 EC under such circumstances would not only amount to an abuse of this provision but would also run counter to the *raison d'être* of Article 301 EC. Finally, the fact that Article 297 EC was abandoned by the Member States in relation to collective sanctions against a third country well prior to the introduction of Article 301 EC indicates that there is a significant *acquis politique* against recourse to the former in the case referred to above.

---

[47] See R Fornassier, "Quelques réflexions sur les sanctions internationales en droit communautaire", (1996) 402 *Revue du Marché commun et de l'Union européenne* 670; C Stefanou and H Xanthaki, *A Legal and Political Interpretation of Articles 224 and 225 of the Treaty of Rome: The Former Yugoslav Republic of Macedonia Cases* (Aldershot: Dartmouth and Ashgate, 1997); R Toxopeus, "The Greek Embargo and Articles 224 and 225 EEC—A Political Question Looked at from a Juridical Point of View" (1996) 49 *Revue hellenique de droit international* 187.

[48] See *supra* note 44. On the Opinion of Jacobs AG, see *infra* at ch. 6.

The second possibility regarding the role of Article 297 as a justification for collective sanctions against a third country deals with recourse being had by some Member States to Article 297; in this case, the Member States would claim that they could not satisfy the voting requirements regarding the adoption of a common position or a joint action under Title V TEU and, hence, the only medium available for sanctions to be imposed was through national measures justified under Article 297 EC. It has been argued that in the light of Article 297 as a "reserve of sovereignty", "there is little or no argument" against the position that the Member States may impose sanctions under national law justified under Article 297 in cases where no common position is reached or no joint action is adopted under Title V.[49]

The above assumption may be questioned on two grounds. First, to construe Article 297 EC as "a reserve of sovereignty"[50] is tantamount to rejecting the strict interpretation that its "wholly exceptional character" entails according to the Court. Moreover, it clearly runs counter to the Treaty itself; indeed, the provision for a consultation procedure amongst the Member States, between the Member State invoking Article 297 EC and the Commission and, finally, the extraordinary jurisdiction of the Court under Article 297 EC indicates that recourse to Article 297 EC is subject to certain conditions, adherence to which is to be ensured by the Court.

The second argument against the assumption that Member States may invoke Article 297 EC in order to justify sanctions imposed under national measures focuses on cases where the sanctions under consideration are collective, that is imposed by some Member States when no common position is reached or joint action adopted. It is suggested that, in such cases, reliance upon Article 297 may run counter to the spirit underpinning the imposition of sanctions on the basis of an inter-pillar procedure. The requirement that a common position or joint action be adopted under Article 12 TEU entails an extensive consultation process aimed at reaching consensus amongst the Member States and, ultimately, recourse being had to a Community instrument under Article 301EC. If the Member States have the right to rely upon Article 297 EC in order to justify collective sanctions imposed under national rules, the procedure envisaged under Article 301 EC prior to the adoption of the Council regulation would be seriously undermined. The implications of this phenomenon would be two-fold. On the one hand, the Union would hardly act as "a cohesive force in international relations",[51] and its objective "to assert its identity on the international scene"[52] would be seriously questioned. These implications become more apparent in the light of the role of economic sanctions against third countries as

---

[49] Konstadinidis, *supra* note 41 at 30. This argument is qualified by the requirements that no improper use of the powers provided for in Art. 297 EC be made and that, if the adoption of Community law becomes feasible, the Member State concerned fall in line with it.

[50] C-D Ehlermann, "Communautés européennes et sanctions internationales" [1984–85] *RBDI* 79.

[51] Art. 14 TEU.

[52] Art. 2 TEU.

one of most powerful instruments at the disposal of the Union, widely used in order to give some teeth to its Common Foreign and Security Policy. On the other hand, given that the adoption of a Council Regulation under Article 301 EC is subject to the prior adoption of a common position or a joint action, to evade the latter by having recourse to Article 297 EC would inevitably be tantamount to further marginalising the former. Therefore, it may be argued that reliance upon Article 297 EC by some Member States in order to justify collective sanctions against a third country would constitute misuse of powers and, hence, trigger the procedure envisaged in Article 298 EC, ultimately giving rise to the Court's exceptional jurisdiction provided thereunder.

6.3. The implementation of UN Security Council Resolutions and Article 297 EC

A separate, albeit interrelated, issue is whether Member States may rely upon the third ground laid down in Article 297 EC, that is "in order to carry out obligations [they] ha[ve] accepted for the purpose of maintaining peace and international security", so as to justify national measures implementing sanctions imposed under a United Nations Security Council Resolution. As was highlighted above,[53] this was standard practice in the 1970s under the so-called "Rhodesia doctrine", which was based on the assumption that the Member States' obligation to implement sanctions imposed by Security Council Resolutions was independent of their Treaty obligations: given that deviation from the Treaty as a whole is allowed for reasons related to "obligations [the Member State in question] has accepted for the purpose of maintaining peace and international security", no involvement of the Community was envisaged. However, this view long ago became *de facto* obsolete; indeed, subsequent practice, seeking to ensure the effectiveness of sanctions through uniform implementation, abandoned the "Rhodesia doctrine" and had recourse to a Community instrument, first under Article 133 EC and then under an autonomous legal basis provided by Article 301 EC.

While it is not in dispute that the Community is under no direct duty to enforce Security Council resolutions, given that it is not a member of the United Nations,[54] the question which arises is whether it is under an indirect legal duty to implement them in so far as they cover areas which give rise to exclusive

[53] See *supra* at ch. 3.
[54] Under Art. 4 UN Charter, only states can become full members of the UN. Furthermore, according to Art. 48(1) UN Charter, "[t]he action required to carry out the decisions of the Security Council for the maintenance of international peace and security shall be taken by all the Members of the United Nations or by some of them, as the Security Council may determine". The Community, however, participates in the UN General Assembly in the capacity of observer. On the Community's participation in the UN General Assembly see P Brueckner, "The European Community and the United Nations" (1989) 1 *EJIL* 175. On its participation in other international organisations see *supra* at ch. 2.

Community competence. In addressing this question, the following two factors must be taken into account: on the one hand, all Member States are full members of the United Nations and therefore bound, under Article 48(3), to implement the Security Council resolutions; on the other hand, according to the long and consistent case law of the Court, the Member States are precluded from acting in areas over which the Community is exclusively competent.[55] This has serious implications regarding Security Council Resolutions whose implementation involves measures which give rise to the Community's exclusive competence. As far as such measures are concerned, it is suggested that the only way for the Member States to comply with their duty under Article 48(3) UN Charter without violating their Treaty obligations entails their implementation at Community level. This proposition is supported by Article 297 EC itself, for its "wholly exceptional character" renders it applicable in so far as the exceptional circumstances required thereunder cannot be dealt with under the Treaty. The introduction of an autonomous legal basis provided under Article 301 EC underlines that, in the case of United Nations Security Council Resolutions imposing sanctions on third states, this is clearly not the case.

It is noteworthy that the inapplicability of Article 297 regarding implementation of Security Council Resolutions does not render the third ground provided therein of no significance. It remains directly relevant in cases of Resolutions which give rise to obligations excluded from the scope of the Treaty, namely those with defence or security implications. The same applies to obligations related to areas over which the Member States are jointly competent. Moreover, there are obligations imposed on Member States by other international agreements, such as NATO.[56]

Finally, implementation of United Nations Security Council Resolutions at Community level where the former require actions touching upon the exclusive competence of the latter does not run counter to Article 307 EC. The reason for this is the inapplicability of both these provisions in the cases under consideration.[57] Indeed, the central point is not one of "compatibility" between the obligations of Member States under the United Nations Charter, on the one hand, and the EC Treaty on the other; in this respect, there seems to be no conflict

---

[55] See Case 22/70 *Commission v. Council (ERTA)* [1971] ECR 263, [1971] CMLR 335 at paras. 17–18; Joined Cases 3–4 and 6/76 *Kramer and Others* [1976] ECR 1279, [1976] 2 CMLR 440; *Opinion 1/76 (Re Draft Agreement for a Laying-up Fund for Inland Waterway Vessels)* [1977] ECR 741, [1976] 2 CMLR 440; *Opinion 1/94 (Re WTO Agreement)* [1994] ECR I–5267, [1995] 1 CMLR 205.

[56] See J-L Dewost in *Commentaire Mégret* (Brussels: Presses Interuniversitaires de Bruxelles, 1987) xv, at 437, Verhoeven in *supra* note 38; and H Smit and PE Herzog, *The Law of the European Community—A Commentary on the EEC Treaty* (New York: Matthew Bender, 1996) at 6–216.85.

[57] Art. 234(1) reads as follows: "The rights and obligations arising from agreements concluded before the entry into force of this Treaty between one or more Member States on the one hand, and one or more third countries on the other, shall not be affected by the provisions of this Treaty", whereas Art. 234(2) reads: "To the extent that such agreements are not compatible with this Treaty, the Member State or States concerned shall take all appropriate steps to eliminate the incompatibilities established. Member States shall, where necessary, assist each other to this end and shall, where appropriate, adopt a common position".

between them. Instead, it is the implementation of the former obligations through the procedures established by the latter Treaty which is at issue. The Member States' action in conformity with the Treaty does not undermine their obligations under the United Nations Charter.

6.4. Unilateral sanctions under Article 297 EC

It has been argued above that, since the inclusion of Article 301 in the Treaty, Article 297 EC cannot be invoked by the Member States for sanctions either stemming from a European Union initiative or implementing United Nations Security Council Resolutions. However, it is suggested that Article 301 EC has not precluded a Member State from relying upon Article 297 EC in order to justify national measures imposing unilateral sanctions on a third country. In this respect, there are two cases whereby Article 297 EC can be relied upon. The first deals with a Member State taking the initiative to impose economic sanctions against a third country. This was the case of the embargo imposed by Greece against FYROM. Given its "wholly exceptional" character, Article 297 EC does cover such sanctions in so far as the conditions set therein are met; this conclusion was also reached by Advocate General Jacobs in his Opinion in the *FYROM* case.[58]

The second case in which Article 297 EC may be invoked is for unilateral deviations from sanctions imposed under Article 301 EC.[59] In the past, such recourse to Article 297 was made in the case of sanctions against Argentina. Italy and Ireland relied on this provision and did not apply the Community measures adopted under Article 133 EC and extending the embargo against Argentina. It needs to be stressed that such use of Article 297 EC must be accompanied by the strictest possible compliance with the substantive and procedural requirements laid down therein. It follows that Member States cannot invoke Article 297 EC and deviate from sanctions imposed under Article 301 EC for reasons of political convenience. Were this the case, Article 297 EC would be rendered an all-encompassing political clause and the inclusion of Article 301 EC in the Treaty would become of little practical significance.

7. PROBLEMS RAISED BY THE APPLICATION OF THE INTER-PILLAR PROCEDURE ESTABLISHED UNDER ARTICLE 301 EC

The inclusion of a separate legal basis in the Treaty may seem to facilitate the swift adoption of sanctions by the Member States and, hence, contribute to their effectiveness. However, the express linkage between the Community legal

---

[58] For further comments, see *infra* at ch. 6.
[59] See Schmitter in Constantinesco et al., *supra* note 38 at 759.

framework and the CFSP provided under Article 301 EC raises an important legal problem in cases where the Council Regulation is adopted with considerable delay in relation to the Title V measure. This is by no means uncommon in practice under Article 301 EC; the case of Regulation 1901/98 concerning a ban on flights of Yugoslav carriers between the Federal Republic of Yugoslavia and the European Community is a case in point: it was adopted approximately 70 days after the adoption of the accompanying Common Position 98/426/CFSP. In addition, a whole series of sanctions regimes under Article 301 EC may be identified whereby the adoption of the Council Regulation is characterised by a significant delay in relation to that of the accompanying Common Position.[60]

This problem has practical, substantive and procedural implications. One of the factors ensuring the effectiveness of a sanctions regime consists of the ability of the sender states to act rapidly and decisively. This is not the case when sanctions are actually implemented with considerable delay following their announcement. On the other hand, this problem is of questionable significance if the announcement of the sanction measures in the Common Position entails their effective implementation by the Member States.

This point touches upon the effect that the Common Position pursuant to which the Council Regulation is adopted under Article 301 EC may have on the Member States. As common positions under Title V TEU are legally binding on Member States, the latter are clearly under a duty to abide by those which require that sanctions be imposed. However, this point is obscured by the very content of the Common Position. The main provision of common positions requiring that sanctions be imposed is worded in the shortest and most general terms. Common Position 98/426/CFSP concerning a ban on flights by Yugoslav carriers between the Federal Republic of Yugoslavia and the European Community, for instance, states that "[f]lights by Yugoslav carriers between the Federal Republic of Yugoslavia and the European Community will be banned", no reference being made to the regulation to be adopted subsequently.

The generality of this provision may weaken the obligation actually imposed upon the Member States. This might be read as a statement of intention to have recourse to a Community instrument as soon as possible. However, this

---

[60] See Reg. 1607/98 [1998] OJ L209/16 concerning the prohibition of new investment in the Republic of Serbia which was adopted 46 days after the adoption of its accompanied Common Position 98/374/CFSP; Reg. 462/96 [1996] OJ L65/1 concerning the interruption of economic and financial relations with the Federal Republic of Yugoslavia, the United Nations-protected areas in the Republic of Croatia and those areas in the Republic of Bosnia and Herzegovina under the control of Bosnian Serb forces was adopted more than three months after the adoption of the accompanying Common Position; Reg. 1733/94 [1994] OJ L182/1 prohibiting the satisfying of claims with regard to contracts and transactions the performance of which was affected by the UN sanctions on Yugoslavia was adopted approximately a month after the adoption of the accompanying Common Position 94/366/CFSP; the same delay characterised the adoption of Reg. 1705/98 [1998] OJ L215/1 concerning the interruption of certain economic relations with Angola; Reg. 1295/98 [1998] OJ L178/33, concerning the freezing of funds held abroad by the Governments of the Federal Republic of Yugoslavia and the Republic of Serbia was adopted 45 days following the adoption of the accompanying Common Position 98/326/CFSP.

approach seems at odds with both the absence of any reference to the Council Regulation whose adoption is to follow under Article 301 EC and the standard provision in all Common Positions imposing sanctions that they are to take effect from the date of their adoption. Moreover, and most importantly, to confine the significance of the content of the common position to that of a political statement, however strong that may be, is tantamount to undermining the legally binding character of common positions under Title V.

Alternatively, a generally worded Common Position requiring that sanctions be imposed on third states may be interpreted as requiring the Member States to implement those sanctions. However, once all 15 Member States are bound to implement sanctions, various serious and complex issues arise which cannot be handled on the basis of the vaguely drafted Common Position alone. This was clearly illustrated in the long negotiating process prior to the adoption of Regulation 1901/98[61] imposing a ban on flights by Yugoslav carriers between Yugoslavia and the Community. The United Kingdom and Greece relied upon bilateral agreements with Yugoslavia and argued that they could only suspend flights between them following one year's and six months' notice respectively.[62] This led to a deadlock which prevented the adoption of Council Regulation 1901/98 for more than two months. The inherent limitations of a duty imposed on Member States under Common Position 98/240/CFSP to implement the sanctions provided therein are manifest in the fact that, pursuant to the adoption of this instrument, the British Government did ban charter flights, for they were excluded from the scope of its agreement with Yugoslavia.[63]

It thus becomes apparent that, pending the adoption of a Council Regulation under Article 301 EC, the legally binding effect of a vaguely phrased provision of a Common Position adopted under Article 15 TEU requiring that sanctions be imposed by the Member States is confined to the nature of the obligations arising under Title V. In other words, the exact scope of the obligations assumed by the Member States is not subject to the authoritative determination of an independent institution and, hence, lack of uniformity regarding the implementation of sanctions is inevitable. The problematic ramifications of this are illustrated in the rather blunt statement of President Santer himself: "decisions taken by the fifteen Member States have to be applied by fifteen. If one or more countries refuses to play the game, it strips the decision to impose sanctions of any meaning".[64]

In the light of the instrumental role that uniformity of implementation has played in the choice of the legal regulation of sanctions, the practical problem analysed above has serious legal repercussions. Indeed, in the period prior to the adoption of Article 301 EC, sanctions were implemented by the Member States under Article 297 EC following a decision in the framework of European

---

[61] [1998] OJ L248/1.
[62] See *Agence Europe*, 7286 25–26 Aug. 1998 at 2 and *The European*, 14–20 Sept. 1998 at 6.
[63] *Agence Europe*, 7298 11 Sept. 1998 at 5.
[64] *European Voice*, 17–23 Sept. 1998 at 15.

Political Co-operation. It was the ensuing lack of uniformity that led to the implementation of sanctions through recourse to Article 133 EC following a decision in the framework of European Political Co-operation. This is clearly illustrated in the regulations adopted under Article 133 EC which include a standard provision in the preamble according to which "the Community and its Member States have agreed to have recourse to a Community instrument, *inter alia* in order to ensure a uniform implementation throughout the Community [of the measures provided in the sanctions regime]".[65]

This rationale clearly underpins the very *raison d'être* of the adoption of Article 301 EC itself. This is clearly illustrated in the considerably broader scope of Article 301 EC in relation to that of Article 133. Therefore, pending the adoption of the Council Regulation under Article 301 EC, it is unacceptable to allow the implementation of the sanctions regime to be undermined by the problems the adoption of Article 301 EC was itself intended to remedy.

Another problem raised by the express linkage between the Community legal framework and the CFSP provided under Article 301 EC is of a procedural nature. Under the autonomous legal basis incorporated in the Community legal order by the Maastricht Treaty, sanctions are imposed by means of a Council regulation adopted by a qualified majority; however, this measure is to follow a common position or a joint action adopted according to Title V TEU, that is unanimously under Article 23(1) TEU.[66] Given that the adoption of a Council Regulation by a qualified majority is preceded by the unanimous adoption of a common position, it follows that the decision-making procedure provided under Article 301 EC may lose any practical relevance. In relation to this problem, two points need to be made. First, this problem is by no means new; it underpinned the imposition of sanctions prior to the Maastricht Treaty, when a Council regulation was adopted by a qualified majority under Article 133 EC pursuant to a decision of the Member States adopted unanimously within the framework of European Political Co-operation, the precursor of the CFSP. Amongst other factors, this dependence of the decision-making procedure provided under Article 133 EC upon that provided beyond the Community legal framework substantiated the view that sanctions had already been construed, adopted and applied as a *sui generis* category of trade measures; in short, while imposed within the Common Commercial Policy, they had, in fact, been dissociated from it. Secondly, the practical implications of this problem should not be overstated. It has been argued, for instance, that, the imposition of sanctions "on an issue of common defence policy" under Article 301 EC following a European Council joint action under Article 13 TEU would have the following effect: "in the case of Denmark, binding CCP measures may result from

---

[65] Reg. 1432/92 prohibiting trade between the [then] EEC and the Republics of Serbia and Montenegro, para. 10 of the preamble.

[66] Art. 15 TEU is the relevant provision, for it has been invariably Common Positions that expressed the Union's decision to impose sanctions on third countries by means of a Community instrument.

non-binding [due to its opt-out from EU decisions with defence implications] decisions".[67] This is a rather far-fetched scenario. There is still considerable progress to be made towards the framing of the common defence policy of the European Union. Moreover, CCP measures do not result from the application of Article 301 EC. More importantly, sanctions on arms, that is those with the most obvious defence implications, are imposed by means of a common position under Article 15 TEU rather than a Council Regulation under Article 301 EC.

The legal problems analysed above, while stemming from the application of the inter-pillar procedure provided for under Article 301 EC, are not inherent in it. They are due to the inability of the Member States to agree upon whether to impose sanctions and how to apply the relevant measures. In other words, it is the political reality rather than the legal provision that may undermine the effectiveness of the sanctions regimes the European Union imposes. This phenomenon reveals how difficult it is for the Member States to forge and implement a truly common stance on the international scene and, hence, address the problem that led them to adopt an autonomous legal basis for the imposition of sanctions in the first place. In this respect, and given the reliance of the inter-pillar formula upon Title V, the success of its application is to a significant extent dependent upon the main features of that framework. Having argued that the effect of the *sui generis*, incremental and dynamic system provided under Title V relies upon the extent to which it is used to its full potential by the Union institutions involved, it follows that it is this feature of Title V that inevitably affects the application of the inter-pillar approach under Article 301 EC. Viewed from this angle, there is an inherent limit to how effective Article 301 EC may be: the more effectively the CFSP procedures are relied upon by the Union institutions, the more effectively the inter-pillar formula under Article 301 will be applied. Therefore, it may be concluded that the inter-pillar procedure provided thereunder may be capable of ensuring the swift imposition of sanctions on the basis of the synergy between EC and CFSP in so far as the Union institutions are politically committed to use it to its full potential.

8. CONCLUSION

This chapter argued that the application of the inter-pillar approach to the imposition of sanctions under Article 301 EC and its relationship with potential alternative legal bases within the Community legal framework cannot be studied in isolation; instead, they must be analysed in the light of developments within the CFSP framework. The above analysis illustrates that the arguments against the formula provided under Article 301 EC were based on the inability of the Union institutions to agree within Title V rather than insurmountable

---

[67] Konstadinidis, *supra* note 41 at 29.

legal obstacles inherent in the inter-pillar approach. Therefore, if the external relations of the Union are understood as a "system"[68] whose underlying characteristics are coherence, consistency and effectiveness, the question which needs to be addressed is the following: is the inter-pillar procedure for the imposition of sanctions incapable of being a part of this system, in that it relies upon the legal characteristics of both EC and CFSP?

---

[68] *ERTA, supra* note 55 at para. 19.

5

The Community Regime on Exports of Dual-use Goods to Third Countries

1. INTRODUCTION

The previous chapter concluded by questioning whether an inter-pillar approach to the interactions between trade and foreign policy is so fraught with problems, due to the distinct legal character of the EC and CFSP, that it is inherently incapable of ensuring the consistency, coherence and effectiveness of the external relations of the European Union. The examination of this issue would be incomplete without an analysis of the rules applicable to exports of dual-use goods. The reason for this is that the legal regulation of these measures raises issues similar to those examined in the previous chapter; however, these issues have been addressed *de lege lata* in a different way.

Dual-use goods are products "which can be used for both civil and military purposes".[1] On the one hand, they are industrial products involving a huge market the development of which is determined to a large extent by economic considerations. On the other hand, their export may be instrumental in the exercise of foreign policy. This two-fold function of dual-use goods raises the question of the legal framework within which their exports are to be regulated. Their role in the conduct of foreign policy may seem to point towards the Common Foreign and Security Policy, whereas the Common Commercial Policy under Article 133 EC may equally seem to be the appropriate legal basis under which any measures applicable to the export of dual-use goods may be adopted.[2]

The question of the appropriate legal framework regarding trade measures serving foreign policy objectives has already been addressed in relation to trade sanctions against third countries: under Article 301 EC, an inter-pillar approach has been adopted on the basis of a Common Position under Title V and a Council Regulation. The regulation of exports of dual-use goods is related to that of trade sanctions, for an inter-pillar approach has been adopted by the Union institutions, hence following the rationale underpinning Article 301 EC;

---

[1] Art. 2(a) of Reg. 3381/94 [1994] OJ L367/1.

[2] It is not only in the context of the EU and the legal arrangements underpinning its constitutional order that the legal regulation of exports of dual-use goods may cause controversy. In the USA, the export control policies applied to high-technology products which may be used for military purposes have been the target of criticism from both trade promoters and champions of non-proliferation: see R Johnston, "U.S. Export Control Policy in the High Performance Computer Sector" [1998] *The Non-Proliferation Review* 44.

the common rules on exports of dual-use goods have been adopted pursuant to a Common Position under Title V TEU and a Council Regulation under Article 133 EC. However, this similarity notwithstanding, the approach to the regulation of exports of dual-use goods under the law of the European Union is distinct from that of trade sanctions against third countries on two inter-related grounds: first, the structure of the specific measures adopted under this approach is inconsistent with that envisaged under Article 301 EC in so far as the material scope and the *modus operandi* of the Council Regulation is incorporated in the Title V measure; secondly, the adoption of the Council Regulation under Article 133 EC raises legal issues regarding specifically the Common Commercial Policy; these issues include the extent to which the Community's exclusive competence is undermined by the structure of the measures in question and the extent to which the principle whereby the Member States may not deviate from the CCP without an express and specific Community law authorisation is affected.

In examining these issues, this chapter[3] will be structured as follows. First, it will outline the main principles underpinning the Community regime on exports of dual-use goods. Secondly, it will focus on a two-fold critical examination: on the one hand, it will assess the guidelines on the basis of which national authorities are to apply the rules under consideration; on the other hand, it will focus on the legal formula underpinning these rules and its consistency with the principles underlying the constitutional order of the European Union. Thirdly, the Commission proposals on the reform of the Community regime on exports of dual-use goods will be outlined, special emphasis being put on the legal formula suggested therein.

2. THE ESTABLISHMENT OF COMMON RULES ON THE CONTROL OF EXPORTS OF DUAL-USE GOODS UNDER REGULATION 3381/94

The adoption of a legal framework regarding exports of dual-use goods was the result of an acrimonious negotiating process which lasted approximately three years. It was not the need for common rules to be adopted that was in dispute; it had been acknowledged that, in the context of the single market, the absence of common export policies in relation to dual-use goods would enable exporters to evade strict export regimes by exporting their products to Member States with lax export rules and subsequently re-export them to third countries. This would lead to serious economic advantages being accrued to the Member State with more lax export controls and, consequently, to the eventual scaling down of national export policies. Furthermore, the absence of common export rules on dual-use goods would enable Member States, in order to prevent the evasion of their export policies, to impose restrictions on intra-Community trade of

---

[3] This ch. draws upon ideas first put forward in P Koutrakos, "Exports of Dual-use Goods under the Law of the European Union" (1998) 23 *ELRev.* 235.

dual-use goods. In the light of the increasing relevance of civil goods to military production and, hence, the increase in products which could be classified as dual-use goods, the absence of common rules on exports of dual-use goods would seriously impair intra-Community trade and question the very establishment of the single market.

The problems which arose in the course of the negotiations leading to the adoption of common rules on exports of dual-use goods were related mainly to the mechanism which would make them operational and the legal basis under which these rules were to be adopted. The former problem revealed national concerns over waiving the right to control exports from their territories in so far as they have been authorised by the competent authorities of another Member State. The latter problem was focused on the list of products to be covered by the rules under consideration, the destinations of the exports to be allowed and the criteria under which the exports would be authorised.[4] The question whether a common regime on exports of dual-use goods falls within the scope of the CCP and, hence, gives rise to the Community's exclusive competence or is excluded from the Community legal framework altogether and falls within the scope of the CFSP was resolved *de lege lata* by a compromise: on the one hand, the rules setting out the principles underpinning the common rules on exports and the procedures under which they were to be applied were laid down in a Council Regulation adopted under Article 133 EC, namely Regulation 3381/94 setting up a Community regime for the control of exports of dual-use goods[5]; on the other hand, the lists of products and destinations covered by this Regulation, along with the guidelines under which the common rules were to be applied, were set out in a Joint Action adopted under Article J.3 (now 14) TEU, incorporated in Council Decision 94/942/CFSP.[6]

2.1. The objectives of the Community regime for the control of dual-use goods

The main principle of the common rules established under Regulation 3381/94 is that exports of dual-use goods falling within its ambit require an authorisation which is granted by the competent authorities of the Member State in which the exporter is established and is valid throughout the Community. Regulation

---

[4] For the negotiations prior to its adoption see P Cornish, "Joint Action "The Economic Aspects of Security" and Regulation of Conventional Arms and Technology Exports from the EU" in M Holland (ed.), *Common Foreign and Security Policy. The Record and Reforms* (London: Pinter, 1997) 73 at 81–2.

[5] *Supra* note 1.

[6] Dec. 94/942/CFSP [1994] OJ L367/8 was amended consecutively by Decs. 95/127/CFSP [1995] OJ L90/2, 95/128/CFSP [1995] OJ L90/3, 96/173/CFSP [1996] OJ L52/1, 96/613/CFSP [1996] OJ L278/1, 97/100/CFSP [1997] OJ L34/1, 97/419/CFSP [1997] OJ L178/1, 97/633/CFSP [1997] OJ L266/1, 98/106/CFSP [1998] OJ L32/1, 98/232/CFSP [1998] OJ L92/1. The date of application of Reg. 3381/94 had already been amended by Reg. 837/95 [1995] OJ L90/1.

3381/94 is not intended to provide a complete harmonising framework for dual-use goods; instead, "th[e] system [established by the Regulation] represents a first step towards the establishment of a common system for the control of exports of dual-use goods which is complete and consistent in all respects". [7]

The objectives of the Regulation include the elimination of controls by Member States on intra-Community trade in certain dual-use goods,[8] the improvement of the international competitiveness of European industry[9] and effective control on exports of dual-use goods on a common basis.[10]

2.2. The material scope of the Community regime for the control of exports of dual-use goods

Article 2(a) defines dual-use products as "goods which can be used for both civil and military purposes". However, under Article 3, the material scope of Regulation 3381/94 is confined to a list of products annexed to Decision 94/942/CFSP. This list refers to the following nine generally phrased categories of products: nuclear materials, facilities and equipment; materials, chemicals, "microorganisms" and "toxins"; materials processing; electronics; computers; telecommunications and "information security", sensors and lasers; navigation and avionics; marine; propulsion systems, space vehicles and related equipment. Annex I to Decision 94/942/CFSP further specifies a variety of products, namely equipment, assemblies and components, test, inspection and production equipment, materials, software and technology referring to the above general categories. It is interesting that the above list and those subsequently amending it[11] include high technology goods rather than products whose proximity to the military end of the spectrum is doubtful; it may, therefore, be assumed that, for instance, boots or combat trousers are to be governed by the Community export rules applicable to all products. Moreover, the incorporation of the above list of dual-use goods in a Title V instrument illustrates the determination of the Member States to keep what they deem "considerations of a strategic nature" beyond the Community legal framework. Finally, under Article 3(3) of Regulation 3381/94, goods in transit are not covered by its provisions.

In addition to the products incorporated in the above list, the export of certain dual-use goods not listed therein is subject to an authorisation under Article

---

[7] Tenth recital of the preamble to Reg. 3381/94 *supra* note 1. In addition, it is stated that "in particular, it is desirable that the authorization procedures applied by the Member States should be harmonized progressively and speedily". In addition, according to Art. 3(3) of this Reg., goods in transit are not covered by its provisions. In this respect, the content of Reg. 3381/94 would not have changed the Court's approach in Case 367/89 *Criminal Proceedings against Aimé Richardt and Les Accessoires Scientifiques SNC* [1991] ECR I–4621.

[8] See the fourth recital of the preamble to Reg. 3381/94 *supra* note 1.

[9] See the fifth recital of the preamble to Reg. 3381/94 *supra* note 1.

[10] See the tenth recital of the preamble to Reg. 3381/94 *supra* note 1.

[11] Decs. 95/127/CFSP, 96/613/CFSP, 97/100/CFSP and 97/419/CFSP.

4(1) of Regulation 3381/94. This constitutes the so-called "catch-all" clause and refers to goods which "are or may be intended, in their entirety or in part, for use in connection with the development, production, handling, operation, maintenance, storage, detection, identification or dissemination of chemical, biological or nuclear weapons or the development, production, maintenance or storage of missiles capable of delivering such weapons, as covered by the corresponding non-proliferation arrangements".

2.3. The central principle of the Community regime on exports of dual-use goods

The central feature of the system established under Regulation 3381/94 is that exports of dual-use goods falling within its ambit require an authorisation which is to be granted by the competent authorities of the Member State in which the exporter is established and is valid throughout the Community. This principle is similar to that of mutual recognition, whereby the attribution of certain legal characteristics by one Member State is recognised as binding on all Member States save in exceptional circumstances.[12] Under the Regulation, all Member States are bound by the authorisation granted by another Member State. In this respect, Member States seem to rely on the evaluation made by the national authorities of another Member State of the threat that any export of dual-use goods may entail.

This principle also draws upon mutual confidence between national authorities of different Member States[13] which is itself the expression of the co-operation upon which the Member States' conduct must be based under the Regulation.[14] This is expressed in various ways. In cases where an export authorisation is sought for a product located in another Member State, the competent authorities of the Member State where the authorisation has been made shall "immediately consult" the authorities of the Member State in question; if the latter express any objections to the granting of the export authorisation, those are binding on the authorities of the Member State where the authorisation has

---

[12] In the area of free movement of goods the principle of mutual recognition can be exemplified by the idea that a product lawfully produced and marketed in one Member State is entitled to free circulation within the Community save in exceptional circumstances: see Case 120/78 *Rewe-Zentrale* v. *Bundesmonopolverwaltung für Branntwein (Cassis de Dijon)* [1979] ECR 649, [1979] 3 CMLR 494. As far as the right of establishment is concerned see, for instance, Dir. 89/48 on recognition of higher education diplomas [1989] OJ L19/16. On the central role of this principle in the new approach to harmonisation and the establishment of the internal market see H Wallace and AR Young, "The Single Market" in H Wallace and W Wallace (eds.), *Policy-Making in the European Union*, (Oxford: Oxford University Press, 1996) 125.

[13] On this principle in the area of free movement of goods see, for instance, Case 25/88 *Esther Bouchara, née Wurmser* [1989] ECR 1105.

[14] In this respect, recourse must be had to Council Reg. 1468/81 on mutual assistance between the administrative authorities of the Member States and co-operation between the latter and the Commission to ensure the correct application of the law on customs or agricultural matters [1981] OJ L144/1 as amended by Reg. 945/87 [1987] OJ L90/3.

been sought. Furthermore, Article 13 of the Regulation provides for "direct cooperation and exchange of information between competent [national] authorities".[15] In addition, Article 7(3) states that "[i]f an exportation might prejudice its essential interests, a Member State may request another Member State not to grant an export authorization or, if such authorization has been granted, request its annulment, suspension, modification or revocation. The Member State receiving such a request shall immediately engage in consultations of a non-binding nature with the requesting Member State, to be terminated within 10 working days." Even though this consultation provided for is of a non-binding nature, this provision implies an effort to accommodate various concerns over the binding character of an authorisation given by the authorities of another Member State.

Furthermore, Regulation 3381/94 requires that the actions of the Member States be co-ordinated at Community level in a two-fold way: on the one hand, it establishes a Co-ordinating Group under Article 16 which, comprised of one representative of each Member State and chaired by a Commission representative, deals with any question concerning the application of the Regulation and the national measures that are necessary in order to inform exporters of their obligations[16]; on the other hand, it sets up a mechanism whereby each Member State must inform the Commission of all measures adopted in implementation of both Regulation 3381/94 and Decision 94/942/CFSP. These measures shall be forwarded by the Commission to the other Member States.[17]

2.4. Scope for unilateral action left to the Member States

Under the Community regime on exports of dual-use goods, Member States retain under the Regulation the right to impose unilateral measures in order to ensure effective control of exports of dual-use goods.[18] In addition, they may "carry out controls on dual-use goods in order to safeguard public policy or public security".[19] In relation to intra-Community trade, the Member States shall require authorisations regarding a list of products considered to be of a

[15] The administrative co-operation provided thereunder aims "in particular [at] eliminat[ing] the risk that possible disparities in the application of export controls may lead to a deflection of trade, which could create difficulties for one or more Member States".
[16] Under Art. 16(2)(a), a question regarding the application of Reg. 3381/94 may be raised by either the chairman of the Coordinating Group or a representative of a Member State. Moreover, under para. 3, the Group "may, whenever it considers it to be necessary, consult organizations representative of exporters concerned by th[at] Regulation".
[17] See Art. 18, which also provides that a report on the application of Reg. 3381/94 be presented to the European Parliament and the Council by the Commission every two years.
[18] According to the thirteenth recital of Reg. 3381/94, "[Arts. 4 and 5 of this Regulation] do not prevent Member States from adopting or maintaining, for the same purpose [that is to ensure effective control of exports of dual-use goods] and with due regard for the internal market, additional export control measures which are compatible with this Regulation's objectives".
[19] Fifteenth recital, according to which this right is retained by the Member States "pursuant to and within the limits of Article 36 of the Treaty, and pending a greater degree of harmonization".

highly sensitive nature and annexed to Decision 94/942/CFSP.[20] In addition, under Article 20(1) of Regulation 3381/94 some Member States are expressly allowed to maintain national controls for consignments of dual-use products dispatched to other Member States; the products covered by this clause are specifically referred to in a list annexed to Decision 94/942/CFSP.[21]

In relation to the "catch-all" clause of Article 4 of Regulation 3381/94, the Member States enjoy two rights. First, in cases where an exporter is aware that the goods to be exported are indeed related to programmes of weapons of mass destruction, the national authorities must be notified and then will determine "whether or not it is expedient to make the export concerned subject to authorization".[22] Secondly, Member States may adopt or maintain legislation requiring that the exporters notify the competent national authorities when they have grounds for suspecting that the goods to be exported are intended to assist programmes of weapons of mass destruction covered by the "catch-all" clause.[23]

Finally, Member States are free to determine the penalties which will be imposed in the event of breach of the regulation in question or the national measures implementing it; these penalties "must be effective, proportionate and dissuasive".[24]

2.5. Typology of export authorisations granted by national authorities under Regulation 3381/94

The main type of export authorisation provided under Regulation 3381/94 to be granted by the competent authorities of the Member State in which the exporter is established covers individual exports of goods listed in Annex I to Council Decision 94/942/CFSP.[25] In addition to this individual authorisation, three other types are also provided for in Article 6, namely a general, a global and a simplified one. A general authorisation may be granted regarding a type or category of products within the scope of the Regulation and on the basis of the criteria listed in Annex III. This general authorisation will be granted for exports to countries listed in Annex II to Decision 94/942/CFSP upon request by the exporter, without any further formalities. This list constitutes an exception to the exclusion of a country list from the ambit of the Regulation. A global authorisation may be granted to a specific exporter for exports to one or more specified countries of goods within the scope of the Regulation. Article 6(1)(b) does not mention the criteria of Annex III to be taken into account for a global authorisation to be granted. However, there can be no objective reasons to justify their exclusion

---

[20] Art. 19(1)(b) of Reg. 3381/94 applying to the products referred to in Annex IV to Dec. 94/942/CFSP.

[21] See Annex V to Dec. 94/942/CFSP.

[22] Art. 4(2) of Reg. 3381/94 *supra* note 1.

[23] See Art. 4(3) of Reg. 3381/94 *supra* note 1.

[24] Art. 17.

[25] Art. 7(1) of the Reg.

regarding the global authorisation. The fact that Article 6(1) provides for the Member States to apply simplified formalities in respect of these types of authorisation is not sufficient to exclude consideration of the general criteria. This becomes even more so in the light of their express inclusion in Article 6(1)(a); there is no reason to apply different procedures regarding a general and a global authorisation. Therefore, Article 6(1)(b) must be interpreted as requiring the national authorities to consider an application for global authorisation on the basis of the criteria listed in Annex II. Finally, Member States are allowed to apply simplified procedures regarding an application for authorisation of exports of dual-use goods not listed in Annex I to Decision 94/942/CFSP.[26] Any export authorisation granted under Article 6 shall be valid throughout the Community.[27]

2.6. The criteria to be taken into account be national authorities

The criteria that national authorities must take into account in order to determine whether or not to grant an export licence are listed in Annex III to Decision 94/942/CFSP. They consist of the commitments that the Member States have undertaken under international agreements on non-proliferation and the control of sensitive goods their obligations under sanctions imposed by the UN Security Council or agreed in other international fora, considerations of national foreign and security policy and considerations about intended end-use and the risk of diversion.

It is noteworthy that the Commission's proposal included a list of criteria in the body of the proposed regulation, despite its preambular statement that such lists "are clearly of a strategic nature and consequently fall within the competence of the Member States".[28]

---

[26] See Arts. 6(1)(c) and 5 of the Reg.

[27] Art. 6(3) of the Reg.

[28] Para. 6 of the preamble of the proposed Reg. A second significant difference lies in the criteria themselves. According to the Commission, respect for human rights in the country of final destination must be taken into account by the competent national authorities; however, this criterion is not included in the Regulation finally adopted. In addition, a number of other criteria considered to be of importance by the Commission were actually excluded by the Reg., namely tensions or internal armed conflicts in the country of final destination, the preservation of regional peace, security and stability, the behaviour of the buyer country regarding the international community and particularly its attitude to terrorism, the nature of its alliances, and respect for international law and the existence of a risk that the equipment will be diverted within the buyer country or re-exported under undesirable conditions. In addition, the Reg. finally adopted does not include as a criterion the national security of the Member States along with that of friendly and allied countries, which the Commission had included in its proposal. See Art. 8 at paras. (b), (c), (d), (f), (g) and (e).

3. COMMENT ON THE COMMON RULES ON EXPORTS OF DUAL-USE GOODS
ESTABLISHED UNDER REGULATION 3381/94 AND DECISION 94/942/CFSP

The system of controls on exports of dual-use goods to third countries established under Regulation 3381/94 and Decision 94/942/CFSP is a decentralised one: national authorities are to grant export authorisations following common rules and procedures. The effectiveness of such a system is determined by the scope of competence of national authorities and the content and nature of the criteria to be applied. However, the objective of the Community regime, that is the effective control of dual-use goods, is seriously undermined by its very content. This argument is supported by the absence of a list of prohibited destinations, contrary to the Commission proposal. This omission increases the scope of the power of national authorities and compromises the significance of the establishment of common rules.[29] However, the most important criticism against the common rules established under Regulation 3381/94 and Decision 94/942/CFSP focuses on the guidelines that the competent authorities of the Member States must take into account in order to determine whether to grant an export licence.

3.1. The criteria provided for in Decision 94/942/CFSP as amended by Decision 96/613/CFSP

The list initially annexed to Decision 94/942/CFSP is problematic in terms of the nature of both the criteria it comprises and those that it excludes. Of the four criteria initially listed in Annex III to Decision 94/942/CFSP, only conformity with sanctions obligations appears to have any teeth. However, its inclusion in the Annex neither adds anything new nor clarifies any legal issue on the interaction between Community and national competence. Sanctions imposed by the UN Security Council are implemented at Community level by a common position under Title V TEU and a Council Regulation under Article 301 EC. Leaving aside the legal problems to which this formula may give rise,[30] the joint action is adopted prior to the Community measure and by unanimity.[31] Therefore, all Member States need to have agreed on the imposition of the sanctions and, in any case, are legally bound by the Community Regulation. The amendment introduced by Decision 96/613/CFSP which makes express reference to the European Union does not add anything significant, for the original list of

---

[29] See FG Jacobs, "The Completion of the Internal Market v the Incomplete Common Commercial Policy" in SV Konstadinidis. (ed.), *The Legal Regulation of the European Community's External Relations after the Completion of the Internal Market* (Aldershot: Dartmouth, 1996) 3 at 10.

[30] See *infra* ch. 4.

[31] The possibility of a unanimous decision defining matters to be adopted by qualifying majority under the ex Art. J.3(2) TEU was only used in relation to the land-mines.

Decision 94/942/CFSP mentioned, in a note, the embargoes imposed by the EU. As for the international commitments of Member States, they impose an obligation on national authorities which is of an autonomous nature. Their inclusion in the guidelines of Annex III merely repeats the self-evident fact that Member States' international legal obligations in this field must be taken into account.[32]

As regards national foreign policy and security considerations, the Member States would take them into account without any need to have recourse to the Annex. They would be allowed to do so for two reasons: first, on the basis of the interpretation of Article 11 of the export regulation that the Court put forward in *Richardt*,[33] a case concerning a Luxembourg prohibition on the export of dual-use goods from Paris to Moscow via Luxembourg under national rules protecting national security; secondly, under the public security proviso retained by Regulation 3381/94. Ultimately, this is the very reason export controls on dual-use goods were considered to touch upon national competence. The last factor mentioned in Annex III to Decision 94/942/CFSP, namely considerations about intended end-use and the risk of diversion, is expressed in such vague wording that hardly any significance can be ascertained. The very definition of dual-use goods lies in their capacity to be used for military purposes. Does the above factor imply that authorisation can be denied only when a degree of proximity is presumed between the use of the good in question and an objective military purpose in the country of destination? It must be admitted that such a conclusion is not supported by the text of the Annex and could be characterised, on the basis of the Regulation under consideration, as too *communautaire*.

It is noteworthy that, in the context of "considerations of national foreign and security policy", Annex III to Decision 94/942/CFSP makes further reference "where relevant, [to] those covered by the criteria agreed at the European Council in Luxembourg in June 1991 and in Lisbon in June 1992 with regard to the export of conventional arms". Of the criteria agreed at the Luxembourg European Council, Member States' commitments stemming from international non-proliferation agreements and sanctions imposed by the United Nations, along with the risk of diversion of the product in question, were expressly included in the list of Annex III to Decision 94/942/CFSP. The other criteria consisted of the purchasing country's human rights record and internal situation, the preservation of regional peace, security and stability, the national security of Member States, their territories and allied countries and the purchasing coun-

---

[32] The attribution of a Community dimension to the relevant international obligations of the Member States seems to be dependent on the extent to which the legal effectiveness of Dec. 94/942/CFSP is supervised by the Court. On the basis of the Court's approach in the field of the external relations, it seems unlikely that the international legal obligations in question will be strengthened within the Community legal order.

[33] *Supra* note 7.

try's behaviour towards the international community.[34] An additional criterion dealing with the effect of the export in question on the purchasing country's economy was added at the Lisbon European Council.[35]

It is not apparent on what basis the Council decided which of these criteria were expressly to be provided for. However, the absence of a clear and express reference to the above criteria, as suggested by the Commission,[36] in Decision 94/942/CFSP is open to criticism for it blurs their practical effect. In the case of the requirement of respect for human rights in the country of destination, its omission is indefensible in view of the increasing practice of including human rights clauses in association agreements concluded by the Community and third states.[37] This omission is yet more questionable in the context of a Union "attach[ed] to the principles of liberty, democracy and respect for human rights and fundamental freedoms and of the rule of law".[38] Article 7 of the TEU as amended in Amsterdam reinforces this point by providing for the suspension of Treaty rights in cases where a Member State commits a "a serious and persistent breach" of the above principles.

The same objections apply to the omission of express reference to the other criteria. As regards to the preservation of regional peace, security and stability, for instance, can Germany justify its export restriction to Iraq while another Member State justifies its authorising exports of the same product to the same country? Would the conclusion have varied had the European Union urged

---

[34] Annex VII to the Conclusions of the Presidency after the Luxembourg European Council: *Bull. EC* 6–1991 at 19. It was then stated that "[i]n the perspective of political union, the European Council hopes that on the basis of criteria of this nature a common approach will be made possible leading to a harmonization of national policies".

[35] Namely "the compatibility of the arms exports with the technical and economic capacity of the recipient country, taken into account the desirability that States should achieve their legitimate needs of security and defence with the least diversion for armaments of human and economic resources": *Bull. EC* 6–1992 at 17. Reference to all the above criteria was made in the Conclusions of the Amsterdam Summit in 1997.

[36] See Art. 8(b), (c), (d), (f), (g) and (e) of the Commission's proposal, *supra* note 14. The Commission's proposal recognised that the elaboration of criteria on the basis of which an authorisation would be granted was a task within national competence. However, it included the list of criteria in the body of the proposed Reg. Can this approach be reconciled with the preambular statement that any criteria applied by the Member States were "clearly" excluded from the Community competence? Is this inconsistency to be attributed to careless draftmanship? The significance of the Reg. and the important legal consequences of this inconsistency seem to suggest otherwise. Besides, the goods and destinations covered by the Reg. were not included in the proposed measure because of their strategic nature. A possible explanation of the Commission's *lapsus* could be the legal problem itself which it was trying to avoid, that is a clear delimitation between commercial measures covered by the Community competence and foreign policy and security considerations covered by national competence. This interaction is of central importance, because it determines the legal formula chosen for the measure in question. It is assumed that the Commission had in mind a decision of the representatives of the Governments of the Member States meeting in Council, that is a measure under the umbrella of the then European Political Cooperation, prior to a measure on issues covered by Community competence.

[37] See M Cremona, "The Human Rights Clause in the Association Agreements" in N Emiliou and D O'Keeffe (eds.), *The European Union and World Trade Law After the GATT Uruguay Round* (Chichester: John Wiley, 1996) 62.

[38] Preamble to the TEU, third recital.

efforts to be made in order to prevent further disruption of peace, security and stability in a country in crisis?[39] Are national authorities not asked to take into account the widespread allegations against Libya, for example, when the export of technologies easily adapted to the manufacture of chemical weapons is at stake?

An important point needs to be clarified. The elaboration of the criteria on the basis of which an export authorisation is to be given in a Title V instrument might be viewed as a positive development. This argument relies upon the interpretation of these criteria as being a central parameter of the right of the Member States to determine whether their public security is threatened; hence, the incorporation of these criteria in a Title V instrument may be viewed as an indication that, in the area under consideration, the national approach is to be substituted by a common approach. It might even be argued that such a step reflects the evolution of the foreign policy in the Union context, that is something more than 15 national foreign policies but something less than a single Union foreign policy. However, the criteria elaborated in Annex III to Decision 94/942/CFSP are drafted in such a way as to leave no scope for defining threats to security and foreign policy on a common basis. In addition, it is expressly stated that "considerations of national foreign and security policy" are to be taken into account.

3.2. The legal formula—inconsistencies and problems

It was argued above that the limited practical significance of the criteria expressly mentioned in Decision 94/942/CFSP and the vague reference to fundamental parameters of national behaviour on the international scene seriously undermine the effectiveness of the established rules. A further problem is raised by the legal formula under which the common rules regarding exports of dual-use goods were introduced. To the question whether the Community legal order or the CFSP is the appropriate framework, a combination of a Community regulation and a Title V measure was put forward. This approach follows that underpinning Article 301 EC regarding economic sanctions against third countries, according to which a common position adopted under Title V is implemented by a Community regulation.[40] However, all similarities between the above approaches end at that. A decision taken in the CFSP framework in the area of sanctions expresses the determination of Member States to use a commercial measure in order to achieve a political aim. Decision 94/942/CFSP, on

---

[39] See, e.g., the conclusions of the General Affairs Council of 24 Feb. 1997 urging a ceasefire in the Great Lakes area, in *Agence Europe*, 6921 24–25 Feb. 1997 at 3.

[40] Before the TEU, Community sanctions on third countries were imposed on the combined basis of a Decision adopted within the European Political Co-operation framework and initially Art. 297, subsequently Art. 133: see *supra* at ch. 3.

the other hand, does not only express the political will of all Member States[41]; by incorporating the criteria to be taken into consideration, it deprives the Community measure of the most important feature of its *modus operandi*, that is any ground of control over national authorities. The result is that national authorities are to grant export authorisation on the basis of vaguely expressed criteria excluded from the Community framework. National authorities are hence enabled to manipulate the control system established by Regulation 3381/94 to protect national exports and hence accommodate national concerns of an essentially economic nature. It follows that the legal protection of the individual exporter is at risk.

This distinction between the inter-pillar approach underpinning the imposition of sanctions on third countries and the establishment of a Community regime on exports of dual-use goods illustrates that the establishment of a legal system within the current constitutional order of the Union may be based on both the first and second pillars and yet follow different patterns. In this respect, a conclusion on whether a legally sensible system of rules may be based on the distinct frameworks of the Union is inevitably tantamount to a generalisation; what is essential is to examine the specific terms in which this inter-pillar approach is adopted.

To examine the specific terms in which the inter-pillar approach underlies the current regime on exports of dual-use goods raises the issue of the exclusion of the scope and the *modus operandi* of Regulation 3381/94 from the Community legal framework. In doing so, the Council illustrated a conception of trade and foreign policy as two rigidly distinct areas of activity. In legal terms, the approach underpinning Regulation 3381/94 and Decision 994/942/CFSP seeks to serve two main objectives: on the one hand, the controversial issue of exports of dual-use goods is subject to unanimity which prevails under Title V, whereas, on the other hand, the guidelines under which an export authorisation is to be given are excluded from the Court's control under Article 46 TEU.

This approach is unacceptable in legal terms and unrealistic in practical terms. As regards the latter, the interdependence between trade and foreign policy makes it increasingly difficult to ascertain the exact degree to which a commercial measure serves a foreign policy objective.[42] It is interesting, for instance, that assistance to Russia which would enable it to convert and restructure former chemical weapon factories and destroy its stockpile of weapons in conformity with the United Nations Chemical Weapons Convention will be offered from the TACIS programme, that is a programme based on Article 308 EC. In legal terms, the justiciable character of Regulation 3381/94 would be of no significance if a Member State were allowed to rely upon the non-justiciable nature of its *modus operandi* and protect national exporters by refusing to grant authorisation to Community traders. Therefore, the express objective of Regulation

---

[41] According to Art. 1, "[the] joint action [is] aimed at protecting Member State's essential security interests".

[42] See *European Voice*, 5 June 1997 at 6.

3381/94 and Decision 94/942/CFSP to "constitute an integrated system"[43] is reduced to a statement of merely rhetorical significance if the legal guarantees enjoyed by the latter are denied to its most essential element, namely the criteria upon which the principles underpinning the system established thereunder are to be applied. The material interdependence between Regulation 3381/94 and the substance of Decision 94/942/CFSP is so close that this formula undermines the objective they purport to serve.

Furthermore, the argument that the intergovernmental character of a Title V instrument may not undermine the legal effectiveness of a Community measure follows from the main principles underpinning the constitutional order of the European Union under Article 3 TEU. Indeed, the requirement that the consistency between the activities undertaken within the distinct pillars be ensured and the *acquis communautaire* respected entails that the Community and the CFSP measures are deemed parts of a truly "integrated approach". However, to exclude the guidelines upon which Regulation 3381/94 is to operate from the Community legal framework is tantamount to enabling national authorities to apply that Community law measure in a manner contrary to its objectives. In addition to running counter to the rationale underpinning Article 3 TEU, such action by national authorities would be contrary to the duty of co-operation which binds all the organs of the state under Article 10 EC. Whereas it is the role of the Court, under Article 220 EC, to ensure that the competent national authorities comply with this duty, the *modus operandi* of the export regime is incorporated in a measure excluded, under Article 46 TEU, from its jurisdiction. What renders the rules under discussion more problematic is the fact that the effectiveness of the Community measure is subject to a Title V measure which makes reference to European Council Summit conclusions. In other words, the effectiveness of every measure concerned is subject to another measure of considerably weaker legal qualities. This further highlights the inability of the rules under consideration to operate as "an integrated system" and the prospect of the effectiveness of the *acquis communautaire* becoming of symbolic significance.

4. THE COMMISSION'S PROPOSALS ON REFORMING THE COMMON RULES ON EXPORTS OF DUAL-USE GOODS

The Commission addressed both the legal and practical problems to which the Community regime on exports of dual-use goods initially under Regulation 3381/94 and Decision 94/942/CFSP gave rise. In doing so, it adopted a document entitled *Proposal for a Council Regulation (EC) setting up a Community regime for the control of dual-use goods and technology*[44] wherein it suggested the amendment of the system initially established under Regulation 3381/94 and

[43] Para. 6 of the preamble to Reg. 3381/94 *supra* note 1, and Art. 1 of Dec. 94/942/CFSP.
[44] COM(1998)257 final, adopted in Brussels on 15 May 1998.

Decision 94/942/CFSP. This document was accompanied by a second one entitled *Report to the European Parliament and the Council on the application of Regulation (EC) 3381/94 setting up a Community system of export controls regarding dual-use goods*[45] in which it pointed out the deficiencies of the system under consideration.

4.1. The substantive issues examined by the Commission regarding the functioning of the Community regime on exports of dual-use goods

In its evaluation of the functioning of Regulation 3381/94 and Decision 94/942/CFSP, the Commission referred to two main achievements: the first deals with the establishment, in practical terms, of the free movement of dual-use goods within the Community from which both companies and national administrations have benefited; the second achievement refers to the development of the administrative co-operation between the competent authorities of the Member States. In this respect, not only has a network of national officials responsible for export controls been developed, but also practical difficulties were dealt with efficiently by the Co-ordinating Group.[46]

As regards to the problems to which the application of the common regime has given rise, the Commission focused on the following two: first, the discrepancy between national licensing systems has enabled national authorities to inquire about the validity of authorisations given by other Member States, hence causing considerable delays for the exporter; secondly, the administrative co-operation between the Member States is inherently limited because it is confined to the Member States directly involved, hence excluding the possibility of a supervisory role being played by the Commission itself.[47]

In addressing the above problems, the Commission proposal is underpinned by three principles. The first consists of the harmonisation of trade-related issues regarding the exports of dual-use goods. In this respect, it suggests the introduction of a general Community licence; this licence would cover exports to ten countries which raise no proliferation concern and towards which the export policies of the Member States have already converged.[48] In order to cut down on the delay caused by differing authorisation policies, the Commission suggests the adoption of a common licence form in relation to exports of dual-use goods not covered by the Community General licence. Furthermore, the

[45] COM(1998)258 final, adopted in Brussels on 15 May 1998.

[46] A list of practical issues over which the Co-ordinating Group has reached agreement is annexed to COM(1998)268 final at 13 *et seq.* under the title "Elements of consensus".

[47] Another practical problem highlighted by the Commission is the fact that the "catch all" clause of Reg. 3381/94 has been applied inconsistently due to the varying extent to which national governments inform their exporters of sensitive end-users.

[48] The destinations covered by a Community general licence are suggested to be Australia, Canada, Japan, New Zealand, Norway, Switzerland, USA, Poland, the Czech Republic and Hungary.

Commission suggested the reinforcement of the administrative co-operation between the Member States and the imposition of a duty to provide a similar level of guidance to exporters affected by the Community regime on exports of dual-use goods.

The second principle underlying the Commission proposals is the abolition of controls over the intra-Community trade in dual-use goods. This would cover, on the one hand, the authorisations all Member States were required to impose in relation to certain dual-use goods and, on the other hand, those that certain Member States were allowed to maintain regarding other, specifically defined, goods under Regulation 3381/94 and Decision 94/942/CFSP. However, in order to ensure that free intra-Community trade will not undermine the effective control of exports to third countries, the licensing requirement covering the intra-Community trade of specifically defined sensitive products under Regulation 3381/94 and Decision 94/942/CFSP is to be replaced by an *ex post* notification requirement.

The final suggestion put forward by the Commission deals with the enhancement of the effectiveness of the Community regime on exports of dual-use goods by closing two main loopholes. On the one hand, the "catch-all" clause is proposed to cover transactions not only potentially related to programmes of weapons of mass destruction, as is the case under the current system, but also to conventional armaments in so far as the exports in question are directed to countries subject to a United Nations arms embargo. On the other hand, the ambit of the common rules is proposed to extend to technology transfers by intangible means.[49]

4.2. The legal formula of the Community regime on exports of dual-use goods

The Commission proposals are based on the idea of the abolition of the inter-pillar approach. The framework suggested therein is to be established under a Council regulation adopted pursuant to Article 133 EC. This measure is to incorporate the substantive content of Decision 94/942/CFSP, namely both the material scope of the common rules and the guidelines on the basis of which national authorities are to grant export authorisations.

However, the discussion of the Commission proposals in the Council's Working Group on dual-use goods has indicated that the abandonment of the inter-pillar approach has not been wholly welcomed; certain Member States insist on the revised Community regime on exports of dual-use goods being adopted under both Article 133 EC and Article 14 TEU. The arguments put forward against the adoption of common rules on exports of dual-use goods solely under Article 133 may be summarised as follows. First, the inherent sensitive character of dual-use goods and the foreign and security policy implications of

---

[49] These would cover PC, fax and telephone.

their exports render their legal regulation a matter entirely for the Member States to determine; this central role may only be ensured within the CFSP framework. Secondly, in authorising exports of dual-use goods, the competent national authorities exercise the right of the Member States to determine whether their security is at risk; any interference by the Court in how the authorisation process is carried out would impinge upon the Member States' right to conduct their foreign policy.

The first of the above concerns has been addressed by the Commission in its proposals on the amendment of the current regime. In these proposals, it is stressed that the central role of the Member States in authorising exports to third countries is fully safeguarded within the Community legal order. On the one hand, the provision for certain dual-use goods to be covered by the Community general licence merely formalises what has already been standard practice amongst the Member States. On the other hand, decisions over exports of dual-use goods not covered by a Community general licence are to be taken by the competent national authorities, who, therefore, remain solely responsible for determining the effect of the exports in question on national security. Furthermore, the case of the amendment of the lists of products covered by the scope of the common rules illustrates the central role of the Member States in the export system; these lists are to by amended by the Group List, that is the representatives of the Member States, upon common agreement, whereas the Commission does not enjoy the exclusive right of initiative.[50]

It follows that the main tenet of the rationale underpinning the Commission proposal is not fundamentally distinct from that of Regulation 3381/94 and Decision 94/942/CFSP, namely the separation of trade and foreign policy within the constitutional order of the European Union. Indeed, the Commission proposal seeks to address the main interests upon which this rationale draws, that is, on the one hand, the right of the Member States to determine whether their security is in danger and, on the other hand, the effectiveness of Community law. The feature of the Commission proposal that is fundamentally distinct from the existing Community regime on exports of dual-use goods is how these interests are addressed: instead of conflicting, they are viewed as essentially interdependent. In this respect, they are viewed as capable of being fully protected within the Community legal order.[51]

Therefore, it is the second concern in relation to the abolition of the inter-pillar approach that needs to be examined, namely the judicial interference in an area lying beyond the Community legal framework. This requires an analysis of

[50] See Art. 12 of the proposed Council Reg. in COM(1998)257 final at 14.

[51] In this respect, it is interesting that the head of the unit of Commission's DG I responsible for dual-use goods, in a speech delivered at the University of Münster/Westfalen, does not cease to emphasise that, according to the Commission proposals, a Community regime should focus on trade matters, for decisions on security-sensitive exports will be taken by national administrations in accordance with national policies; this speech is entitled "Dual-use Export Controls: The Common European Export Control Regime and How to Improve It" (http://www/europa.eu.int/comm/dg01/dualuse5.htm).

the Court's jurisprudence on exports of dual-use goods which will be carried out in the next chapter.

5. CONCLUSION

The above analysis suggested that the inter-pillar approach to the legal regulation of exports of dual-use goods, as adopted under Regulation 3381/94 and Decision 94/942/CFSP, is fundamentally flawed. It argued that it relied upon an obsolete distinction between trade and foreign policy and, by excluding the Community measure's *modus operandi* from the Community legal framework, rendered it ineffective. Therefore, the Commission proposal to amend the current legal regime by the adoption of rules based solely on Article 133 EC is to be welcomed; while ensuring that it would not encroach upon the right of the Member States to protect their security, the legal regulation of exports of dual-use goods within the Community legal order effectively addresses the problems raised by the inter-pillar approach underpinning the existing regime. The legal effectiveness of the Council Regulation is not subject to non-Community instruments and, hence, is to be protected on the basis of the legal guarantees provided under Community law and supervised by the Court.

However, its main premise does not necessarily entail the *a priori* abandonment of the inter-pillar approach in relation to the economic aspects of security *in toto*. This argument is based on the different patterns on the basis of which the inter-pillar approach has been adopted; indeed, the approach underpinning the imposition of sanctions on third countries pursuant to Article 301 EC is significantly distinct from that of the existing Community regime on exports of dual-use goods.

It follows that the role of the inter-pillar approach regarding the legal regulation of the economic aspects of security requires an assessment of how it materialises in legal terms and whether it is consistent with the main principles underpinning the constitutional order of the European Union. If the requirement that the European Union be served by a single institutional framework ensuring the consistency of activities carried out by the Union and building upon the *acquis communautaire* is not respected, the inter-pillar approach must be abandoned. However, the assessment of the above issues inevitably entails that the inter-pillar approach, namely the establishment of common rules on both the Community legal order and the Common Foreign and Security Policy, is not in itself fundamentally flawed. In other words, the extent to which an inter-pillar approach may ensure the legal regulation of trade measures with express foreign policy dimensions in a legally sensible and realistically effective way relies upon the way it is adopted and implemented. This is illustrated in the difference between the formula followed in the case of sanctions against third countries and that of the common rules on exports of dual-use goods. It follows that the inter-pillar approach may be adopted and applied in different ways, whose compliance with the principles of the constitutional order of the Union ought to be assessed *in concreto*. In the case of the interaction between trade and foreign policy, a central part of this analysis focuses on the Court's jurisprudence: has it put forward an approach which would ensure the effectiveness of Community law while respecting the competence of the Member States to determine their foreign policy?

6

The Court's Approach to Exports of Dual-use Goods to Third Countries

1. INTRODUCTION

In the previous chapters, the imposition of trade sanctions on third countries under Article 301 EC and the legal regulation of exports of dual-use goods under Regulation 3381/94 and Decision 94/942/CFSP were studied as two typical examples of direct interactions between the Community legal framework and CFSP. However, the inter-pillar approach they put forward varies considerably: in the case of trade sanctions, the Community and CFSP measures are of distinct scope, the latter being confined to expressing the political will of the Member States to have recourse to the former; in the case of the common rules on exports of dual use goods, both the material scope and the *modus operandi* of the Community measure are incorporated into the CFSP instrument. It was then argued that the inter-pillar approach reflected in Regulation 3381/94 and Decision 94/942/CFSP is fundamentally flawed. It is only at a superficial level that it acknowledges the interrelationship between trade and foreign policy, its underlying objective being to define a legal sphere enjoying the effectiveness ensured within the Community legal framework and the wide scope for national action maintained under CFSP; in order to achieve this objective, it puts forward a formula which relies upon both the above legal frameworks but belongs to neither.

The different pattern of the inter-pillar approach to sanctions and exports of dual-use goods indicates that its merits as a form of legal regulation of trade measures with express foreign policy dimensions may not be assessed in general terms; instead, it is the specific way in which this inter-pillar approach is adopted and implemented that must be analysed. In particular, in order to establish whether the inter-pillar formula provides a legally sensible and realistically effective framework within the constitutional order of the European Union, it must be examined whether it complies with the main constitutional principles of the Union, namely a single institutional framework ensuring the consistency of the activities of the Union and building upon the *acquis communautaire*.

The analysis of the problems and potential of the inter-pillar approach for the legal regulation of the interactions between trade and foreign policy needs to be focused on the role of the European Court of Justice. Given the importance of its contribution to the development of the Community legal order, its approach to issues at the margins of that order is of the utmost importance. This is even more so in the light of Article 46 TEU which brings within the Court's jurisdiction the application of Article 47 TEU, according to which the EC Treaty is not to be affected by TEU.

Prior to the analysis leading to the above conclusion, a more general point needs to be made. Dealing with trade measures with foreign policy and security implications, the legal regulation of exports of dual-use goods raises issues regarding the scope of the exclusive competence of the Community and the right of the Member States to act beyond the Community legal order. A central feature of this debate involves the role of the Court and the extent to which it may exercise its jurisdiction in spheres of activities touching upon, albeit excluded from, the Community legal framework. This is a problem inherent in the jurisdiction of any court of law and has arisen in various legal orders. It is for this reason that an outline of how this problem has been dealt with beyond the European Union will precede the analysis of the Court's approach to the interaction of trade and foreign policy in the case of exports of dual-use goods.

The structure of this chapter will be as follows. First, the problems regarding the role of the judiciary raised by legal disputes with significant foreign policy components will be outlined as inherent in any legal order established under the rule of law, while the specific approach adopted by American and German courts will be summarised. Secondly, the case law on unilateral restrictions on exports of dual-use goods will be outlined and, thirdly, it will be analysed along with the Court's construction of the common commercial policy in broad terms, account being taken of the wide discretion enjoyed by national authorities. Fourthly, the implications of the Court's judgments on exports of dual-use goods for Council Regulation 3381/94 and Decision 94/942/CFSP will be assessed.

2. THE GENERAL FRAMEWORK: POLITICAL ISSUES BEFORE THE JUDICIARY

In terms of the jurisdiction of the Court, the interactions between trade and foreign policy may schematically be perceived as the juxtaposition between the justiciable and the non-justiciable. Indeed, whereas the former has been the basis upon which the Court has formulated the main principles underpinning the Community legal order, the latter has been considered the area *par excellence* excluded from its control. This has been clearly illustrated in the Treaty on European Union in Article 46, under which Title V is expressly excluded from the Court's jurisdiction.[1]

[1] Art. 46 TEU reads as follows: "The provisions of the Treaty establishing the European Community, the Treaty establishing the European Coal and Steel Community and the Treaty establishing the European Atomic Energy Community concerning the powers of the Court of Justice of the European Communities and the exercise of those powers shall apply only to the following

The issue of the extent to which, if at all, the judiciary is to exercise its jurisdiction over foreign policy decisions undertaken by the executive is by no means
unique in the Community legal order; it has arisen in national legal systems too
and has been the subject of controversy not only between the judiciary and the
executive but also amongst legal scholars. A brief outline of how the issue of judicial control over foreign policy issues has arisen in national legal orders and the
approach adopted by national judicial organs will assist the analysis to follow, for
it will provide a canvass of various aspects of essentially the same problem.
However, before this canvass is briefly set, two points need to be made. First, the
purpose of this outline is by no means to provide an exhaustive analysis of how
the issue of judicial control over foreign policy has been settled within various
legal orders, for such an analysis is clearly excluded from the scope of this book.
The second and related point is that the following outline in no way suggests any
parallels to be drawn between the role of the Court and that of national courts. In
other words, the inherently limited significance of any analysis seeking to examine the constitutional order of the European Union in general and the Community
legal order in particular with national legal orders, be they federal or confederal,
is fully taken into account. Indeed, such an attempt would ignore the *sui generis*
legal character of the Union and the interplay between Community competence,
national competence and common action of the Member States under the
umbrella of the Union, unique in the constitutional order of the Union, that lies
upon the very core of the adjudicating role of the Court.

In his informative analysis of the approach adopted by the American courts
when being called upon to adjudicate on issues with foreign policy dimensions,
Professor Franck[2] refers to the "political-question doctrine"; according to this
doctrine foreign policy is perceived to be a domain exclusively reserved under
the constitution to the President of the United States and, hence, impervious to
judicial control. This approach led to what he calls, "the abdicationist tendency" widely followed by the American courts,[3] in which issues related to the

provisions of the Treaty: (a) provisions amending the Treaty establishing the European Economic
Community with a view to establishing the European Community, the Treaty establishing the
European Coal and Steel Community and the Treaty establishing the European Atomic Energy
Community; (b) provisions of Title VI, under the conditions provided for by Article 35; (c) provi-
sions of Title VII, under the conditions provided for by Article 11 of the Treaty establishing the
European Community and Article 40 of this Treaty; (d) Article 6(2) with regard to action of the insti-
tutions, insofar as the Court has jurisdiction under the Treaties establishing the European
Communities and under this Treat; (e) Articles 46 to 53".

[2] *Political Questions/Judicial Answers. Does the Rule of Law Apply to Foreign Affairs?*
(Princeton, NJ: Princeton University Press, 1992).

[3] One of the first federal decisions excluding issues bearing on foreign policy from its jurisdiction,
The Cherokee Nation v. *Georgia*, 30 US (5 Pet.) 1 (1831), relied upon an English decision delivered
in the 1790s; it was the *Nabob of Arcot* case, wherein it was stated that "for their political acts states
were not amenable to tribunals of justice" in Franck, *supra* note 2 at 12, where he describes this
approach as of "monarchical" character. Franck explains this approach of American federal courts
on what he calls "the Faustian pact between the judiciary and the executive", that is the price federal judges suggested paying in order to render the judicially inspired expansion of their jurisdiction
over domestic issues acceptable to the executive.

exercise of foreign policy were declared beyond their jurisdiction. Franck argues that this approach was adopted not only on theoretical grounds, that is constitutional interpretation, but also pursuant to prudential reasons; these include the unusually evidentiary problems that cases related to the conduct of foreign policy raise, the absence of determinate and manageable legal standards to be judicially applied, the implications that their judgment may have upon the security of their state and the absence of means of rendering a judgment on foreign policy enforceable.[4] However, he argues that, contrary to the lower federal courts which are reluctant to exercise their jurisdiction over issues they perceive to be of a sensitive nature, "[cases underpinned by] a clash between political powers and a countervailing legal interest [are] clearly seen by the Supreme Court to call for adjudication rather than deference, even where there are foreign policy implications".[5] Having criticised the failure of American courts to construe and consistently apply a doctrine regarding their adjudication upon cases with foreign policy implications, the main thrust of Professor Franck's thesis deals with what he calls "judicial double-entry bookkeeping"[6]; this term describes the tendency of American courts to combine, on the one hand, general statements of deference to the executive and inability to adjudicate upon issues bordering on foreign affairs and, on the other hand, application of traditional legal reasoning to decide these very same issues.[7] Franck concludes that "when judges take jurisdiction in a case involving foreign affairs or national security, they never reject the political-question doctrine as such. Instead, they circumnavigate it, and they have developed several pragmatic ways to do this, . . . , most simply . . . by silently passing over the doctrinal or theoretical shoals, gliding past the prudential problems, while studiously avoiding all disquisition on jurisprudential issues".[8]

Contrary to the American case law, the German Constitutional Court has expressly and consistently interpreted the Basic Law as the foundation of its jurisdiction to adjudicate upon any case brought before it by parties with standing.[9] However, in both cases the control exercised by the courts over decisions related to the conduct of foreign policy by the executive by no means substituted the will of the former for that of the latter; what was at issue was the consistency of the expression of the political will of the executive with the constitution. As the analysis provided by Professor Franck illustrates, both the wide discretion enjoyed by the executive in the conduct of foreign policy and the political

---

[4] *Supra* note 2 at 45–60.

[5] *Ibid.* at 95; for an analysis substantiating his conclusion, see *ibid.* at 61–96.

[6] *Ibid.* at 23.

[7] *Ibid.* at 21–30.

[8] *Ibid.* at 61. It is interesting to note a circuit court judgment which quite explicitly referred to his method of avoiding to deal with the theoretical problem at issue by stating that "[w]ithout necessarily disapproving the District Court's conclusion [that a claim by members of Congress and Nicaraguan citizens in relation to the involvement of the United States in hostilities in Nicaragua be rejected on political-question grounds] . . . we choose not to resort to that [political question] doctrine. . . . [W]e find other bases for dismissing the suit" cited in *ibid.* at 94.

[9] *Ibid.* at 107–25.

context within which this discretion is exercised are parameters fully taken into account by American and German courts; this has led to "a middle course between judicial abdication and rampant judicial interference in the making and execution of foreign and security policy, one that satisfies systemic imperatives of the rule of law and political flexibility".[10]

The fundamentally different normative context characterising the American and German national orders and the Community legal order notwithstanding, Professor Franck's analysis is relevant to the subject under discussion in a two-fold way: on the one hand, it raises the issue of the extent to which the judiciary should define its jurisdiction by what is perceived to be the sensitive nature of foreign affairs issues brought before it in the context of a specific dispute; on the other hand, it points out that the problem in question is not unique in the task performed by the European Court of Justice but is inherent in any legal order governed by the rule of law.

3. THE COURT'S APPROACH TOWARDS EXPORTS OF DUAL-USE GOODS: TRADE AND FOREIGN POLICY AS WITHIN A SINGLE NORMATIVE FRAMEWORK

In its case law on unilateral restrictions on exports of dual-use goods, the Court subtly introduces the principles underpinning its approach to the legal regulation of specific issues arising from the interaction of trade and foreign policy and the different competences involved. The existing case law examines the legal position of exports of dual-use goods in both its internal and external aspect; the *Richardt* judgment[11] is about the compatibility of export restrictions with new Article 30 EC, whereas the *Werner*[12] and *Leifer*[13] judgments examine the compatibility of export restrictions with the Common Commercial Policy.

3.1. The *Richardt* case—the facts

A French company undertook to deliver to the Soviet central purchasing agency certain high-technology goods. All the necessary formalities had been followed but the flight from Paris was cancelled and the goods were transported to Luxembourg airport in order to be sent later by plane to Moscow. However, the Luxembourg authorities prohibited the transportation of the goods in question on the basis of a national law implementing the export restrictions agreed

---

[10] *Ibid.* at 107. Franck argues that this has been pursued by the German Constitutional Court on an immensely more coherent and consistently applied basis.

[11] Case C–367/89 *Criminal proceedings against Aime Richardt and Les Accessoires Scientifiques SNC* [1991] ECR I–4621.

[12] Case C–70/94 *Fritz Werner Industrie-Ausrustungen GmbH* v. *Federal Republic of Germany* [1995] ECR I–3189.

[13] Case C–83/94 *Criminal proceedings against Peter Leifer and Others* [1995] ECR I–3231.

multilaterally by Western states within the Co-ordinating Committee (COCOM).[14] Hence, the transit of the goods in question was subjected to a licence requirement and, in the absence of any special transit licence request, the Luxembourg customs authorities confiscated the goods and initiated criminal proceedings.

3.2. The *Richardt* judgment

The *Cour de Cassation de Luxembourg* referred to the Court under the preliminary references procedure the question whether Luxembourg was entitled to impose restrictions additional to those provided for under Regulation 222/77 on Community transit in cases of goods considered by the competent national authorities to be of strategic nature and on external security grounds. The Court, contrary to the Opinion of Advocate General Jacobs,[15] held that the whole problem was one of transit on the basis that the goods, even though physically in Luxembourg, had to be examined as exported from France. In this respect, the Court reiterated its previous case law on transit,[16] adding that the general principle that the Community transit regime applies to all movements of goods within the Community irrespective of their nature[17] is supplemented by the exceptional provision of Article 10 of Regulation 222/77, whereby prohibitions and restrictions on importation, exportation and transit by a Member State apply to the extent that they are compatible with the Treaties establishing the Communities. The Court held that this provision entailed the need to examine the special transit licence required by the Luxembourg regulation and the subsequent confiscation of the goods on the basis of the Treaty and particularly Article 30. Consequently, it held that the above measures must serve the interest which that Article protects, be proportionate and not restrict intra-Community trade more than absolutely necessary.[18]

The Court expressed the principle that "the concept of public security within the meaning of Article [30] of the Treaty covers both a Member State's internal security and its external security".[19] Then, it stated that "[i]t is common ground

---

[14] On the COCOM and its demise after the end of the Cold War, see *infra* at ch. 9.

[15] Jacobs AG argued that what was at issue was a problem of export rather than of transit. He argued that the restriction imposed by Luxembourg was a measure having equivalent effect to a quantitative restriction on exports and covered by the Export Reg. He then concluded that the measure in question was covered by Art. 11 of the Export Reg., that is an exceptional clause similar to that of Art. 30 EC, but he did not make any analysis of the public security proviso contained therein. It must also be noted that Jacobs AG examined the problem at issue in the context of Arts. 296 and 297; regarding the former, he pointed out that the products in question have not been argued to be covered by the Art. 296(2) list and hence concluded that Art. 296 was not relevant. The Court did not examine Arts. 296 and 297 at all, indicating that they were of no relevance.

[16] Case 266/81 *SIOT* v. *Ministero delle Finanze* [1983] ECR 731; Case C–117/88 *Trend-Moden Textilhandel GmbH* v. *Hauptzollamt Emmerich* [1990] ECR I–631.

[17] Art. 1 of Reg. 222/77 [1977] OJ L38/1.

[18] Para. 20.

[19] Para. 22.

that the importation, exportation and transit of goods capable of being used for strategic purposes may affect the public security of a Member State, which it is therefore entitled to protect pursuant to Article [30] of the Treaty".[20] Finally, regarding the sanction imposed for failure to obtain the special transit licence, the Court held that it was for the national court to examine it on the basis of the proportionality test. However, it stated that the penalty in question, that is confiscation of the goods, "may be considered disproportionate to the objective pursued, and thus incompatible with Article [30] of the Treaty, in a case where the return of the goods to the Member State of origin could suffice".[21]

3.3. The *Werner* case—the facts

The *Werner* case reached the Court through the preliminary reference procedure of Article 234 EC. The plaintiff received an order to supply some sensitive materials to Libya.[22] The competent German authorities refused to issue a licence for this export on the basis of a national provision protecting the security of Germany, the peaceful coexistence of nations and the prevention of the external relations of Germany from being disrupted. In addition, the German authorities were permitted to make contracts and activities subject to a licence requirement or to prohibit them, provided that the principle of proportionality was respected. The German authorities claimed that the products in question could enable Libya to produce missiles capable of reaching countries such as Italy and Israel.

3.4. The *Werner* judgment

In *Werner* the Court reiterated its broad interpretation of the common commercial policy.[23] Consequently, a measure preventing or restricting the export of certain products was held to come within the ambit of the CCP despite the fact that it has foreign policy and security objectives, for the Member States cannot "freely decid[e], in the light of [their] own foreign policy or security requirements, whether a measure is covered by Article 133".[24] Having made reference to the exclusive Community competence over the CCP, the Court reiterated that

---

[20] *Ibid.*
[21] See para. 24 of the judgment.
[22] Namely a vacuum induction, smelting and cast oven along with industion spools for that oven.
[23] "[S]o as to avoid disturbances in intra-Community trade by reason of the disparities which would then exist in certain sectors of economic relations with non-member states": para. 9. See also Case 8/73 *Hauptzollamt Bremerhaven* v. *Massey Fergusson* [1973] ECR 897; Cases 37–38/73 *Sociaal Fonds voor de Diamantarbeiders* [1973] ECR 1609, [1976] 2 CMLR 222; *Opinion 1/75* [1975] ECR 1355, [1976] 1 CMLR 85; and *Opinion 1/78* [1979] ECR 2871, [1979] 3 CMLR 639.
[24] Para. 9 of the judgment.

Member States can act in this area only on the basis of a specific Community authorisation.[25]

Then, the Court examined whether the contested decision of the German authorities ran counter to the common rules for exports, established by Council Regulation 2603/69.[26] The Export Regulation introduces the rule that exports to third countries must be unrestricted,[27] but also provides an exceptional clause similar to Article 30 EC.[28] The Court held that a licence requirement, that is a measure having equivalent effect to a quantitative restriction within the meaning of Article 29 EC, comes within the ambit of the Export Regulation, even though it is not specifically mentioned, on the grounds of both its legal basis, that is Article 133 providing for the CCP, and its objective, that is the implementation of the principle of free exportation from the Community to third countries.

The Court made express reference to *Richardt* and the broad interpretation given therein to the notion of public security as encompassing both its internal and external aspects. The same approach was adopted regarding the same term referred to in Article 11 of the Export Regulation.[29] Furthermore, in agreement with the argument put forward by the German Government, the Court held that "the risk of a serious disturbance to foreign relations or to peaceful coexistence of nations may affect the security of a Member State"[30] for "it is becoming increasingly less possible to look at the security of a State in isolation, since it is closely linked to the security of the international community at large, and of its various components".[31]

The Court left it to the national court to decide whether Article 11 of the Export Regulation could be invoked under the specific circumstances by the national authorities; however, it stated that "it is common ground that the exportation of goods capable of being used for military purposes to a country at war with another country may affect the security of a Member State within the meaning [of the concept of public security given by the Court]".[32]

---

[25] The Court referred to Case 41/76 *Donckerwolke v. Procureur de la République* [1976] ECR 1921, [1977] CMLR 535 and Case 174/84 *Bulk Oil v. Sun International* [1986] ECR 559, [1986] 2 CMLR 732.

[26] [1969] OJ L324/25; amended by Council Reg. No 3918/91, [1991] OJ L372/31.

[27] According to Art. 1, products are to be exported from the Community to third countries without being subject "to any quantitative restriction, with the exception of those restrictions which are applied in conformity with the provisions of this Regulation".

[28] According to Art. 11 of the Reg., Member States can impose export restrictions on exports "on grounds of public morality, public policy or public security; the protection of health and life of human, animals or plants; the protection of national treasures possessing artistic, historic or archaeological value, or the protection of industrial and commercial property".

[29] The Court argued that this interpretative analogy was based on the fact that "[t]o interpret the concept more restrictively when it is used in Article 11 of the Export Regulation would be tantamount to authorizing the Member States to restrict the movement of goods within the internal market more than movement between themselves and non member countries": para. 25 of the judgment.

[30] Para. 27.

[31] Para. 26.

[32] Para. 28.

3.5. The *Leifer* case—the facts

The *Leifer* case was another Article 234 EC reference by a German court. Mr. Leifer was facing criminal proceedings for having exported without licence sensitive goods[33] to Iraq from 1984 to 1988, that is during the war between Iraq and Iran. The German government argued that the abovementioned goods were capable of being used for the production of chemical weapons and hence were covered by the provisions previously invoked in *Werner*. Their export to one of the parties involved in the first Gulf War was argued to have put the external security of the Federal Republic of Germany in danger. In this respect, the prohibition on their export helped to prevent the use of chemical weapons in the war and hence protected the life and health of numerous people.

3.6. The *Leifer* judgment

The Court reiterated a number of points already made in *Werner*, namely the broad interpretation of the scope of the common commercial policy, its approach towards export restrictions on dual-use goods as within the ambit of Article 133 EC and, hence, the requirement that any national restriction needed specific Community authorisation; furthermore, it confirmed that an export licence requirement, as a measure of equivalent effect to a quantitative restriction, is covered by the Export Regulation and reiterated its broad interpretation of public security as encompassing both its internal and external aspects and, as far as the latter were concerned, the risk of a serious disturbance to foreign relations or to the peaceful coexistence of nations.

Addressing the specific question referred to by the German *Landgericht* Darmstadt regarding the legality of a national measure imposing the burden on the applicant for an export licence of proving that the dual-use products are for civil use or entailing a refusal to license where the goods are objectively suitable for military use, the Court held that Article 11 of the Export Regulation needed to be interpreted restrictively, having regard to the principle of proportionality, for it is an exception to the principle of free exportation at Community level. According to the Court, it is up to national courts to establish whether the measures adopted on the basis of the exceptional provision of Article 11 are necessary and appropriate. In addition, the national court must ascertain whether less restrictive measures could have served the same aim. However, the Court held that "depending on the circumstances, the competent national authorities have a certain degree of discretion when adopting measures which they consider to be necessary in order to guarantee public security in a Member State within the meaning [given by the Court]. When the export of dual-use goods involves a threat to the public security of a Member State, those measures may include a

---

[33] Namely industrial plant, plant parts and chemical products.

requirement that an applicant for an export licence show that the goods are for civil use and also, having regard to specific circumstances such as *inter alia* the political situation in the country of destination, that a licence be refused if those goods are objectively suitable for military use".[34]

Furthermore, the Court held that a Member State may initiate criminal proceedings for failure to comply with the export licence requirement "provided that the penalties applicable do not exceed what appears to be proportionate in relation to the public security aim pursued",[35] reference being made to the criteria provided for in *Richardt*, that is the nature of the goods in question, the circumstances in which the breach was committed and whether the defendant's non-compliance was due to good faith. Finally, the Court held that Article 1 of the Export Regulation, establishing the general principle of free exportation of goods at Community level, was directly effective.

4. COMMENT ON THE COURT'S RULINGS ON EXPORTS OF DUAL-USE GOODS

In adjudicating upon the *Richardt*, *Werner* and *Leifer* cases, the Court did not take into account the rules established by Regulation 3381/94 and Decision 94/942/CFSP on exports of dual-use goods, for they were adopted after proceedings had been initiated. It will be recalled that the underlying theme of these rules[36] consists of a rigid distinction between trade and foreign policy: by incorporating the *modus operandi* of Regulation 3381/94 in Decision 94/942/CFSP, the Member States sought to exclude it from the Court's jurisdiction and hence safeguard their competence to determine foreign policy. However, the thrust of the Court's approach, illustrated in these judgments, is fundamentally different, for it suggests that national competence over foreign policy be protected within a Community law system of external relations which may also ensure the effectiveness of the CCP.[37]

4.1. Exports of dual-use goods as within the CCP

First in *Richardt* and more clearly in *Werner* and *Leifer*, the Court opined that, on the one hand, exports of dual-use goods do fall within the Common Commercial Policy, for "the[ir] [strategic] nature cannot take them outside the scope of the common commercial policy"[38]; on the other hand, it held that

---

[34] Para. 35.

[35] Para. 42.

[36] For an analysis of the Community regime on exports of dual-use goods see *supra* ch. 4.

[37] This comment on the rulings on exports of dual-use goods will not examine the Court's refusal to answer the question submitted by the German court in *Leifer* whether the measure under consideration was justifiable under Art. 296(1)(b) EC. The scope of this provision in general and the question whether it covers national restrictions on exports of dual-use goods in particular will be dealt with *infra* at Ch. 7.

[38] *Leifer* judgment at para. 11.

national restrictions may be justified under the public security exception provided that they conform with Community law guarantees. The significance that this statement may seem to bear cannot be overstated, for, being viewed as within the scope of CCP, exports of dual-use goods are covered by the exclusive competence of the Community and, hence, the Member States may deviate by imposing unilateral restrictions only on the basis of a specific Community law authorisation. This is a far-reaching conclusion, given that the regulation of exports of dual-use goods constitutes an area which touches upon the less integrationist reflexes of Member States.

However, the significance of the application of this principle to the exports of dual-use goods must be assessed on the basis of how the Court interpreted the right of Member States to deviate from the CCP and the conditions introduced therewith. In other words, too broad a construction of the scope for unilateral national action in relation to exports of dual-use goods may seem to reduce the significance of the extension of the ambit of CCP in the first place.

4.2. Broad definition of public security

The Court has adopted a broad definition of the public security proviso.[39] First, the *Richardt* conclusion that public security must be understood on the basis of both its internal and external aspects was reiterated. Secondly, having recourse to identical wording in both *Werner* and *Leifer*, it explicitly adopted the argument put forward by Advocate General Jacobs in his Opinion regarding the increasing interrelationship between national security and the security of the international community.[40] The Court, by recognising that states take foreign policy considerations into account in order to determine whether their external security is at risk, does not merely acknowledge a rather self-evident fact; the interdependence between states within an increasingly globalised international

---

[39] It has been subject to debate whether the public security proviso included in both the Transit Reg., in relation to the *Richardt* case, and the Export Reg., in relation to the *Werner* and *Leifer* cases, may be considered "specific" enough an authorisation under Community law to justify the national unilateral action in question; see Eeckhout, P., *The European Internal Market and International Trade: A Legal Analysis* (Oxford: Clarendon Press, 1994) at 254; N Emiliou, annotation on *Werner* and *Leifer* in (1997) 22 *ELRev.* 68 at 73–4 and I Govaere and P Eeckhout, "On Dual Use Goods and Dualist Case Law: The *Aimé Richardt* Judgement on Export Controls" (1992) 29 *CMLRev.* 941 at 957–8, arguing that Art. 11 of the Export Reg. leaves a number of important issues undetermined, namely the measures to be taken, their material scope and the destinations subject to controls. Therefore, they argue, it cannot be considered a specific Community authorisation. However, Kuyper points out in "Trade Sanctions, Security and Human Rights and Commercial Policy" in M Maresceau, (ed.), *The European Community's Commercial Policy after 1992: The Legal Dimension* (Deventer: Kluwer Law International, 1993) 387 at n. 35 that after *Bulk Oil*, *supra* note 25, this discussion is meaningless.

[40] Para. 26 in *Werner* and para. 27 in *Leifer*. Therefore, the Court concluded, in para. 27 in *Werner* and para. 28 in *Leifer*, that "the risk of serious disturbance to foreign relations or to peaceful coexistence of nations may affect the security of a Member State".

environment is what the Court relies upon in order to ascertain the scope enjoyed by Member States for unilateral action in areas covered by the Common Commercial Policy. In construing the public security proviso in relation to the CCP in broad terms, the Court inevitably recognises the broad scope left to Member States to rely upon it.

A question that the broad construction of the definition of the public security proviso may raise is whether, in practical terms, it reduces the significance of the extension of the scope of CCP to exports of dual-use goods. In other words, given that the broad interpretation of the public security proviso increases the scope for Member States to deviate from the CCP, the construction of exports of dual-use goods within the latter may seem to become of questionable legal significance. It is suggested that, in terms of intellectual consistency, the Court could not have decided otherwise. Its judgments relied upon, on the one hand, the widespread practice of having recourse to trade measures in order to serve foreign policy objectives and, on the other hand, the often considerable difficulty of distinguishing between the various objectives served by a specific measure. In the light of these considerations, to render the existence of a foreign policy dimension the decisive criterion for whether a measure is excluded from the CCP would be tantamount to depriving the latter of any substance. In parallel, too restrictive a construction of public security to reduce the scope of Member States for unilateral action would deny the very basis of the extension of the scope of CCP over exports of dual-use goods in the first place, namely the acknowledgement of the interdependent nature of foreign politics and trade in the current international environment. In other words, if the judicial recognition that exports of dual-use goods fall within the ambit of Article 133 is understood as relying upon a broad construction of trade in the current international environment, it follows that an equally broad construction of security should be adopted. Indeed, this line of reasoning is followed in both the Opinion of Advocate General Jacobs and the *Richardt*, *Werner* and *Leifer* judgments.

4.3. The issue of judicial control

The merit of the approach put forward by the Court is not confined to its intellectual consistency; it also refers to the legally sensible and realistic solution it suggests regarding the exercise of judicial control over national export controls on dual-use goods. Advocate General Jacobs argued that "it is not easy for this Court, or for a national court, to examine the reality of the threat posed to the security of the Federal Republic by the exportation of the goods in issue". He then concluded that "in the absence of Community legislation it is essentially for the competent authorities of each Member States to decide in which case exports of certain dual-use products may raise security concerns" and that "judicial review is confined to ensuring that manifest errors of appraisal have not occurred and that national authorities have not abused the powers conferred by [the exceptional provision in question]".[41]

In other words, in the case of national restrictions on exports of dual-use goods imposed on the basis of foreign policy considerations, the role of the judiciary is confined to ensuring that Member States comply with the principles of proportionality[42] and less restrictive alternative means, and hence that neither manifest errors nor abuse of powers has occurred. Therefore, the *acquis communautaire* is to be safeguarded.

In the *Werner* and *Leifer* judgments, the Court did not address the issue of the exercise of judicial control over exports of dual-use goods in such express terms as the Advocate General had in his Opinion, but nonetheless seemed impliedly to support his line of reasoning. In this respect, it is a positive development that, in setting out in its *Leifer* judgment certain factors that national courts are to consider while assessing whether the principle of proportionality has been adhered to, the Court refers to the "objective suitability [of the dual-use goods in question] for military use" and, hence, adopts a different approach from that in *Richardt*. It will be recalled that, in the latter judgment, the Court had ignored the type of dual-use goods in question and implied that all dual-use goods were intrinsically linked to the public security proviso. Such a conclusion would constitute a blanket exception to a whole category of products whose link with the public security exception might not always be apparent; hence, it would automatically justify national restrictions and render the application of Article 133 in that area meaningless.[43] There is no reason, for example, for

---

[41] Para. 45 of his Opinion in *Werner*. This argument of Jacobs AG on the inherently limited role of the Court when the security of a Member States is at stake was also put forward in relation to the application of the principle of proportionality in the *Leifer* case, whereby he stated at para. 55 of his Opinion that "once it is accepted that the security of a Member State may be at stake, there is little scope for the courts to review whether export restrictions serve the aim of safeguarding that security. Nor could it really be suggested that the aim could be achieved by less restrictive means, since the requirement of authorization to export must be the minimum requirement necessary to prevent exports which may threaten the security of a State." Consistently, Jacobs AG argued in Case C–120/94 *Commission* v. *Greece (Re FYROM)* [1996] ECR I–1513 at para. 60 that the scope for judicial review is "extremely limited" in cases which involve foreign and security policy considerations.

[42] For an analysis of the principle of proportionality see N Emiliou, *The Principle of Proportionality in European Law. A Comparative Study* (London: Kluwer Law International, 1996), especially at 171–94 and 227–265; T Tridimas, *The General Principles of EC Law* (Oxford: OUP, 1999) ch. 4. For the application of the principle in the area of free movement of goods see P Oliver, *Free Movement of Goods in the European Community* (3rd edn., London: Sweet and Maxwell, 1996) at 182–9 and LW Gormley, *Prohibiting Restrictions on Trade within the EEC* (Amsterdam: Elsevier, 1985) at 124 *et seq.*

[43] The extent to which civil technologies are increasingly used in arms production renders the above restrictive approach of enormous practical significance. An argument in favour of the Court's approach in *Richardt* based on the division of jurisdictions between the Court and national courts is not valid. The task of national courts to determine the compatibility of the measure in question with Community law would not only be respected but also facilitated if the Court elaborated a test to ascertain the legality of the specific measure. This is what the Court did in other areas in which it considered that national courts might have found it difficult to apply Community requirements in the case in question: see, e.g., Case C–392/93 *R.* v. *HM Treasury, ex. p. British Telecommunications Plc* [1996] ECR I–1631.

national export restrictions on uniforms required by the military in peacetime to be automatically justified on the basis of the public security proviso.[44]

4.4. The issue of the definition of commercial policy

The case law on exports of dual-use goods raises questions regarding the scope of the Common Commercial Policy in general. In relation to the longstanding debate over its definition,[45] although the Court might seem to adopt the instrumentalist approach in defining the scope of CCP and hence delineating the exclusive Community competence,[46] it has been argued that this was not the case; the argument that the instrumentalist approach was not in fact adopted in *Werner* and *Leifer* relies upon the reference that the Court made to "the effects of the contested measures in the light of the objectives of the common commercial policy", a method incompatible with the main thrust of the instrumentalist argument, that is the use of measures of a commercial nature.[47]

However, it must be stressed that the Court, in order to determine whether the national measure in question is covered by Article 133, refers to the objective of the Community provision rather than the objective of the national measure. Indeed, the Court makes reference to "national measures whose *effect*[48] is to prevent or restrict the export of certain products".[49] Therefore, it does not follow, from the simple use of the word "effect", that the instrumentalist approach is denied. This would have been the case had the Court made reference to the aim of the national measure being of a non-commercial character and hence excluded from the scope of Article 133 EC. In other words, the Court seems to distinguish between the effect and the objective of the measure in question. The former is defined in the light of the Treaty and brings the measure in question into the ambit of Article 133; the latter is examined on the basis of exceptions granted by Community law and justifies the national measure. This distinction seems to question the significance of the traditional instrumentalist/teleological debate about the definition of the scope of the CCP. Even if the Court does not expressly endorse the instrumentalist approach, in effect, it reaches the same conclusion through a different line of reasoning. It could have argued that, because of their aim, that is to protect public security in general, national export restrictions on dual-use goods are not covered by Article 133. The Court, instead, refers to their effect which initially brings them into the

---

[44] See A Evans, *The Integration of the European Community and Third States in Europe: A Legal Analysis* (Oxford: Clarendon Press, 1996) at 89.

[45] See *supra*, ch. 5, 2.2.

[46] The same approach seemed to have been put forward by Jacobs AG in his Opinion in *Richardt*, in which national export controls on dual-use goods were examined in the light of Art. 133 and the Export Reg.

[47] See Emiliou, *supra* note 39 at 73–5.

[48] Emphasis added.

[49] Para. 10 in *Leifer* and para. 10 in *Werner*.

ambit of Article 133 EC and only then, because of their objective, can they be justified on the basis of Community law exceptions. Either way, the outcome of the dispute is the same. What is important is how the exceptions recognised by Community law are interpreted by the Court. Indeed, a test broadly defining the scope of both CCP and its exceptions is not in effect considerably different from a restrictive approach to CCP and the exceptions recognised by Community law. This may explain the Court's reluctance to address directly the issues raised in the theoretical debate explained above.

In view of the foreign policy dimensions inherent in various commercial policy measures, the Court's approach on exports of dual-use goods indicates the limits of the instrumentalist/teleological theories regarding the scope of Article 133 EC. The extent to which a commercial policy measure serves a foreign policy objective cannot always be ascertained. Such rigid distinctions are not valid in the increasingly interdependent international environment. Therefore, if the CCP is deemed a part of a system of external relations, the focus must be on how the exceptional national competence will be reconciled with the principle of the Community's exclusive competence. The dual-use goods case law constitutes a clear illustration of this approach. On the one hand, by extending the scope of Article 133 EC in order to cover export restrictions on dual-use goods, the Court underlines the need for this category of measure to be regulated on the basis of common rules and hence for the ultimate aims of the common commercial policy to be achieved. On the other hand, it makes clear that, even though the effective realisation of the single market demands in principle the Community's exclusive competence under Article 133 EC, this exclusivity is to be interpreted in such a way as to take into account prevailing national concerns.[50]

5. THE IMPLICATIONS OF THE COURT'S APPROACH FOR THE LEGAL REGULATION OF EXPORTS OF DUAL-USE GOODS

The legal formula adopted by the Council regarding Council Regulation 3381/94 and Decision 94/942/CFSP, whereby the *modus operandi* of a Community system is incorporated into an instrument excluded from the Community legal order and the Court's jurisdiction, runs counter to the thrust of the Court's judgments. The latter made it clear that the foreign and security policy implications of a trade measure do not necessarily exclude it from the ambit of Community law. It was on this basis that exports of dual-use goods were viewed as within the CCP, while the public security proviso applied therein was interpreted broadly and the role of judicial control was limited. Viewed from this angle, the legal formula adopted in the case of the current Community regime on exports of dual-use goods is flawed and must be abandoned. This

---

[50] On the Court's pragmatism in its external relations case law, see T Tridimas and P Eeckhout, "The External Competence of the Community and the Case-Law of the Court of Justice: Principle versus Pragmatism" (1994) 14 *YEL* 143.

argument constitutes the very foundation for the Commission's proposals that, in amending Council Regulation 3381/94 and Decision 94/942/CFSP, the new rules must be based solely on Article 133 EC.[51] During the discussions in the relevant Working Group, certain concerns were expressed. It was argued that to accept the jurisdiction of the Court over the whole system of exports of dual-use goods would open the door to judicial interference in the area of foreign policy.

The Court's jurisprudence on exports of dual-use goods addresses this concern both effectively and convincingly. It makes it clear that in no way does the exercise of the Court's jurisdiction encroach upon the right of the Member States to assess whether their security is at risk; in ensuring that the legal effectiveness of Community law is in no way undermined, judicial control over deviation from the CCP on the basis of the public security protection is confined to cases of blatant disregard of Community law and violation of the principle of proportionality and alternative means. It does not follow that national courts are to dictate how foreign policy should be conducted by national governments. As Advocate General Jacobs stressed in his Opinion in *Commission v. Greece*, the subjective point of view of a Member State is of central importance in the assessment of foreign policy considerations.[52] It is for this reason that, consistently with the exercise of national competence, judicial control is limited to abuse of powers and manifest errors of appraisal. The Member States' competence to protect their national security would be safeguarded on a two-fold basis, namely the public security proviso of Regulation 3381/94 which is to be construed as encompassing both its internal and external aspects and the caution that the Court has demonstrated in *Richardt*, *Werner* and *Leifer* not to transgress the boundaries between national sovereignty and Community competence. In addressing these issues, the *Werner* and *Leifer* judgments rely on the intrinsic link characterising the trade and foreign policy dimensions of a measure and imply the following point: the conduct of foreign policy, lying beyond the Community legal framework and reserved to the Member States, and the protection of the effectiveness of Community law, entrusted to the Court, must be carried out within a single framework rather than rigidly compartmentalised ones. Viewed from this angle, the inter-pillar formula reflected in Regulation 3381/94 and Decision 94/942/CFSP is fundamentally flawed.

Having argued that the inter-pillar approach adopted in Regulation 3381/94 and Decision 94/942/CFSP must be abandoned, the following question arises: given the concerns expressed over its abolition, does its maintenance rule out an effective review of the legal problems raised by the current regime on exports of dual-use goods? In other words, is the protection of the legal effectiveness of Regulation 3381/49 dependent solely upon the adoption of the relevant rules under Article 133 EC?

The answer to this question is negative. In the light of the fundamental role of the principle of "full effectiveness of Community law" in the development of

[51] COM(1998)257 final at 4.
[52] *Supra* note 41 at paras. 54–56.

the Community legal order[53] and the intrinsic link between Regulation 3381/94 and Decision 94/942/CFSP, the justiciable nature of the Regulation may enhance the effectiveness of the Title V Decision. This entails that the Court may exercise its jurisdiction over the interpretation of the guidelines set by Decision 94/948/CFSP as a matter of Community law. It follows that, in so far as the guidelines set out in Annex III to Decision 94/94/CFSP are concerned, the adoption of the latter pursuant to Title V must not be considered sufficient to exclude it from the Court's jurisdiction under Article 46 TEU; it is, therefore, to be viewed as being incorporated by reference into Regulation 3381/94.[54] To argue otherwise would be tantamount to reducing Regulation 3381/94 into a mere implementing medium of Decision 94/942/CFSP and, hence, rendering its application an issue beyond the Community legal framework. This view is supported by Advocate General Jacobs' argument in *Centro-Com* about "[t]he need for measures adopted in the framework of the common commercial policy to be effective (the principle of effectiveness or *effet utile*)".[55] It is also supported by his conclusion that that "the interpretation of a Community act depends on its objectives, its terms and its context. The fact that it has a foreign or security policy dimension may therefore have an impact on its interpretation, but it does not in principle mean that the Member States have more leeway".[56] It follows that judicial protection over Regulation 3381/94, both directly under Article 226 and indirectly under Article 234, cannot possibly exclude consideration of the guidelines included in Decision 94/942/CFSP.[57]

However, one point of central significance must be clarified. The above analysis does not argue that the interdependence of any Title V measure and a Community instrument is to attribute to the former all the Community law qualities of the latter. An interesting comparison may be drawn with the case of economic sanctions on third countries: the Title V instrument pursuant to which a regulation is adopted under Article 301 EC expresses the political will of the Member States to have recourse to a Community measure. It is clearly implausible to argue that the Court may exercise its adjudicatory role over the expression of the political will of the Member States beyond the Community legal framework; it is only when the Member States choose to express their political will in a way which violates the constitutional principles of the Union and runs counter to Community law that the role of the Court becomes relevant. However, in the case of the common rules on export of dual-use goods, it is the

[53] Case C–213/89 R. v. *Secretary of State for Transport, ex parte Factortame Ltd and Others* [1990] ECR I–2433, [1990] 3 CMLR 1 at para. 21; Cases C–6 and 9/90 *Francovich and Bonifaci v. Italy* [1991] ECR I–5357, [1993] 2 CMLR 66 at para. 33; Cases C–46 and 48/93 *Brasserie du Pêcheur v. Germany and R v. Secretary of State for Transport, ex parte Factortame Ltd (III)* [1996] ECR I–1029, [1996] 1 CMLR 889 at para. 20.

[54] On how the Court may protect its jurisdiction in determining the broderline between the first and second pillars see *infra* at ch. 7, 5.

[55] Para. 53 of his Opinion.

[56] Para. 43 of his Opinion.

[57] See A von Bogdandy and M Nettesheim, "Ex Pluribus Unum: Fusion of the European Communities into the European Union" (1996) 2 *ELJ* 267 at 283.

intrinsic link between Regulation 3381/94 and Decision 94/942/CFSP which distinguishes them from other inter-pillar systems; to disregard this link would be tantamount to undermining the legal effectiveness of a Community law measure. In this context, the Court's control over any blatant misapplication of the relevant criteria is essential in order to ensure that the effectiveness of the *acquis communautaire* is not subject to extra-Community features and hence is not to become of symbolic significance.

6. CONCLUSION

Contrary to the rationale underpinning the current regime on exports of dual-use goods, the Court's dual-use goods jurisprudence is based on an approach which is progressive and functional in nature. Instead of approaching trade and foreign policy as two rigidly separate spheres of activities, the Court acknowledges their interactions and accommodates national concerns congruent with the conduct of foreign policy within the Community legal order. In doing so, it makes it clear that the effectiveness of Community law will be safeguarded, while the right of the Member States to determine whether their security is at risk will be fully respected. In this respect, the significance of the Court's dual-use goods jurisprudence is not confined to an alternative approach which may effectively address the fundamental flaws of the current regime of exports of dual-use goods; it also provides an indicator of how the Court is to exercise its jurisdiction at the margins of the Community legal order.

7

A Fully-fledged Approach to the Interactions between Trade and Foreign Policy: The Court's Case Law on Sanctions against Third Countries

1. INTRODUCTION

In viewing exports of dual-use goods as within the scope of the Common Commercial Policy while fully respecting the right of the Member States to determine whether their security is at risk, the Court adopted a dynamic approach to a specific aspect of interactions between trade and foreign policy. The question which then arises is whether this approach relies upon an isolated view of these increasingly interlinked areas of activity or constitutes a part of a coherent conception of how the interactions between Community law and the Common Foreign and Security Policy may be regulated within the constitutional order of the European Union. The Court's jurisprudence on sanctions against third countries illustrates that the latter is the case; in other words, it has developed a fully-fledged approach to the legally distinct, albeit interdependent, legal frameworks upon which the European Union is based as a functional whole. This approach draws upon the main principles laid down in Article 3 TEU, namely that the pillars are to operate within a single institutional framework which is to ensure the consistency of the activities of the Union and respect and build upon the *acquis communautaire*. The implications of the Court's approach are not confined to the scope of activities that the Member States may carry out beyond the Community legal framework and their relationship with their Community law duties. Quite significantly, in its case law on sanctions, the Court outlines its role as the constitutional guarantor of the principles underpinning the structure of the European Union, which must not be reduced to statements of rhetorical significance.

It must be pointed out that the Court's case law on sanctions against third countries has, so far, addressed problems arising from the implementation of sanctions regimes imposed under Article 133 EC pursuant to a decision adopted by the Member States within the framework of European Political Co-operation. However, the Court's conclusions are relevant to Article 301 EC, for this provision formalises the pre-Maastricht practice regarding the imposition of sanctions.

This chapter will be structured as follows. The first three parts will focus on the Court's case law on sanctions against third countries, while the fourth one will identify the thread that links these judgments and ascertain a fully-fledged approach to the interactions between trade and foreign policy. The fifth part will examine the Court's case law on sanctions in the light not only of its past jurisprudence but also its exceptional jurisdiction under Article 298 EC. Finally, the sixth part will focus on the extent to which the Court is prepared to exercise its jurisdiction at the margins of the Community legal order by determining the borderline between the pillars.

2. THE FIRST STEP: THE *BOSPHORUS* CASE

The first case that reached the Court in relation to sanctions against third countries dealt with an economic embargo imposed by the international community on Yugoslavia pursuant to a number of Security Council Resolutions. First, the embargo concentrated on weapons and military equipment under Resolution 713(1991), adopted on 27 September 1991.[1] Under Resolution 724(1991), a Committee was established to examine control and facilitate the implementation of the sanctions.[2] Then it covered trade and financial transactions pursuant to Resolution 757(1992), adopted on 30 May 1992.[3] Furthermore, under Resolution 787(1992), the sanctions covered the transshipment through the Federal Republic of Yugoslavia of various economically vital products, whereas Resolution 820(1993) provided for the freezing of funds belonging to or controlled by the authorities or undertakings in the Federal Republic of Yugoslavia

---

[1] Under para. 6, "all States shall, for the purposes of establishing peace and stability in Yugoslavia, immediately implement a general and complete embargo on all deliveries of weapons and military equipment to Yugoslavia until the Security Council decides otherwise following consultations between the Secretary-General and the Government of Yugoslavia".

[2] Under para. 5, this Committee consists of all the members of the Security Council, to which it is set to report on its work with its observations and recommendations. Its role is "(i) to examine the reports [submitted by all States in relation to the implementation of the embargo]; (ii) to seek from all States further information regarding the action taken by them concerning the effective implementation of the embargo; (iii) to consider any information brought to its attention by States concerning violations of the embargo, and in that context to make recommendations to the Council on ways of increasing the effectiveness of the embargo; (iv) to recommend appropriate measures in response to violations of the general and complete embargo on all deliveries of weapons and military equipment to Yugoslavia and provide information on a regular basis to the Secretary-General for general distribution to Member States".

[3] Under para. 4, this embargo covered all commodities and products originating in the Federal Republic of Yugoslavia and was applicable to their imports, any activities which would promote or are calculated to promote their export or transshipment, including any transfer of funds to the Federal Republic of Yugoslavia for the purposes of such activities or dealings, their sale or supply to any person or body in the Federal Republic of Yugoslavia or to any person or body for the purposes of any business carried out in or operated from the Federal Republic of Yugoslavia and any activities which promote or are calculated to promote such sale or supply. All states were required to apply this embargo in relation to all such activities carried out by their nationals or in their territory or using their flag vessels or aircraft. This embargo did not apply to supplies intended strictly for medical purposes and foodstuffs notified to the Sanctions Committee.

and elaborated on the provision of services and commercial maritime traffic. The latter Resolution was implemented at Community level through Council Regulation 990/93 concerning trade between the Community and the Federal Republic of Yugoslavia.[4]

2.1. The *Bosphorus* case—the facts

The *Bosphorus* case[5] reached the Court under the preliminary reference procedure at the request of the Irish Supreme Court[6] and dealt with the interpretation of Council Regulation 990/93 concerning trade between the Community and the Federal Republic of Yugoslavia.[7] Two aircraft owned by the Yugoslav National Airlines (JAT) were leased to Bosphorus Airways, a Turkish airline which thus acquired complete control over their management. Under Article 8 of the above-mentioned Regulation, "all vessels, freight vehicles rolling stock and aircraft in which a majority or controlling interest is held by a person or undertaking in or operating from the Federal Republic of Yugoslavia (Serbia and Montenegro) shall be impounded by the competent authorities of the Member States".[8] Under Article 9, "[a]ll vessels, freight vehicles, rolling stock, aircraft and cargoes suspected of having violated, or being in violation of, Regulation (EEC) No 1432/92 or this Regulation shall be detained by the competent authorities of the Member States pending investigations".[9]

The question referred by the Irish Supreme Court under the Article 234 procedure was whether the aircraft owned by an undertaking the majority or controlling interest in which was held by a Yugoslav undertaking but leased to an undertaking whose majority or controlling interests in which was not held by an undertaking in or operating from Yugoslavia was covered by Article 8 of Regulation 990/93.

2.2. The *Bosphorus* judgment

In order to answer this question, the Court held that "in interpreting a provision of Community law it is necessary to consider its wording, its context and its

---

[4] [1993] OJ L102/14.

[5] Case C–84/95 *Bosphorus Hava Yollari Turizm ve Ticaret AS* v. *Minister for Transport, Energy and Communications, Ireland and the Attorney General* [1996] ECR I–3953, [1996] 3 CMLR 257.

[6] For the ruling of the Irish High Court, the appeal against which before the Supreme Court resulted in the preliminary reference under consideration being made see [1994] 3 CMLR 464.

[7] [1993] OJ L102/14.

[8] Under this provision, "[e]xpenses of impounding vessels, freight vehicles, rolling stock and aircraft may be charged to their owners".

[9] The territorial and personal scope of the Reg. was defined under Art. 11 as "within the territory of the Community, including its air space and in aircraft or vessel under the jurisdiction of a Member State, and to any person elsewhere who is a national of a Member State and any body elsewhere which is incorporated or constituted under the law of a Member State". The date of its entry into force was 28 Apr. 1993.

aims".[10] In relation to the former, the Court held that nothing in the wording of Article 8 of Regulation 990/93 suggests that the management of an aircraft by an undertaking both alien to its owner and excluded from the personal scope of Regulation 990/93 can render the latter inapplicable in so far as the owner is covered by its scope.[11] This conclusion was supported by reference to the wording of Resolution 820(1993),[12] for "the Council gave effect to the decision of the Community and its Member States, meeting within the framework of political cooperation, to have recourse to a Community instrument to implement in the Community certain aspects of the sanctions taken against the Federal Republic of Yugoslavia by the Security Council of the United Nations".[13] Finally, the Court made reference to the aim of the Regulation in question, namely "to put pressure on [the Federal Republic of Yugoslavia]" and held that, had the management rather than ownership of the aircraft been the criterion rendering Regulation 990/93 applicable, "the effectiveness of the strengthening of the sanctions" would have been jeopardised.[14] This conclusion was based on the Court's interpretation of the "effectiveness of the strengthening of the sanctions [as consist[ing] in impounding all means of transport of the Federal Republic of Yugoslavia and its nationals, including aircraft, in order further to increase the pressure on that republic".[15] The Court added that "the mere transfer of day-to-day operation and control of means of transport, by a lease or other method, without transferring ownership would allow that republic or its nationals to evade application of those sanctions".[16]

The second issue that the Court examined was whether the above conclusion ran contrary, on the one hand, to the right of the undertaking which leased the aircraft in question to peaceful enjoyment of its property and its freedom to pursue a commercial activity and, on the other hand, the principle of proportionality. As for the fundamental rights invoked by Bosphorus, the Court referred to its previous case law which had established that "their exercise may be subject to restrictions justified by objectives of general interest pursued by the Community".[17] In this respect, it pointed out that trade sanctions by definition

---

[10] Para. 11.

[11] See para. 12.

[12] The Court held in para. 15 of the judgement that "it is not necessary for th[e owner of the aircraft in question] to have actual control of the aircraft. The word 'interest' in Paragraph 24 cannot, on any view, exclude ownership as a determining criterion for impounding. Moreover, that word is used in that paragraph in conjunction with the word 'majority', which clearly implies the concept of ownership"; in support of this conclusion, the Court makes reference to both most of the language versions of Regulation 990/93, which "use terms with explicit connotations of ownership" and Art. 8(2) of Reg. 990/93, according to which "the expenses of impounding aircraft may be charged to their owners", at para. 16.

[13] Para. 13.

[14] Para. 18.

[15] *Ibid.*

[16] *Ibid.*

[17] Para. 21; the Court referred to Case 44/79 *Hauer* v. *Land Rheinland-Pfalz* [1979] ECR 3727, [1980] 3 CMLR 42; Case 5/88 *Wachauf* v. *Bundesamt für Ernährung und Forstwirtschaft* [1989] ECR 2609, [1991] 1 CMLR 328; and Case C–280/93 *Germany* v. *Council* [1994] ECR I–4973.

affect economic rights of persons not responsible for the situation covered by the sanctions and added that "the importance of the aims pursued by the regulation at issue is such as to justify negative consequences, even of a substantial nature, for some operators".[18] The Court concludes that "[a]s compared with an objective of general interest so fundamental for the international community, which consists in putting an end to the state of war in the region and to the massive violations of human rights and humanitarian international law in the Republic of Bosnia-Herzegovina, the impounding of the aircraft in question, which is owned by an undertaking based in or operating from the Federal Republic of Yugoslavia, cannot be regarded as inappropriate or disproportionate".[19]

2.3. Comment on the *Bosphorus* judgment

The most significant feature of the *Bosphorus* judgment was the Court's approach towards Council Regulation 990/93 as fully within the Community legal order. Indeed, the Court's interpretation relied upon the assessment of the relevant provision's wording, context and aim, that is a method already underpinning the whole *corpus* of its case law. The important characteristic of this pattern lies upon its minimalistic application by the Court: the briefest of references was made to the Council Regulation's adoption pursuant to a decision of the Member States' Representatives within the framework of European Political Co-operation; furthermore, no reference whatever was made to whether this formula would give rise to issues of division of competence between the Member States and the Community. Hence, the issue of the extent to which judicial control could be exercised over a Community measure adopted pursuant to a decision beyond the Community legal framework was not directly addressed. It follows that the Community instrument's reliance upon a political decision adopted beyond the Community legal framework by no means undermines the judicial control to be exercised over its interpretation and application and, consequently, its status as a Community act.

The above issues would be likely to arise in relation to the Court's assessment of the objective of the Community Regulation. In contrast to the Court's brief reference to the aim of the sanctions as "put[ting] pressure on [the Federal

---

[18] Paras. 22–23. At para. 24, the Court explicitly refers to the preamble to Reg. 990/93 *supra* note 5; it also refers to its seventh recital, according to which "the Bosnian Serb party has hitherto not accepted, in full, the peace plan of the International Conference on the Former Yugoslavia in spite of appeals thereto by the Security Council". At para. 25 the Court goes on to note that "[i]t is in the light of those circumstances that the aim pursued by the sanctions assumes especial importance, which is, in particular, in terms of Regulation No 990/93 and more especially the eighth recital in the preamble thereto, to dissuade the Federal Republic of Yugoslavia from further violating the integrity and security of the Republic of Bosnia-Herzegovina and to induce the Bosnian Serb party to cooperate in the restoration of peace in this Republic".

[19] Para. 26.

Republic of Yugoslavia]", Advocate General Jacobs addressed the issue of interpretation of Resolution 820(1993) in detail.[20] He pointed out that "it is likely ... to be much more difficult to divine the precise purpose of a Community measure implementing a resolution of the United Nations Security Council than it would normally be to ascertain the purpose of an ordinary Community measure[, for w]hat is in issue is . . . the intention of the Security Council, an organ composed of many diverse States acting in highly charged political circumstances".[21] It was for this reason that he opined in favour of "a literal interpretation of the text [as] carry[ing] more weight".[22] In the light of this position and in relation to the "interest" referred to in paragraph 24 of the above Resolution, he argued that "[i]t is not possible to establish that, on the basis of the text of the resolutions, the requirement to impound means of transport was only intended to strengthen the trade embargo"[23]; therefore, he concluded that "it is by no means excluded that the Security Council intended to go further", namely "freezing assets abroad even if there is no immediate risk of their being used to circumvent the trade embargo".[24]

The literal interpretation expressly put forward by Advocate General Jacobs and impliedly relied upon by the Court was criticised as too positivist.[25] It was argued that the above approach was too restrictive and indicative of the Court's reluctance to have recourse to the teleological interpretation generally underpinning its case law; furthermore, the support apparently being given to the Commission's interpretation of the provision in question was criticised as

---

[20] Prior to the *Bosphorus* judgment, the Court had been asked to deal with the interpretation of a UN Security Council Resolution in Case 204/86 *Greece* v. *Council* [1988] ECR 5323. In this case, the Greek Government challenged the legality of the provision of financial assistance to Turkey under the Association Agreement signed in 1971. One of the arguments put forward by the Greek Government relied upon a number of UN Security Council Resolutions condemning the Turkish invasion and occupation of the northern part of Cyprus. The Court refused to address this argument, for "it is sufficient to observe that the resolution of the Security Council of the United Nations . . . is completely extraneous to relations between the Community and Turkey in the context of the Association" (para. 28). The legality of this aid was again challenged in Case 30/88 *Greece* v. *Council* [1989] ECR 3711.

[21] Para. 40 of his Opinion.

[22] *Ibid.* Jacobs AG also referred to the Commission's observations, according to which it would be "hazardous to attempt to assess the exact purposes of the Security Council's decision".

[23] This was the argument of the High Court judge, *supra* note 7 at para. 18, according to whom "[s]urely the purpose of the regulation is to deprive the guilty party of recourse to the aircraft, vehicle or whatever mode of transport is involved and which could itself be used to transport goods in breach of the embargo imposed by the regulations". Hence, he had concluded that "the 'interest' referred to in Article 8 [of Regulation 990/93] is essentially the interest in possession or the right to enjoy control or regulate the use of the asset rather than an income derived from it".

[24] Para. 39 of his Opinion. In this respect, Jacobs AG referred to the written observations submitted by the defendants, according to which the object of the sanctions provision in question might be "to deprive the Yugoslav undertaking in a case such as the present of even the indirect benefit of the fact that a means of transport will continue to operate and continue to be maintained and insured".

[25] See I Canor, " 'Can Two Walk Together, Except They Be Agreed?'. The Relationship Between International Law and European Law: The Incorporation of United Nations Sanctions Against Yugoslavia Into European Community Law Through the Perspective of the European Court of Justice" (1998) 35 *CMLRev.* 137 at 145–9.

demonstrating the Court's deference to the executive.[26] This criticism is misplaced for three reasons. First, the exercise of the judicial function is by no means associated with the rejection of the arguments put forward by the executive. To argue otherwise would be tantamount to transforming a judgment on the substance and the implications of the dispute in question into the outcome of an inter-institutional conflict devoid of legal significance. Secondly, the criticism of the literal interpretation of the Regulation and Resolution adopted by both the Advocate General and the Court as positivist ignores its substantive implications. In relying upon the literal interpretation of the wording of the Regulation provision in question and ultimately that of the Resolution provision, Advocate General Jacobs in effect construed the objectives of Resolution 820 (1993) in broad terms. Indeed, it was the general wording of the term "interest" that led the Court to hold Regulation 990/93 applicable to all potential means, direct and indirect, of accruing benefit to the Federal Republic of Yugoslavia. Thirdly, the critique referred to above ignores the legal implications of the Court's approach. In having recourse to Resolution 820(1993), the Court raises an important legal issue, namely the extent to which it has jurisdiction under the Treaty to provide an authoritative interpretation of Security Council Resolutions.[27] In this respect, a distinction must be made. In practical terms, it is indeed questionable why both the Advocate General and the Court deemed it necessary to refer to Resolution 820(1993) in order to support their interpretation of Article 4 of Regulation 990/93, for the wording of the two provisions is identical. Be that as it may, it would be nonsensical in legal terms to argue that the Court may not seek to ascertain the goals of the United Nations Security Council Resolution whose implementation has been rendered a matter of Community law under a Council Regulation. In seeking to ascertain the main objectives of the sanctions imposed by the United Nations, the Court does not transgress the boundaries of jurisdiction set out in the Treaty. This is illustrated in its general stance regarding the relationship between Community law in general and public international law. Having consistently held that Community competences must be exercised in accordance with international law,[28] the Court's adjudication upon the latter has inevitably involved an assessment of the rules and the objectives of the former. This is *a fortiori* the case in relation to legally binding international obligations imposed on all Member States under the United Nations Charter and being implemented by means of a Community measure, hence becoming part of the Community legal order.

---

[26] *Ibid.* at 157–8.

[27] See N Burrows, "Caught in the Cross-Fire", (1997) 22 *ELRev.* 170 at 172 who argues that the Court's interpretation is in no way more valid than that adopted by national courts.

[28] See Cases C–286/90 *Poulsen/Diva* [1992] ECR I–6019 and C–61/94 *Commission* v. *Germany* [1996] ECR I–3989.

3.   A STEP FURTHER: THE *CENTRO-COM* CASE

It was argued above that, in its *Bosphorus* judgment, the Court put forward a minimalistic approach toward the interpretation of Community measures adopted pursuant to a political decision by the Member States beyond the Community legal framework and implementing international obligations imposed upon them by the United Nations Security Council Resolution. This approach consisted, on the one hand, of analysing the Community measure under consideration as fully within the Community legal framework and, on the other hand, the Court's reluctance to formulate general principles dealing with the extent to which the political source of the Regulation affected its interpretation and application. The following analysis will indicate that, in response to the second preliminary reference on the interpretation of a sanctions regulation, the Court took up the opportunity offered by the questions referred by the national court and provided an answer to how the external relations of the Union can be viewed within the current constitutional framework of the Union.

The ruling of the Court in *The Queen, ex parte Centro-Com Srl v. HM Treasury and Bank of England*[29] was delivered under the preliminary reference procedure at the request of the English Court of Appeal[30] and dealt with the interpretation of Regulation 1432/92,[31] amended by Regulation 2015/92,[32] prohibiting trade between the Community and the Republics of Serbia and Montenegro in implementation of Resolution 757(1992).[33]

Centro-Com was an undertaking which had obtained the approval of the United Nations Sanctions Committee and the authorisation of the Italian authorities to export 15 consignments of pharmaceutical goods and blood-testing equipment from Italy to Montenegro. Payment had been agreed to be debited to a bank account held by the National Bank of Yugoslavia with Barclays Bank in Great Britain. Pursuant to an Order adopted by Great Britain in order to implement the above Resolutions and Regulation, Centro-Com had to be given permission from the Treasury before its account could be credited.[34]

---

[29]   Case C–124/95 [1997] ECR I–81.

[30]   The High Court judgment was published in [1994] 1 CMLR 109.

[31]   [1992] OJ L151/4, adopted on 1 June 1992.

[32]   [1992] OJ L205/2.

[33]   In its preamble, Reg. 1432/92 [1992] OJ L151/4 makes reference to UN Security Council Res. 757(1992). Reg. 1432/92 make reference to "the prolonged direct and indirect activities of the Republics of Serbia and Montenegro in and with regard to the Republic of Bosnia-Herzegovina [which] are the main cause for the dramatic developments in the [latter]"; it also adds that "a continuation of these activities will lead to further unacceptable loss of human life and material damage, and to a breach of international peace and security in the region". Furthermore, it points out that "the President of the Republic of Bosnia-Herzegovina has asked the international community to assist his country against the intervention of the Republics of Serbia and Montenegro in the internal affairs of the [former]".

[34]   This Order was adopted on 4 June 1992 under s. 1(1) of the UN Act 1946. It is Art. 10 which is at issue, according to which: "[e]xcept with permission granted by or on behalf of the Treasury, no person shall (a) make any payment or part with any gold, securities or investments; or (b) make any

Eleven of the 15 applications submitted by Centro-Com were approved and hence the account held by the Yugoslav Bank was debited on the basis of the policy of the Treasury to provide such authorisation irrespective of the country authorising the export of products for medical and humanitarian purposes in so far as the procedure laid down in the applicable Resolutions was followed. However, after reports of abuse of the authorisation procedure followed by the Sanctions Committee, the Treasury decided to allow payment from Serbian and Montenegrin funds held in United Kingdom only in cases of exports actually made from the United Kingdom.[35]

The question asked by the Court of Appeal was the following: in the light of the Common Commercial Policy in general and the Sanctions Regulation in particular which allows that products classified by the United Nations Sanctions Committee as intended for strictly medical purposes be exported to Serbia and Montenegro provided that they are authorised by the competent authorities of a Member State, is it lawful under Community law for a Member State to prevent Serbian or Montenegrin accounts located in its territory from being debited in order to pay for goods exported pursuant to the above procedure unless the export in question is authorised by this Member State's competent authorities and actually takes place from its territory? It is the far-reaching significance of the Court's judgment that requires detailed examination.

3.1. The requirement of consistency with Community law

The Court first addressed an argument put forward by the British Government, that national measures adopted in order to ensure the effective application of sanctions are covered by national competence in the field of foreign and security policy and in relation to the performance of national obligations under the United Nations Charter and the United Nations Resolutions; in this respect, the British Government maintained that the validity of these measures could not be affected by either the exclusive competence enjoyed by the Community under Article 133 EC or the Sanctions Regulation whose role is confined to

---

change in the persons to whose credit any sum is to stand or to which order any gold, securities or investments are to be held, where any such action is action to which this article applies. (2) Action to which this article applies is action which is likely to make available to or for the benefit of any person connected with Serbia and Montenegro any funds or other financial or economic resources, whether by their removal from the United Kingdom or otherwise, or otherwise to remit or transfer funds or other such resources to or for the benefit of any person connected with Serbia and Montenegro. (3) Any permission granted by or on behalf of the Treasury under this article may be granted either absolutely or subject to conditions and may be varied or revoked at any time by, or on behalf of the Treasury".

[35] The reason for this change of policy was the conviction of the British authorities that they could thereby "exercise effective control over goods exported to Serbia and Montenegro so as to ensure that the goods exported actually matched their description and that no debiting of accounts held with British banks was authorized for payments for non-medical or non-humanitarian purposes": para. 16 of the judgment.

"implementing at Community level the exercise of Member States' national competence in the field of foreign and security policy".[36]

This argument was answered by the straightforward statement of the Court that "the powers retained by the Member States must be exercised in a manner consistent with Community law".[37] The Court repeated the principle already spelled out in *Werner*[38] that the foreign policy and security objectives of a national measure whose effect is to prevent or restrict the export of certain products cannot render it outside the scope of the Common Commercial Policy.[39] Furthermore, the Court stressed that "[i]t was indeed in the exercise of their national competence in matters of foreign and security policy that the Member States expressly decided to have recourse to a Community measure, which became . . . Regulation [990/93], based on Article [133] of the Treaty".[40]

3.2. The issue of compatibility with the Common Commercial Policy

The Court then addressed a second argument put forward by the British Government, according to which national measures imposing restrictions on the release of funds are not measures of commercial policy and, hence, are excluded from the common commercial policy.

The Court did not examine whether the measure in question constituted a measure of commercial policy; instead, it examined whether its adoption was inconsistent with the common commercial policy "if and insofar as [it] contravene[s] Community legislation adopted in pursuance of [the common commercial policy]".[41] The Court pointed out that, whereas Regulation 990/93 prohibited exports to Serbia and Montenegro and hence deviated from the Community export regime adopted under Article 133, exports of products for strictly medical purposes satisfying the conditions set out under Articles 2(a) and 3 of Regulation 990/93 are not covered by this Community deviation and hence are regulated by the Exports Regulation.[42] Having stressed that restrictions on the release of funds held at a bank do constitute quantitative restrictions on

---

[36] Para. 23 of the judgment.

[37] Para. 25; the Court referred to Joined Cases 6/69 and 11/69 *Commission* v. *France* [1969] ECR 523; [1970] CMLR 43 at para. 17; Case 57/86 *Greece* v. *Commission* [1988] ECR 2855 at para. 9; Case 127/87 *Commission* v. *Greece* [1988] ECR 3333 at para. 7; and Case C–221/89 *Factortame and Others* [1991] ECR I–3905, [1991] 3 CMLR 589 at para. 14.

[38] Case C–70/94 *Fritz Werner Industrie-Ausrustungen GmbH* v. *Federal Republic of Germany* [1995] ECR I–3189 at para. 10.

[39] See para. 26 of the judgment.

[40] Para. 28. The Court further added in para. 29 that "[a]s the preamble to the Sanctions Regulation shows, that regulation ensued from a decision of the Community and its Member States which was taken within the framework of political cooperation and which marked their willingness to have recourse to a Community instrument in order to implement in the Community certain aspects of the sanctions imposed on the Republics of Serbia and Montenegro by the United Nations Security Council".

[41] Para. 32.

[42] See paras. 33–6.

exports to third countries and hence fall within the scope of Regulation 2603/69,[43] the Court proceeded to examine the British argument that the adoption of the measure in question was justified on grounds of public security.[44] The Court, while accepting the British argument that the measure in question fell within the public security proviso of Article 11 of the Regulation 2603/69, held that national recourse to this exceptional provision is not justified "if Community rules provide for the necessary measures to ensure protection of the interests enumerated in that article".[45] The Court held that "effective application of the sanctions can be ensured by other Member States' authorization procedures, as provided for in the Sanctions Regulation, in particular the procedure of the Member State of exportation"[46] and concluded that "the Member States must place trust in each other as far as concerns the checks made by the competent authorities of the Member State from which the products in question are dispatched".[47] Furthermore, the Court stressed the exceptional character of Article 11 of Regulation 2603/93 and held that "it must, on any view, be interpreted in a way which does not extend its effects beyond what is necessary for the protection of the interests which it is intended to guarantee".[48] In this respect, it was held that "a Member State may secure the protection of the interests involved by measures less restrictive of the right to export than a requirement that all goods should be exported from its territory. So, where a Member State has particular doubts about the accuracy of descriptions of goods appearing in an export authorization issued by the competent authorities of another Member State, it may, in particular, before giving authorization for accounts held in its territory to be debited, have resort to the [collaboration procedures between national administrative authorities established under Community law]".[49]

---

[43] See paras. 39–42. The Court, contrary to the argument put forward by the British Government, referred to the definition of measures of equivalent effect to quantitative restrictions on exports within the meaning of Art. 1 of Reg. 2603/69 [1969] OJ L324/25 given in *Werner, supra* note 38 at para. 22 and Case C–83/94 *Criminal Proceedings against Peter Leifer and Others* [1995] ECR I–323 at para. 23. The Court held that the measure in question "is an essential element of the export transaction" (para. 41) and "[its] application precludes the making of payments in consideration of the supply of goods dispatched from other Member States and thus prevents such exports" (para. 42).

[44] The British Government argued that the measure allowing the release of Montenegrin funds for exports of products for medical purposes only in so far as the products in question are actually exported from the British territory pursuant to an export authorisation granted by the competent British authorities in order to ensure that the sanctions are applied effectively "since it allows the United Kingdom authorities themselves to check the nature of the goods exported to Serbia and Montenegro" (para. 44).

[45] Para. 46; the Court made reference to Case 72/83 *Campus Oil and Others* v. *Minister for Industry and Energy* [1984] ECR 2727, [1984] 3 CMLR 544 at para. 27 in relation to the public security proviso under Art. 30 EC.

[46] Para. 48.

[47] Para. 49. The Court added that there was no evidence suggesting that the system established under Reg. 990/93, namely the requirement for the exporter to notify the export of products strictly for medical purposes to the Sanctions Committee and seek export authorisation from the competent authorities of the exporting Member State, was malfunctioning.

[48] Para. 51.

[49] Para. 52; the Court referred to the procedure estabilised by Council Reg. 1468/81 of 19 May 1981 on mutual assistance between the administrative authorities of the Member States and

3.3. The issue of the justification of national export restrictions under Article 307 EC

The Court then addressed the second question submitted by the Court of Appeal, namely whether the British restriction on release of Montenegrin funds were justified under Article 307 EC.[50] The Court made reference to its previous *Evans* judgment[51] which clarified the aim of this provision by identifying the commitment of Member States to comply with obligations arising under international agreements predating the EC Treaty; accordingly, it held that the British measure preventing Montenegrin funds in the United Kingdom from being released unless the export in question has been authorised by the competent British authorities and the export actually takes place from British territory may by justified under Article 307 only in so far as it is necessary in order to enable Great Britain to perform its obligation under the United Nations Charter and Security Council Resolution 757(1992).[52] Despite the determination of whether this is the case being left to the national court to make, the Court pointed out that "when an international agreement allows, but does not require, a Member State to adopt a measure which appears to be contrary to Community law, the Member State must refrain from adopting such a measure".[53]

3.4. Comment on the *Centro-Com* judgment

In *Centro-Com*, the Court formulated with greater clarity and force what had already been spelled out in *Werner* and *Leifer*, namely that, in the exercise of their competence within the foreign and security policy domain, Member States must conform with Community law. In putting forward this principle, the Court expressly relied upon its formulation in previous case law.[54] However, it is of interest to ascertain whether the context in which it was introduced was similar to that in *Centro-Com*. The Court makes reference to two judgments regarding monetary measures, the former dealing with a preferential rediscount rate for exports granted by a Member State in favour of national products exported to other Member States[55] and the latter with interest rebates on export

cooperation between the latter and the Commission to ensure the correct application of the law on customs or agricultural matters [1981] OJ L144/1.

[50] Art. 307 EC reads as follows: "The rights and obligations arising from agreements concluded before the entry into force of th[at] Treaty between one or more Member States on the one hand, and one or more third countries on the other, shall not be affected by the provisions of th[at] Treaty".

[51] Case C–324/93 R. v. *Secretary of State for the Home Department, ex parte Evans Medical Ltd. and MacFarlane Smith Ltd* [1995] ECR I–563.

[52] See paras. 57–59.

[53] Para. 60; the Court also referred to the *Evans* judgment *supra* note 51.

[54] See para. 25 of the judgment.

[55] Joined Cases 6 and 11/69 *Commission* v. *French Republic* [1969] ECR 523.

credits.[56] Furthermore, the Court makes reference to its *Factortame* judgment,[57] whereby the same principle was expressed in relation to the competence left to Member States to determine the conditions for the registration of vessels.

In relying upon the above judgments in order to substantiate the duty of the Member States to conduct their foreign and security policy consistently with Community law, the Court may become subject to criticism. It may be accused of extending the application of the principle that national competence be conducted in accordance with Community law over the sphere of foreign policy on the basis of an arbitrary parallelism. Indeed, it may be argued that the phrase "the powers retained by the Member States" that the Court has recourse to in all the above cases is too general to cover areas so inherently diverse as the competence to adopt measures of monetary character and that of conducting foreign and security policy. This argument draws upon the qualitatively different nature of the above spheres of activities, for the latter touches directly and unequivocally upon the national sovereignty of Member States.

Two counter-arguments may be put forward to refute the above suggestion. The first one relies upon the rationale of the Court's proposition that the conduct of foreign and security policy by Member States be consistent with Community law. It is suggested that this arguably consists of the inherently indeterminate character of any attempt to distinguish with clarity and precision the foreign policy implications of a trade measure in the increasingly globalised post-Cold War international environment. The judgment of the Court is regrettably short on this point, in contrast to the Opinion of Advocate General Jacobs, who succinctly argued that "[m]any measures of commercial policy may have a more general foreign or security policy dimension. When for example the Community concludes a trade agreement with Russia, it is obvious that that agreement cannot be dissociated from the broader political context of the relations between the European Union, its Member States, and Russia".[58] In the light of the foreign policy implications inherent in most trade measures, to rely upon them in order to absolve the Member States from their Community law obligations would be tantamount to undermining the effectiveness of Community law. In this respect, it is interesting to note the observation made by Advocate General Jacobs in its Opinion that "[t]he interpretation of a Community act depends on its objectives, its terms and its context. The fact that it has a foreign or security policy dimension may therefore have an impact on its interpretation, but it does not in principle mean that the Member States have more leeway".[59]

A second argument supporting the Court's reliance upon previous case law in elaborating the requirement that the conduct of foreign policy be compatible

---

[56] Case 57/86 *Greece* v. *Commission* [1988] ECR 2855.

[57] Case C–221/89 *The Queen* v. *Secretary of State for Transport, ex parte Factortame Ltd and Others* [1991] ECR I–3905.

[58] Para. 41 of his Opinion in *Centro-Com supra* note 29.

[59] Para. 43 of his Opinion.

with Community law lies upon its position within the Court's relevant jurisprudence. The Court did not spell out this proposition in isolation; had this been the case, the principle under consideration would have been cryptic, incomplete in terms of its legal reasoning and of questionable significance in practical terms. Instead, the principle that Member States conduct their foreign and security policy consistently with Community law constitutes a part, albeit a central one, of a more general and consistent approach towards the external relations of the Union.

This approach may be understood as the Court's response to two principal, albeit conflicting, claims regarding an inter-pillar approach to the legal regulation of sanctions. The first holds that the instrumentalisation of Community law measures pursuant to political decisions adopted by the Member States beyond the Community framework may open the door to judicial intervention in a sphere in which Member States retain their competence to act. In elaborating upon the principle that Community law be the outer limit of the exercise of national competence over the sphere of foreign and security policy, the Court effectively addresses this concern. It makes it clear that it is not the expression of the political will of the Member States beyond the Community legal framework that is subject to the Court's control, but the extent to which Community law in general and the Common Commercial Policy in particular are affected by the expression of the political will of the Member States. This distinction is of the utmost importance and is highlighted by the Court itself; indeed, it specifies that it is the *exercise* of the powers retained by the Member States in the foreign and security policy domain in general and their express decision to have recourse to a Community measure in particular that give rise to the requirement of respect for Community law. At a more general level, the Court's determination not to be drawn into an examination of the expression of the political will of the Member States beyond the Community legal framework is clearly illustrated in its approach to the formula whereby sanctions are imposed on third states. The arrangement whereby Article 133 EC was relied upon only following a political decision beyond the Community legal order was not questioned by the Court, the absence of an express Treaty provision notwithstanding. Already relied upon regarding the imposition of sanctions on third countries since the early 1980s, this arrangement preceded not only the introduction of the Maastricht Treaty but also that of the Single European Act. Indeed, it is suggested that it was the introduction of Article 301 EC into the Maastricht Treaty, which attributed to this practice Treaty status, that deterred the Court from actually examining the validity of this arrangement in respect of its repercussions over the application of Community law in general and the Common Commercial Policy in particular.[60]

---

[60] See the annotation on *Centro-Com* and *Ebony Maritime* by C Vedder and H-P Folz, (1998) 35 *CMLRev*. 209 at 215. It is interesting to note that the judgment itself makes no reference to either Art. 301 or Art. 60 EC, as opposed to the Opinion of Jacobs AG.

The contrasting argument on the formal interactions between the Community legal framework and the foreign and security policy impliedly addressed by the Court may be summarised as follows. Given the different nature of the decision-making process under the Community legal framework and the CFSP and the different normative effect of the decisions adopted thereunder, a decision under the latter to have recourse to a Community law measure would undermine the legal integrity of the former. In substantive terms, this might be due to the fact that the genesis of a Community measure beyond the Community legal order might question the judicial control likely to be exercised over its application and interpretation. The Court made it clear that a Community measure to which recourse had been made following a decision in the framework of European Political Co-operation is to be treated as entirely within the Community legal order. Therefore, the fact that the Community measure finds its political source beyond the Community framework by no means undermines its status as a Community act or renders its interpretation and application impervious to judicial control. An illustration of how this principle is understood by the Court is provided by the pattern it followed in respect of Regulation 1432/92 imposing sanctions on Serbia and Montenegro. It identified its objectives, namely "[the] achieve[ment of] a peaceful solution to the situation in Bosnia-Herzegovina, which forms a threat to international peace and security"[61]; then, it examined them in relation to the national measure which, pursuant to the public security proviso of the Export Regulation, purported to serve them. It proceeded by setting them against the procedures already set out in Regulation 1432/92 and the extent to which they ensure the fulfilment of these objectives. Having determined that they do so properly, it opined that consistency with the restrictive interpretation stemmed from the exceptional nature of the public security proviso of the Export Regulation and the proportionality principle applicable thereto requires that Member States have recourse to "measures less restrictive of the right to export than a requirement that all goods should be exported from its territory".[62] Significantly, the Court confined this to cases raising national concerns regarding the achievement of the aims of the Regulation 1432/92 that lie upon "particular doubts about the accuracy of descriptions of goods appearing in an export authorization issued by the competent authorities of another Member State",[63] whereby recourse to Community rules on collaboration between national administrative authorities should be had.

---

[61] *Supra* note 29 at para. 45.
[62] *Ibid.* at para. 52.
[63] *Ibid.*

4. THE COURT'S APPROACH FULLY APPLIED: THE *EBONY MARITIME* CASE

In the *Ebony Maritime* case,[64] a vessel, owned by one of the plaintiffs carrying cargo owned by the other, began to take on water while sailing the Adriatic Sea. It sent out signals indicating that it had changed its route and headed towards the Montenegrin coast in order to run aground. However, while the vessel was still on the high seas, the Dutch crew of a NATO/WEU helicopter which landed on its deck and took charge, changed course and handed the vessel over to the Italian authorities in Brindisi.

Regulation 990/93 prohibited both the entry into the territorial sea of the Federal Republic of Yugoslavia by all commercial traffic[65] and all activities whose object or effect would be to promote directly and indirectly any transaction covered by the Regulation.[66] Furthermore, under Article 10 of the Regulation the Member States are to determine the penalties imposed upon infringement of its provisions.[67]

4.1. The *Ebony Maritime* judgment

Before engaging in the analysis of the issues put forward by the *Consiglio di Stato*, the Court examined the scope of Regulation 990/93 relying heavily upon the wording of the applicable provisions, namely the references to the prohibition on entry into the territorial sea of the Federal Republic of Yugoslavia by all commercial traffic in Article 1(1)(c), the detention of all vessels suspected of or engaging in violation of the embargo by the competent national authorities under Article 9 and the confiscation of such vessels upon the establishment of the violation under Article 10. In interpreting the wording of these provisions as rendering the occurrence of the violation outside the territorial jurisdiction of a Member State irrelevant to the scope of Regulation 990/93, the Court relied upon United Nations Security Council Resolution 820(1993) itself and the identical wording of its paragraph 25 in order to support the above conclusion. Hence, it concluded that Regulation 990/93 is applicable "to all vessels suspected of having breached the sanctions imposed against the Federal Republic of Yugoslavia, even if they are flying the flag of a non-Member country, belong to non-Community nationals or companies, or if the alleged breach of sanctions occurred outside Community territory".[68]

---

[64] Case C–177/95 *Ebony Maritime SA and Loten Navigation Co. Ltd.* v. *Prefetto della Provincia di Brindisi and Ministero dell' Interno* [1997] ECR I–1111, [1997] 2 CMLR 24.

[65] See Art. 1(1)(c).

[66] See Art. 1(1)(d).

[67] Art. 10. Moreover, the Member States whose authorities have detained vessels, freight vehicles, rollingstock, aircraft and cargoes which violated the Reg. may forfeit them.

[68] Para. 18. Therefore, the territorial scope of Reg. 990/93, defined under its Art. 11, was interpreted as referring to the detention of the vessels in question once they are within the territorial

The Italian court asked whether Regulation 990/93 was applicable to the following two situations: first, to a vessel flying the flag of a non-Member State, navigating in international waters and belonging, along with its cargo, to a non-Community undertaking; secondly, to conduct which there is sufficient reason to believe constitutes an attempt illicitly to enter the territorial sea of the Federal Republic of Yugoslavia. The Court answered both these question in the affirmative, relying upon the effectiveness of the sanctions imposed by Regulation 990/93 and emphatically concluded that "[a]ny other interpretation would risk rendering the prohibition [of any entry whatever of commercial traffic into the territorial sea of the Federal Republic of Yugoslavia] ineffective".[69]

The last question asked by the referring Italian court was whether a national provision prescribing compulsory or discretionary confiscation of the cargo carried by any means of transport covered by Regulation 990/93 was lawful under Article 10 of that Regulation. The Court answered this question in the affirmative by referring, in the absence of any provision regarding confiscation of cargo in the Italian version of Article 10, to the translation given in other official languages. Furthermore, the Court made express reference to Security Council Resolution 820(1993), which was intended to be implemented by Regulation 990/93 in general and its paragraph 25 in particular, mentioned above. Finally, the Court examined the argument put forward by the applicants in the main proceedings that the Italian provision in question, on the one hand, imposes a system of strict criminal liability, hence running counter to the principle *nulla poena sine culpa* and, on the other hand, it violates the principle of proportionality by unjustifiably penalising the owner of the cargo in the same way as the owner of the vessel. The Court held that a system of strict criminal liability in relation to breach of a regulation had already been accepted as not being in itself incompatible with Community law[70] and further stated that it was for the national court to determine whether the penalty in question was indeed effective, proportionate and dissuasive. However, the Court pointed out that, in

jurisdiction of a Member State (para. 19). In support of this argument, the Court pointed out that "the prohibition on entry into the territorial sea of the Federal Republic of Yugoslavia . . . can be breached only outside Community territory" (para. 17). It also supported this conclusion by reference to Security Council Resolution 920 (1993), whose para. 25 states that "all States shall detain pending investigation all vessels . . . and cargoes found in their territories and suspected of having violated or being in violation of Resolution 713(1991), 757(1992) and 787(1992) or the present Resolution, and that, upon a determination that they have been in violation, such vessels . . . shall be impounded and, where appropriate, they and their cargoes may be forfeit to the detaining State".

[69] Para. 25. According to the Court, this conclusion was supported by the broad scope of the prohibition of Art. 1(1)(d) of Reg. 990/930 [1993] OJ L102/14.

[70] See Case C–326/88 *Hansen* [1990] ECR I–2911 at para. 19. In relation to this point, the Court made reference to its previous case law consistently stating that in the absence of a Community rule specifically providing for a penalty or referring to national rules, Member States are under a Community law duty based on Art. 5 EC to determine the penalties to be imposed while ensuring that "infringements of Community law are penalised under conditions, both procedural and substantive, which are analogous to those applicable to infringements of national law of a similar nature and importance and which, in any event, make the penalty effective, proportionate and dissuasive".

carrying out the above task, the national court should take into account "that, the objective pursued by the Regulation, which is to bring an end to the state of war in the region concerned and the massive violations of human rights and humanitarian international law in the Republic of Bosnia-Herzegovina, is one of fundamental general interest for the international community".[71]

4.2. Comment on the *Ebony Maritime* judgment

The *Ebony Maritime* judgment was criticised for extending Community jurisdiction into areas which cannot be covered by it and, hence, running counter to customary international law, whereby "a vessel on the High Seas is subject only to the regulatory jurisdiction of the flag State".[72] An examination of the consistency of the Court's ruling with customary international law is excluded from the scope of this book.[73] It is the consistency of the Court's approach with that already followed in the *Bosphorus* and *Centro-Com* judgments that is of relevance to the argument put forward in this chapter. The point of reference of the *Ebony Maritime* judgment is the relevant UN Security Council Resolution and the Court's approach is underpinned by two strands: first, reference to the objectives of the sanctions imposed thereunder in the broadest terms and, second, literal interpretation of the terms of the Resolution so as not to restrict in any way the scope of its application. In other words, the Court adjudicated upon the issues before it by approaching, in interpretive terms, the United Nations Security Council Resolution in the least interventionist way.

The above reading of the case law on exports of dual-use goods and sanctions on third countries does not imply that it was merely serious national concerns that the Court addressed in its rulings. On the contrary, it engaged in a broad construction of the Community legal order and did not enable foreign political considerations, often inherent in the adoption of the Community measures in question, to dilute the latter's normative characteristics, namely their application in pursuance of their full effectiveness and subject to judicial control and their interpretation consistently with the principles underpinning Community law. It was in the light of this consideration that the Court applied its interpretive technique of focusing on the wording, the context and the objectives of the Community measure under consideration; in doing so, it sought to assess the objectives of a measure otherwise, that is in the absence of its implementation by means of a Council Regulation, excluded from its jurisdiction, namely a UN Security Council Resolution.

---

[71] Para. 38.

[72] *Supra* note 60 at 221 *et seq.*

[73] For a comment on *Ebony Maritime* in terms specifically of the application of the universality principle of jurisdiction to Community circumstances see N Burrows, Reinforcing International Law, (1998) 23 *ELRev.* 79.

A counter-argument against the above contentions may hold that the Court's apparently minimalistic approach towards the UN Security Council Resolutions conceals its attempt to achieve maximalistic objectives, namely effectively to extend its jurisdiction and, in principle, establish its authority over areas of activities beyond the Treaty framework. These areas would directly touch upon the action of Member States on the international scene as fully sovereign subjects of international law. This argument ignores the fact that the interpretation of the UN Security Council resolution, that is the expression of the political will of the Member States beyond the Treaty, was rendered a matter directly relevant to the Court's jurisdiction by the Member States' decision to implement the resolution by means of an Article 133 regulation. In the light of this consideration, there is no basis for arguing that the Court's ruling, along with the previous ones dealing with sanctions, further a hidden agenda to transform the Community judicature into the ultimate adjudicator upon the international actions of the Member States.

5. THE EMERGENCE OF A FULLY-FLEDGED APPROACH TO THE LINKAGE BETWEEN TRADE AND FOREIGN POLICY

In its jurisprudence dealing with, on the one hand, exports of dual-use goods and, on the other hand, sanctions imposed under a United Nations Security Council resolution and implemented by the Member States pursuant to an Article 133 Regulation, the Court has addressed the legal issues raised by the adoption of trade measures with significant foreign policy implications. Before the thread linking the Court's judgments on these two instances of interaction between the Community legal order and the CFSP is analysed, the thrust of the Court's approach will be recalled. In relation to the judgments on exports of dual-use goods, the main elements of the Court's approach may be summarised as follows. First, in the light of the increasing instrumentalisation of trade measures for foreign policy objectives and the increasingly interdependent international environment, both the Common Commercial Policy of the Community and the concept of public security upon which the Member States may justify their deviation from Article 133 are broadly construed. Secondly, the discretion enjoyed by the Member States in determining the measures they deem necessary in order to protect their security is fully taken into account. Thirdly, the role of national courts is confined to examining whether, in deviating from the Common Commercial Policy, the public security proviso has been legitimately invoked and the principles of proportionality and alternative means complied with by national authorities. As regards sanctions against third countries, the main principles underpinning the Court's approach may be outlined as follows. First, notwithstanding their adoption pursuant to a decision taken in the framework of European Political Co-operation, the Community regulations adopted under Article 133 were approached by the Court as fully within the Community legal order. Secondly, the interpretive method that this approach entails, namely an assessment of the wording, the context and the objectives of the measures in question, leads to the examination of the goals pursued by the UN Security Council Resolution which the Community measure under consideration implements. Thirdly, in examining the UN Security Council measure, the Court demonstrates great reluctance to restrict in any way its scope, hence rendering the effectiveness of the sanctions imposed thereunder its prevailing interpretative aim.

The combined effect of the principles underlying the Court's case law on exports of dual-use goods and sanctions against third countries contributes to the construction of an approach which would ultimately establish "a system of external relations" of the European Union within its current constitutional framework.[74] In doing so, the Court does not merely seek to strike a balance between two spheres of competence, namely, the exclusive competence enjoyed by the Community over its Common Commercial Policy and that shared by the Member States within the *sui generis* framework of Title V in order to pursue a common foreign policy. A third sphere of competence enjoyed by the Member States in areas which remain beyond the reach of both the EC Treaty and Title V as they currently stand must be taken into account in terms of the effect that its exercise may have upon Community law. While approaching these levels of competence, the Court relies upon the following guiding principle: the inherent link between trade and foreign policy entails that they cannot be viewed as rigidly compartmentalised spheres of activities. Applying this principle to the legal frameworks within which these areas are regulated, it follows that the Community legal order and the CFSP, legally distinct though they are, must be viewed in functional terms. This entails their construction in such a way as to ensure that they perform a variety of legal functions: protect the effectiveness of Community law and build upon the *acquis communautaire*, respect the expression of the political will of the Member States under the procedures provided in the second pillar and respect the right of the Member States to determine whether their security is at risk.

Can this approach provide a legally coherent, realistically effective and politically sensible view of the legal regulation of trade measures with significant foreign and security policy dimensions? The Court has answered this question in the affirmative. Its dual-use goods jurisprudence ensures the effectiveness of the CCP while safeguarding the right of the Member States to determine whether their security is at risk. The Court's jurisprudence on sanctions against third countries ensures that Community law is not undermined by the conduct of the foreign policy of the Member States without interfering with the substance of the political will of the Member States expressed beyond the Community legal

---

[74] In Case 22/70 *Commission* v. *Council (ERTA)* [1970] ECR 263, [1971] CMLR 335 at para. 18, the Court referred to the system of external relations of the Community which may not be separated from that of internal Community measures. It is suggested that reference to this notion is not without significance, for it may be understood as denoting the substantive coherence and the consistent application which must characterise the external relations of the Community.

framework. The construction of the external relations as a "system" by the Court is also evident in its broad interpretation of the duty of co-operation imposed on the Member States. The core of this duty is encapsulated in Article 10 EC, which provides that the Member States "are to take all appropriate measures, whether general or particular, to ensure fulfilment of the obligations arising out of th[e EC] Treaty" and to "facilitate the achievement of the Community's tasks".[75] In the field of external relations, this duty was underlined and refined in *Opinion 1/94* in cases where the Member States' competence in the area of external trade relations is shared with that of the Community. The Court held that "it is essential to ensure close co-operation between the Member States and the Community institutions, both in the process of negotiation and conclusion and in the fulfilment of the commitments entered into. That obligation to co-operate flows from the requirement of unity in the international representation of the Community".[76] Viewed from this perspective, the *Centro-Com* requirement that the Member States' conduct of their foreign policy must be consistent with Community law further develops a thread seeking to weave the external relations of the Union into a "system".

In the light of the Court's approach to the interactions between trade and foreign policy, the debate over the pillar-structure of the European Union has become redundant. Indeed, in consolidating the pillar-structure, the Amsterdam Treaty illustrates that, unless the constitutional model of the Union is drastically changed, there will always be a core of activities performed by the Member Sates beyond the Community legal order.[77] Therefore, the question which must be addressed is not whether this should be the case, for the answer would rely upon inherently indeterminate criteria, often extraneous to legal analysis, such as political ideas underpinning the construction of a political union, internal political developments of the Member States, the foreign relations systems developed by other collective international actors. Instead, the question which must be addressed is whether, given that the pillar structure of the Union is a legal reality, a viable framework is provided within which neither the status of Member States as fully sovereign subjects of international law is diminished nor the competence of the Community and the effectiveness of its policies undermined. In answering this question in the affirmative, the Court relies heavily upon the principles the Treaty itself sets out, namely "the consistency and the continuity of the activities carried out [by the Union and ensured by the single

[75] On Art. 10 EC and its interpretation by the Court, see O Due, "Article 5 du traité CEE. Une disposition de caractére federal" in *Collected Courses of European Law* (Dordrecht: Martinus Nijhoff, 1991); J Temple Lang, "The Core of the Constitutional Law of the Community—Article 5 EC" in L Gormley (ed.), *Current and Future Perspectives on EC Competition Law. A Tribute to Professor M.R. Mok* (London: Kluwer Law International, 1997) 41 and "Community Constitutional Law: Article 5 EEC Treaty" (1990) 27 *CMLRev*. 645.

[76] *Opinion 1/94 (World Trade Organisation Agrement)* [1994] ECR I–5267, [1995] 1 CMLR 205 at para. 108.

[77] Dashwood writes that "[n]o longer . . . can the division between EC external competence and the CFSP be regarded as merely temporary" in External Relations Provisions of the Amsterdam Treaty: (1998) 35 *CMLRev*. 1019 at 1020.

institutional framework] in order to attain its objectives while respecting and building upon the *acquis communautaire*".[78] Indeed, the Court does not view the requirement of consistency as merely connoting the absence of contradictions between the Community framework and the second pillar; instead, it approaches the issue of the interaction of Community competence and the specific aspects of national sovereignty related to foreign policy and security as within a single, albeit multipolar, framework whose operation depends upon the synergy between its component parts, namely the first and second pillars. Having dealt with the requirement of a single institutional framework as a legal reality, the Court's jurisprudence renders concerns over a gradual and implied transfer of Community policies to the intergovernmental pillars[79] largely irrelevant.

In practical terms, the Court's construction of the interactions between trade and foreign policy and, essentially, the Community legal framework and the CFSP assure the institutional actors of the Union and the Member States alike that the constitutional choices regarding the delimitation of powers between the Member States, the Community and the Union which underpin both the Maastricht and Amsterdam Treaties will not be challenged by the Community judiciary. In the context of the jurisprudence analysed above, this is illustrated in the Court's approach towards those issues which essentially involved the expression of the political will of national authorities. Indeed, in relation to the assessment by the Member States of whether their public security was at stake, the Court pointed out the discretion they enjoyed and, consequently, the limited degree of judicial control that could be exercised over their conclusions as a matter of Community law. Furthermore, the Court did not question at all the choice made by the Member States to recourse being had to a Community measure in the area of sanctions against a third country pursuant to a decision reached beyond the Community legal framework. In addition, while seeking to ascertain the objectives of the UN Security Council Resolution implemented by a Community measure before it, the Court did not seek to engage in an active attempt to impose in any way the UN Security Council measure, that is the expression of the collective will of the Member States in their capacity as fully sovereign subjects of international law.

6. THE COURT'S DYNAMIC APPROACH WITHIN THE BROADER CONTEXT OF ITS JURISPRUDENCE

The dynamic approach that the Court put forward in approaching exports of dual-use goods and sanctions on third countries must not be viewed in isolation. It is in full accordance with the view it has adopted in other trade disputes with

[78] Art. 3 TEU.
[79] See D Obradovic, "Repatriation of Powers in the European Community" (1997) 34 *CMLRev,* 59 and, specifically, in relation to exports of dual-use goods and trade sanctions against third countries at 69–70.

significant foreign policy implications. Furthermore, it is supported by the elaborate analysis of Advocate General Jacobs in the only case that reached the Court under its exceptional jurisdiction provided for in Article 298 EC regarding cases in which a Member State deviates from Community law as a whole under extraordinary circumstances.

6.1. Early indications of the Court's approach

The Court's interpretive approach in cases with considerable foreign policy dimensions is by no means a novelty in the Community legal order. In its *Anastasiou* judgment[80] the Court indicated the parameters which would prove central to its subsequent interpretation of cases dealing with trade sanctions on third countries. In that case, a number of producers from the Republic of Cyprus challenged before the High Court the practice followed by English national authorities to accept origin and phytosanitary certificates issued by the self-proclaimed "Turkish Republic of Northern Cyprus" as valid under the 1977 Protocol regarding products originating from Cyprus[81] and Council Directive 77/93/EEC on protective measures against the introduction into the Community of organisms harmful to plants or plant products[82] respectively. A preliminary reference was made by the English High Court essentially asking the Court whether, following the Turkish invasion of the northern part of Cyprus, the unilateral declaration of an independent state recognised by neither the Member States nor any other member of the international community required a broad interpretation of the terms of the Association Agreement and the Phytosanitary Certificates Directive. The British Government and the Commission argued that origin and phytosanitary certificates issued by the Turkish-occupied part of Cyprus should be accepted as valid with the above Community legislation, mainly because the Association Agreement was concluded in order to be valid to the Cypriot territory and also, given that under Article 5 of the Agreement no discrimination should be exercised between nationals or companies of Cyprus, the population of the northern part of Cyprus should not be deprived from the benefits of the Association Agreement.[83]

---

[80] Case C–432/92 *The Queen* v. *Minister of Agriculture, Fisheries and Food, ex parte S.P. Anastasiou (Pissouri) Ltd and Others* [1994] ECR I–3087, annotated by M Cremona in (1996) 33 *CMLRev*. 125 and N Emiliou in (1995) 20 *ELRev*. 202.

[81] This protocol defining the concept of "originating products" and providing for methods of administrative co-operation between the Community and national authorities and Cypriot authorities was incorporated in Council Reg. 2907/77 on the conclusion of the Additional Protocol to the Agreement establishing an Association between the European Economic Community and the Republic of Cyprus [1977] OJ L339/1. The original Association Agreement between the Community and Cyprus was adopted under Council Reg. 1246/73 [1973] OJ L133/1.

[82] [1977] OJ L26/20.

[83] The Commission also relied upon the Opinion of the International Court of Justice on Namibia [1991] ICJ Reports 16, in which it was held that, following the illegal administration of Namibia by South Africa, the sanctions imposed on the latter should not deprive the population of the former of any advantages derived from international cooperation.

The Court's ruling may be summarised as follows. First, having determined the direct effect of the 1977 Protocol on origin, it held that strict adherence to the rules set out therein was required, the repercussions of the *de facto* partition of Cyprus on the application of this Agreement notwithstanding. The Court held that the non-recognition of the self-proclaimed state in the northern part of Cyprus[84] excluded the possibility of mutual reliance and recourse being had to administrative co-operation between the latter's authorities and those of the Member States at the level envisaged under the 1977 Protocol.[85] To hold otherwise would constitute, according to the Court, "denial of the very object and purpose of the system established by the 1977 Protocol".[86] Secondly, the Court held that the non-discrimination clause of Article 5 of the Association Agreement does not entail a broad interpretation of the 1977 Protocol on origin, for the proper functioning of the administrative co-operation between the authorities of the Member States and Cyprus is crucial to the proper operation of the Association Agreement. What is of direct relevance to the argument put forward in this chapter is the Court's reference, in addition to various arguments supporting its conclusion,[87] to the need to "ensure uniform application of the Association Agreement in all the Member States".[88] The Court referred to Article 31 of the Vienna Convention on the Law of Treaties, under which in the interpretation of an international treaty due regard must be taken of the object and purpose of this treaty and of subsequent practice in its application, and concluded that the approach of the Member States towards origin and phytosani-

---

[84] It is suggested that the Court seemed somewhat confused when, referring to the self-proclaimed state of the northern part of Cyprus, it said that it is recognised "*neither* by the Community *nor* by the Member States" in para. 40 (emphasis added). The possibility of the Community recognising a State under international law separately from its Member States may not be easily envisaged. However, this confusion seems quite justified in the light of the past practice which hardly clarifies the issue of recognition by the Member States in legal terms. Indeed, in relation to the recognition of the states resulting after the dissolution of the Federal Republic of Yugoslavia, the new Republics were recognised by "the Community and its Member States" pursuant to a decision adopted in the framework of European Political Co-operation; on this legal entanglement see *supra* ch. 2, 2.4.

[85] The Court held in para. 39 of its judgment that the relationship between the competent authorities of the exporting state and those of the importing state should be based on "total confidence in the system of checking the origin of products as implemented by the competent authorities of the exporting State" and that "the importing State [must be] in no doubt that subsequent verification, consultation and settlement of any disputes in respect of the origin of products or the existence of fraud will be carried out efficiently with the cooperation of the authorities concerned".

[86] *Ibid.* at para. 41.

[87] In this respect, the Court referred to the following three points. First, it held in para. 45 that, on several occasions, the whole population of Cyprus has benefited from advantages stemming from the Association Agreement, especially in relation to the financial protocols concluded pursuant to the Agreement. Secondly, from Art. 3 of the Agreement, according to which the Community is under a duty to refrain from jeopardising the achievement of the aims of the Agreement, the Court concluded in para. 46 that no means of proof of the origin of products other than that expressly provided for in the 1977 Protocol may be unilaterally adopted by the Community; if other means are to be accepted as valid, this should be done, account being taken of the Community's contractual partner, that is the Republic of Cyprus and within the framework of the institutions established under the Association Agreement itself.

[88] *Ibid.* para. 54.

tary certificates issued by the authorities of the northern part of Cyprus was far from uniform. The Court concluded that "[t]he existence of different practices among the Member States thus creates uncertainty of a kind likely to undermine the existence of a common commercial policy and the performance by the Community of its obligations under the Association Agreement".[89] It is noteworthy that, contrary to the Opinion by Advocate General Gulmann which stressed the lack of uniform practice amongst the Member States and its repercussions on the Common Commercial Policy in emphatic terms,[90] the Court's ruling was regrettably short on this issue.

In dealing with an issue of a seemingly technical nature but essentially of considerable political significance, the Court adopted a cautious approach. This is illustrated in a two-fold way: on the one hand, in relying upon its premise that "Article 5 [of the Association Agreement] cannot in any event confer on the Community the right to interfere in the internal affairs of Cyprus[, for] the problems resulting from the *de facto* partition of the island must be resolved exclusively by the Republic of Cyprus, which alone is internationally recognised",[91] the Court was very reluctant to depart from the express wording of the Association Agreement; in doing so, it avoided being called upon to resolve a dispute with essentially political repercussions that the Member States themselves were unable or unwilling to deal with. It is not without significance that the Court totally ignored the argument put forward by the Greek Government that the acceptance of certificates from the Turkish occupied northern part of Cyprus would be tantamount to violating a number of Resolutions adopted by the United Nations Security Council that condemn the Turkish occupation and urge all members of the international community not to recognise the self-proclaimed state. This leads to the second main feature of the Court's ruling, that is its reliance on the practice followed by the Member States in relation to the origin and phytosanitary certificates issued from the northern part of Cyprus. In relying upon the lack of uniformity, the Court managed to justify its reluctance to adopt too active an approach to the interpretation of the Association Agreement while making clear that the positions of the Member States are fully taken into account.

[89] *Ibid.* para. 53. The Court also referred in para. 51 to the express position of the Republic of Cyprus, according to which only products accompanied by certificates issued by its official Government should be imported in the Community under the terms of the Association Agreement and to its contrast to the Commission's practice.

[90] In para. 62 of his Opinion, he argued that "[i]t would . . . be a significant factor with regard to [the] interpretation [of the Association Agreement] if it could be assumed that the Member States had, in fact, in the period after the problem arose, accepted certificates of origin issued by authorities other than the competent R[epublic] O[f] C[yprus] authorities". Furthermore, dealing with the significance of this lack of uniformity in relation to the CCP, Gulmann AG argued that "it is unacceptable . . . for Community rules to be interpreted and applied in different ways in the Member States, unless there is a clear basis otherwise. In the area of common commercial policy it is especially important for the Community rules to be treated uniformly, because application of the law of the importing State can directly affect other Member States as a consequence of the free movement of products in the internal market" (para. 66).

[91] *Ibid.* para. 47.

The relevance of this approach to that subsequently adopted by the Court in relation to unilateral restrictions on exports of dual-use goods and the interpretation of Community regulations implementing at Community level trade sanctions imposed pursuant to United Nations Security Council Resolutions is clear: the Court provided a legally sensible solution to a dispute with important foreign policy repercussions by ensuring the uniformity and effectiveness of Community law, taking fully into account the positions shared by the Member States and intervening as little as possible in an issue which was highly charged in political terms.

6.2. The exceptional jurisdiction of the Court under Article 298(2) EC

The Court's approach to unilateral restrictions on exports of dual-use goods and trade sanctions on third countries was viewed as the exercise of judicial review over disputes with foreign policy implications rather than foreign policy review. It is suggested that this approach of the Court is supported not only by the general principles underpinning the constitutional order of the Union but also by the exceptional jurisdiction it enjoys under the EC Treaty on issues touching upon the very core of national sovereignty. Under Article 298(2) EC, "by way of derogation from the procedure laid down in Articles 222 and 227, the Commission or any Member State may bring the matter directly before the Court of Justice if it considers that another Member State is making improper use of the powers provided for in Articles 296 and 297. The Court of Justice shall give its ruling *in camera*".[92] The interpretation of this provision in relation to Article 296 will be dealt with elsewhere.[93] It is its application in the context of Article 297 which is of relevance here.

The only precedent regarding recourse to the Article 298 EC procedure was the action brought by the Commission against Greece regarding the economic and trade sanctions imposed by the latter against the Former Yugoslav Republic of Macedonia (FYROM).[94] The Greek Government claimed that the embargo in question was justified under Article 297 EC, whereas the Commission argued that the latter provision had been improperly used.[95] That case has not been decided upon by the Court, for an agreement between Greece and FYROM was

[92] Art. 297 reads as follows: "Member States shall consult each other with a view to taking together the steps needed to prevent the functioning of the common market being affected by measures which a Member State may be called upon to take in the event of serious internal disturbances affecting the maintenance of law and order, in the event of war or serious international tension constituting a threat of war, or in order to carry out obligations it has accepted for the purpose of maintaining peace and international security".

[93] See *infra* at ch. 8, 4.4.

[94] Case C–120/94 *Commission* v. *Greece (Former Yugoslav Republic of Macedonia)* [1996] ECR I–1513.

[95] For the detailed arguments put forward by both parties, see *The European Commission's action before the ECJ following the counter-measures adopted by the Hellenic Republic against F.Y.R.O.M.* (in Greek) (Athens: A.N. Sakkoulas, 1996) at 13–183.

reached before the Court's judgment. However, in his Opinion, Advocate General Jacobs stressed the following three points as underpinning the role of the Court under Article 298(2) EC: first, the determination of whether the conditions laid down in Article 297 are met clearly constitutes a justiciable issue. Not only did Advocate General Jacobs explicitly mention this, but he also examined whether the first of the grounds justifying national action under Article 297 was met, namely a serious internal disturbance affecting the maintenance of law and order.[96] Secondly, the nature of the determination of a complex foreign policy issue, such as the existence of war or serious international tension constituting a threat of war, "severely limit[s] the scope and intensity of the review that can be exercised by the Court" due to "a paucity of judicially applicable criteria"[97] and hence renders the judicial control over such matters of "extremely limited nature".[98] Thirdly, it follows from the above two points that the determination of the valid use of the rights conferred under Article 297 EC is dependent to a great extent upon the subjective point of view of the Member State concerned.[99]

The arguments of Advocate General Jacobs that the determination of issues of extreme national importance, while being a matter for the national government, is not beyond the Court's jurisdiction, exceptional though it may be under Article 298(2) EC, proceeds on the assumption that the role of the Court is confined to ensuring that this determination, and hence any deviation from the Treaty, will involve neither manifest errors nor abuse of powers. This is illustrated by the very carefully worded conclusion of his Opinion: first, to the subjective view expressed by the Greek government, he added reference to various objective factors, namely "the geopolitical environment and . . . the history of ethnic strife, border disputes and general instability that characterised the Balkans for centuries, including of course the series of armed conflicts that have engulfed the former Yugoslavia in recent years"; then, he concluded that "Greece is [not] acting wholly unreasonably by taking the view that the tension

---

[96] Jacobs AG argued that "Greece has failed to establish that in the absence of the trade embargo decreed against FYROM civil disturbances would take place on such a scale that the means at its disposal for maintaining law and order would be insufficient" in *supra* note 94 at para. 48, and concluded that "Greece has not in fact come anywhere near establishing the massive breakdown of public order needed to justify recourse to Article [297] on grounds of serious internal disturbances affecting the maintenance of law and order" at para. 49.

[97] *Ibid.* at para. 50.

[98] *Ibid.* at para. 60.

[99] *Ibid.* at paras. 54–56, where Jacobs AG argues that under Arts. 297 and 298, the Court must ascertain "whether in the light of all the circumstances" a Member State "c[an] have . . . some basis for considering, from its own subjective point of view" that one of the three conditions laid down in Art. 297 is fulfilled. Jacobs AG stresses that "the question must be judged from the point of view of the Member State concerned. Because of the differences of geography and history each of the Member States has its own specific problems and preoccupations in the field of foreign and security policy. Each Member State is better placed than the Community institutions or the other Member States when it is a question of weighing up the dangers posed for it by the conduct of a third State. Security is, moreover, a matter of perception rather than hard fact."

between itself and FYROM bears within it the threat—even if it may be long-term and remote—of war".[100]

The line of reasoning followed by Advocate General Jacobs in his Opinion in the *FYROM* case clearly suggests that, in exercising the right provided for under the wholly exceptional rule of Article 297, the Member States are not to act entirely beyond judicial control; the scope for deviation provided for under the Treaty, considerably wide though it may be, cannot amount to abuse of powers.[101] The relevance of this argument, recently reaffirmed in quite strong terms by Advocate General La Pergola in *Sirdar*,[102] in relation to the Court's adjudication upon unilateral restrictions on exports of dual-use goods and trade sanctions on third countries is clear: if national competence in a sphere touching upon the very core of national sovereignty, as in the case of Article 297, is to be exercised subject to the minimum substantive and procedural guarantees set out by the Treaty, trade measures with foreign policy components must *a fortiori* be applied and interpreted consistently with the requirement of respect for the *acquis communautaire*, in both cases account being taken of the relevant political context by the Court.

---

[100] *Ibid.* at para. 56.

[101] An interesting point, though one not related to the subject under consideration, deals with the procedure set out under Art. 297. In the light of the "wholly exceptional character of this provision", repeatedly and consistently stated by the Court, e.g. in Case 13/68 *Salgoil SpA* v. *Italian Ministry for Foreign Trade* [1968] ECR 453 at 463 and Case 222/84 *Marguerite Johnston* v. *Chief Constable of the Royal Ulster Constabulary* [1986] ECR 1651, [1986] 3 CMLR 240 at paras. 26–27, it is suggested that adherence to the procedure set out thereunder be a condition of legality of the invocation of this clause by a Member State. Furthermore, this procedure must be construed restrictively, hence consisting of consultation between the Member States carried out, prior to the adoption of the unilateral measures and in a way which does not constitute a mere formality. It is regrettable that Jacobs AG did not address this issue at all in his Opinion, despite the fact that the Greek government had not adhered to the procedure. *Cf.* C Stefanou and H Xanthaki, *A Legal and Political Interpretation of Articles 224 and 225 of the Treaty of Rome: The Former Yugoslav Republic of Macedonia Cases* (Aldershot: Dartmouth and Ashgate, 1997).

[102] Case C–273/97 *Angela Maria Sirdar* v. *The Army Board and Secretary of State for Defence* [1999] 3 CMLR 559. This case was an Art. 234 reference by an Industrial Tribunal and one of the questions referred was whether Art. 297 EC may justify deviation from the Equal Treatment Dir. 76/207 [1976] OJ L39/40 during peacetime and/or in preparation for war. In his Opinion, La Pergola AG stressed that the judicial review provided under Art. 298 "is a power of review clearly conferred on the Court in the fullness of its attributes as the judicial body which guarantees compliance with Community law" (para. 26); he then went on construe Art. 297 in strict terms, for, given "the qualified nature of the exception provided for [thereunder], . . . by bringing the normal organisation of the armed forces within the ambit of [that provision], . . . , the Member States would be authorised to apply the exception in a practically 'normal' manner, thereby unduly extending the scope within which the rule providing for that exception can be invoked" (para. 27). However, the issue of the interpretation of Article 297 EC was not raised by the Court. For a comment on *Sirdar* and the subsequent Case C–285/98 *Tanja Kreil* v. *Bundesrepublik Deutschland* of 11 Jan. 2000, not yet reported, see P Koutrakos, "EC Law and Equal Treatment in the Armed Forces" (2000) 25 *ELRev.* 433. For reliance upon Art. 297 in relation to employment in armed forces see A Arnull, "EC Law and the Dismissal of Pregnant Servicewomen" (1995) 24 *Industrial Law Journal* 215 at 233–4.

7. THE EMERGENCE OF THE FUNCTIONAL JURISDICTION OF THE COURT:
ADJUDICATING UPON THE PILLARS

The main thrust of the argument put forward so far may be summarised as follows. The Court's judgments on exports of dual-use goods and trade sanctions against third countries exemplifies an approach to the interactions between trade and foreign policy both coherently constructed and consistently applied: on the one hand, by avoiding general statements regarding its role within the constitutional order of the Union, the Court examined the compatibility of the expression of the political will of the Member States, put forward either unilaterally or under the umbrella of the precursor of the Common Foreign and Security Policy, that is European Political Co-operation, with the principles underpinning the constitutional order of the Union; on the other hand, the Court was acutely aware not only of the wide degree of discretion enjoyed by national authorities when decisions with foreign policy implications are to be made, but also of the political context within which these decisions are taken and, hence, the inherently limited role of the judiciary. In doing so, the Court renders the European Union a functional legal framework within which trade and foreign policy may be conducted by distinct actors with overlapping competence in a legally sensible and effective way.

The Court's jurisprudence, as outlined above, begs the question who is entitled to ensure that the constitutional order of the European Union will indeed operate as a dynamic interrelated system of rules. Having approached the trade and foreign policy issues that underpin the Union's external relations as a fully-fledged system within the existing framework established under the TEU, it delivered a judgment which displays in no uncertain terms its intention to determine where the dividing line between the pillars lie.

This judgment was delivered in relation to an action brought by the Commission under Article 230 challenging the validity of a Joint Action adopted by the Council under Article K.3(2) of the Maastricht Treaty.[103] The measure in question provided for harmonised rules on granting airport transit visas and the Commission's action was based on its contention that such rules should have been adopted under the then Article 100c (now repealed) of the EC Treaty rather than Title VI TEU. This was a clear case in which the Court was called upon to adjudicate on the dividing line between the pillars and could not do so without examining the content of the Title VI measure.

As far as the admissibility of the Commission's action was concerned, the Court held that "[i]n accordance with Article [46] . . . , the provisions of the EC Treaty concerning the powers of the Court of Justice and the exercise of those

---

[103] Case C–170/96 *Commission* v. *Council*, [1998] ECR I–2763, [1998] 2 CMLR 1092. The Commission's action was supported by the European Parliament. Art. 100c EC dealt with visas to nationals of third countries crossing the external borders of the Member States.

powers apply to Article [47] of the Treaty on European Union";[104] given that the latter provision "makes it clear that a provision such as Article K.3(2) . . . does not affect the provisions of the EC Treaty",[105] the Court concluded that it "has jurisdiction to review the content of the Action in the light of ex-Article 100c of the Treaty in order to ascertain whether the Action affects the powers of the Community under that provision and to annul the Action if it appears that it should have been based on Article 100c of the EC Treaty".[106]

Despite the fact that the Court rejected the Commission's action on substantive grounds,[107] its judgment is of immense significance. It confirmed that, in relation to Title VI, the mere adoption of a measure beyond the Community framework does not automatically render it immune to judicial control, for this would be tantamount to enabling Member States to ignore the legal bases provided under the Treaty for the adoption of legislation.[108] In this respect, the Court's ruling reflects the widely supported view in academic circles that it falls within the Court's jurisdiction to ensure that no measure adopted under the procedures provided in Title V threatens the *acquis communautaire*.[109] In the light of the combined effect of these provisions, the Court's role entails an assessment of where the dividing line between the pillars lies and, in practical terms, inevitably consists of indirectly exercising its jurisdiction over measures brought before it for having been adopted under the wrong legal framework.

[104] *Ibid.* at para. 15.
[105] Art. 47 TEU provides that "nothing in this Treaty shall [a]ffect the Treaties establishing the European Communities or the subsequent Treaties and Acts modifying or supplementing them".
[106] *Ibid.* at para. 17. Fennelly AG had argued that the Commission's action was inadmissible "as the Court has no jurisdiction under Article [230] of the Treaty to review the legality of a Council act which falls outside the sphere of the Community competence": para. 46 of his Opinion. However, this conclusion was not based on adoption of the Joint Act under the third pillar, but on its content being outside the scope of Art. 100c(1) EC.
[107] The Court held that Art. 100c EC "applies to measures concerning the crossing of Member States' external borders by nationals of third countries only in so far as they relate to the entry into and movement within the internal market by those nationals who must, for that purpose, be in possession of a visa", the phrase "crossing the external borders of the Member States" being interpreted as referring, "in the case of an airport, to the crossing of those borders at a border control point, permitting the holder of the visa to enter and to move within the internal market". However, Art. 1 of the Joint Action in question "presupposes that the holder [of a visa provided under that instrument] will remain in the international area of th[e] airport [of a Member State] and will not be authorised to move within the territory of that Member State". Therefore, the Court concluded that the subject matter of the Joint Action in question did not fall within the scope of Art. 100c EC and dismissed the Commission's action. For a comment on the substance of the judgment, see the annotation of A Oliveira in (1999) 36 *CMLRev.* 149.
[108] See the references of Fennelly AG to the previous case law illustrating the Court's functional approach on this issue at paras. 12–15 of his Opinion.
[109] P Allott, Written Evidence to the *House of Lords Scrutiny of the Intergovernmental Pillars of the European Union* (1992–93) HL 124 at 50; M Cremona, "The Common Foreign and Security Policy of the European Union and the External Powers of the European Community" in D O'Keeffe and P Twomey (eds), *Legal Issues of the Maastricht Treaty* (London: Chancery Law, 1994) 247 at 256; A Dashwood (ed.), *Reviewing Maastricht. Issues for the 1996 IGC* (Cambridge: LBE, 1996) 218; I MacLeod, ID Hendry and S Hyett, *The External Relations of the European Communities* (Oxford: Clarendon Press, 1996) at 414; and JHH Weiler, "Neither Unity Nor Three Pillars—The Trinity Structure of the Treaty on European Union" in J Monar, W Ungerer and W Wessels (eds.), *The Maastricht Treaty on European Union. Legal Complexity and Political Dynamics* (Brussels: European Interuniversity Press, 1993) 49 at 53.

Furthermore, by accepting the admissibility of the Commission's claim, the Court raised an issue of considerable constitutional significance: in implementing the principle of consistency within the single institutional framework of the Union, the latter's institutions must respect the *acquis communautaire* not as a proclamation of merely rhetorical significance but as a principle adherence to which is to be controlled by the Court. In practical terms, this entails that it is the role of the Court to ensure that no measure adopted under Title V undermines either the powers of institutions within the Community legal order or the procedural rules regarding the adoption of Community measures or the latter's substantive content.[110]

However, the *Airport Transit Visa* judgment must not be construed as an attempt by the Court to exercise an all-encompassing jurisdiction. In this respect, it is recalled that in the *Gomis* case, it declined to respond to a preliminary reference by a Spanish court on, amongst others, Article 2 of the Maastricht Treaty, holding that it "clearly has no jurisdiction to interpret that article in the context of such proceedings".[111]

8. CONCLUSION

In adjudicating upon disputes which arose out of unilateral restrictions on dual-use goods and trade sanctions on third countries, the Court has been called upon essentially to address two questions: first, is there "a zone of twilight"[112] between what the Community is exclusively competent to do and what the Member States are sovereign to do and, secondly, if the answer is affirmative, to what extent can the Court ensure that the limits on both the Community and the Member States will be applied as envisaged in the Treaty?

In addressing the first question, the Court clearly implied that there are no tightly compartmentalised spheres of activity and, consequently, the issue of competence between the Community and the Member States should be resolved accordingly. In the light of the increasingly interdependent and globalised post-Cold War international environment, this assertion may seem self-evident;

---

[110] The significance of the *Airport Transit Visa* judgment is illustrated in the argument that, in accordance with Case 314/85 *Foto-Frost (Firm)* v. *Hauptzollamt Lübeck-Ost* [1987] ECR 4199, [1988] 3 CMLR 57, national courts are under a duty to make a reference under Art. 234 EC on the validity of a measure adopted under the second or third pillar: see DM Curtin and IG Dekker, "The EU as a 'Layered' International Organization: Institutional Unity in Disguise" in P Craig and G de Búrca (eds.), *The Evolution of EU Law* (Oxford: OUP, 1999) 83 at 123.

[111] Case C–167/94 *Juan Carlos Grau Gomis and Others* [1995] ECR I–1023 at para. 6.

[112] This expression was used by Supreme Court Justice Rehnquist in order to describe a sphere of activities in which the President and Congress may have concurrent authority or in which its distribution is uncertain; cited in T Franck, *Political Questions/Judicial Answers. Does the Rule of Law Apply to Foreign Affairs?* (Princeton, NJ: Princeton University Press, 1992) at 74. In the context of the European Union, the less evocative but more valid term "parallel competences" was used by I Govaere and P Eeckhout, "On Dual Use Goods and Dualist Case Law: The *Aimé Richardt* Judgement on Export Controls" (1992) 29 *CMLRev.* 941 at 963 to denote the fact that both the Community and the EU are competent regarding export controls.

indeed, taking into account the unlimited scope of the areas of foreign and security policy covered by the CFSP,[113] to argue that it is to be pursued as a sphere distinct from that of trade would result in rendering the scope of the Community legal framework virtually non-existent. The Court then examined how the limits between the materially interdependent but legally distinct areas of competence will be respected. It provided an answer firmly based upon the principles the Member States themselves established as the foundation of the European Union. On the assumption that the Union is to be served by a single institutional framework ensuring both the consistency between the activities under its constituent legal frameworks and respect for the *acquis communautaire*, the Court took it upon itself to ensure that neither the Community competence nor national sovereignty regarding the conduct of foreign policy would be undermined. This conclusion, clearly supported by the fact that Article 47 TEU is not excluded from the scope of the Court's jurisdiction under Article 46 TEU.

In exercising its jurisdiction over disputes with significant foreign policy overtones, the Court neither reduced its role on the basis of the indeterminate and inherently general criterion of the "sensitive nature" defining the dispute before it, nor lost sight of the clear political parameters that may be attached to its judgments.[114] Furthermore, it makes clear that the *acquis communautaire* does not draw too heavily upon extra-Community features on the basis of a "pragmatic" interpretation,[115] for otherwise it will become of symbolic significance. More importantly, the Court's approach is characterised by intellectual coherence, may be workable in practice and consistently applied. This cannot be said

[113] According to Art. 11(1) TEU, "[t]he Union and its Member States shall define and implement a common foreign and security policy covering all areas of foreign and security policy". As regards the relationship between the Community legal framework and the CFSP, it might be understood as an antithesis between the supranational and intergovernmental elements of the EU. However, it is suggested that such an antithesis is potentially misleading. Indeed, it may under-estimate variables of major significance, such as the Court's tendency to apply the broadly defined CCP in a very restrained manner. This trend indicates that the antithesis "supranationalism–intergovernmentalism" in the external relations of the EU does not apply as such. It is more accurate to argue that both supranational and intergovernmental elements underlie in parallel the system of the external relations of the EU.

[114] Thus, the Court demonstrated a considerable degree of self-restraint; judicial self-restraint within the German legal order has been described by the German Constitutional Court as requiring the judges to "refuse to play politics" by "trenching upon the area created and circumscribed by the Basic Law as appropriate for the unrestricted operation of the political institutions": the *Inter-German Basic Treaty Case* (1973) cited in Franck, *supra* note 112 at 122. For the revival of the debate on whether the Court has generally been judicially activist see TC Hartley, "The European Court, Judicial Objectivity and the Constitution of the European Union" (1996) 112 *LQR* 95 and A Arnull, "The European Court and Judicial Objectivity—A Reply to Professor Hartley" (1996) 112 *LQR* 411; for a more elaborate analysis of the same theme see T Hartley, *Constitutional Problems of the European Union* (Oxford: Hart Publishing, 1999) and A Arnull, *The European Union and its Court of Justice* (Oxford: OUP, 19999) especially at 538–65.

[115] See C Flaesch-Mougin, "Le traité de Maastricht et les compétences externes de la Communauté Européenne: à la recherche d'une politique externe de l'union" (1993) 29 *CDE* 350 at 375–6 and J-V Louis, "Les relations extérieures de l' Union européenne: unité ou complémentarité" (1994) 4 *Revue du Marché Unique Européen* 5 at 7.

for the legal regime on exports of dual-use goods set out under Regulation 3381/94[116] and Decision 94/942/CFSP, with the latter incorporating the scope and *modus operandi* of the former; neither can it be said for Community practice in general, whereby, while export controls on dual-use goods were regulated on the basis of an EC *cum* CFSP legal formula, assistance to Russia which would enable it to convert and restructure former chemical weapon factories and destroy its stockpile of weapons in conformity with the United Nations Chemical Weapons Convention will be offered from the TACIS programme,[117] that is a programme based on Article 308 EC. It hardly seems the case that the objectives of the latter action are more closely linked to the objectives of the Community than those of the former.

[116] [1994] OJ L367/1.
[117] See *European Voice*, 5 June 1997 at 6.

8

The Regulation of Defence Products under the Law of the European Union

1. INTRODUCTION

The analysis of the imposition of trade sanctions on third countries and of regulation of exports of dual-use goods highlighted the legal problems that their foreign policy objectives and implications raise in the context of the European Union. These problems are of a more direct nature in the case of the legal regulation of armaments: not only do these products perform a variety of inextricably linked functions, but also their regulation touches upon issues not dealt with in a fully-fledged way within the framework of the European Union. It is on these grounds that the so-called "sensitive character" of defence products has been used to justify the prevailing view that they fall within a grey area of law in the context of the European Union.

This chapter will examine the validity of the above perception under the law of the European Union. Its structure will be as follows. First, it will outline the multifarious aspects of security, namely military, political and economic, and the approach of the European Union and the Member States towards them. Secondly, it will examine the practice of the Community institutions and Member States regarding the legal regime of defence industries within the Community legal order. Thirdly, it will put forward an interpretation of Article 296(1)(b) EC consistent with both its wording and character as "a wholly exceptional" Community provision. Fourthly, it will assess the arguments for the deletion of Article 296(1)(b) EC and analyse the intrinsic link between its interpretation and the development of Title V TEU.

2. THE MULTIFARIOUS FUNCTIONS OF SECURITY

The terms "security" and "defence" are interrelated but not identical. Security is to be analysed as a generic concept[1] encompassing defence. Defence may be understood as connoting the preparation and utilisation of military force and

---

[1] For a philosophical analysis of the concept of security see J Huysmans, "Security! What do You Mean? From Concept to Thick Signifier" (1998) 4 *European Journal of International Relations* 226. For an analysis of the notion of security on the basis of political science and international relations see DA Baldwin, "The concept of security" (1997) 23 *Review of International Studies* 5.

strategies aiming at protecting the territorial integrity of a state or entity from external threat or aggression likely to result in conquest or destruction.[2] In this respect, if the primary function of security is of a military character, national defence may be identified as its core. The secondary function of security is of a political nature and focuses on how state entities construct their position in the broader geopolitical environment through unilateral initiatives or participation in multilateral institutional mechanisms. Finally, the tertiary function of security is economic and deals with armaments as industrial products whose trade is determined to a great extent by economic considerations.

While the above distinction between the military, political and economic functions of security constituted the basis upon which the foreign policy system of the Union was originally founded,[3] it was criticised as impossible to follow in practical terms and hence of only academic significance.[4] However, this criticism is not directly relevant to the subject-matter of this book. To examine the validity of the distinction between the military, political and economic aspects of security within the context of the European Union requires a detailed assessment of both the political currents underpinning its development and structure and the geopolitical context within which the Union has evolved.[5] The scope of this book, on the other hand, is confined to the approach of the European Union regarding the regulation of the economic aspects of security and analyses the legal problems that it gives rise to within the constitutional structure of the Union in general and the Community legal order in particular. Therefore, the three-fold distinction put forward above is intended merely as an analytical tool: its aim is to disentangle the multifarious functions of security and, hence, to facilitate the examination of the broader context that this book must take into account, while not purporting to analyse exhaustively the notion of "security".[6]

---

[2] See WJ Feld, "Defence and security policy issues" in L Hurwitz and C Lequesne (eds.), *The State of the European Community* (London: Lynne Rienner Publishers, 1991) 425.

[3] Indeed, the Solemn Declaration on European Union, adopted by the European Council in 1983, made reference to the "co-ordination of the positions of the Member States on the political and economic aspects of security", whereas Art. 30(6)(a) of the Single European Act provided that "the High Contracting Parties . . . are ready to co-ordinate their positions more closely on the political and economic aspects of security". For a more elaborate analysis, see *supra* ch. 2.

[4] See K de Gucht and S Keukeleire, "The European Security Architecture: The Role of the European Community in Shaping a New European Geopolitical Landscape" (1991) XLIV/6 *Studia Diplomatica* 29 at 39–42; also A van Staden, "After Maastricht: Explaining the Movement towards a Common European Defence Policy" in Q Carlsnaes and S Smith (eds.), *European Foreign Policy— The EC and Changing Perspectives in Europe* (London: SAGE, 1994) 138 at 141–2 where it is argued that the Community's intervention in the Yugoslav War illustrated the untenable character of the pursuit of a foreign policy on the basis of the distinction between the political, economic and military aspects of security.

[5] For an analysis of the relationship between the geopolitical changes of the last decade and the economic aspects of security construed in the broad terms of economic security see J Sperling and E Kirchner, "Economic Security and the Problem of Cooperation in Post-Cold War Europe" (1998) 24 *Review of International Studies* 221.

[6] In other words, the distinction between the military, political and economic aspects of security does not purport to define exhaustively the generic term "security" and categorise all the functions likely to be assumed by it. This is illustrated by forms of action such as crisis management,

2.1. The defence and political aspects of security

Article 2 TEU provides that the implementation of a common foreign and security policy "includ[es] the progressive framing of a common defence policy, which might lead to a common defence". The especially careful wording of this provision makes it clear that the common defence of the Union has yet to be attained,[7] the primary function of security remaining a national matter.

However, the European Union co-operates with two European security organisations which encompass defence functions.[8] The first is the North Atlantic Treaty Organisation, established in 1949 in order to provide the institutional framework for the defence of Western democracies against the communist countries.[9] The post-Cold War era has forced NATO to redefine its role[10]; this development is clearly illustrated not only by the membership of Poland, Slovakia and Hungary and the participation of Russia in its institutional structure,[11] but also NATO's recent intervention in Kosovo.

humanitarian intervention, peace-enforcement and peacekeeping, which are not confined to the political aspects of security and yet seem not fully covered by its military function, either. It follows that other criteria enabling the categorisation of the various security functions may be put forward. In JM Gabriel, "The Integration of European Security: A Functionalist Analysis" (1995) 50 *Aussenwirtschaft* 135 at 142, the primary function of security is defined in terms of national defence, whereas the secondary one focuses on the utilisation of force for the purpose of crisis management, humanitarian intervention, peace-enforcement and peacekeeping. Another approach was adopted by the European Parliament which, in its Resolution on the formulation of perspectives for the common security policy of the European Union, [1997] OJ C167/99, views the notion of security as all-encompassing and distinguishes between its external and internal matters. The former cover various diverse issues, such as the territorial integrity of the Union and its Member States and the protection of its citizens, the control of armaments, the existence of frontier problems, unresolved minority problems or inter-ethnic rivalries which are liable to spread and ultimately threaten the Member States of the Union and the political turmoil and instability in certain countries bordering the Community territory. The internal security area covers equally wide-ranging matters, such as the threats represented by terrorism, the activities of organised crime, the economic and social crisis in European societies.

[7] Approximately 40 years after the failure to establish the European Defence Community, the Declaration on WEU, annexed to the TEU, characterises the establishment of a defence policy as "a gradual process involving successive stages". For a concise analysis of the effect of the regional and international geopolitical environment on the development of the defence and security identity of the Union see M Pugh, "Combating the Arms Proliferation Problem-Time to Embark in an Integrated Approach" (1994) 42 *NATO Review* 24.

[8] For a recent detailed analysis of the security dimension of the Union and both its position and potential within the general European security context see P Tsakaloyannis, *The European Union as a Security Community: Problems and Prospects*, (Baden-Baden: Nomos, 1996). For an analysis of the relevant provisions of the TEU see W Wessels, "Rationalizing Maastricht: The Search for an Optimal Strategy of the New Europe" (1994) 70 *International Affairs* 445.

[9] The membership of NATO is not identical to that of the Union. Ireland, Austria, Sweden and Finland are not members of NATO, whereas five non-Member States, namely Iceland, Norway, Turkey, United States and Canada, are.

[10] See J Woodliffe, "The Evolution of a New NATO for a New Europe", (1998) 47 *ICLQ* 174.

[11] The formula "19+1", often used to indicate Russia's link with NATO's institutional structure, illustrates the *sui generis* character of this relationship. On this relationship see R Muellerson, "NATO Enlargement and the NATO-Russian Founding Act: the Interplay of Law and Politics" (1998) 47 *ICLQ* 192.

The second organisation of direct relevance to the European Union is the Western European Union.[12] Of different membership from that of the Union,[13] it was reactivated in 1984 in order to address the problem of the development of the security identity of the Member States of the then EEC[14]; however, its operation has not been intended to undermine the existing structures of NATO,[15] hence its definition as "a very ambiguous compromise between Europeanism and Atlanticism".[16] Under Article 17(1) TEU, despite being "an integral part of the development of the Union", the WEU is not a part of the latter's constitutional structure. However, there is provision not only for the Union to "avail itself of the WEU to elaborate and implement decisions and actions of the Union which have defence implications",[17] but also for the Union to "foster closer institutional relations with the WEU with a view to the possibility of the integration of the WEU into the Union, should the European Council so decide".[18] The most important current role of the WEU is illustrated by the so-called Petersberg tasks which consist of combat forces being engaged in crisis management, humanitarian and rescue tasks and peacekeeping. This function, already introduced prior to the TEU,[19] constitutes a direct linkage between the Union and WEU under the Amsterdam Treaty; the Council may take political decisions in relation to these Petersberg tasks and Union may "avail itself" of the WEU for their implementation.[20]

---

[12] The WEU originated in the Brussels Treaty, concluded in 1948 between Belgium, the Netherlands, Luxembourg, France and Great Britain, and was established in 1954 with the addition of Germany and Italy. For the text of this Treaty and other related documents see A Bloed, and RA Wessel (eds.), *The Changing Function of the Western European Union (WEU)—Introduction and Basic Documents* (Dordrecht: Martinus Nijhoff, 1994).

[13] Austria, Ireland, Denmark, Finland and Sweden have the status of observer, whereas Ireland, Norway and Turkey are associate members. The Czech Republic, Estonia, Lithuania, Latvia, Bulgaria, Hungary, Poland, Romania and Slovakia are associate partners.

[14] See P Tsakaloyannis (ed.), *The Reactivation of the WEU: Its Effects on the EC and its Institutions* (Maastricht: EIPA, 1985). During the first three decades of its existence, the WEU did not have a significant record to present, hence its description as a "sleeping beauty" by M Jopp, "The Defence Dimension of the European Union: The Role and Performance of the WEU" in E Regelsberger, P de Schoutheete de Tervarent and W Wessels (eds.), *Foreign Policy of the European Union. From EPC to CFSP and Beyond* (London: Lynne Rienner Publishers, 1996) 153 at 154.

[15] On the complex and ambiguous relationship between NATO and WEU see J Walch, "L'européanisation de l'OTAN" [1997] *Revue du Marché commun et de l'Union européenne* 238.

[16] P Lawrence, "European Security: A New Era of Crisis?" in R Bideleux and R Taylor (eds.), *European Integration and Disintegration. East and West* (London: Routledge, 1996) 46 at 53.

[17] Art. 17(3) TEU, whereby the necessary practical arrangements are to be agreed upon by the Council and the WEU institutions.

[18] Art. 17(1) TEU.

[19] This function was introduced under the Petersberg Declaration, issued on 19 June 1992 by the WEU Council of Ministers. On this role and its relationship with the Union under the TEU see T Taylor, "West European Security and Defence Cooperation: Maastricht and Beyond" (1994) 70 *International Affairs* 1 at 2–7.

[20] Art. 17 TEU which also provides for the participation of the military non-aligned Member States on an *ad hoc* basis. Moreover, in the context of the general relationship between the Union and WEU, the Amsterdam Treaty makes reference to joint defence and institutional relations, whereas a Declaration by the WEU concerning its relations with both the Union and NATO is annexed.

The relationship between the Union and NATO is less direct. This is illustrated in the careful wording of Article 17 TEU, according to which "[t]he policy of the Union in accordance with this Article shall not prejudice the specific character of the security and defence policy of certain Member States and shall respect the obligations of certain Member States, which see their common defence realised in the North Atlantic Treaty Organisation (NATO), under the North Atlantic Treaty and be compatible with the common security and defence policy established within that framework".[21]

The relationship between the EU and the WEU and NATO has evolved in the context of the post-Cold War geopolitical environment prevailing in Europe. As the perception of an immediate and direct threat to Western democracies *en bloc* was removed, the primary function of security is being reconsidered and associated with the development of transnational co-operation mechanisms. As far as national armed forces are concerned, the emphasis has now shifted to the exercise of a global role by intervention in areas of crisis under the umbrella of security co-operation mechanisms.[22] It must be pointed out, however, that this development is not entirely relevant to all EU Member States: the position that no European state is under threat is challenged by Greece in view of Turkish claims over its territorial integrity. Furthermore, the conflict in Kosovo may give rise to developments affecting the security of both Member States and states directly related to the European Union.

2.2. The economic aspects of security

Armaments are industrial products involving a huge market the development of which is largely determined by economic considerations. However, the link between this function and the defence and political role of armaments has determined the unique nature of the defence market[23] which is due to the following

---

[21] The relationship between the Union, on the one hand, and NATO and WEU, on the other, is further defined under Art. 17(4) TEU which reads as follows: "[t]he provisions of this Article shall not prevent the development of closer co-operation between two or more Member States on a bilateral level, in the framework of the WEU and the Atlantic Alliance, provided such co-operation does not run counter to or impede that provided for in this Title". It is noteworthy that this provision leaves the question of future developments within the Union open while seeking not to undermine developments beyond the structure of the Union.

[22] This is illustrated by the main objectives of the reorganisation of the armed forces of the big European countries. It is noteworthy that the Strategic Defence Review recently put forward by the British Government aims at enhancing its ability to intervene globally by improving its long-range strike capability. Broadly the same objective had already been set by the French government in its plan to reorganise its armed forces: see *The Economist*, 2 Mar. 1996 at 45–6. A sweeping overhaul of the Swedish and Danish armed forces has already been undertaken: see *Financial Times*, 12 Oct. 1998 at 6 and 27 May 1999 at 3 respectively. It is interesting that the Foreign Affairs Committee of the European Parliament has suggested that a recommendation for the Council be adopted to examine the possibility of creating a civilian peace corps under Title V TEU: see *Agence Europe*, 7389 23 Jan. 1999 at 6.

[23] See K Hartley, "The European Defence Market and Industry" in P Creasey and S May (eds.), *The European Armaments Market and Procurement Cooperation*, (London: MacMillan Press, 1988) 31 *et seq*.

characteristics. First, national governments play a dominant role on the buying side of the market. This fact illustrates that political parameters, namely national perceptions of security threats and defence needs, not only influence to a great extent the volume and content of the industrial supply but may also determine the very structure of the market.[24] This results in a regulated market which does not follow the traditional liberal model of the consumer-determined market. Secondly, the defence market is highly diversified and specialised; it involves various "sub-markets", such as air, land and sea systems, and various "sub-sectors", such as components of the final product, electronics and other equipment, which illustrates the close relationship between the defence and civil industries.

On the one hand, the economic recession in the mid-1980s and, on the other hand, the *rapprochement* between the Western countries and the Communist block and the post-Cold War era led the Member States to introduce significant cuts in defence spending.[25] As a result, unemployment in this sector has been rising[26] and the defence market has become export-oriented.[27] This is problematic, for, on the one hand, the volume of defence exports has been considerably reduced in the post-Cold War era[28] and, on the other hand, the defence industries are highly fragmented not only within the Union but often within the Member States themselves.[29] As a result, their international competitiveness is undermined and their export gains minimised. Furthermore, as research on and

[24] This argument is supported by the close links between defence undertakings and governments maintained in several countries. France is a case in point, where until very recently defence undertakings were state-controlled. In general, the extent to which the links between defence undertakings and governments influence the structure of the market relies heavily upon the general economic tradition and policy of each state. In Great Britain, for example, the heavily regulated defence market model followed in France is alien to the prevailing liberal economic philosophy.

[25] Total military spending fell by 5.3% between 1985 and 1994: see *European Voice*, 5 May 1997 at 8. This development is not limited to the Community Member States but rather constitutes an international phenomenon: see H Wulf, "Arms industry limited: the turning point in the 1990s" in H Wulf (ed.), *Arms Industry Limited* (Oxford: OUP, 1993) 3 at 4–5.

[26] The significance of this phenomenon is underlined by the fact that the defence industry generally provides jobs for 1m people in the Member States. The total of industrial jobs dependent on defence in United Kingdom in 1997 is a third less than in 1985: see *Financial Times*, 15–16 Nov. 1997 at 1.

[27] For the post-Cold War drive of arms exports see T Taylor, "Conventional Arms: The Drives to Export" in T Taylor and I Ryukichi (eds.), *Security Challenges for Japan and Europe in a Post-Cold War Wolrd. Vol. III: The Defence Trade. Demand, Supply and Control* (London: Royal Institute for International Affairs and Institute for International Relations, 1994) 95. For a general analysis of the economic challenges that the defence industries face in the post-Cold War increasingly competitive international market see RA Bitzinger, "The Globalization of the Arms Industry—The Next Proliferation Challenge" (1994) 19 *International Security* 170 at 174.

[28] According to the International Institute for Strategic Studies, the total value of arms deliveries in 1987 was $88.5bn, in 1997 it was $46bn and a further decrease is expected: see *Independent*, 23 Oct. 1998 at 15.

[29] It is noteworthy that, whereas the combined defence budget of Germany, Great Britain, France, Sweden, Italy and Spain is less than half of that of the United States, their national defence contractors are three times as many: see *Financial Times*, 27 Mar. 1998 at 2. On French, German, Italian, Dutch and British national defence policies in particular see T Taylor. (ed.), *Reshaping European Defence* (London: Royal Institute of International Affairs, 1994).

development and manufacturing of new generations of weapon systems have become more costly, indigenous defence industries, while collectively characterised by excess production capability,[30] find it increasingly difficult to engage in both research and development and international trade on an individual basis.[31] This problematic state of the defence industries of the Member States is further underlined by the competition from US firms which has become more intense[32] and already affected the European market.[33]

2.3. Political and economic approaches to the problems of defence industries

The economic problems that defence industries encounter have been subject to discussions and developments at two different levels.[34] The first consists of efforts initiated by national governments within the existing European security organisations. Under the aegis of NATO, the Conference of National Armaments Directors (CNAD) has been set up in order to examine political, economic and technical aspects of development and procurement of equipment for the national forces of the NATO members. However, its role is advisory[35] and all efforts to restructure it have been confined to administrative changes. Another attempt in the NATO framework was the EUROGROUP,[36] which operated on an informal basis and provided for the elaboration of joint studies on research and development.

In addition, there were efforts of a European character, such as the Comité FINABEL de Coordination, which preceded EUROGROUP and had the same aim.[37] Subsequently, the Independent European Programme Group (IEPG) was created[38] and operated on an independent basis. IEPG can be characterised as

[30] In R Beard, "NATO Armaments Cooperation in the 1990s" (1993) 41 *NATO Review* 2, an elaborate analysis is provided regarding the excess capacity in the context of a NATO multinational airmobile division in the Rapid Reaction Corps. Four national brigades are expected to act with six kinds of helicopter, six kinds of artillery and mortars, ten different makes of vehicle, seven kinds of anti-tank weapon, nine kinds of small arms and four different communications systems.

[31] It was because of these problems that defence industry was described as "a fragmented jumble of national champions" in *The Economist*, 22 Nov. 1997 at 103.

[32] Compared with 1991, the increase of the overseas orders for military equipment in 1992 was approximately 130%: see Bitzinger, *supra* note 27 at 174; see also I Anthony, "The United States: Arms Exports and Implications for Arms Production" in Wulf, *supra* note 25 at 66 *et seq*. On the other hand, the EU industry exports amount to less than half as much as those of the US; see COM(96)10 final at 6.

[33] According to the Commission's Communication, *The Challenges Facing the European Defence-Related Industry, A Contribution for Action at European Level*, COM(96)10 final, 75% of the major conventional weapons bought by the Member States is imported from the USA.

[34] See the very good analysis by P Cornish, *The Arms Trade and Europe* (London: Pinter, 1995).

[35] See A Cox, "The Future of European Defence Policy: The Case for a Centralised Procurement Agency" (1994) 3 *Public Procurement Law Review* 65 at 70.

[36] France and Ireland did not participate.

[37] This forum involved initially France, Italy, the Netherlands, Belgium and Luxembourg and later the UK and Germany.

[38] It was created in 1976 and consists of the European members of NATO, apart from Iceland, including France.

the first serious European attempt to address the issue of co-ordination of defence industries.[39] However, it has not been limited to Community Member States[40] and hence cannot benefit from the institutional sophistication characterising the Community. In addition, it has not been particularly successful; various far-reaching proposals by IEPG studies advocating open defence markets and harmonised military requirements were not adopted,[41] whereas the action plan finally adopted consisted of considerably less radical and significant measures.[42] IEPG was dissolved in 1992 and its functions were transferred to the WEU within the structure of which the Western European Armaments Group was established. This body deals with issues regarding armaments co-operation and aims in particular to introduce conditions of competition in national defence markets, promote the technological and industrial basis of defence industries and achieve closer co-operation on research and development. A European Armaments Agency, envisaged in the Declaration on WEU annexed to the Maastricht Treaty, is to be established under a WEAG decision but no agreement has been reached regarding its principles and priorities.

An initiative originating from IEPG is the European Defence Equipment Market (EDEM) which is aimed at, among other things, establishing open procurement procedures. This objective is set to be achieved by a competitive approach, that is advertising major contracts and rendering economic considerations the basis for making awards. This initiative contains a number of exceptions[43] and lacks both formal legal status and a binding system for ensuring its effective application.[44]

The second approach towards the economic problems of defence industries consists of efforts initiated by the industry forces themselves. The need for indigenous defence industries to share the costs and reduce the risks has inevitably led various European firms to co-operation[45] of various forms,

[39] See G Coeme, "The Role of the IEPG" (1991) 39 *NATO Review* 15.

[40] Norway and Turkey also participate.

[41] In this respect see H Vredeling, *Towards a Stronger Europe* (Brussels: IEPG, 1986), who proposed the gradual independence of public procurement procedures from national administrations and the creation of an harmonised regime of military requirements by IEPG.

[42] Among other measures, the Member States of IEPG committed themselves to establishing a defence research programme, that is what would subsequently be the European Co-operative Long-Term Initiative for Defence (EUCLID). For a critical evaluation of these measures and the structural deficiencies of the concept on the basis of which the IEPG was adopted see Cox, *supra* note 35 at 71 *et seq.*

[43] There are both specific products excluded, such as warships, and general exception clauses involving "emergencies", "national security" and "other national imperatives": see S Arrowsmith, "The Application of the E.C. Treaty Rules to Public and Utilities Procurement" (1995) 6 *Public Procurement Law Review* 255 at 263–4.

[44] For the deficiencies of EDEM in particular and the inherent ineffectiveness of the incremental and minimalistic approach it adopts in general see Cox, *supra* note 35.

[45] It is noteworthy that this co-operation often involves American firms. This is illustrated in the armed scout vehicle and the Joint Strike Fighter built by the British American Aerospace and the American Lockheed Martin: see *The Economist*, 22 Nov. 1997 at 20. In relation to transatlantic co-operation, the managing director of British Aerospace argued that "if the Europeans do not restructure their industry, the Americans would do it for them": see *The Economist*, 22 Nov. 1997

namely co-production and co-development projects,[46] strategic alliances,[47] which usually constitute loose agreements towards future collaboration, joint venture companies,[48] mergers and acquisitions,[49] which are characterised by a more permanent link between the parties.[50] Another response to the problems faced by defence industries consists of production diversification which may take the form of either total conversion from producing military units to civilian production or merely expansion to non-military markets.

The initiatives undertaken at a political level under the aegis of NATO and WEU constitute a first step towards the reorganisation of the defence-related industries. On the one hand, they illustrate the Member States' acknowledgement of the critical position of the defence-related industries; on the other hand, by having recourse to multilateral bodies the Member States recognise the inefficiency of nationally confined solutions in an area intrinsically linked with national sovereignty. In this respect, a culture of co-operation has been established upon which future developments may build. However, positive though these developments may be, they are of questionable potential in terms of their effect on defence industries, for they are confined to either consultative procedures or declaratory positions. The limited effect of initiatives such as IEPG and EDEM is accentuated not only by the differing membership of the mechanisms they involve but also the differing aims of these mechanisms. It is not enough to say that differing membership of mechanisms of differing aims is the very model upon which the European Union has been developed. The Union and the pillar model on which it is based have been equipped with the institutional structures necessary to attribute to the Union normative coherence and substantive consistency.[51] This conceptual construction does not characterise either the structure or the actions of the security mechanisms to which various Member States have resorted in relation to the consolidation of their defence industries.

In relation to the market-driven approach of the defence industries, it must be pointed out that, as a spontaneous response of the market forces to the changing environment characterising the defence market, it develops on an incremental basis and has not addressed the problems that the industry needs to overcome as a whole. In other words, it is not a part of a coherent strategy and hence is often characterised by the very problems in response to which it was put

---

at 107. On defence co-operation with the American defence industry in the general context of the transatlantic trade relationship see J Van Scherpenberg, "Transatlantic Competition and European Defence Industries: A New Look at the Trade–Defence Linkage" (1997) 73 *International Affairs* 99.

[46] E.g. the Franco-Belgian-Dutch tripartite minesweeper.

[47] E.g. British Aerospace and Aerospatiale on fighter aircraft designs.

[48] E.g. Thomson-Shorts Systems, joining the missile production of France's Thomson-CSF and UK's Short Brothers.

[49] E.g. the joint purchase of the British Plessey by Siemens and GEC-Marconi.

[50] For an analytical account of the various forms of co-operation see E Skoens, "Western Europe: internationalisation of the arms industry" in Wulf, *supra* note 25 at 160 *et seq.* For the application of Reg. 4064/89 [1989] OJ L395/1, see *infra* this ch., 3.1.

[51] See *supra* ch. 2.

forward in the first place, namely over-administration, insufficient co-ordination on research and development and creation of excess production capabilities.[52] Moreover, the dependence of indigenous defence industries in some Member States upon the state will raise a permanent obstacle to their market-led consolidation.[53]

2.4. The intrinsic link between the multifarious functions of security

The intrinsic link between the multifarious functions of security is illustrated by the effects that any developments regarding one of them may have on the others. The end of the Cold War not only redefined the geopolitical climate in Europe but also set a whole range of new economic parameters affecting the structure and operation of the defence market. It is also illustrated by the extent to which the association, in the collective subconsciousness, of indigenous defence industries with security self-reliance has evolved, hence responding to the prevailing political climate and economic problems. In this respect, the example of France and its gradual privatisation of state-owned defence companies is revealing, for it marks the abandonment of a long tradition of market regulation in an area which evokes national security concerns.[54]

It is because of this intrinsic link between the various aspects of security that only parallel and combined initiatives can succeed in addressing effectively the problems of defence industries. Recent developments seem to indicate that this has been acknowledged by both national governments and market forces. A report commissioned by the governments of Great Britain, Germany and France on Europe's leading aerospace and defence companies[55] stressed both the role and limits of co-operation between undertakings and pointed out areas of consolidation involving most of those covered by defence industries in general.[56]

---

[52] See Bitzinger, *supra* note 27 at 172–88 and GC Berkhof, "The American Strategic Defence Initiative and West European Security: An Idea" in J De Vree, P Coffey and RH Lauwaars (eds.), *Towards a European Foreign Policy—Legal, Economic and Political Dimensions* (Dordrecht: Martinus Nijhoff Publishers, 1987) 205 at 242.

[53] This may be regarded as the major difference from the United States' defence industry, whose consolidation resulted in the rationalisation of its production and the enhancement of its international competitiveness. It is this very model of restructuring that the American defence undersecretary for acquisition and technology put forward as ideal in the case of the European defence industry: see *Financial Times*, 27 Mar. 1998 at 5.

[54] The privatisation of Thomson-CSF which manufactures defence electronic equipment is a case in point; important though this trend may be, it resulted in the state owning approximately a third of the company's shares through the state-owned Thomson and Aérospatiale because of the political crisis it caused: see *Financial Times*, 23 July 1998 at 26.

[55] Namely British Aerospace, Daimler-Benz Aerospace and Aérospatiale.

[56] The report under consideration suggested that Airbus Industrie, that is the consortium owned by the above three companies which manufacture the aircraft, become a single company with its own management and hence constitute the first step towards a single aerospace and defence company. The areas in which, according to the report, pan-European manufacturers could arise include a missile-maker, a defence-electronics and an aerospace company: see *International Herald Tribune*, 15 Apr. 1998 at 6.

Two options were put forward in the report, namely the formation of a single European defence conglomerate in the aftermath of the consolidation which has taken place in the United States or the *ad hoc* consolidation of producers of identical categories of products under a single management. However, its authors, that is representatives of the defence industry itself, recognised that both the above options seemed unrealistic; this conclusion relied upon the argument that, the security co-operation culture prevailing in Europe notwithstanding, national defence and political concerns still determine the regulation of defence products.

However, in a move which indicates awareness of the economic problems and the intense international competition in the defence industry, the French, British and German industry ministers responded positively to the report's proposals and required a detailed report from the undertakings involved in the process leading to the establishment of the so-called European Aerospace and Defence Company as well as the latter's shareholding, structure and management.[57] The seriousness of the problems and the increased awareness on behalf of national governments are illustrated by the addition of Italy, Spain and Sweden to the three governments initially involved in this process.

3. COMMUNITY PRACTICE UNDER ARTICLE 296(1)(b) EC

It was indicated above that both political and economic developments regarding the consolidation of defence industries take place either within institutional frameworks of overlapping scope and differing membership or on the basis of multilateral yet *ad hoc* initiatives. A reason for this extremely cautious approach is the entrenched view that the political character of the defence market renders defence products *a priori* beyond any supranational legal framework. In the case of the Community legal order, this view is often based on Article 296(1)(b) EC, the only Treaty provision making explicit reference to defence products.

Article 296(1)(b) reads as follows: "[a]ny Member State may take such measures as it considers necessary for the protection of the essential interests of its security which are connected with the production of or trade in arms, munitions and war material; such measures shall not adversely affect the conditions of competition in the common market regarding products which are not intended for specifically military purposes".

The approach adopted by the Community institutions in general and the Commission in particular in its capacity as the guardian of the Treaty regarding the interpretation of Article 296(1)(b) EC is of central significance in determining the legal regime governing arms, munitions and war material under Community law. This section will outline the legal position of defence products under competition, public procurement and import duties law. These areas

---

[57] See *Financial Times*, 11 July 1998 at 1.

touch upon important issues regarding defence industries: competition law is directly relevant to the increasing co-operation between undertakings as put forward by the defence market forces; defence procurement represents a substantial part of total procurement of Member States; finally, the imposition of duties on imported defence products reveals a conflict between the Commission and the Member States which touches upon the proper interpretation of Article 296(1)(b) EC.

3.1. The defence industries under Community competition law

The response of the defence industries to the post-Cold War economic context based on production rationalisation through co-operation increases the importance of the application of Community competition law in that area. The Commission's approach is based on the general premise that Article 296(1)(b) must be construed restrictively.[58] In practical terms, this position is illustrated in the Commission's effort to protect competition in dual-use goods markets from national measures adopted under Article 296(1)(b) EC. In the *French State/Suralmo* case, the Commission held that this provision could not be invoked in the case of a clause restricting the right of the licencee to grant sub-licences regarding a patented invention, if "the engines to which the patents related, far from being intended for specifically military purposes, were on the contrary intended primarily for non-military use".[59] The Commission reached this conclusion despite the fact that the restriction in question applied only to military use. However, this approach does not seem to address a question of central significance, namely which criteria determine the primary function of the product under consideration.[60] The absence of such criteria may result in an interpretive vacuum undermining in practical terms the significance of the application of competition law, in principle, over the defence industries.

In relation to the Merger Regulation,[61] the Commission has dealt with two categories of cases. The first category consists of mergers where applications for clearance were made by the defence undertakings without Article 296(1)(b) EC being invoked by their national governments.[62] In these cases, the Commission

---

[58] *Supra* note 33 at 13–14; see also Answer to Written Question 1088/89 [1991] OJ C130/2.

[59] European Commission, *Ninth Report on Competition Policy* (Luxembourg: Office for Official Publications of the European Communities, 1979), point 115.

[60] See JB Wheaton, "Defence Procurement and the European Community: The Legal Provisions" (1992) 1 *Public Procurement Law Review* 432 at 434. For the approaches adopted by various countries in order to distinguish purely military from dual-use products see M Bothe and T Marauhn, "The Arms Trade: Comparative Aspects of Law" (1993) 26 *RBDI* 20 at 27 *et seq.*

[61] Reg. 4064/89 [1989] OJ L257/13.

[62] Case IV/M.527 *Thomson CSF/Deuthsce Aerospace* [1995] OJ C65/4 (in the field of armaments and missile propulsion); Case IV/M.86 *Thomson/Pilkington* [1991] OJ C279/19 (optronics, mainly in the defence sector); Case IV/M.318 *Thomson/Shorts* [1993] OJ C136/4 (very short range missiles, electronic command and control systems and firing units); Case IV/M.17 *Aérospatiale/MBB* [1991] OJ C59/13 (helicopters); Case IV/M.953 *Thomson/Siemens/ATM* [1997] OJ C255/8 (air transport

stresses two points. The first is the Commission's view of geographic markets for defence products as national, where a Member State has an established producer of the relevant product, due to the connection between the existence of national suppliers and military independence.[63] The second point that the Commission takes seriously into account is the important role played by the main purchasers of defence products, namely the national Ministries of Defence, which consists mainly of exercising great bargaining power by formulating the operational requirements and technical specifications of the products under consideration. Finally, it is noteworthy that in a merger decision regarding defence undertakings, the Commission made reference to "a move towards a more international approach to procurement over the recent years" and "increased competition from non-national suppliers".[64]

The second category of merger cases the Commission deals with involves Member States requesting the parties, under Article 296(1)(b) EC, not to notify parts of the concentration in question to the Commission, as would otherwise be required under the Merger Regulation, which remains in principle applicable in the defence sector.[65] In these cases, the Commission focuses its attention on ensuring compliance with the prohibition of adverse effect on competition regarding dual-use goods markets. This is illustrated by a number of cases involving both military and civilian activities in which the concentration was required to be notified, even though the civilian activities, in one of those, represented only 2.5 per cent of the company's turnover.[66] The Commission's

management systems and air turnkey systems); Case IV/M.767 *Thomson/CSF/Finmeccanica/ Elettronica* [1996] OJ C310/9 (electronic warfare and space electronics); Case IV/M.620 *Thomson CFS/Teneo/Indra* [1995] OJ C264/9 (electronics); Case IV/M.437 *Matra Marconi Space/British Aerospace Space Systems* [1994] OJ C245/9 (space equipment); Case IV/M.945 *Matra Bae Dynamics/ Dasa/LFK* [1998] OJ C149/4 (guided weapons, guided weapons systems and unmanned air vehicles).

[63] The Commission also argues that, given the national governments' insistence that subcontractors are also of the same nationality, the markets for such products are also generally national.

[64] *Matra BAe Dynamics/DASA/LFK* case, *supra* note 62 at 6.

[65] See Case IV/M.17 *Aérospatiale/MBB supra* note 62. It must be noted that, under Art. 21(3) of the Merger Reg., public security constitutes one of the "legitimate interests" which Member States are allowed to protect through "appropriate measures . . . compatible with the general principles and other provisions of Community law". The Commission made clear that this provision is without prejudice to Art. 296 but refers to the scope of this provision in rather broad and ambiguous terms: see the Commission's statement regarding Art. 21(3) entered in the minutes of the Council [1989] 4 CMLR 314 at 318, whereby Art. 296 is construed as allowing a Member State "to intervene in respect of a concentration which would be contrary to the essential interests of its security and is connected with the production of or trade in arms, munitions and war material". The Commission also notes the self-evident conclusion that the restriction under Art. 296(1)(b) concerning products not intended for specifically military purposes should be complied with.

[66] See Case IV/M.528 *British Aerospace/VSEL* [1994] OJ C348/6 and Case IV/M.529 *GEC/VSEL* [1994] OJ C368/20; in both cases, the application of Art. 296(1)(b) EC was considered separately from that of Art. 21(3) of the Merger Reg. *supra* note 61. The proposed merger was declared compatible with the Merger Reg. on the grounds of the absence of any spillover effect on the non-military activities of the parties involved and in the absence of significant impact on suppliers, subcontractors and Ministries of Defence in the Member States. In this respect, it is interesting to note the similar concerns expressed by the Commission in Case No IV/M.877 *Boeing/McDonnell Douglas* OJ C136/3; see *Agence Europe*, 6980 24 May 1997 at 11 and *Financial Times*, 22 May 1997 at 17 and 23 May 1997 at 6.

approach is typified in the merger between British Aerospace and Lagardère SCA which deals with the areas of guided weapons and associated weapons systems.[67] According to the decision, the products that both companies would contribute "are used almost entirely in military applications". Under the instructions of the British and French Governments, the notification of the joint venture was confined to the dual-use goods produced by the two undertakings and in particular to their non-military applications, for the military products were exempted from the ambit of Regulation 4064/89 under Article 296(1)(b) EC. The Commission, however, examined the applicability of this provision by ensuring that the conditions laid down therein are fulfilled. In particular, the Commission noted that, "on the basis of the information provided by the Governments of the United Kingdom and France", the non-notified products were mentioned in the Article 296(2) list; that list, drawn up unanimously by the Council in 1958, refers to products to which the exception of Article 296(1)(b) EC is applicable.[68] The Commission Decision also confirmed the necessity of the measures for the protection of the essential interests of the security of the states concerned and the absence of spillover effects on the non-military applications of the dual-use goods. Moreover, the Commission noted "the absence of a significant impact on suppliers and subcontractors of the undertakings concerned and on Ministries of Defence of other Member States" and the fact that "intermediate consumers in the sector involved would be little affected" by the joint venture under consideration.[69]

The analysis of the Commission outlined above is consistent with the general premise put forward in its decision regarding a merger of manufacturers of engines for missiles.[70] In that case, the Commission accepted the application of Article 296(1)(b) but made it clear that the Member State concerned had to enable it to check that the conditions for its application were met and that the merger would not have any adverse effects for the suppliers of the undertakings concerned and intermediate consumers and final consumers, that is the defence ministries, in other Member States. In addition, it reserved the right to initiate the Article 298(1) EC procedure, that is consultation with the Member State in order to ensure that the measure in question does not deviate from the Treaty.

The approach adopted by the Commission regarding the application of Article 296(1)(b) EC in merger cases seems to be based on an assessment of whether all the requirements laid down in that provision are met. However, in various other instances it has adopted less than clear positions. In *GEC-*

---

[67] Case IV/M.820 [1997] OJ C22/6.

[68] For the content of the list and the debate over its relationship with the definition of the scope of Art. 296(1)(b) EC, see *infra* this ch., 4.2.

[69] The Commission justified, on the same rationale, the non-notification by GEC and Thomson-CSF of their joint venture regarding the military applications of their sonar activities: see Case IV/M.724 [1996] OJ C186/2.

[70] This merger involved Aérospatiale and SNPE; see the Commission's *XXIIIrd Report on Competition Policy* (Luxembourg: Office for Official Publications of the European Communities, 1993), point 324 *et seq.*

Siemens/Plessey, the Commission, "leaving aside the question to what extent and under which conditions the competition rules of the EEC Treaty apply to products [intended] exclusively for defence purposes", reached the conclusion that the proposed merger "does not give rise to any appreciable restrictions of competition within the meaning of Article 85(1), insofar as it relates to products destined for defence purposes".[71] This Decision neither takes a position on the applicability of Community competition law to defence industries nor elaborates on the scope of Article 296(1)(b) EC.

3.2. Defence procurement

Public procurement law is of major importance in relation to defence industries, for the latter rely almost exclusively upon public purchases.[72] However, Community procurement legislation has adopted a very cautious approach towards public contracts covering defence products. The reason for this is twofold. The first is that they exclude "the products to which Article 223(1)(b) of the EEC applies" from their ambit.[73] However, they specify that "products covered by contracts awarded by contracting authorities in the field of defence" come within their scope. The second reason is that a security clause is included in all applicable public procurement Directives in standard form excluding services, supply contracts, works contracts and contracts in the water, transport and telecommunications sectors "which are declared secret or the execution of which must be accompanied by special security measures in accordance with the laws, regulations or administrative provisions in force in the Member State concerned or when the protection of the basic interests of that State's security so requires".[74]

The above general security clause has been construed in academic writings as a generally applied express exclusion of military products from the ambit of Community procurement legislation.[75] The foundation for this view is that

---

[71] Case IV/33.18 [1990] OJ C239/2 at 8.

[72] According to the Green Paper on Public Procurement in the European Union: Exploring the Way Forward at 9; for an analysis of this paper see A Mattera, "La politique communautaire des marchés publics: necessité ou souci de perfectionnisme?" (1996) 4 *Revue du marché de l'Union Européenne* 9.

[73] See Art. 4 of Dir. 92/50/EEC relating to the co-ordination of procedures for the award of public service contracts [1992] OJ L209/1 and Article 3 of Dir. 93/36/EEC [1993] OJ L199/1; the latter provision had already been inserted by Directive 88/295/EEC [1998] OJ L127/1 amending Dir. 77/62/EEC relating to the co-ordination of procedures on the award of public supply contracts and repealing certain provisions of Dir. 80/767/EEC [1980] OJ L 215/1 [1988] OJ L127/1.

[74] Arts. 4(2) of Dir. 92/50/EEC on services, *supra* note 73, 2(2) of Dir. 93/36/EEC on supply contracts, *supra* note 73, 4(b) of Dir. 93/37/EEC concerning the co-ordination of procedures for the award of public contracts [1993] OJ L199/54 and 10 of Dir. 93/38/EEC co-ordinating the procurement procedures of entities operating in the water, transport and telecommunications sectors [1993] OJ L199/84.

[75] See C Bovis, *EC Public Procurement Law* (London: Longman, 1997) 123 and "The European Public Procurement Rules and their Interplay with International Trade" (1997) 31 *JWT* 63 at 89;

public procurement of military products is excluded from the scope of the Treaty altogether and, hence, deprives the Community of the power to regulate it.[76] In practical terms, this view may be illustrated by the complaint of an Austrian manufacturer that the United Kingdom had awarded a £35 million battlefield ambulance contract to Land Rover against the recommendation of its own procurement department.[77]

3.3. Imports of defence products

It has been argued that the Commission approaches the application of Article 296(1)(b) EC within an interpretive vacuum. This becomes all the more apparent as far as imports of armaments from third countries are concerned. This gives rise to different interpretations concerning the applicability of the Common Customs Tariff (CCT). Member States argue that such goods must be exempted from Common Customs duties, on both economic and practical grounds. They are usually very expensive, because of the high technology they involve, and the application of the CCT would impose too heavy a burden on national industries and therefore undermine the security of the Member States.[78] The Commission has failed to put forward a consistent and fully fledged interpretation of Article 296(1)(b) EC regarding this issue. On the one hand, it argues that "charging a customs duty is not likely to harm the 'essential interests' of the security of the Member States concerned" and therefore the latter "may not rely on Article [296(1)(b) EC] . . . in order unilaterally to allow duty-free entry for dutiable defence equipment imported from non-member countries".[79] It is noteworthy that, in 1985, the Commission initiated infringement proceedings under Article 226 EC against five Member States on grounds of duty-free importation of jeeps and inflight tanker aircraft and, hence, violation of Article 26 EC.[80] On the other hand, this strict approach based on the *in concreto* fulfilment of the conditions laid down in Article 296(1)(b) was effectively undermined by the Commission's suggestion that the legal position of the imposition of customs duties on imports of defence material was ambiguous and "a solution must be found which, while respecting national defence policies, nevertheless remains fully compatible with the basic objectives of the

---

JMF Martin, *The Public Procurement Rules: A Critical Analysis* (Oxford: Clarendon Press, 1996) at 139–41; and M Trybus, "European Defence Procurement: Towards a Comprehensive Approach" (1998) 4 *EPL* 111 at 113.

[76] See S Arrowsmith, *The Law of Public and Utilities Procurement* (London: Sweet & Maxwell, 1996) at 860.

[77] *Irish Times*, 22 Jan. 1996 at 5.

[78] See A Collet, "Le développement des actions communautaires dans le domaine des matériels de guerre, des armes et des munitions" (1990) 26 *Rev. trim. dr. europ.* 75.

[79] Answer to Written Question 277/80 [1980] OJ C198/39–40.

[80] MA Chatterji, "The EC Internal Armaments Market: A New Aspect of the New Security" (1991) XV *Journal of European Integration* 25 at 38.

Community".[81] In its effort to achieve a *modus vivendi*, the Commission submitted a proposal for a Council Regulation temporarily suspending, under Article 26, import duties on certain weapons and military equipment.[82] The proposed regulation was based on a two-fold premise; on the one hand, it accepted the need for Member States to import military products duty-free[83] and, on the other hand, it argued that tariff suspensions "should be strictly limited and should cover only major items of military procurement"[84] and be applied uniformly. The suspension of import duties would be based on an end-user certificate issued by the authorities of the Member State for whose armed forces the goods were destined and would be confined to a list of seven categories of items, their component parts and equipment needed for their repair.[85] However, the proposed regulation was not adopted due to various objections by Member States before it was even discussed in the Council.[86] The Member States were reluctant to imply that, by discussing this subject in the Council, they accepted that import duties were in principle payable.

3.4. The emerging interpretative vacuum surrounding Article 296(1)(b) EC

The above outline of the legal position of defence products under Community law illustrates an inconsistent approach. The Commission has adopted an idiosyncratic approach by focusing on some aspects of Article 296(1)(b) EC and tacitly refusing to put forward its fully fledged interpretation. On the one hand, it states that "some Member States have interpreted this Article broadly and divergently . . . applying exemptions to a wider range of products without reference to the 1958 list" and requires that the Member States "no longer interpret the exemptions authorised by Article [296] so broadly".[87] It also argues that Member States invoke this wholly exceptional clause in order to compartmentalise the

---

[81] *Ibid.*

[82] COM(88)502 final.

[83] Under para. 7 of the preamble to the proposed reg., "it is in the interests of the defence of the Community as a whole that the Member States should be enabled to procure for the use of their armed forces the most technologically advanced and suitable weapons and military equipment and that Community manufacturers should be able to meet the greater part of these needs; . . . it is compatible with the interests of the Community that certain of these weapons and equipment may be imported free of import duties; . . . it is appropriate to suspend the charging of import duties on such weapons and equipment and to this end a common list of duty suspensions for weapons and military equipment should be established; . . . uniform measures are required for the purpose of creating the single market".

[84] See *supra* note 82 at 5.

[85] The categories of products, annexed to the proposed reg., comprised tanks and other armoured fighting vehicles, helicopters, helicopters and other aircraft, bombs, grenades, torpedoes, mines and missiles. The proposed measure indicates that it applies to these products in so far as they are of military use.

[86] See Chatterji, *supra* note 80 at 38.

[87] See *supra* note 33 at 14.

Community market and effectively undermine the single market.[88] On the other hand, the Commission contradicts this argument for a strict construction of Article 296(1)(b) EC by suggesting that "there is a grey area of products to which it is unclear, to say the least, whether Article [296] . . . applies".[89]

Despite its assertion that armaments are not beyond the Community legal framework altogether,[90] the Council has been as reluctant as the Commission to put forward a fully fledged interpretation of Article 296(1)(b) EC, as the case of customs duties on imports of defence products in Member States illustrates. Furthermore, the European Parliament has interpreted Article 296(1)(b) as an absolute clause of exclusion: a Report of the Committee on Foreign Affairs and Security argued that "trade in arms is not covered by Community rules"[91] and "urges that matters pertaining to armaments production and the arms trade be brought within the Community ambit".[92]

4. THE INTERPRETATION OF ARTICLE 296(1)(b) EC IN THE CONTEXT OF THE EC TREATY

The approach of the Community institutions to Article 296(1)(b) which has emerged so far views the legal position of defence products at the margins of the Community legal order. Whereas in theory military products are treated within the Community legal order, their multifarious functions give rise too often to reference being made to their "sensitive nature" which, in practical terms, excludes them from the ambit of Community law. However, to argue that "the sensitive character" of military products renders them, in practical terms, beyond the Community framework is tantamount to determining the legal regime of a whole category of products on the basis of an inherently indeterminate attribute rather than the Treaty itself. The effective exclusion of defence products *in toto* from the remit of Community law is not supported by a close analysis of Article 296(1)(b) EC.

4.1. The wholly exceptional character of Article 296(1)(b) EC

Article 296(1)(b) EC is one of a number of Treaty Articles providing derogation from Community law on the basis of public security. Articles 30, 39(3) and 46(1) provide derogations from the freedom of movement of goods, persons and

[88] See the extract from a speech by Commissioner Sir Leon Brittan in Wheaton, *supra* note 60 at 433–4. Sir Leon also argued that national approaches regarding the application of Art. 296(1)(b) complicated the formulation of the common security policy.

[89] See Answer to Written Question 508/86 [1986] OJ C19/10.

[90] See Answers to Written Questions 574/85 [1985] OJ C287/9, 1306/86 [1986] OJ C277/57 and 865/91 [1991] OJ C315/20.

[91] Session Document A3–0260/92 at 5.

[92] *Ibid.* at 6.

establishment respectively and, as such, "deal with exceptional cases which are clearly defined and which do not lend themselves to any wide interpretation".[93] The strict interpretation applied by the Court aims at ensuring the maximum protection of the *acquis communautaire* and the attainment of the Treaty objectives by allowing the minimum deviation from Community law within limits set under Community law and interpreted by the Court. However, the derogation introduced by Article 296(1)(b) authorises the Member States to deviate from all the rules relating to the common market. In this respect, its effect is significantly different from that of the above exceptional clauses.[94] This special feature of Article 296 justifies its status as of a "wholly exceptional character".[95] However, the unlimited scope of national measures and the deviation from Community law *in toto* it may justify render Article 296(1)(b) subject to abuse by a Member State seeking to invoke it to an extent not envisaged by the Treaty.[96] Therefore, the need for protection of the Community legal order from unduly extensive application of exceptional clauses and hence from abuse applies *a fortiori* in the case of Article 296(1)(b) whose "wholly exceptional character" further underlines the argument that it must be strictly construed.

4.2. The scope of Article 296(1)(b) EC

The definition of the scope of Article 296(1)(b) in relation to the Article 296(2) list has been the subject of a longstanding debate. This was illustrated in the Commission's argument that "there is a grey area of products to which it is unclear, to say the least, whether Article [296] . . . applies".[97]

Article 296(2) reads as follows: "[t]he Council may, acting unanimously on a proposal from the Commission, make changes to the list, which it draw up on April 1958, of the products to which the provisions of paragraph 1 (b) apply". This list has neither been published[98] nor modified since 1958.[99] It comprises 15

[93] Case 13/68 *Salgoil SpA* v. *Italian Ministry for Foreign Trade* [1968] ECR 453 at 463 and Case 222/84 *Marguerite Johnston* v. *Chief Constable of the Royal Ulster Constabulary* [1986] ECR 1651, [1986] 3 CMLR 240 at paras. 26–7.

[94] See the Opinion of Jacobs AG on Case C–120/94 *Commission* v. *Greece* [1996] ECR I–1513 at para. 46.

[95] *Johnston, supra* note 93 at para. 27.

[96] *Ibid.* at paras. 26, 27 and 60; in addition, the Opinions of Jacobs AG in *Commission* v. *Greece*, *supra* note 38 at para. 46 and in Cases C–70/94 *Fritz Werner Industrie-Ausrüstungen GmbH* v. *Federal Republic of Germany* [1995] ECR I–3189 and C–83/94 *Criminal proceedings against Peter Leifer and Others* [1995] ECR I–3231 at para. 64.

[97] See Answer to Oral Question H–558/85, *Debates of the European Parliament* (Feb. 1986). It is noteworthy that, in reply to the critical points put forward in the subsequent Written Question 508/86 [1986] OJ C19/10, the Commission did not clarify its stance. Instead, it stated that, in the light of "a detailed examination of the complex and sensitive issues [involved,] [i]t would be premature to comment upon the specific aspects cited in the question" regarding the scope of Art. 296(1)(b) and that of the Art. 296(2) list.

[98] The list, based on the 1958 COCOM Munitions List has been included in Wulf, *supra* note 25 at 214.

[99] See Answer to Written Question 573/85 [1985] OJ C269/21. The fact that the list has not been

generally worded categories of products, namely (i) portable and automatic firearms, (ii) artillery and smoke, gas and flame-throwing weapons, (iii) ammunition for the above weapons, (iv) bombs, torpedoes and guided missiles, (v) military fire control equipment, (vi) tanks and specialist fighting vehicles, (vii) toxic or radioactive agents, (viii) powders, explosives and liquid or solid propellants, (ix) warships and their specialist equipment, (x) aircraft and equipment for military use, (xi) military electronic equipment, (xii) camera equipment specially designed for military use, (xiii) other equipment and material, (xiv) specialised parts and items of material included in this list as they are of a military nature and (xv) machines, equipment and items exclusively designed for the study, manufacture, testing and control of arms, munitions and apparatus of an exclusively military nature included in this list.[100]

The contention that the scope of Article 296(1)(b) is confined to the Article 296(2) list is supported by the wording of the Treaty. The French version of Article 296(1)(b) refers to "*la* liste *des* produits" and the German to "die Liste *der* Waren" and, hence, provide overwhelming evidence that the Member States can only invoke it for products included in the Article 296(2) list.[101]

It is sometimes suggested, however, that the scope of Article 296(1)(b) EC extends beyond the Article 296(2) list and that the latter is of a non-exhaustive character. This was suggested by the British Government which, in its intervention in the *Leifer* case, argued that Article 296(1)(b) could be invoked in relation to dual-use goods. However, this broad construction of the Article 296(2) list and, hence, the scope of application of Article 296(1)(b) runs counter to the restrictive interpretation that the "wholly exceptional character" of Article 296 entails.[102]

---

modified so far seems to be at odds with the national governments' insistence on retaining Art. 296(1)(b) in the 1992 IGC.

[100] The scope of some of these categories is clarified by reference to particular items. Category (xiii), for instance, comprises parachutes and parachute fabric, water purification plant specially designed for military use, military command relay electrical equipment. However, some others, such as category (x), are included without further clarification.

[101] See also the Council's reply to Written Question 574/85, [1985] OJ C287/9 at 10, where reference is made to "[t]he list of products covered by Article 223(1)(b)" (emphasis added). Also see LW Gormley, *Prohibiting Restrictions on Trade within the EEC* (Amsterdam, Elsevier, 1985) at 248. Another indication that the material scope of Art. 296(1)(b) EC is not to be construed broadly is provided by the fact that Community legislation has already been adopted in relation to certain arms. Dir. 91/477 [1991] OJ L256/51, adopted under Art. 95 EC, harmonises the conditions under which an authorisation of the acquisition and possession of weapons is granted within the Member States by providing for a European firearms pass. Subsequently, the Commission annexed to Recommendation 93/216 [1993] OJ L93/51 a specimen of a European firearms pass and called upon the Member States to conform with it. This specimen was later modified by Recommendation 96/129 [1996] OJ L30/47. However, Art. 2(2), of Directive 91/477 states that this directive "shall not apply to the acquisition or possession of weapons and ammunition, in accordance with national law, by the armed forces, the police [and] the public authorities . . . [n]or shall it apply to commercial transfers of weapons and ammunition of war". On the right of national authority to invoke Art. 30 EC regarding the personal firearms sector see Answer to Written Question 259/97 [1997] OJ C319/47.

[102] See Dewost et al. (eds.), *Commentaire Mégret* (Brussels: Presses Interuniversitaires de Bruxelles, 1987) xv at 430; P Eeckhout, *The European Internal Market and International Trade: A Legal Analysis* (Oxford: Clarendon Press, 1994) at 251; H Smit and PE Herzog, *The Law of the European Community—A Commentary on the EEC Treaty* (New York: Matthew Bender, 1996) at 6–216.89.

Another argument for the construction of the Article 296(2) list as of a non-exhaustive character is based on the fact that it has never been updated.[103] However, the outdated character of the Article 296(2) list is not to be attributed to its purported non-exhaustive character; instead, it may be explained by the Member States' reliance upon the inherently indeterminate "sensitive nature" of defence products which, in turn, has given rise to the perception that Article 296(1)(b) excludes defence products altogether from the remit of Community law.

The exclusion of specifically dual-use goods from the scope of Article 296(1)(b) EC is supported on various grounds. First, these products, by definition of civil use but potentially rendered of military use, cannot be identified with any of the categories covered by Article 296(1)(b), that is arms, munitions or war materials.[104] Secondly, the second limb of Article 296(1)(b) provides that the conditions of competition regarding dual-use goods must not be adversely affected by recourse to its first limb. If dual-use goods were covered by Article 296(1)(b) EC, the increasing relevance of dual-use goods and technologies in the military industry[105] and the considerable expansion of defence-related companies in civil-use production[106] would effectively render this provision of unlimited scope. This conclusion would not only run counter to the wholly exceptional character of Article 296(1)(b) EC, but would also contravene two specific provisions: the very wording of the second limb of Article 223(1)(b), which qualifies the first in the case of dual-use goods, and Article 298, which provides a mechanism for enforcing this qualification.

Thirdly, the exclusion of dual-use goods from the scope of Article 296(1)(b) EC is also supported by the content of the Article 296(2) list. This list does not include arms such as very low calibre weapons,[107] even though the latter items may be described as "arms". In this respect, it would be inconsistent with the *rationale* underlying the composition of the Article 296(2) list to extend its application to dual-use goods. A counter-argument that dual-use goods are by their very nature connected with the scope of Article 296(1)(b) is seriously questioned by the insistence of the authors of the Article 296(2) list on underlining the military use of all the items included therein. The components included in the list are only those "*specially designed* for the handling, assembly,

---

[103] Arrowsmith, *supra* note 76 at 858, where it is pointed out that the analysis of the Art. 296(2) as exhaustive "would certainly render the current list very outdated".

[104] See I Govaere and P Eeckhout, "On Dual Use Goods and Dualist Case Law: The *Aimé Richardt* Judgment on Export Controls" (1992) 29 *CMLRev.* 941 at 956; *cf.* O Lhoest, "La production et le commerce des armes, et l'article 223 du Traité instituant la Communauté Européenne" (1993) 26 *RBDI* 176.

[105] See *The Economist*, 8 Mar. 1997 at 23–5.

[106] See B Adam, "Evolution du Contexte Politique et Economique du Commerce des Armes" (1993) 26 *RBDI* 3 at 12.

[107] The exclusion of such weapons does not seem to have been mandatory for the Council. However, it is a sensible choice, for their link with the "essential interests of [the Member States'] security" seems tenuous.

dismantling, firing or detection of the articles [in category (i) of the list]"[108] and "specialised parts and items of material [are included in that list] insofar as they are of a military nature".

Fourthly, the intention of the Council to exclude dual-use goods from the scope of Article 296(1)(b) is illustrated in a comparison between the Article 296(2) list and its main source of inspiration, namely the COCOM munitions list.[109] The former is confined to armaments and war materials, whereas the latter included many dual-use goods.[110] Had the Member States envisaged such an extensive list, they would have followed the list which they draw upon and hence would have included some dual-use goods expressly.

The arguments put forward above lead to the conclusion that national governments may not adopt measures under Article 296(1)(b) regarding products not covered by the Article 296(2) list. Dual-use goods in particular, either put forward by the Member States themselves or included in multilaterally set lists, cannot be covered by Article 296.[111]

4.3. The notion of "security" under Article 296(1)(b) EC

In addition to being confined to the exhaustive Article 296(2) list, Article 296(1)(b) is applied in so far as the conditions provided therein are fulfilled. Member States may invoke this clause and hence deviate from Community law when they deem it "necessary for the protection of the essential interests of [their] security".

The wording of Article 296(1)(b) EC indicates that the notion of security provided therein must be interpreted in exceptionally restrictive terms. The reference to "the essential interests" of the security of Member States underlines that the aim served by the national measure adopted under Article 296(1)(b) EC must be directly linked with the very core of national sovereignty.

The interpretation applied by the Court to the notion of public security contained in exceptional Treaty clauses supports this conclusion. In *Campus Oil*, the Irish Government argued that national legislation requiring petroleum products importers to purchase a certain proportion of their supply from the only Irish refinery was justified under the public security proviso of new Article 30 EC, for, otherwise, that refinery would not be kept in operation and hence supplies, especially in the event of a crisis, could not be guaranteed. In defining the

---

[108] Emphasis added.

[109] The Co-ordinating Committee on Multilateral Export Controls (COCOM) was an international arrangement between Western democracies which was intended to regulate exports of armaments and sensitive materials to the Soviet bloc. For an analysis of it and its successor, namely the Wassenaar Arrangement on Export Controls for Conventional Arms and Dual-Use Goods and Technologies see *infra* ch. 9.

[110] See PJ Kuyper, "European Economic Community" in KM Meessen (ed.), *International Law of Export Control: Jurisdictional Issues* (London: Graham and Trotman, 1992) 57 at 71.

[111] See Govaere and Eeckhout, *supra* note 104 at 956.

public security clause of Article 30 EC, the Court stressed two points: first, in order to be justified under the public security proviso, the national measure in question must seek to avoid circumstances that would affect the very core of the country's existence[112]; secondly, these circumstances must be objective and not give rise to purely economic considerations.[113] In addition to these features, the Court held in *Richardt* that the public security proviso connotes both the internal and external aspects of the security of the Member States.[114]

Regarding the relationship of the notion of security referred to in the wholly exceptional clause of Article 296(1)(b) with that of public security referred to in exceptional Treaty provisions, Advocate General Slynn, in his Opinion in *Campus Oil*, implied that the former must be construed more restrictively than the latter; he argued that Article 30 "is clearly not limited to external military security which largely fall to be dealt with under Articles [296 to 298]".[115] The Commission also argued for the Article 30 clause to be construed in more general terms than Article 296(1)(b) but suggested a more restrictive definition than that put forward by Advocate General Slynn, namely that it should be confined

---

[112] In Case 72/83 *Campus Oil v. Minister for Industry and Energy* [1984] ECR 2727, the Court held at para. 34 that "petroleum products, because of their exceptional importance as an energy source in the modern economy, are of fundamental importance for a country's existence since not only its economy but above all its institutions, its essential public services and even the survival of its inhabitants depend upon them. An interruption of supplies of petroleum products, with the resulting dangers for the country's existence, could therefore seriously affect the public security that Article [30] allows States to protect." For a critique of the above formula in general and its unclear wording, see Gormley, *supra* note 101 at 136–9. Finally, the Court stressed the need for the national measures in question to adhere to the principles of proportionality and alternative means.

[113] The Court held at para. 35 that "in the light of the seriousness of the consequences that an interruption in supplies of petroleum products may have for a country's existence, the aim of ensuring a minimum supply of petroleum products at all times is to be regarded as transcending purely economic considerations and thus as capable of constituting an objective covered by the concept of public security". The Court subsequently pointed out that "to come within the ambit of Article [30], the rules in question must be justified by objective circumstances corresponding to the needs of public security. Once that justification has been established, the fact that the rules are of such a nature as to make it possible to achieve, in addition to the objectives covered by the concept of public security, other objectives of an economic nature which the Member States may also seek to achieve, does not exclude the application of Article [36]". In Case C–347/88 *Commission v. Greece* [1990] ECR I–4747, the Greek Government put forward the interpretation of public security given in *Campus Oil* in order to justify legislation enabling national authorities to approve or amend annual procurement programmes for petroleum products submitted by undertakings. However, this argument was rejected by the Court due to the absence of evidence that the above measure was indeed essential.

[114] The same definition was given by the Court in the public security clause provided for under Art. 11 of Council Reg. 2603/69 [1969] OJ L324/25 amended by Council Reg. 3918/91 [1991] OJ L372/31.

[115] *Supra* note 112 at 2764 where he also argued that the public security clause of Art. 30 "is not limited to internal security, in the sense of the maintenance of law and order, falling short of "serious internal disturbances affecting the maintenance of law and order" which is covered by Article 297 EC, though it may include this". As for the strict interpretation of the public security proviso, a parallel may be drawn with Case 30/77 *R. v. Bouchereau* [1977[ECR 1999 [1977] 2 CMLR 800; in that case, a French national working in England was convicted of unlawful possession of drugs and fought proposed deportation. In interpreting the public security proviso in Art. 39(3) EC, the Court referred to the need for "a genuine and sufficiently serious threat to the requirements of public policy affecting one of the fundamental interests of society"; para. 35 of the judgment.

to "such matters as national defence and the maintenance of civil peace in so far as those matters are not covered by the more specific provisions of Articles [296, 297 and 298] of the [EC] Treaty".[116] In interpreting Article 30, the Court seemed to have accepted *sub silentio* the construction of the public security clause provided thereunder in more general terms than that of "security" under Article 296(1)(b).[117]

The Court's ruling that the exceptional clause of Article 30 EC may be invoked in the light of fundamental objectives such as safeguarding the institutions of the Member States, their essential public services and the survival of their inhabitants may lead to the conclusion that recourse to the wholly exceptional clause of Article 296(1)(b) EC must require conditions of extraordinary significance. In other words, the definition of the term "security" under Article 296(1)(b) must reflect the "wholly exceptional nature" of this provision by being construed in more restrictive terms than that of the public security clause of the other exceptional Treaty provisions.[118] This is supported not only by the reference to the "external military security" by Advocate General Slynn in his Opinion in *Campus Oil*, but also by the ratio of Article 296(1)(b) itself: the nature of the material scope of the national measures envisaged therein, namely arms, munitions and war material, focuses on the exercise of the most fundamental aspects of national sovereignty and hence must be viewed as underpinning the definition of "security". In the light of the above considerations, the term "security" under Article 296(1)(b) EC may be construed as referring to interests of such fundamental significance as the territorial integrity of a state from external threat or aggression or the protection of the institutions of the state from terrorists.

A point of importance needs to be clarified. The interpretation of "security" under Article 296(1)(b) EC in more restrictive terms than that of "public security" under the exceptional Treaty clauses[119] does not render Article 296 a *lex specialis* in relation to Article 30. If that were the case, the principle *lex specialis legis generalis derogat* would preclude recourse to the latter provision in a scenario fulfilling the conditions laid down by the former provision. However, this conclusion is illogical. The construction of Article 296 as a wholly exceptional provision is based upon, on the one hand, the highly exceptional effect that its recourse entails, namely deviation from the Treaty, and, on the other hand, the fundamental national interests it acknowledges. Consequently, its strict interpretation seeks to avoid abuse by Member States. If the latter deem their fundamental interests envisaged under Article 296(1)(b) EC to be adequately protected under exceptional Treaty clauses, then they are free to invoke them.

---

[116]   *Supra* note 112 at 2740.

[117]   It is noted that in *Campus Oil*, the Court held that the national rules under consideration were justified.

[118]   See Verhoeven in *Commentaire Mégret*, *supra* note 102 at 1390.

[119]   On the notion of "security" in general under Community law see S Peers, "National Security and European Law" (1996) 16 *YEL* 363.

This line of reasoning also suggests that, if the reverse was the case, that is, if the interests they sought to protect fell within the definition of public security under Article 30, the Member States would be precluded from invoking Article 296(1)(b), for its wholly exceptional character justifies its invocation only when absolutely necessary.

4.4. The discretion enjoyed by Member States under Article 296(1)(b) EC and the role of the Court under Article 298(2) EC

It was argued above that the wholly exceptional clause of Article 296(1)(b) EC must be invoked only in so far as the conditions required thereunder are fulfilled. In other words, the Member State concerned must aim at protecting the very core of its sovereignty, confine its measures deviating from the Treaty to products included in the exhaustive list of Article 296(2) EC and not adversely affect the conditions of competition in the common market regarding dual-use goods. Article 296(1)(b) EC itself suggests that Member States are under a discretion to determine whether the essential interests of their security must be protected by recourse to measures deviating from the Treaty. Indeed, the absence of a consultation procedure between the Member State deviating from the Treaty and the other Member States, in contrast to Article 297, indicates that, under Article 296(1)(b) EC, the Member States are *a fortiori* solely responsible for determining whether the measures are "necessary".

However, recourse to Article 296(1)(b) is subject to judicial control under the extraordinary procedure of Article 298(2) EC which reads as follows:

> By way of derogation from the procedure laid down in Articles 226 and 227, the Commission or any Member State may bring the matter directly before the Court of Justice if it considers that another Member State is making improper use of the powers provided for in Articles 296 and 297. The Court of Justice shall give its ruling *in camera*.

The question which then arises is the extent to which the discretion of national governments, to determine whether recourse to Article 296(1)(b) EC is necessary in order to protect the essential interests of their security, is subject to judicial control under Article 298(2).

The only precedent regarding recourse to the Article 298 procedure was the action brought by the Commission against Greece on the economic and trade sanctions imposed by the latter on the Former Yugoslav Republic of Macedonia (FYROM). The Greek Government claimed that the embargo in question was justified under Article 297 EC, whereas the Commission argued that the latter provision had been improperly used. That case was not decided by the Court, for an agreement between Greece and FYROM was reached before the Court's judgment but after Advocate General Jacobs had delivered his Opinion.[120] His

---

[120] Case C–120/94 *Commission* v. *Greece* [1996] ECR I–1513.

approach was analysed above.[121] Its thrust was that, while the determination of whether the conditions laid down in Article 297 are met clearly constitutes a justiciable issue, the nature of the determination of a complex foreign policy issue such as the existence of war or serious international tension constituting a threat of war, renders the judicial control over such matters of "extremely limited nature".[122] For this reason the determination of the valid use of the rights conferred under Article 297 EC is dependent to a great extent upon the subjective point of view of the Member State concerned.[123]

It is suggested that the above arguments of Advocate General Jacobs regarding the role of the Court under Article 298(2) are only partly relevant when the Court is called upon to exercise its jurisdiction over national measures adopted under Article 296(1)(b) EC. In being called upon to determine whether "improper use" of Article 297 has been made, the Court must focus on the definition of the ambiguous and broadly worded terms "serious internal disturbance affecting the maintenance of law and order, war or serious international tension constituting a threat of war, obligations the Member States have accepted for the purpose of maintaining peace and international security". However, in being called upon to determine whether "improper use" of Article 296(1)(b) EC has been made, the Court's role is not confined to the definition of the equally broadly worded "essential interests of [national] security"; it also consists of determining whether the national measure in question covers products included in the Article 296(2) list and respect the conditions of competition in the common market regarding dual-use goods. The assessment of whether a national measure sought to be justified under Article 296(1)(b) EC meets these requirements does not touch upon issues so inextricably linked with the core of national sovereignty as to be inherently alien to the exercise of judicial control.[124]

Therefore, the role of the Court under Article 298(2) EC in relation to national measures sought to be justified under Article 296(1)(b) EC is by no means non-existent for the "extremely limited nature" of judicial control does not alter the Court's duty to ascertain whether the application of the Article 296 clause is reasonable.[125] In this respect, the Court has jurisdiction under Article 298 to strike down two categories of national measures sought to be justified

[121] *Supra* ch. 7, 6.2.
[122] *Supra* note 120 at para. 60.
[123] *Ibid.* at paras. 54–56.
[124] The limited nature of the judicial control under Art. 298(2) EC raises an issue regarding the decision under which the Art. 296(2) list was set. In its Answer to Written Question 574/85 [1985] OJ C287/9 at 10, the Council stated that the instrument under which the Art. 296(2) list was drawn up was an Art. 249 decision; the logical conclusion of this is that the drafting of the list consistently with the wording and the aims of Art. 296(1)(b) would be subject to the ordinary jurisdiction of the Court. This would lead to the following paradox: in establishing the Art. 296(2) list, the Council would be subject to the Court's general jurisdiction, whereas, in adopting national measures applicable to the products included in that list, the Member States would be subject to the Court's extraordinary and limited jurisdiction under Art. 298.
[125] *Ibid.* For other cases in which misuse of Art. 296 might occur, for example measures concerning products not included in the Art. 296(2) list, see Smit and Herzog, *supra* note 102 at 6–216.89. It is noteworthy that, in Case C–273/97 *Angela Maria Sirdar* v. *The Army Board and*

under Article 296(1)(b). The first consists of measures adopted fo other than those envisaged under the latter provision, namely "the prc the essential interests of [national] security". Such measures may inclu obstacles to the free movement of goods in order to boost national ment.[126] They may also include measures adopted as a result of a flagrantly unreasonable exercise of the discretion enjoyed by the Member States under Article 296(1)(b) EC. The argument that the determination of this matter is covered by the jurisdiction of the Court under Article 298(2) is supported by Advocate General Jacobs in his Opinion in *Commission* v. *Greece (FYROM)*, whereby he suggests that, in determining whether the conditions laid down in Article 297 EC are met, "it can[not] be said that Greece is acting *wholly unreasonably*".[127] In the light of the above, it becomes clear that the power of review enjoyed by the judiciary is confined to extreme cases.

The second category of measures which the Court may strike down in exercising its Article 296(2) EC jurisdiction includes those which run counter to the requirements laid down in Article 296(1)(b) EC either by covering products excluded from the material scope of that provision or by affecting competition in the common market regarding dual-use goods. Such measures may include the purchase of military material at an excessive price in order to subsidise the production of non-military material by the same producer[128] or a state aid not notified to the Commission when it is intended to boost national industry to the detriment of other Community firms.

4.5. The requirement of respect for the conditions of competition in the common market regarding dual-use goods under Article 296(1)(b) EC and the role of the Commission under Article 298(1) EC

Reliance upon Article 296(1)(b) EC gives rise to a procedure involving the Commission. Under Article 298(1) EC, "[i]f measures taken in the circumstances referred to in Articles 296 and 297 have the effect of distorting the conditions of competition in the common market, the Commission shall, together with the State concerned, examine how these measures can be adjusted to the rules laid down in this Treaty".

It is noteworthy that the terminology of Articles 296, 297 and 298 in relation to competition is not identical. Under Article 296(1)(b), the national measures shall not "adversely affect" the conditions of competition regarding dual-use

---

Secretary of State for Defence, La Pergola AG did construe Art. 297 in strict terms and reached the conclusion that the normal organisation of national armed forces is excluded from its ambit, for, otherwise, the latter's scope would be "unduly extend[ed]": para. 27 of his Opinion [1999] 3 CMLR 559.

[126] See Smit and Herzog, *supra* note 102 at 6–216.89.

[127] *Supra* note 120 at para. 56; emphasis added.

[128] See PJG Kapteyn and P VerLoren van Themaat, *Introduction to the Law of the European Communities* (3rd edn., London: Kluwer, 1998) at 406.

goods in the common market. This term, albeit not strictly identical,[129] is construed in the same way as the reference in Article 297 to "the functioning of the common market being affected".[130] However, it is different from the reference in Article 298(1) to the "effect of distorting the conditions of competition in the common market".[131] The adverse effect on competition seems to be produced by less important practices than those distorting competition.

The implications of the different terms used under Articles 296(1)(b) and 298(1) are illustrated by reference to the substantive content of those provisions: the former specifies that national measures deviating from the Treaty must not adversely affect competition in dual-use goods; the latter, while providing that the Member State under consideration and the Commission will consult each other regarding national measures which distort competition in the common market, makes no specific reference to dual-use goods markets. It follows that reliance upon Article 296(1)(b) EC to justify measures covering products included in the Article 296(2) list does give rise to the Article 225(1) EC procedure when these measures distort competition not only in dual-use goods markets but also in the market for military products.

Indeed, it would be nonsensical for recourse to the Article 298(1) EC procedure to be had in order "to . . . adjust to the rules laid down by th[e] Treaty" measures that are not justified under the Treaty. Furthermore, in the light of the exclusion of dual-use goods from the scope of Article 296(1)(b) EC, to confine the Article 298(1) EC procedure to measures distorting the competition in dual-use goods markets would be equally nonsensical. To argue otherwise would lead to the absurd conclusion that measures not covered by the wholly exceptional clause of Article 296(1)(b) EC would be subject to the limited judicial control that the extraordinary Article 298 procedure entails.

The procedure provided under Article 298(1) does not constitute a sanction against the Member States for deviating from the Treaty; instead, it draws upon a specific aspect of the general duty of Member States to "take all the appropriate measures, whether general or particular, to ensure fulfilment of the obligations arising out of th[e] Treaty" under Article 10 EC.

5. THE INTERPRETATION OF ARTICLE 296(1)(b) EC WITHIN THE CONSTITUTIONAL STRUCTURE OF THE EUROPEAN UNION

What the above analysis sought to refute was the view that the inherent military and political nature of armaments renders them beyond the Community legal

---

[129] In its French version, Art. 296(1)(b) EC provides that national measures "ne doivent pas *alterer les conditions de concurrence dans le marché commun*", whereas under Article 297 "le fonctionnement du marché commun ne soit [pas] *affecté*".

[130] See V Constantinesco, R Kovar and D Simon (eds.), *Traité sur l'Union européenne: (signé le 7 février 1992): commentaire article par article* (Paris: Economica, 1996) at 1394.

[131] In its French version, Art. 298(1) refers to measures which "ont pour effet de fausser les conditions de la concurrence dans le marché commun".

order altogether. It was argued that this approach has relied upon a highly problematic and legally inconsistent interpretation of Article 296(1)(b) EC. Instead, an alternative interpretation was put forward: the Member States may deviate from Community law as a whole in so far as their decision is confined to the products laid down in the Article 296(2) EC list, is necessary to protect the "essential interests of their security" strictly construed, while reliance upon Article is subject to judicial control under Article 298 EC. This approach is consistent not only with its character as a "wholly exceptional provision" but also its wording and scope.

Having dealt with one extreme approach to Article 296(1)(b) EC, an opposite, albeit equally extreme, position must be addressed. This questions the very position of Article 296(1)(b) EC within the constitutional order of the Union. It has been argued, in particular, that the introduction of Title V TEU has rendered Article 296(1)(b) EC redundant.[132] The following analysis will challenge this view as fundamentally flawed.

5.1. The interrelationship between Article 296(1)(b) EC and Title V TEU

The main objection to the argument that Article 296(1)(b) EC should be deleted relies upon the current constitutional structure of the European Union. The multifarious functions of armaments are not in dispute. One of their primary functions, namely their defence dimension *stricto sensu*, touches upon the very core of national sovereignty. However, the current constitutional structure of the European Union, as established under the Maastricht Treaty and consolidated under the Amsterdam Treaty, does not suggest the abandonment of the totality of functions performed under the aegis of the Member States as fully sovereign subjects of international law. It follows that, *a fortiori,* neither has it signalled the transfer of the core of national sovereignty to the normative structure of the Union.[133] Therefore, and in the light of the absence of an operative and fully-fledged EU defence dimension, it remains for the Member States to protect what a strict definition of the "essential interests of their security" may entail. Viewed from this angle, the decision in the 1996 Intergovernmental Conference to retain Article 296(1)(b) EC in the EC Treaty must be welcomed, for that provision accurately reflects the role of the Member States within the current constitutional structure of Union. [134]

---

[132] XA Giataganas, *The Member States of the European Union facing the Community Legality. Contribution to the Theory of European Integration* (in Greek) (Athens: A.N. Sakkoulas, 1996) at 80.

[133] See the analysis in ch. 2.

[134] In this respect, it is noteworthy that Verhoeven argues that the right of each Member State to protect its security is independent of Community law; see Constantinesco et al., *supra* note 130 at 1329. In the light of the Court's pronouncement in *Centro-Com* that the conduct of national foreign policy be consistent with Community law, the accuracy of Verhoeven's view is limited to the extent that the very core of national sovereignty, the territorial integrity of the Member States, for instance, is at stake.

However, what the development of the CFSP has affected is the conditions under which the Member States can "protect the essential interests of their security" by deviating from the Treaty. In other words, a link between Article 296(1)(b) EC and the development of the CFSP has been established. This entails that the definition of the conditions under which the Member States can protect the essential interests of their security is dependent upon the extent to which these interests are protected under Title V. The more the "independence and integrity of the Union" is safeguarded and its security is strengthened "in all ways", the more restrictively the conditions under Article 296(1)(b) enabling Member States to deviate from the Treaty in order to protect "the essential interests of their security" must be construed.

Whether the strict construction of Article 296(1)(b) EC and the attainment of the objectives of the Union under Article 2 TEU will ultimately question the necessity of the deviation itself from Community law under the former provision is relevant. It depends upon the extent to which the procedures and instruments provided under Title V are used to their fullest potential to enable the Union to achieve its objectives and safeguard the independence and integrity of the Union and strengthen its security in all ways.

In this respect, recent developments regarding the Defence and Security Identity of the European Union are very important. Not only did the Defence Ministers of the Member States meet for the first time within the framework of the CFSP,[135] but also a number of proposals have been put forward regarding the establishment of the military capability of the Union independently from NATO. It was the British Government that first raised the issue of "an autonomous European military capability"[136] which then became the subject of British–French proposals[137]; finally, the German Presidency submitted a comprehensive proposal to the EU informal foreign ministers meeting on 13–14 March 1999; this document suggested that the EU develop "credible military capabilities" and that decisions dealing with them be adopted within the institutional framework of the Union and facilitated by the establishment of a military committee.[138] No safe conclusion may be drawn regarding the establishment of the defence dimension of the EU on the basis of these proposals[139]; suffice it to say that the starting point of the above proposals is to facilitate the role of the Union to carry out the Petersberg tasks, incorporated within the CFSP under the Amsterdam Treaty; their common thrust is that the role of

---

[135] See *Agence Europe*, 7336 5 Nov. 1998 at 3. It is interesting that the first ever meeting of the EU defence ministers took place at the initiative of the Austrian Presidency, that is a neutral country.

[136] See *Independent on Sunday*, 4 Oct. 1998 at 1.

[137] These proposals were put forward at the annual summit between the two governments in St Malo in Dec. 1998.

[138] The document of the German Presidency is entitled Strengthening the Common Policy on Security and Defence and may be found on the internet (http://www.basicint.org/natosum6-1.htm).

[139] The tentative nature of the discussion is illustrated in an article by Prime Minister Blair entitled "Time for Europe to Repay the American Soldier" in *International Herald Tribune*, 14–15 Nov. 1998 at 8, where he states that he "ha[s] an open mind about what [the proposals regarding the establishment of an autonomous military capability within the EU] might mean institutionally".

NATO as "the foundation of the collective defence of its members"[140] should not be undermined and defence should not be removed from the control of national governments. This was stressed by the Helsinki European Council which expressed "its determination to develop an autonomous capacity to take decisions and, where NATO as a whole is not engaged, to launch and conduct EU-led military operations in response to international crises" and made it clear that "this process . . . does not imply the creation of a European army".[141] What is of significance, however, is the pace of the developments: whereas the development of a European military capability did not attract much support in the 1996 IGC, consensus in this direction seems to be emerging within a period of less than two years after its conclusion. This is illustrated in the establishment of interim bodies which would act as the precursor of the Military Committee consisting of the Member States' Chiefs of Staff.

While these developments deal with the military and political aspects of security, they cannot but affect its economic dimension. The harmonisation of defence procurement, for example, is an essential concomitant to the development of a military capability within the EU structure, however limited its scope may be, as was expressly recognised in the Vienna meeting of the Defence Ministers of the Member States. In other words, the developments outlined above, should they materialise, may eventually lead to a common position setting out common operational requirements for forces of the Member States; this may be interpreted as depriving the Member States of the right to invoke Article 296(1)(b) EC in order to justify procurement of military equipment alien to that prescribed in the common position. In other words, there is an intrinsic link between Article 296(1)(b) EC and the CFSP framework which requires that reliance upon the former cannot be justified when the "essential interests of [national] security" are protected by measures adopted within the latter. It should be noted, however, that this link is inevitably underpinned by the essential characteristics of the second pillar: its dynamic nature and incremental development entail that, in practical terms, the extent to which Member States would consider themselves bound by a Title V common position not to invoke Article 296(1)(b) EC would be contingent upon the development of the CFSP in general and the system of compliance developed amongst them within it in particular.

---

[140] *Supra* note 138.

[141] Presidency Conclusions, Helsinki European Council, 10 and 11 Dec. 1999, para. 27. This was also stressed by High Representative Solana, according to whom European Security and Defence Identity "is not about collective defence. NATO will remain the foundation of the collective defence of its members. . . . ESDP [does not] attempt to undermine the right of Member States to retain their own specific security and defence policy": speech entitled "The Development of a Common Security and Defence Policy—The Integration Project of the Next Decade", delivered on 17 Dec. 1999.

5.2. The limited effect of Article 296(1)(b) EC

The proposition that the development of the CFSP entails the strict construction of the conditions under which Article 296(1)(b) EC is to be invoked indicates the latter's limited effect. Indeed, it would be rather rarely the case that the "essential interests of the security" of a Member State would necessitate the adoption of wholly exceptional unilateral measures. For example, the exemption of imports of armaments from third countries from the Common Customs Tariff could very rarely indeed, if ever, be considered necessary for the protection of "the essential interests of [national] security".[142] At any rate, if such a scenario occurs, in a case, for example, of a Member State at war with a third country or in preparation for one, then it would have the right to protect its territorial integrity, that is the most essential interest of its security, by any means. The limited effect of Article 296(1)(b) EC is also illustrated by the definition of its material scope on the basis of the Article 296(2) EC list and the increasing relevance of dual-use goods, which are not covered by the proviso under consideration. Furthermore, the increasing participation of the Member States in various multilateral efforts to regulate the production of and trade in armaments and to control proliferation would render the link between a closed defence market and national security tenuous; this would question too frequent an invocation of Article 296(1)(b) EC by the Member States.

5.3. Article 296(1)(b) EC and political realities

The deletion of Article 296(1)(b) EC is rendered not only less significant, in the light of its proper construction and the development of the CFSP, but also unrealistic on political grounds. This has recently been accepted not only by the Commission,[143] contrary to proposals it had submitted in the past,[144] but also the European Parliament, that is the most enthusiastic advocate of its deletion.[145] Responding to the Commission Communication on the challenges

---

[142] See *Commentaire Mégret, supra* note 102 at 432.

[143] See COM(96)10 final, *supra* note 32 at 14.

[144] See COM(90)600 final, *Opinion on Political Union*, at 5 and J Cloos, G Reinesch, D Vignes and J Weyland, *Le Traité de Maastricht. Genèse, Analyse, Commentaire* (Brussels: Bruyland, 1993) at 364–5. The hostile reception its proposal received, however, made the Commission, in its Opinion for the 1996 IGC, adopt the more flexible suggestion of "une meilleure intégration du secteur de l'armement dans les règles générales du traité": see COM(96)90 final, *supra* note 32 at 15.

[145] For the Parliament's previous approach regarding the deletion of Art. 296(1)(b), see Resolution on (i) the Parliament's opinion on the convening of the Intergovernmental Conference; and (ii) evaluation of the work of the Reflection Group and definition of the political priorities of the European Parliament with a view to the Intergovernmental Conference at 9, Resolution on the need for European controls on the export or transfer of arms [1995] OJ C43/89 at 90, Resolution A3–0260/92, Report on the Community's role in the supervision of arms exports and the armaments industry [1992] OJ C284/138 at 142.

facing the European defence-related industry,[146] the Parliament adopted a considerably more flexible approach[147]; it suggested that Article 296 EC be considered in depth, possibly adapted[148] and ultimately revised[149] and called upon the Member States, in the meantime, to invoke it only under exceptional circumstances. It is noteworthy that the Parliament even suggested that Article 296(1)(b) EC may play a positive role within the Union structure by "protect[ing] industries which are crucial for development of the European security and defence identity from coming under the control of third-country undertakings".[150]

6. CONCLUSION

The thrust of the above analysis is two-fold: on the one hand, the deeply entrenched perception of armaments as entirely beyond the Community legal order is inconsistent with the proper interpretation of Article 296(1)(b) EC; on the other hand, an intrinsic link between the interpretation of that provision and the development of the CFSP must be acknowledged within the current constitutional structure of the European Union. This conclusion has important implications for how the pillar-structure of the Union may be construed in practical terms; to argue that the interpretation of a wholly exceptional Community provision depends to a considerable extent upon developments beyond the Community legal framework is tantamount to understanding EC and CFSP as parts of a functional whole. Viewed from this angle, not only is the rhetoric of the "single institutional framework" transformed into a legal reality, but also the requirements of "consistency and continuity" and respect for the *acquis communautaire* are met. Finally, the above conclusion effectively questions the view that the establishment of the Union on distinct, albeit interdependent, legal frameworks undermines the effectiveness of its activities; indeed, viewed as parts of a functional whole, the Community legal order and the CFSP may contribute to the attainment of the objectives of the Union. It is not the structure of the Union itself but the way in which its institutions and the Member States have recourse to the legal means provided therein that may undermine its effectiveness.

---

[146] *Supra* note 33.

[147] Report A4–76/97.

[148] According to the Parliament, the adaptation of Art. 296(1)(b) EC is required particularly in relation to the Art. 296(2) list "so as to encourage the creation of a European armaments industry" in *ibid*. at 6.

[149] The Parliament "believes that the gradual establishment of [a common armaments policy incorporating scientific and technological components] will ultimately require Article [296] to be revised in order to achieve integrated production, trading and monitoring of armaments" in *ibid*.

[150] *Ibid*.

9

The European Union Code of Conduct on Arms Exports and the Commission's Proposals on Defence Industries

1. INTRODUCTION

The thesis that the development of the CFSP is relevant to the extent to which recourse may be had to Article 296(1)(b) EC establishes an intrinsic link between the first and second pillars. This, in effect, questions the view of the pillars as rigidly distinct legal frameworks and establishes a functional link which seeks to build upon the *acquis communautaire* while not impinging upon the inter-governmental features of Title V. The question which then arises is whether the Community legal framework and CFSP have indeed been viewed as parts of a functional whole by the Union institutions. In other words, has their intrinsic link been relied upon in order to facilitate the adoption of a legally sensible and effective approach towards the economic aspects of security? The answer to this question is obscured by mixed signals: while the regulation of the external aspects of arms, which resulted in the adoption of an EU code of conduct on arms exports, suggests a negative answer, the relatively recent Commission proposals on the defence industries illustrate a more positive approach.

In examining these issues, the structure of this chapter will be as follows. First, the substantive content of the EU code of conduct on arms exports and the legal formula under which it was adopted will be analysed. Secondly, the Commission's Communications on the defence-related industries will be examined, special attention being paid to the legal formula they put forward. Thirdly, these proposals will be viewed as encapsulating a coherent approach encompassing both the first and second pillars and, hence, an alternative to the legal confusion prevailing in the area of the legal regulation of armaments under the law of the European Union.

2. ARMS EXPORTS AND THE EUROPEAN UNION CODE OF CONDUCT

One of the most important aspects of the regulation of armaments deals with their export. This issue raises two questions of central significance. The first question focuses on the role of arms export control regimes in general, as operating on the basis of criteria set up unilaterally by the exporting states or agreed upon collectively by groups of states. This question touches upon not only the political necessity of such controls in the post-Cold War geopolitical environment, but also the role of human rights in the elaboration of the export control systems. While the examination of the former issue has been confined to academic circles,[1] the latter has been widely debated during recent years in the light of the initiative of the British Government to add an "ethical dimension" to its foreign policy in general and its arms exports in particular.[2] A wide range of divergent opinions have been expressed: a former British Minister of Defence characterised human rights concerns in international relations "crap"[3] while a former European Commissioner argued that "a foreign policy purged of any ethical value [may] produc[e] monsters".[4] For the purpose of this book, both the political necessity of arms export control regimes and the role of human rights in their development is approached as an accepted part of the political reality prevailing in current international relations: this is evident, in the case of the former, in the proliferation of multilateral arms export control regimes, whereas, in the case of the latter, in its role underpinning the initiative of the British and French Governments which eventually led to the adoption of the EU code of conduct on arms exports.[5]

The second question regarding the regulation of arms exports is of a legal character and raises a dilemma similar to that regarding the exports of dual-use goods. Given their character as trade measures serving foreign policy objectives, within which legal framework are they to be regulated? The issues related to the regulation of arms exports are underpinned by a two-fold dimension of considerable significance which was analysed above: on the one hand, the intrinsic link of armaments with the development of the defence and security identity of the Union and, on the other hand, the longstanding perception of armaments as beyond the Community legal order altogether pursuant to an arbitrary interpretation of Article 296(1)(b) EC. Viewed from this angle and in the light of the difficulties regarding the establishment of common rules on exports of dual-use

---

[1] For an analysis supporting the establishment of arms control regimes and their typology see S Croft, "In Defence of Arms Control" (1996) XLIV *Political Studies* 888.

[2] See *Independent*, 17 Oct. 1998 at 9. For an analysis of this initiative from the viewpoint of international relations see NJ Wheeler T and Dunne, "Good International Citizenship: A Third Way for British Foreign Policy?" (1998) 74 *International Affairs* 847.

[3] A Clark, *Diaries* (London: Phoenix, 1994) at 161.

[4] E Bonino, in a speech made on the occasion of the fifth anniversary of the ECHO, *Agence Europe*, 7097 11 Nov. 1997 at 3.

[5] Whether the "ethical dimension" added in British foreign policy has actually materialised is an entirely different issue, clearly exceeding the bounds of this book. However, it is interesting to note that there is no shortage of reports claiming that, in practical terms, no "ethical dimension" has been added regarding exports of arms authorised by the British Government: see details from reports prepared by Saferworld, an independent research group, in *The Guardian*, 24 June 1998 at 1 and Amnesty International in *The Guardian*, 23 Sept. 1998 at 2. In addition, see *Financial Times*, 4 May 1998 at 6 for concerns over exports to Sierra Leone and *The Sunday Times*, 13 Dec. 1998 at 1 to Indonesia. For an overall critique, see *The Sunday Times*, 14 Mar. 1999 at 1.

goods, it is hardly surprising that the regulation of arms exports had been the subject of long and tortuous negotiations. However, given the considerable interest that the regulation of arms exports has attracted from the international community in general, the EU code of conduct must be examined in the light of other multilateral initiatives undertaken prior to its adoption.

2.1. International initiatives on the regulation of arms exports

The establishment of multilateral export control regimes in relation to arms was considered a *sine qua non* of the Cold War geopolitical environment. The most prominent initiative was the Co-ordinating Committee on Multilateral Export Controls (COCOM) which was intended to regulate exports to the Soviet bloc[6]; this regime dealt with nuclear equipment, munitions and dual-use goods. Operating on a semi-secret basis and lacking treaty status, the COCOM system offered Western democracies, that is the USA, its NATO allies (except Iceland), Japan and Australia, the chance to present a common front, albeit not without problems.[7] In the post-Cold War era, international initiatives regarding the introduction of common export rules have still been undertaken; instead of a potential common enemy, these initiatives have been justified in the light of the trend towards multilateralism that characterises the international community.[8] The successor of COCOM in the post-Cold War geo-political climate is the Wassenaar Arrangement on Export Controls for Conventional Arms and Dual-Use Goods and Technologies.[9] This regime deals with the same range of goods covered by COCOM and focuses mainly on preventing the transfer of advanced conventional weapons if the situation in a region or the behaviour of a state is, or is likely to become, a cause for serious concern to the participating states.[10] The main features of the Wassenaar Arrangement are laid down in its Initial Elements, agreed upon by its members on 19 December 1995.[11] The participating states have

---

[6] See generally P D'Argent, "Les enseignements du COCOM" (1993) 26 *RBDI* 500.

[7] For the structural problems of the COCOM regime and its ineffectiveness that ensued at various instances see DJ Fitzpatrick, "Of Ropes, Buttons and Four-By-Fours: Import Sanctions for Violations of the COCOM Agreement" (1989) 29 *Va J. Int'l L.* 249.

[8] For an analysis of the proliferation of multilateral export control regimes see A Latham and B Bow, "Multilateral Export Control Regimes" (1998) 53 *International Journal* 465 and J Spear, "Arms and Arms Control" in B White, R Little and M Smith (eds.), *Issues in World Politics* (London: MacMillan, 1997) 111.

[9] In addition to the Wassenaar Arrangement, the following four major multilateral export control regimes have been undertaken: the Nuclear Suppliers' Group (NSG) and Zangger Committee (ZAC) deal with technologies related to nuclear weapons; the Australia Group (AG) deals with goods and technologies related to chemical and biological weapons; the Missile Technology Control Regime (MTCR) deals with the specific missile system capable of delivering nuclear, biological or chemical warheads.

[10] There are 33 participating states, including, amongst others, all the EU Member States, the USA and the Russian Federation.

[11] The list of dual-use goods and technologies and munitions submitted to its plenary meeting can be found on the internet (http://www.wassenaar.org).

agreed to notify each other of any transfers and denials of transfers to non-participating states based on items laid down in a list of dual-use goods and technologies and in a munitions list.[12] The participating states are to take into account a study paper on criteria for assessing destabilising weapons accumulations entitled *Elements for Objective Analysis and Advice Concerning Potentially Destabilising Accumulations of Conventional Weapons*. The defining feature of the Wassenaar Arrangement is its complete reliance upon the participating states' discretion: it is their sole responsibility to grant or deny an export authorisation, while it is clear that all measures undertaken will be in accordance with national policies.

2.2. Objective, scope and criteria laid down in the EU code of conduct on arms exports

The code of conduct on arms exports was adopted by the Council on 25 May 1998 in order to "set high common standards which should be regarded as the minimum for the management of, and restraint in, conventional arms transfers by all EU Member States, and to strengthen the exchange of relative information with a view to achieving greater transparency".[13] Its material scope is not expressly laid down therein; no list of products is attached, while it is stated that the Member States "will work for [its] early adoption . . . based on similar national and international lists".[14]

   The code of conduct refers to eight criteria on the basis of which national authorities of the Member States are to authorise exports. The thrust of these criteria, as put forward by the then President of the Council, is that "weapons cannot be sold to countries which could use them for external aggression or internal repression".[15] The first criterion consists of respect for the international commitments of the Member States, in particular the sanctions decreed by the Security Council and those decreed by the Community, agreements on non-proliferation and other subjects, as well as other international obligations.[16] The second criterion is respect for human rights in the country of final destination. Adherence to this entails a two-fold obligation: on the one hand, the Member States are not to issue an export licence if there is a clear risk that

---

[12] These lists are to be reviewed regularly in order to take into account technological developments.

[13] Third recital of the preamble. See *Bull EU* 5–1998, I–3.6.

[14] Until then, the competent national authorities are to apply the code of conduct on the basis of national lists incorporating, where appropriate, elements from relevant international lists.

[15] *Agence Europe*, 7228 25–26 May 1998 at 4.

[16] The code stresses that an export licence should be refused if approval would be inconsistent with, *inter alia*, the following: the international obligations of Member States and their commitments to enforce UN, OSCE and EU measures; the international obligations of Member States under the Nuclear Non-Proliferation Treaty, the Biological and Toxic Weapons Convention and the Chemical Weapons Convention; their commitments in the frameworks of the Australia Group, the Missile Technology Control Regime, the Nuclear Suppliers Group and the Wassenaar Agreement; finally, their commitment not to export any form of anti-personnel landmines.

the proposed export might be used for internal repression[17]; secondly, caution and vigilance should be exercised in issuing a licence to a country where serious violations of human rights have been established by the competent bodies of the UN, the Council of Europe or the EU. These cases are to be examined on an *ad hoc* basis while the competent authorities of the Member States are to take into account the nature of the equipment to be exported.

The third criterion on the basis of which the competent authorities of the Member States are to grant an export authorisation consists of the internal situation in the country of final destination, as a function of the existence of tensions or armed conflicts. The following two criteria consist of the preservation of regional peace, security and stability[18] and the national security of the Member States and of the territories whose external relations are the responsibility of a Member State, as well as that of friendly and allied countries. In relation to the latter, it is noteworthy that, while the potential effect of the proposed export on the defence and security interests of the Member States is to be taken into account, the code of conduct points out that this cannot affect consideration of the criteria on respect for human rights and on regional peace, security and stability. The sixth criterion refers to the behaviour of the buyer country with regard to the international community, as regards in particular its attitude to terrorism, the nature of its alliances and respect for international law. The following one consists of the existence of a risk that the equipment will be diverted within the buyer country or re-exported under undesirable conditions. Finally, in granting an arms export authorisation, the competent authorities of the Member States must take into account the compatibility of the arms exports with the technical and economic capacity of the recipient country, taking into account the desirability that states should achieve their legitimate needs of security and defence with the least diversion for armaments of human and economic resources.

2.3. The applicable procedures under the EU code of conduct

Refusal by the competent authorities of a Member State to authorise an export is to be notified and justified through diplomatic channels to the other Member

---

[17] The term "internal repression" is defined as covering, *inter alia*, torture and other cruel, inhuman and degrading treatment or punishment in summary or arbitrary executions, disappearances, arbitrary detentions and other major violations of human rights and fundamental freedoms as set out in relevant human rights instruments, including the Universal Declaration on Human Rights and the international Covenant on Civil and Political Rights.

[18] The code of conduct refers, in particular, to cases where there is a clear risk that the intended recipient would use the proposed export aggressively against another country or assert by force a territorial claim. In examining where these risks do exist, four additional grounds are provided to be taken into account by the national authorities, namely the existence or likelihood of armed conflict between the recipient and another country, a claim against the territory of a neighbouring country which the recipient has in the past tried or threatened to pursue by means of force, whether the equipment would be likely to be used other than for the legitimate national security and defence of the recipient and the need not to affect adversely regional stability in any significant way.

States; if, however, an application for an export licence covering the same products is submitted to the authorities of another Member State, the so-called "no undercutting" rule is to be applied, whereby the latter State shall consult the one which issued the denial. If, nonetheless, it decides to grant an export licence, it shall inform that Member State and justify the authorisation.[19]

The application of the code is to be examined on an annual basis and a report is to be produced by the Council. This report will be based on national reports that each Member State will provide to the other Member States in confidence in relation to its defence equipment and its implementation of the code.[20]

2.4. Comment on the code of conduct

When the code of conduct on arms exports was adopted, it became the subject of debate and criticism. It was criticised on various grounds: the requirement that violations of human rights will prevent an export from being authorised only when established by international "competent bodies" was deemed to have "put the threshold of evidence ominously high"[21]; the requirement, contrary to proposals submitted during the negotiating process,[22] that a Member State asked to authorise an export denied by another Member State consult with only the latter and not all the Member States was seen as undermining the establishment of a consistent approach towards sensitive end-users amongst the Member States[23]; the absence of a permanent list of countries with poor human rights records was criticised by the Nordic Member States as undermining the effectiveness of the code.[24] It is interesting that, following the adoption of the code of conduct, the German Government suggested that another code be adopted in order to restrict arms brokers from circumventing national restrictions by arranging manufacture abroad; however, this suggestion was not received enthusiastically by other governments,[25] even though it would clearly enhance the effectiveness of the code of conduct on arms exports.

Important though the above issues are, what is of utmost relevance to this analysis is the legal nature of the EU code of conduct on arms exports: having been negotiated within the CFSP, it was adopted by means of a Declaration by the Council. As such, instead of being legally binding on the Member States, it constitutes "a political undertaking by Member States".[26]

The decision of the Member States to adopt the code of conduct without recourse to the instruments provided within the CFSP framework, namely

---

[19] See Art. 3 of the Code of Conduct.
[20] See *ibid*. Art. 8.
[21] *The Guardian*, 26 May 1998 at 1.
[22] See *Agence Europe*, 7170 28 Feb. 1998 at 2.
[23] *The Guardian*, 26 May 1998 at 17.
[24] See *Financial Times*, 26 May 1998 at 3.
[25] See *The Sunday Times*, 14 Mar. 1999 at 1.
[26] *Agence Europe*, 7170 28 Feb. 1998 at 2.

common positions and joint actions, indicates the Member States' reluctance to assume any legal obligation stemming from Title V TEU. This is illustrated by the wording of the code, which stresses that "[t]he decision to transfer or deny the transfer of any item of military equipment will remain at the national discretion of each Member State".[27] It is also reflected in the objectives of the code of conduct as set out in the preamble; the criteria incorporated in the code of conduct "should be regarded as the minimum for the management of, and restraint in, conventional arms transfers by all EU Member States" while aiming at "strengthening the exchange of relative information with a view to achieving greater transparency".[28] Moreover, the Council expresses its "wish within the framework of the CFSP to reinforce [the] cooperation [amongst the Member States] and to promote their convergence in the field of conventional arms exports".[29] The careful approach, illustrated by the wording of the preamble to the code of conduct, is even more apparent in the statement of the French Foreign Minister Hubert Védrine who, along with the British Government, took the initiative for its adoption: he stated that the code of conduct illustrates "a realistic approach" based on "progressiveness", while adding that the Member States will "see how to go further".[30]

However, the adoption of the code of conduct on arms exports without recourse being had to the formal instruments provided for under Title V TEU is regrettable on four grounds. First, the effectiveness of the code of conduct is undermined, for it does not impose a legal obligation on the Member States to abide by its content. This does not mean that the code of conduct is of no actual significance; the Member States still have to support its application "actively and unreservedly in a spirit of loyalty and mutual solidarity" under Article 11(2) TEU. However, this duty is not of the legal character that defines those measures identified *par excellence* with the development of the CFSP, namely joint actions and common positions. Furthermore, the Council's decision not to have recourse to the formal instruments of the CFSP is inconsistent with the rationale underpinning the adoption of the code of conduct. Given that all Member States participate in the most comprehensive multilateral control regime of arms exports, namely the Wassenaar Arrangement, the significance of their initiative to set common standards within the EU framework would inevitably rely upon the terms in which it would be established. To ignore the most important part of the CFSP legal machinery seriously questions the actual significance of the initiative.

Secondly, in adopting the code of conduct on arms exports by means of a declaration, the Council undermines the role of common positions and joint actions as the formal instruments of the CFSP. The TEU equipped the Union with these instruments in order to facilitate its ambition to "assert its identity on the

---

[27] Art. 3(2) of the Code.
[28] Third recital of the preamble.
[29] Fifth recital of the preamble.
[30] *Agence Europe*, 7228 25–26 May 1998 at 4.

international scene".[31] Their adoption has underpinned the development of the *sui generis* foreign policy system of the European Union. The Council decision not to have recourse to the formal instruments provided for under Title V is all the more striking in the light of the specific functions performed by them: common positions express an agreed point of view,[32] whereas joint actions are of an operational character[33] and cover issues which have been the subject of guidelines already put forward by the European Council. It would be in conformity with the above requirements for the code of conduct to have been adopted by recourse to a joint action. Indeed, the criteria incorporated in the code of conduct are based on the Common Criteria adopted by the Luxembourg and Lisbon European Councils in 1991 and 1992[34]; furthermore, it is interesting to note that the guidelines upon which the competent authorities of the Member States grant export authorisations of dual-use goods are adopted by means of a Joint Action. However, it must be acknowledged that, in practical terms, the choice of instrument may not always be apparent. Therefore, as it was argued that the *modus operandi* of the common rules on export of dual-use goods could have been adopted by means of a common position and not a joint action,[35] it may also be argued that the code of conduct could have been adopted under a common position. Indeed, this was the suggestion repeatedly put forward by the European Parliament.[36]

Thirdly, the decision not to have recourse to the formal CFSP instruments is inconsistent with past practice under Title V itself, as embargoes on arms against third countries have repeatedly been imposed by means of a Common Position.[37] If the Member States' agreement to prohibit the export of arms *in toto* is adopted by means of a formal Title V instrument, it is not clear why such an instrument was not deemed appropriate to express the Member States' agreement to authorise export of arms on the basis of common criteria. Furthermore, the issue of control of arms exports had already been specified by the Lisbon European Council in 1992 as likely to be subject to a joint action adopted under

---

[31] Art. 2 TEU.

[32] Under the Art. 15 TEU, they "shall define the approach of the Union to a particular matter of geographical or thematic nature".

[33] Under Art. 14(1) TEU, joint actions shall "address specific situations where operational action by the Union is deemed to be required".

[34] Not only is this mentioned in the very first recital of the preamble to the Declaration, but also, according to Art. 12 of the operative provisions of the Code of Conduct, the latter "will replace any previous elaboration of the 1991 and 1992 Common Criteria".

[35] See A Dashwood, "External Relations Provisions of the Amsterdam Treaty" (1998) 35 *CMLRev.* 1019 at n55.

[36] See Art. 8 of the Parliament's *Resolution on a code of conduct for arms exports* [1998] OJ C167/226 and Art. 4 of its *Resolution on a European code of conduct on the export of arms* [1998] OJ C34/163; also *Agence Europe*, 7223 16 May 1998 at 2. Under the Parliament's proposal, this common position would lead to a series of joint actions.

[37] See the embargo on arms, munitions and military equipment to Afghanistan under Council Dec. 96/746/CFSP [1996] OJ L342/1, the prohibition of arms exports to the former Yugoslavia under Council Dec. 96/184/CFSP [1996] OJ L 8/1 and the embargo to Sudan under Council Dec. 94/165/CFSP [1994] OJ L75/1.

Article 14 TEU. Moreover, the decision of the Member States not to have recourse to the formal CFSP instruments is all the more surprising in the light of the express reference to the code of conduct in Joint Action on small weapons.[38]

The fourth argument against the Council's decision to adopt the code of conduct on arms exports by means of a declaration lies upon its undermining effect on the CFSP as a whole. As the development of various international initiatives illustrates, the regulation of arms exports is at the top of the agenda of the international community. For the European Union to attempt to regulate this issue by ignoring the most important instruments provided for under Title V is tantamount to denying the CFSP the opportunity to carry out in a meaningful way a policy lying at its very heart.

3. THE COMMISSION COMMUNICATIONS REGARDING DEFENCE-RELATED INDUSTRIES

In the last four years, the problems that the defence industries face have been the subject of extensive Commission initiatives. This renewed interest may be explained by the structural problems of national defence industries accentuated by reduced national defence budgets and the intensified international competition, namely fragmentation, excess production capability, inability to engage in costly research and development and undermined competitiveness in an increasingly competitive international market. However, it must be noted that, even prior to the Commission's initiatives, Community policies had not been totally irrelevant to defence industries. This is illustrated by the KONVER programme which aims at assisting the conversion of defence industries of Member States to other productions; this programme constitutes part of the structural funds and, hence, is administered by the Commission on the basis of the Community rules applicable to regional aid.[39]

In order to address the problems that the new geopolitical and economic environment has raised for national defence industries, the Commission put forward two documents. The first one, entitled *The Challenges facing the European Defence-Related Industry, A Contribution for Action at European Level,*[40] consists of an outline of the economic problems that defence industries of the Member States face and the political developments in the post-Cold War era in relation to armaments; in addition, it examines the potential of policies and initiatives directly stemming from and indirectly related to the Union which would

[38] Council Dec. 99/34/CFSP [1999] OJL 9/1.

[39] This programme originated in the PERIFRA programme, established in 1991 and aiming at assisting regions of the Member States to cope with post-Cold War consequences such as the effect of disarmament on national defence industries, the trade concessions granted to products imported from CEECs and German unification. For the creation of KONVER and the instrumental role played by the European Parliament in its development see N Hooper and N Cox, "The European Union KONVER Programme" (1996) 7 *Defence and Peace Economics* 75.

[40] COM(96)10 final, adopted on 24 Nov. 1996.

enhance the competitiveness of national defence industries. The second document, entitled *Implementing European Union Strategy on Defence-Related Industries*,[41] on the one hand specifies the Community policies which are of relevance to the problems that national defence industries face and, on the other hand, suggest a specific legal form for the Union's intervention in this area.[42] The following analysis will not provide a detailed study of the specific policy choices that the Commission suggests; instead, it will focus on whether the Commission approaches the various functions of defence industries in a legally sensible and coherent way within the existing constitutional structure of the European Union.

3.1. The thrust of the Commission's proposals: a coherent approach

The starting point for the Commission's proposals based on two assumptions: first, national defence industries perform a variety of functions, namely military, political and economic, which are intrinsically interlinked; secondly, the immense problems that national defence industries face may be effectively addressed only in so far as the above functions are reviewed *in tandem*.[43] It is in the light of this assumption that the Commission argues that "there can be no European defence policy or identity without a healthy and competitive European technological and industrial base" and the proposition that this requires "a clear, reliable political and institutional frame of reference".[44]

The thrust of the Commission's approach is that these functions may be reviewed on the basis of a coherent approach embracing not only all three pillars of the European Union[45] but also developments beyond the structure of the Union.[46]

---

[41] COM(97)583 final, adopted on 12 Nov. 1997.

[42] The following analysis will focus on both Communications as a whole.

[43] This is also illustrated by the following passage of a speech delivered by former Commissioner van den Broek: "A European Defence Identity has three necessary components: a political component, which lies with the EU; a military component which is the joint responsibility of NATO and WEU . . . ; and an industrial, scientific and technological component without which this identity will have no substance. This means that an effective and competitive European armament industry is . . . a precondition for the existence of a credible European Defence Identity": "Challenges facing the European Defence Industry: a contribution for action at European level", a speech delivered to the Symposium on One European Defence Industry, The Hague, 17 Oct. 1996.

[44] To this end, it puts forward its points of convergence with the Council, as identified by the latter's working group on European armaments policy on the basis of COM(96)10 which may be summarised as follows: the maintenance of the industrial and technological base of the Union's defence-related industry is crucial for both security and economic reasons, the former focusing on the establishment of a European defence identity, the latter on competitiveness and jobs in crucial manufacturing sectors. Special reference is also made to the increasing involvement of dual-use goods in the industrial and technological base of defence industries.

[45] The Commission argues that "[i]n an economic area without internal frontiers and with common security interests, consistency demands that the Union institutions implement policies ensuring greater combination of the powers of the institutions in connection with the various pillars of the Union" in *ibid*. at 15.

[46] The Commission stresses the increasingly deteriorating economic conditions which national defence industries face; in particular, it points out that, since its Communication on the Challenges

3.2. The Community legal framework: a strict interpretation of Article 296(1)(b) EC

In both its Communications, the Commission outlines the commonly identified economic and political challenges to which the Member States and their defence industries must respond. The first proposition it advances argues that the fragmentation of the European defence market is partly due to recourse being had to Article 296(1)(b) EC by Member States "broadly and divergently", construing it as "embodying a general principle that all areas concerning national security are not covered by the Treaties".[47] Arguing that this contention has been dismissed by the Court in *Werner* and *Leifer* regarding exports of dual-use goods, the Commission puts forward a strict interpretation of Article 296(1)(b) EC which is consistent with both its wording and context. It is construed as a "wholly exceptional clause" "applicable only under specific circumstances and conditions" and "solely to the products on the [Article 296(2) EC] list", hence "giv[ing] the Member States no exclusive general powers. Instead, it gives them the possibility of invoking an exemption to the discipline imposed by the Treaty under the conditions described [therein] and under the supervision of the Courts".[48]

3.3. The CFSP: the development of the economic aspects of security

In relation to the second pillar, the Commission notes that the economic aspects of security were indicated by the Lisbon European Council as likely to be subject to joint actions adopted under Article 14 TEU[49]; these aspects were specified as comprising control of the transfer of military technology to third countries and control of arms exports. Moreover, in relation to the economic aspects of security, the Foreign Affairs Ministers of the Member States were

Facing the European Defence-related Industries, no action was taken despite further deterioration of the situation in the defence industry, consisting of unemployment between 1993 and 1995 falling by 13%, imports from USA being six times the value of exports and very substantial economic gains for the American defence industries due to the establishment of an American single defence market. It is in the light of these developments that the Commission concludes that "[t]he European market is still too fragmented and the level of intra-Community trade in defence equipment is astoundingly low compared to total procurement by the Member States" in *ibid.* at 3. It is interesting that the Commission puts forward a body of reference upon which the Union's strategy may be based. This consists partly of the recommendations of the working party on European arms policy, which the Commission suggests be formulated as Community or CFSP measures. However, it is pointed out that no such recommendations have been formulated two years after the establishment of the group. According to the Commission, though, "it has made useful progress in defining the special characteristics of this sector and identifying areas in which action should be taken as a priority".

[47] *Supra* note 40 at 14.

[48] *Ibid.* at 14. For an analysis of Art. 296(1)(b), see *supra* ch. 8.

[49] *Bull. EC* 6–1992 at 21. The Lisbon European Council indicated other security issues likely to be subject of joint actions, namely the CSCE process, the policy of disarmament and arms control in Europe, including confidence-building measures and nuclear non-proliferation issues.

asked "to define the necessary basic elements for a policy of the Union . . . [and] in particular consider the elements which will be necessary to the Union in the framework of the CFSP".[50]

Furthermore, the second Commission Communication makes reference to the new parameters set by the Amsterdam Treaty. Under Article 17(2) TEU, "[t]he progressive framing of a common defence policy will be supported, as Member States consider appropriate, by cooperation between them in the field of armaments". In addition, under the Declaration Relating to Western European Union[51] a measure which "can be taken forward now [so as to achieve enhanced cooperation between WEU and EU]" may include "cooperation in the field of armaments, as appropriate within the framework of the Western European Armaments Group (WEAG), as the European forum for armaments cooperation, the EU and WEU in the context of rationalisation of the European armaments market and the establishment of a European Armaments Agency".[52]

3.4. Beyond the structure of the European Union

On the basis of its argument for a coherent approach, the Commission makes extensive reference to developments beyond the Union structure.[53] The significant feature of the Commission's analysis lies on its focus on the interrelationship between the Union and the WEU; it points out that "given that the EU and WEU/WEAG have common political objectives, where their activities cover the same fields there are clear advantages to be gained from mutual information and closer cooperation, particularly in terms of efficiency, costs and consistency".[54]

---

[50] *Ibid.* This was reaffirmed six months later, in the Conclusions of the Edinburgh European Council, *Bull. EC* 12–1992 at 38. Activities have already been undertaken in these areas: under Council Dec. 94/509/CFSP [1994] OJ L205/1, a joint action was adopted regarding the preparation of the 1995 Conference on the Non-proliferation Treaty, whereas in relation to military products, a joint action has been adopted banning exports of anti-personnel mines.

[51] Declaration No 3 annexed to the Amsterdam Treaty.

[52] According to COM(97)583 final, the European Armaments Agency "will have extensive responsibilities for all factors affecting the definition and organization of demand for armaments products [and hence] will facilitate the restructuring and consolidation of the European defence industry".

[53] In addition to the Declaration on WEU annexed to the Maastricht Treaty, reference is made to the establishment of the Western European Armaments Group within the WEU and the failure to establish a European Armaments Agency.

[54] *Supra* note 40 at 16. In relation to the fulfilment of the role of WEU as set out in the Maastricht Treaty, the Commission points out that, "for interoperability and cost reasons and in order to fulfil the common security objectives/tasks, increasingly the equipment requirements of the forces participating in the WEU will in turn become common. Definition by the WEU of European forces' operational requirements will mark a decisive step for European armaments policy" in *ibid.* at 17. Furthermore, it adds that "[c]loser cooperation between the EU institutions and the WEAG would be facilitated by building bridges between the European institutions dealing with defence markets. Such synergies and bridges could be established rapidly and pragmatically on the basis of the Treaty of Rome or of Title V (for example, by extending the existing information and consultation procedures between the WEU and the Commission)" in *ibid.* at 16.

It also points out that "largely common demand for armaments from WEU states would put the EU in a position to define more closely the rules governing the internal market, imports and supplies of military equipment".[55]

3.5. The Commission's proposal to formalise the interactions between EC and CFSP

In formulating a coherent inter-pillar approach, the Commission suggests that a common position be adopted under Article Title V TEU "intended to promote Member States' political commitment to the progressive establishment of a genuine European armaments policy".[56] The important feature of the proposed Common Position is the balance that the Commission strikes between, on the one hand, the relevance of Community policies to the defence industry and, on the other hand, the various national interests identified with the latter's development. The preamble to the proposed Common Position makes this effort apparent: on the one hand, not only does it acknowledge "the important contribution" that "Community policies and instruments can make . . . to the development of a European armaments policy",[57] but it refers specifically to areas within which the Community has acted in various ways, namely employment, intra-Community transfers and public procurement, both of which are mentioned as priority areas for EU action, and imposition of customs duties[58]; on the other hand, it makes special reference to the list adopted under Article 296(2) EC in accordance with Article 296(1)(b) EC.

The body of the proposed Common Position further illustrates the Commission's effort to strike a balance between the various functions of defence industry and the corresponding interests that are involved. The general premise that "an effective European armaments policy entails using CFSP and Community instruments"[59] is defined as follows: on the one hand, the specific features of the armaments sector are to be taken into account[60]; on the other

---

[55] *Ibid.*

[56] *Ibid.*

[57] Fifth recital.

[58] In relation to the latter issue, the tenth preambular para. of the proposed Common Position provides that "it is in the interests of the European Union and the Community that certain imports of arms and equipment for the European armed forces should benefit from exemption from customs duties and a list of equipment suitable for exemption from such duties is therefore needed".

[59] *Ibid.* Art. 2.

[60] *Ibid.* Art. 1. The definition of the special features of the defence market is elaborated in a document drafted by the Council working group on European armaments policy, approved by the Council on 10 Dec. 1996 and annexed to the Common Position. The content of this document is of importance, for Art. 1 refers directly to it. Annex I outlines the economic, political, strategic and security considerations that determine the structure and operation of defence markets. It outlines the influence of national governments over defence markets and the need for confidentiality regarding sensitive military information which may lead to potential constraints of competition; in addition, it refers to the extremely high research and development costs and the increasing application of defence-related technologies to the production of dual-use goods. Finally, Art. 296(1)(b) EC is mentioned as acknowledging the specific characteristics of the armaments sector.

212 Trade, Foreign Policy and Defence under the Law of the EU

hand, the link of a European armaments policy to Community policies is outlined both in general terms[61] and in detail. Indeed, Article 5 of the proposed Common Position refers to a range of Community measures that "will be adopted as soon as possible". The scope of these measures is wide and touches upon policies at the very core of the operation of the internal market, namely free movement of goods, public procurement and imposition of customs duties.

The proposed Common Position is not confined to a mere reference to the areas in which Community initiatives need to be undertaken; instead, it determines their content and outlines the principles upon which they are to be based. In relation to free movement of goods, a simplified system applicable to intra-Community transfers is to be set up along with monitoring and surveillance mechanisms also applicable to exports and export guarantees. In relation to public procurement, rules will be adopted based on binding principles, rules and mechanisms on transparency and non-discrimination and taking current Community public procurement rules as a guiding principle.[62] In the customs area, a list of products which "could be exempt from the Common Customs Tariff in the light of the defence needs of the Member states and the desirability of encouraging the development of a European armaments policy" is to be set up by the Council by the end of 1998. Then, the Commission, "taking account of this list, will, where appropriate, make appropriate proposals for exemptions based on the Treaty establishing the European Community".[63]

Finally, and in addition to the specific measures that the Commission suggested be adopted, regard is being taken of various other long-term objectives through reference to an Action Plan drawn up by the Commission. This Plan defines priority areas of action and suggests specific measures regarding these areas aimed at ensuring progress towards a European market for defence products.[64]

[61] Under Art. 3 of the proposed Common Position, "[t]he Council notes that European armaments policy is linked to Community policies, in particular on industry, trade, the regions, competition, innovation and research".

[62] In its first Communication, *supra* note 40 at 17–19, the Commission had elaborated further on its suggestion for relying upon the main principles of Community procurement rules, namely "a generally applicable non-discrimination and equal treatment principle, competitive tendering, open and transparent procedures based on objective selection and award criteria and an enforcement structure consisting of legal remedies for aggrieved suppliers and an independent enforcement authority which has investigative powers and can seek corrective measures", in order to set up a procurement regime applicable to defence products. Finally, the Commission concludes by stating its intention to co-operate with the other Community institutions and the Member States "taking into account the objective of enhancing in a dynamic way the competitiveness of the European defence-related industry" and noting that any legislative measures that may be adopted will "obvious[ly] have to be binding on all Member States".

[63] Finally, under its Art. 6, the proposed Common Position is to be reviewed 18 months after its adoption.

[64] The Commission's Action Plan suggests the implementation of a wide range of measures, including standardisation of equipment used by the national defence ministries, a simplified licensing system in intra-Community transfers, harmonisation of tariff arrangements in relation to imports of defence products, the creation of a European Company Statute, innovation through civilian use of defence technologies, technology transfer and involvement of small and medium-sized enterprises, application of structural funds to diversification and conversion of defence industries at regional level, extension of the proposed common VAT system, removal of obstacles to European

4. COMMENT ON THE COMMISSION'S PROPOSALS

The Commission's proposals, put forward in the two Communications outlined above, raise important policy issues; these include the extent to which the pursuit of an industrial policy in relation to defence industries is attainable under the current Community rules applicable to mergers[65] and how the principles underlying the Community public procurement regime may assist the defence industries to overcome their critical situation.[66] However, the focus of the following analysis will be on the legal issues that the Commission's proposals raise in relation to the delimitation of competence between the European Union in general, the European Community in particular and the Member States.

4.1. The Commission's proposals as a general thesis

The legal formula put forward by the Commission, namely a Title V formal instrument providing for measures to be taken within the Community legal framework, is not *per se* innovative; substantive interactions between the two frameworks have already been recognised on the basis of the reference that various Title V measures make to specific Community measures either already undertaken or to be adopted.[67] However, there is a significant difference between those measures and the Commission's proposals under consideration: the interactions between the Community legal order and CFSP provided under the former are confined to a specific Community instrument and are aimed at facilitating a specific Union policy; the interactions provided under the latter are of extensive scope and depth, involving a considerable number of Community policies.

This feature may imply that the proposed Title V seeks to provide a framework within which an organic relationship between the Community legal order

exporters, a study of the situation of the defence industry in the Central and Eastern European Countries. Under Art. 4 of the proposed Common Position, the Council "declares its intention of using the Plan to further develop a European armaments policy", while "the Commission will take the appropriate initiatives to ensure that it is implemented".

[65] In COM(97)583 final at 24, the Commission recognises the necessity of concentrations in the defence industry due to the size of certain projects which entails substantial financing and multiple skills; moreover, it argues that any conflict between the objectives served by Community merger policy and the consolidation of defence industry through concentrations would be eliminated as a result of the establishment of the common market for defence equipment. It argues that "[a]s far as geographic markets remain, further concentration may aggravate monopolistic inefficiencies that can extend into civilian areas of business. On the other hand, if progress towards a common market for defence equipment is achieved, and provided that conditions of competition are preserved, business consolidation may contribute favourably to European competitiveness on a global market".

[66] On the extent to which the rules underpinning the existing Community public procurement regime may be applied to defence products and the necessary adaptations, see M Trybus, *European Defence Procurement Law: International and National Procurement Systems as Models for a Liberalised Defence Procurement Market in Europe* (The Hague: Kluwer Law International, 1999).

[67] See *supra* ch. 2.

and the second pillar is established.[68] Viewed from this angle, the significance of the Commission proposal far exceeds the potential attainment of its specific objective, namely to enable national defence industries to respond to their structural economic problems through the establishment of a European defence market. Instead, it marks a new approach to integration within the existing constitutional structure of the European Union.

4.2. The "national" counter argument

A thesis against the approach put forward by the Commission may argue that the proposed Common Position suggests, in effect, the communitarisation of the defence industries. According to this position, to argue for Community policies to be applied in the area of defence industry under a Title V measure is tantamount to establishing a link between the first and the second pillars in relation to so sensitive an area that no substantive measures have yet been adopted even in the intergovernmental sphere.

This proposition may be rebutted on the basis of the substantive content of the proposal which indicates that the Commission is fully aware of both the multifarious functions of defence industries and the ensuing particular features of the defence market. This is clearly illustrated in its proposals on the establishment of common procurement rules in the area of defence products drawing upon the main principles of the Community public procurement regime. In the Action Plan annexed to the proposed Common Position, the Commission stresses the specific character of the defence sector as involving essential security interests and points out, on the one hand, the need to ensure confidentiality of information[69] and, on the other hand, the need to maintain guaranteed sources of supply. In addition, it suggests the insertion of a safeguard clause aimed at allowing Member States "some flexibility in extreme cases involving national security".[70] Furthermore, the Commission does not see its proposals as applying to defence products *en masse*; instead, it divides the materials of the defence sectors into three categories, namely highly sensitive equipment covered by the scope of Article 296 EC, products intended for the armed forces and for military use but not constituting highly sensitive defence equipment and products

---

[68] The Commission argues that "[a]ction should be taken at once, without waiting for a new institutional context to be established, in areas in which it is urgently needed to protect the defence sector's technological and industrial base" in *supra* note 41 at 4.

[69] Confidentiality of information regarding "the essential interests of [national] security" is envisaged under Art. 296(1)(a) EC. The Commission argues that, in relation to the applicability of the Community public procurement regime to defence products, this issue can be addressed by enabling public authorities to consider bids from companies selected on the basis of their ability to fulfil this requirement, provided that this selection would be made under objective criteria and not as a disguised means of arbitrarily eliminating foreign suppliers.

[70] According to the Commission's proposals, this safeguard clause would be applied in so far as both the Commission and the other Member States are informed immediately and provided with sufficiently detailed reasons for the deviation from the Community procurement rules.

intended for armed forces but not for military use. The former category could be exempted in so far as "safety or the protection of vital interests of the country in question so require" and a notification mechanism for this purpose is suggested for reasons of control and transparency. As far as the second category is concerned, the Commission proposes to determine "a fairly flexible set of rules, while respecting the principles of transparency and non-discrimination, inspired by the existing Community public procurement rules". Finally, the third category is viewed as already subject to the Community public procurement provisions and the Commission is committed to specify "where appropriate, in the most suitable form the conditions for the application of these rules". These specific aspects of the Commission proposals make it clear that its approach towards defence industry is cautious.[71]

A related issue consists of the reference in the Commission's proposed Common Position to measures to be adopted under Title V. It is noteworthy that no such measures are mentioned in detail in the body of the Common Position; indeed, only the briefest and most general of references is made to "CFSP measures" which are considered necessary for the development of "an effective European armaments policy". In addition to a very general reference to the development of the defence identity of the Union within the CFSP framework, this formula indicates that the Commission is extremely careful not to be seen as too active in an area where no initiatives have been undertaken even at intergovernmental level.

4.3. The "supranational" counter argument

An argument against the legal formula adopted by the Commission in its proposed Common Position is that any reference, irrespective of its general character, in a common position adopted under Title V to future Community initiatives "would allow the second pillar to become the master of the Union and supersede the Communities".[72] According to this thesis, the common position in question purports to impose a direct legal obligation on the Community institutions to implement it, which is inconsistent with the establishment of the Union on the basis of legally distinct frameworks in general and the preservation of the legal integrity of the Treaty of Rome under Article 47 TEU and the protection of the *acquis communautaire* under Article 3 TEU in particular.[73]

This argument is unconvincing for two reasons. First, the model of interaction put forward by the Commission in its proposed Common Position provides

---

[71] This argument is also supported by the Commission's very careful, albeit inconsistent and vague, approach that it adopted in the period before it put forward its two Communications. This was recognised by the Commission itself in *supra* note 41 at 14.

[72] CWA Timmermans, "The Uneasy Relationship Between the Communities and the Second Union Pillar: Back to the 'Plan Fouchet'?" (1996/1) *LIEI* 61 at 67.

[73] *Ibid.*

for legal safeguards that ensure the integrity of the Community legal order. It is expressly stated that the measures envisaged in the Common Position are to be taken in accordance with Article 47 TEU which prohibits the Treaty of Rome being affected by anything in the TEU which does not expressly amend it. This provision is not excluded from the jurisdiction of the Court under Article 46 TEU, as the *Airport Transit Visas* judgment clearly illustrated.[74] It follows that the provision of Community measures in a Title V common position by no means excludes or reduces the judicial control that the Court is to exercise under Community law over these measures. Furthermore, if a provision to such effect were included in a Title V common position, the Court may be called upon to exercise its Community law jurisdiction over any implementing measure and, hence, indirectly adjudicate upon the effect of the common position. Another legal safeguard against the erosion of the *acquis communautaire* which is expressly spelled out in the body of the proposed Common Position consists of the provision that all the implementing Community measures are to be taken following the appropriate provisions. This clause shows that the provision of Community initiatives in a Title V common position by no means brings the latter within the rules laid down in Title V TEU. In other words, the implementing Community initiatives are not incorporated by reference to the system of rules to which their initial source belongs.

The express provision of both the above clauses in the proposed Common Position does not introduce a new dimension to the interaction between the Community legal order and Title V. Both Article 47 TEU and the principle that Community measures are to be adopted under Community law, clearly stemming from the reference to the *acquis communautaire* in Article 3, would be applicable even in the absence of any express provision to that effect in the proposed Common Position. Furthermore, it is noteworthy that the proposed Common Position refers to Article 296(1)(b) EC only in its preamble stating that that provision applies to the Article 296(2) list of products. This brief reference seems to imply that the interpretation of Article 296(1)(b) EC will no longer be determined on the basis of the "sensitive character" of defence products but pursuant to legal considerations underpinning that provision.

Secondly, the legal effect of the proposed Common Position on the Community institutions in general and the Commission in particular would not be of such an extent as to render their role under Community law subject to the legally distinct rules of Title V. As far as the Council is concerned, according to the proposed Common Position it "notes" that the Commission has suggested on the basis of an Action Plan the adoption of Community initiatives applicable to defence industry and "declares its intention of using the Plan to further develop a European armaments policy". More specifically, the proposed measure states that the Community initiatives outlined therein "will be adopted

---

[74] Case C–170/96 *Commission* v. *Council* [1998] ECR I–2763, [1998] 2 CMLR 1092; for an analysis of this judgment, see *supra* at ch. 7.

as soon as possible" and that the Council "undertakes to draw up, before 31 December 1998, a list of products which could be exempt from the common customs tariff". Should the proposed Common Position be adopted, its legal effect on the Council would be unclear. A failure to draw up the list of products to be exempt from the CCT would not be subject to an action before the Court, for measures adopted under Title V are excluded from the latter's jurisdiction. The fact that the failure in question refers to a Community law measure is irrelevant, because the duty of the Council is not provided under Community law itself and hence its failure does not amount to a violation of Community law.[75]

The role of the Commission provided for under the proposed Common Position may be assessed in similar terms. It must perform its Community law functions by initiating the procedures and participating in the decision-making applicable to the Community initiatives set to achieve the objectives of the proposed Common Position. The Commission's duty to do so in accordance with Community law and respecting the *acquis communautaire* is a matter to be assessed under Community law and subject to the Court's jurisdiction. However, the Commission's role of acting pursuant to the proposed Common Position refers to a legal duty of a different nature; given that its foundation lies upon a Title V instrument, the legal duty of the Commission must be assessed on the basis of Title V itself. Again, whether the lack of means to render this duty enforceable and, hence, ensure the effective application of the common position deprives the latter of practical significance is a question endemic in the character currently attributed to Title V and cannot as such determine the legal effect of the instruments adopted thereunder.

4.4. The significance of the Commission's proposal in practical terms

The arguments put forward above may seem to have led to a paradox. On the one hand, the legal formula suggested by the Commission in the proposed Common Position does not lead to the communitarisation of the defence industry, for the proposals indicate that the multifarious issues inherent in the regulation of the production of and trade in defence products are to be fully taken into account. On the other hand, the legal formula suggested does not lead to the erosion of the *acquis communautaire* either, due to both the legal guarantees provided for in the proposed Common Position and the nature of the duty that the latter gives rise to in relation to the Community institutions. If these propositions are correct, then the question whether the proposed Common Position is of any practical significance arises.

---

[75] In this respect, it is a different issue entirely whether the duty actually imposed on the Council would be significant in practical terms without any means of enforcement. In the light of the legal characteristics attributed to the CFSP framework under the TEU, this concern is valid for any measure adopted under Title V, while it may not alter the legal effect of this measure as provided under the Treaty.

The analysis of this issue requires the examination of the effect of the proposed Common Position on the Member States. It is suggested that while Member States would be bound "to ensure that their national policies conform to the common position", the specific content of the exact legal obligation imposed upon them would not be easily ascertainable. This is due to the general character of the content of the proposed Common Position which sets out the main principles of the Community measures to be adopted rather than specifying their substance. In this respect, the proposed Common Position would have the following effect on the Member States: on the one hand, they would be committed to participating in negotiations under Community rules in order to achieve the objectives referred to in the Common Position; on the other hand, they would be committed to engaging in efforts on the basis of the rules and procedures of Title V leading to "an effective European armaments policy" as specified in the annexed Action Plan. However, the extent to which the Member States would actually commit themselves to this process would essentially rely upon various developments, the actual development of CFSP and the initiatives taken by the Commission being most important.

4.5. The Commission's proposal in the light of related developments

A related issue is whether the all-encompassing, albeit balanced, approach underpinning the Commission's proposal makes it more likely to be adopted. On the one hand, the increasing interest expressed by Member States in the reorganisation of the defence market on the basis of common rules during the last two years is a positive development. The most important such development is the establishment of the Joint Armaments Co-operation Organisation (OCCAR) by Great Britain, France, Italy and Germany in September 1998.[76] Being the embryo of a future European armaments agency, OCCAR aims at managing common arms products, cutting procurement costs, co-ordinating weapons research and development and awarding contracts on behalf of the countries involved but not yet under competitive tenders.[77] The more the Member States will be willing to address the problems of their defence industries on the basis of common rules, the more likely their attention may be focused on the existing legal arrangements within the European Union framework. This conclusion is supported by related initiatives regarding the development of the defence identity of the Union. Indeed, given that these initiatives are focused on the institutional machinery of the Union, they are effectively bound

---

[76] OCCAR originated in a development and procurement agency created jointly by France and Germany in Jan. 1996: see *The Economist*, 13 Jan. 1996 at 63–4.

[77] Focusing on the development of collaborative projects, OCCAR has already been involved in programmes regarding the production of ground-to-air missiles by France and Italy, frigates by France, Germany and Great Britain and combat helicopters by France and Germany: see *Agence Europe*, 7298 11 Sept. 1998 at 4.

to stir initiatives on the organisation of defence markets in that direction too. In the light of these developments, the proposal of the Commission and the all-encompassing approach it puts forward would be of great relevance.

However, OCCAR constitutes an *ad hoc* arrangement, of limited effect which has been undertaken beyond the framework of the European Union.[78] While it remains to be seen whether and to what extent it will evolve into a European armaments agency,[79] OCCAR clearly illustrates that, in dealing with the issue of the economic aspects of security, no comprehensive analysis had been put forward weighing the combined effect of the new geopolitical realities and the consequent economic variables, the globalisation of the market and the various developments within and amongst the Member States both within and beyond the European Union against the potential of both the Community legal order and Title V.

5. CONCLUSION

This chapter argued that the regulation of the external aspects of defence markets has not used the legal means available to the European Union to their fullest potential. Indeed, the formula under which the EU code of conduct on arms exports was adopted is legally inconsistent with the past practice under Title V and undermines not only the effectiveness of the code itself, but also the credibility of the CFSP framework altogether. However, this illustrates yet another facet of the following phenomenon: while acknowledging the multifarious functions of defence industries and the complex legal issues that their intrinsic links raise, both the institutions of the Union and the Member States failed to address them in a legally coherent way within the legal framework of the European Union. This conclusion is valid regarding both the internal and the external aspects of arms regulation: in relation to the former, they have viewed them as within a grey area by relying upon a highly problematic interpretation of Article 296(1)(b) EC; in relation to the latter, the Member States have ignored the legal framework set up to attain the very objectives that the EU code of conduct on arms exports purports to serve.

This approach is underpinned by the inherently indeterminate definition of armaments as "sensitive products". However, the legal analysis of the regulation of arms must not be hindered by this generalisation, as the Commission's proposals on the defence-related industries implied. Its approach, encompassing both the Community legal order and the CFSP framework and referring to

[78] OCCAR was established by an international convention signed by the Defence Secretaries of the states involved on 9 Sept. 1998 in Farnborough.
[79] So far, Spain, Belgium and the Netherlands have expressed interest in joining it. On OCCAR in particular and the rules which should underpin a single defence procurement market see C Bovis, "Defence Procurement, the Single Market and the European Armaments Agency" in A Arrowsmith and A Davies (eds.), *Public Procurement: Global Revolution* (London: Kluwer Law International, 1998) 71.

developments beyond the Union, sought to ensure that action would be taken at various levels while satisfying all conflicting claims regarding the choice of legal formula; indeed, the *acquis communautaire* is to be safeguarded while the defence industries are not to be communitarised.

The pace at which recent initiatives regarding both the economic and the political aspects of security have been undertaken is impressive, all the more so given the contrast with the code of conduct on arms exports, whose adoption became possible only after the criteria referred therein had been subject to discussions within the Council for more than seven years and had already been spelled out twice in the Conclusions of the European Council. These developments may point towards a more positive approach to the existing institutional structures with which the European Union is equipped and the role they could play. However, their substance often illustrates confusion about the legal means to be used in general and the role of the instruments and the institutional machinery of the European Union in particular.

The question that the above problem raises is impossible to answer. An analysis of how the defence industries can become the subject of Community and Union initiatives cannot require a clear prior delimitation of the defence, political and economic aspects of defence products; the reason for this is that the interdependent nature of their relationship inevitably leads to a circular debate: is the regulation of the economic aspects of security the cause or the consequence of the development of the co-operation between Member States regarding the defence and political aspects of security?[80] It is this conundrum that has dominated the debate over defence industries and has effectively excluded a legal analysis of whether the European Union may operate as a framework that provides for safeguards in relation to potential transgressions against either the *acquis communautaire* or national sovereignty. In this respect, the Commission's proposals do constitute "a first but nevertheless important step".[81] The adoption of their substantive content relies heavily upon economic considerations being taken into account, policy choices made and political initiatives undertaken. However, the crux of the problem, namely whether the European Union framework can provide the legal response to the various aspects of defence products, has already been put forward.

[80] For an analysis of developments within the European Union regarding the economic aspects of security in the light of integration theories see TR Guay, *The European Union and Integration Theories: The Case of Europe's Defence Industry* (PhD, Syracuse University, May 1996).

[81] See the speech by former Industry Commissioner Bangemann entitled "The Future of Europe's Defence Industry" at "The Future of Europe's Defence Industry" Conference, Brussels, 18 June 1996.

10

Conclusions

The interdependence between trade and foreign policy being a truism, this book has focused on how their interactions touch upon the relationship between the Community legal framework and the Common Foreign and Security Policy. In particular, this book sought to examine whether the economic aspects of security may be regulated in a legally sensible and realistically effective way within the constitutional order of the European Union. Given that the Amsterdam Treaty made it clear that the European Union structure upon legally distinct frameworks will remain a legal reality for, at least, the foreseeable future, this book analysed the inter-pillar approach adopted either by the Treaty itself or by means of secondary legislation; it asked whether it may perform a variety of functions: ensuring the consistency and coherence between the activities undertaken within the pillars, respecting and building upon the *acquis communautaire* and recognising the position of the Member States within the constitutional structure of the Union as fully sovereign subjects of international law.

The application of the inter-pillar approach to the legal regulation of trade measures with significant foreign policy and security objectives may vary considerably. This is illustrated in the analysis of the implementation of sanctions under Article 301 EC and the current regime on exports of dual-use goods under Regulation 3381/94 and Decision 94/942/CFSP; the former has raised problems of effectiveness due to the Member States' inability to agree upon its application, whereas the latter is structured in such a way as seriously to undermine the nature of the Council regulation as Community law and the effectiveness of the export rules in general. These problems are largely due to the Member States' concern over the dilution of the intergovernmental character of the second pillar, which is reflected in their understanding of trade and foreign policy as two rigidly compartmentalised spheres of activity.

However, the argument that the adoption of the inter-pillar approach may vary implies that there must be a way which would remedy the legal problems and address the concerns raised above. It is the Court's jurisprudence which shows that trade measures with important foreign and security policy dimensions may be regulated within the multi-pillar legal order of the European Union. The underlying assumption of the Court's approach is the self-evident interdependence between trade and foreign policy which illustrates that, as a matter of fact, there is a link between the legal frameworks dealing with these areas, namely the EC and CFSP. Having acknowledged this practical link, it moved on to identify such normative links that would transform the distinct legal frameworks of the Union into a functional whole. It focuses on the principles provided under the Treaty itself, namely a single institutional framework which, on the one hand, would ensure the consistency of the activities of the Union and, on the other hand, would respect and build upon the *acquis communautaire*. In approaching these principles, the Court identified a duty of the Member States to conduct their foreign policy consistently with Community law so as to ensure that the *acquis communautaire* will not be undermined by activities undertaken beyond the Community legal framework. Moreover, the Court makes it clear that by no means does it intend to interfere with the substance of the political will of the Member States, as expressed by the institutions of the Union; the control it is prepared to exercise is confined to whether and to what extent the expression of the political will of the Member States affects the *acquis communautaire*. This line of reasoning is underpinned by the realisation that the Court's role is set by the Treaty itself, which, under Article 47, entrusts the Court with the task of ensuring that the Community legal framework is not affected by the TEU.

The Court's approach illustrates that the constitutional order of the European Union is capable of accommodating several objectives of a divergent nature by recourse to various instruments of a divergent character. This conclusion has been followed up by the Commission in the case of the legal regulation of armaments; the thrust of its proposals is that the economic problems that the defence industries face after the end of the Cold War may be addressed in an effective way by a combination of Community and non-Community instruments. These measures, of a different legal character though they may be, will neither endanger the consistency and coherence of the Union's policies nor undermine the distinct legal character of the first two pillars.

Having argued that the interactions between trade and foreign policy and, hence, those between the EC and CFSP, may be regulated in a legally sensible and effective way within the current constitutional order of the European Union, four general conclusions may be drawn. The first focuses on the role of the European Court of Justice. The fully-fledged approach to the interactions between trade and foreign policy underlying its jurisprudence illustrates its determination to ensure that the Treaty constitutes a workable legal framework rather than a compilation of rhetorical statements. In doing so, it demonstrates acute awareness of the political realities within which the interactions between the EC and CFSP need to be regulated. It makes clear that in no way is it prepared to encroach upon the rights of the Member States safeguarded under the second pillar in general and their right to determine whether their security is at risk in particular. On the other hand, it demonstrates its determination to exercise a functional jurisdiction which is not to be limited by the inherently indeterminate and "sensitive" nature of issues brought before it. This role has serious implications for both the Community legal order and the Union. In relation to the former, the Court approached exports of dual-use good as within the Common Commercial Policy, while fully taking into account the foreign policy objectives they may serve; in doing so, it indicated that the debate over the scope of Article 133 EC has become redundant, for the CCP may accommodate foreign policy considerations without the Community's exclusive competence becoming *de facto* unlimited. As regards the role of the Court in the European Union, its jurisdiction to determine where the borderline between the pillars lies will bring it from the very centre of the Community legal order to the very centre of the European Union. In determining the appropriate framework, the Court will act as the constitutional guarantor in the European Union; its past jurisprudence illustrates that the nature of the Member States as fully sovereign subjects of international law in the conduct of their foreign affairs is in no way undermined.

The second general conclusion that may be drawn follows from the above and deals with the institutions of the Union and the Member States. Since the Court has developed a functional jurisdiction ensuring the effectiveness of Community law while not impinging upon the national competence to conduct foreign policy, the Member States must equally approach the interactions between trade and foreign policy in functional terms. The legal regulation of exports of dual-use goods within the Common Commercial Policy would illustrate such an approach. The fact that such an initiative is not advocated in relation to the legal regulation of sanctions against third countries is not paradoxical. The reason for this is the legal and practical aspects that characterised the imposition of sanctions since the inception of the EC. Despite their adoption under Article 133 EC prior to the establishment of CFSP, trade sanctions had been implemented in a way that dissociated them from the CCP, as the divergence of scope between Articles 301 and 133 EC indicates. Furthermore, they constitute one of the most significant instruments of the foreign policy of the European Union, which explains their heavy reliance upon unanimous implementation. Viewed from this perspective, the imposition of sanctions under the Common Commercial Policy relies on the development both of the CCP itself and of CFSP.

The above point leads to the third general conclusion of this book which touches upon the relationship between the pillars of the European Union. The interdependence between trade and foreign policy and the jurisprudence of the Court illustrate, in both practical and legal terms, that there is a direct link between the EC and CFSP. This is illustrated in the argument that deviation from Community law by relying upon wholly exceptional Treaty clauses must be linked to developments in the CFSP framework: the more progress is made under the second pillar towards safeguarding the essential interests of the Member States, the more difficult the Member States will find it to justify recourse to "wholly exceptional" Treaty provisions in order to protect those interests. In this respect, the *sui generis,* incremental and dynamic development of the foreign policy system of the Union highlights the following point: to enable the Union to act within its pillar-structure in a broad area of external activities with consistency and coherence, albeit following a varying degree of integration, would require that the boundaries between these activities be subject to continuous redefinition. This by no means implies that the reach of Community competence will become *de facto* unlimited; what is argued is that the interactions between trade and foreign policy and, hence, the EC and CFSP frameworks are underpinned by an intrinsic and dynamic relationship whose regulation requires the elaboration of clear, workable and sensible principles. It is the Treaty itself which provided for these principles under Articles 3, 46 and 47 TEU and the Court which elaborated upon them.

The final conclusion draws upon all the above. It argues that the debate over the pillar structure of the European Union has become irrelevant. While this conclusion is supported by the Amsterdam Treaty, it clearly follows not only from an assessment of the foreign policy dimensions inherent in trade measures but, mainly, the legal problems to which they give rise. To assume that the abolition of pillars would solve them is not only naïve but also demonstrates lack of legal judgement and political awareness. The legal regulation of sanctions, exports of dual-use goods and armaments, as approached by the institutions of the Union, the Member States and the Court, illustrates that the dividing line between the pillars is not as rigid as it may originally seem. Therefore, what is of significance is ensuring that what blurs, in practical terms, the dividing line between the pillars will not amount to blurring, in legal terms, the Community legal order and conduct of foreign policy by the Member States as fully sovereign subjects of international law. This may be achieved in a conceptually coherent, legally sensible and realistically effective way within the framework established by the Treaty on European Union.

Epilogue

After this book had been completed, the common rules on exports of dual-use goods under Regulation 3381/94 and Decision 94/942/CFSP were amended. The Council adopted Regulation 1334/2000, [2000] L159/1 which abolished the inter-pillar approach. Accordingly, it adopted Decision 2000/402/CFSP, [2000] L159/218 repealing Decision 94/942/CFSP. It is interesting that Decision 2000/402/CFSP refers to the case-law of the Court in its preamble as a factor which led to the review of system. The abolition of the inter-pillar approach clearly supports the arguments put forward in this book.

Bibliography

ADAM, B., "Evolution du Contexte Politique et Economique du Commerce des Armes" (1993) 26 *RBDI* 3.

ALLEN, D., and WALLACE, W., "European Political Cooperation: The Historical and Contemporary Background" in Allen, D., Rummel, R., and Wessels, W. (eds.), *European Political Cooperation: Towards a foreign policy for Western* Europe (London: Butterworths, 1982).

ALLOTT, P., Written Evidence to the *House of Lords Scrutiny of the Intergovernmental Pillars of the European Union* (1992–93) HL 124, 50.

ANTHONY, I., "The United States: Arms Exports and Implications for Arms Production" in Wulf, H. (ed.), *Arms Industry Limited* (Oxford: OUP, 1993).

ARNULL, A., "EC Law and the Dismissal of Pregnant Servicewomen" (1995) 24 *Industrial Law Journal* 215.

—— "The Scope of the Common Commercial Policy: A Coda on Opinion 1/94" in Emiliou, N. and O'Keeffe, D. (eds.), *The European Union and World Trade Law After the GATT Uruguay Round* (Chichester: John Wiley, 1996) 343.

—— "The European Court and Judicial Objectivity—A Reply to Professor Hartley" (1996) 112 *LQR* 411.

ARON, R., and LERNER, D. (eds.), *France Defeats EDC* (London: Thames and Hudson, 1957).

ARROWSMITH, S., "The Application of the E.C. Treaty Rules to Public and Utilities Procurement" (1995) 6 *Public Procurement Law Review* 255.

—— *The Law of Public and Utilities Procurement* (London: Sweet & Maxwell, 1996).

BALDWIN, D., *Economic Statecraft* (Princeton, NJ: Princeton University Press, 1985).

—— "The concept of security" (1997) 23 *Review of International Studies* 5.

BANGEMANN, M., "The Future of Europe's Defence Industry", speech delivered delievered to the Conference on The Future of Europe's Defence Industry, Brussels, 18 June 1996.

BARENTS, R., "Some Observations on the Treaty of Amsterdam" (1997) 4 *MJ* 332.

BEARD, R., "NATO Armaments Cooperation in the 1990s" (1993) 41 *NATO Review* 23.

BERKHOF, G. C., "The American Strategic Defence Initiative and West European Security: An Idea" in De Vree, J. K., Coffey, P., and Lauwaars, R. H. (eds.), *Towards a European Foreign Policy—Legal, Economic and Political Dimensions* (Dordrecht: Martinus Nijhoff Publishers, 1987) 205.

BIEBER, R., "Democratic Control of European Foreign Policy" (1990) 1 *EJII* 148.

BITZINGER, R. A., The Globalization of the Arms Industry—The Next Proliferation Challenge" (1994) 19 *International Security* 170.

BLIN, O., "L'Article 113 CE Après Amsterdam" (1998) 420 *Revue du Marché Commun et de l'Union Européenne* 447.

BLOED, A., and WESSEL, R.A. (eds.), *The Changing Function of the Western European Union (WEU)—Introduction and Basic Documents* (Dordrecht: Martinus Nijhoff, 1994).

BOHR, S., "Sanctions by the United Nations Security Council and the European Community" (1993) 4 *EJIL* 256.

BOSCO, C., "Commentaire de l'Acte Unique Européen des 17–28 Fevrier 1987" (1987) XXIII *CDE* 355.

BOTHE, M., and MARAUHN, T., "The Arms Trade: Comparative Aspects of Law" (1993) 26 *RBDI* 20.

BOURGEOIS, J.H.J., "The EC in the WTO and Advisory Opinion 1/94: an Echternach Procession" (1995) 32 *CMLRev.* 763.

——Dewost, J.-L., and Gaiffe, M.-A. (eds.), *La Communauté européenne et les accords mixtes. Quelles perspectives?* (Brussels: Presses Interuniversitaires Européennes, 1997).

BOVIS, C., *EC Public Procurement Law* (London: Longman, 1997).

——"The European Public Procurement Rules and their Interplay with International Trade" (1997) 31 *JWT* 63.

——"Defence Procurement, the Single Market and the European Armaments Agency" in Arrowsmith, S. and Davies, A. (eds.), *Public Procurement: Global Revolution* (London: Kluwer Law International, 1998) 57.

BROWNLIE, I., "International Law at the Fiftieth Anniversary of the United Nations. General Course on Public International Law" (1995) 25 *RdC* 9.

——*Principles of Public International Law* (5th edn., Oxford: Clarendon Press, 1999).

BRUECKNER, P., "The European Community and the United Nations" (1989) 1 *EJIL* 175.

BURROWS, N., "Caught in the Cross-Fire" (1997) 22 *ELRev.* 170.

——"Reinforcing International Law" (1998) 23 *ELRev.* 79.

CANOR, I., " 'Can Two Walk Together, Except They Be Agreed?'. The Relationship Between International Law and European Law: The Incorporation of United Nations Sanctions Against Yugoslavia Into European Community Law Through the Perspective of the European Court of Justice" (1998) 35 *CMLRev.* 137.

CHALMERS, D., "Legal Base and the External Relations of the European Community" in Emiliou, N., and O'Keeffe, D. (eds.), *The European Union and World Trade Law After the GATT Uruguay Round* (Chichester: John Wiley, 1996) 46.

CHATTERJI, M.A., "The EC Internal Armaments Market: A New Aspect of the New Security" (1991) XV *Journal of European Integration* 25.

CLARK, A., *Diaries* (London: Phoenix, 1994).

CLOOS, J., REINESCH, G., VIGNES, D., and WEYLAND, J., *Le Traité de Maastricht. Genèse, Analyse, Commentaire* (Brussels: Bruyland, 1993).

COEME, G., "The Role of the IEPG" (1991) 39 *NATO Review* 15.

COLLET, A., "Le développement des actions communautaires dans le domaine des matériels de guerre, des armes et des munitions" (1990) 26 *Rev. trim. dr. europ.* 75.

CONLON, P., "Lessons From Iraq: The Functions of the Iraq Sanctions Committee as a Source of Sanctions Implementation Authority and Practice" (1995) 35 *Va. J Int'l L.* 669.

CONSTANTINESCO, V., KOVAR, R., and SIMON, D. (eds.), *Traité sur l'Union européenne: (signé le 7 février 1992): commentaire article par article* (Paris: Economica, 1996).

CORNISH, P., *The Arms Trade and Europe* (London: Pinter, 1995).

——"Joint Action 'The Economic Aspects of Security' and Regulation of Conventional Arms and Technology Exports from the EU" in Holland, M. (ed.), *Common Foreign and Security Policy. The Record and Reforms* (London: Pinter, 1997) 73.

COX, A., "The Future of European Defence Policy: The Case for a Centralised Procurement Agency" (1994) 3 *Public Procurement Law Review* 65.

CRAVEN, M.C.R., "The European Community Arbitration Commission on Yugoslavia" (1995) LXVI *BYIL* 333.

CREMONA, M., "The Common Foreign and Security Policy of the European Union and the External Powers of the European Community" in O'Keeffe, D., and Twomey, P.M. (eds.), *Legal Issues of the Maastricht Treaty* (London: Chancery Law, 1994) 247.

—— annotation on Case C–432/92 *The Queen* v. *Minister of Agriculture, Fisheries and Food, ex parte S.P. Anastasiou (Pissouri) Ltd and Others* in (1996) 33 *CMLRev.* 125.

—— "The European Union as an International Actor: The Issues of Flexibility and Linkage" (1998) 3 *EFA Review* 67.

—— "External Relations and External Competence: The Emergence of an Integrated Policy" in Craig, P., and de Búrca, G. (eds.), *The Evolution of EU Law* (Oxford: OUP, 1999) 137.

CROFT, S., "In Defence of Arms Control" (1996) XLIV *Political Studies* 888.

CURTIN, D., "The Constitutional Structure of the Union: A Europe of Bits and Pieces" (1993) 30 *CMLRev.* 17.

—— and DEKKER, I.G., "The EU as a 'Layered' International Organization: Institutional Unity in Disguise" in Craig, P., and de Búrca, G. (eds), *The Evolution of EU Law* (Oxford: OUP, 1999) 83.

D'ARGENT, P., "Les enseignements du COCOM" (1993) 26 *RBDI* 500.

DANKERT, P., "Pressure from the European Parliament" in Edwards, G., and Pijpers, A. (eds.), *The Politics of European Treaty Reform. The 1996 Intergovernmental Conference and Beyond* (London: Pinter, 1997) 212.

DASHWOOD, A., *Reviewing Maastricht. Issues for the 1996 IGC* (Cambridge: LBE, 1996).

—— "The Limits of European Community Powers" (1996) 21 *ELRev.* 113.

—— "External Relations Provisions of the Amsterdam Treaty" (1998) 35 *CMLRev.* 1019.

—— "States in the European Union" (1998) 23 *ELRev.* 201.

DAVID, E., "Les sanctions économiques prises contre l'Argentine dans l'affaire des Malouines" (1984–1985) XVIII *RBDI* 150.

DE BURCA, G., "The Principle of Proportionality and its Application in EC Law" (1993) 13 *YEL* 105.

DE GUCHT, K., and KEUKELEIRE, S., "The European Security Architecture: The Role of the European Community in Shaping a New European Geopolitical Landscape" (1991) XLIV/6 *Studia Diplomatica* 29.

DE SCHOUTHEETE DE TERVARENT, P., *La Coopération Politique Européenne* (2nd edn., Brussels: Editions Labor, 1986).

—— "The Creation of the Common Foreign and Security Policy" in Regelsberger, E., de Schoutheete de Tervarent, P., and Wessels, W. (eds.), *Foreign Policy of the European Union. From EPC to CFSP and Beyond* (London: Lynne Rienner Publishers, 1997) 41.

DE WILDE D'ESTMAEL, T., "La politique Etrangère et de Sécurité Commune de l'Union européenne. Essai d'évaluation au-delà du syndrome yougoslave" (1996) 11/3 *Revue politique* 17.

DEHOUSSE, F., "Le Traité d'Amsterdam, Reflet de la Nouvelle Europe" (1997) XXXIII *CDE* 265.

DEHOUSSE, R., and WEILER, J.H.H., "The Legal Dimension" in Wallace, W. (ed.), *The Dynamics of European Integration* (London: Pinter, 1990) 242.

DENZA, E., "The Community as a Member of International Organizations" in Emiliou, N., and O'Keeffe, D. (eds.), *The European Union and World Trade Law After the GATT Uruguay Round* (Chichester: Wiley, 1996) 3.

DEWOST, J.-L., LOUIS, J.-V., SCHWARTZ, I., VAN GRAEYENEST, F., VANDERSANDEN, G., VIGNES, D., and WAELBROECK, M. (eds.), *Commentaire Mégret* (Brussels: Presses Interuniversitaires de Bruxelles, 1987).

DUE, O., "Article 5 du traité CEE. Une disposition de caractère fédéral" in *Collected Courses of European Law* (Dordrecht: Martinus Nijhoff, 1991).

EATON, M.R., "Common Foreign and Security Policy" in O'Keeffe, D., and Twomey, P. (eds.), *Legal Issues of the Maastricht Treaty* (London: Chancery Law, 1994) 215.

EDWARDS, G., "Common Foreign and Security Policy" (1993) 13 *YEL* 497.

——and PHILLIPPART, E., *Flexibility and the Treaty of Amsterdam: Europe's New Byzantium* (CELS Occasional Paper No. 3, Cambridge, Cambridge UP, 1997).

EECKHOUT, P., *The European Internal Market and International Trade: A Legal Analysis* (Oxford: Clarendon Press, 1994).

EHLERMANN, C.-D., "Communautés européennes et sanctions internationales" [1984–85] *RBDI* 79.

——"Communautés européennes et sanctions internationales—Une Réponse à J. Verhoeven" [1984–85] *RBDI* 96.

——*Differentiation, Flexibility, Closer Cooperation: the New Provisions of the Amsterdam Treaty* (Florence: Robert Schumann Centre, European University Institute, 1998).

EMILIOU, N., annotation on Case C–432/92 *The Queen* v. *Minister of Agriculture, Fisheries and Food, ex parte S.P. Anastasiou (Pissouri) Ltd and Others* in (1995) 20 *ELRev.* 202.

——*The Principle of Proportionality in European Law. A Comparative Study* (London: Kluwer Law International, 1996).

——"The Death of Exclusive Competence?" (1996) 21 *ELRev.* 294.

——annotation on *Werner* and *Leifer* in (1997) 22 *ELRev.* 68.

EVANS, A., *The Integration of the European Community and Third States in Europe: A Legal Analysis* (Oxford: Clarendon Press, 1996).

EVERLING, U., "Reflections on the Structure of the European Union" (1992) 29 *CMLRev.* 1053.

FAVRET, J.-M., "Le Traité d'Amsterdam: Une Revision *A Minima* de la 'Charte Constitutionnelle' de l'Union Européenne—De l'integration a l'incantation?" (1997) XXXIII *CDE* 555.

FELD, W.J., "Defence and Security Policy Issues" in Hurwitz, L., and Lequesne, C. (eds.), *The State of the European Community* (London: Lynne Rienner Publishers, 1991) 425.

FINK-HOOIJER, F., "The Common Foreign and Security Policy of the European Union" (1994) 5 *EJIL* 173.

FITZPATRICK, D.J., "Of Ropes, Buttons and Four-By-Fours: Import Sanctions for Violations of the COCOM Agreement" (1989) 29 *Va J. Int'l L.* 249.

FLAESCH-MOUGIN, C., "Le traité de Maastricht et les compétences externes de la Communauté Européenne: à la recherche d'une politique externe de l'union" (1993) 29 *CDE* 350.

FLINTERMAN, C., "Editorial: The European Union and China" (1997) 4 *MJ* 217.

FORNASSIER, R., "Quelques reflexions sur les sanctions internationales en droit communautaire" (1996) no 402 *Revue du Marché Commun et de l'Union européenne* 670.

FRANCK, T., *Political Questions/Judicial Answers. Does the Rule of Law Apply to Foreign Affairs?* (Princeton, NJ: Princeton University Press, 1992).

FREESTONE, D., and DAVIDSON, S., "Community Competence and Part III of the Single European Act" (1986) 23 *CMLRev.* 793.

FRID, R., *The Relations Between the EC and International Organizations. Legal Theory and Practice* (The Hague: Kluwer Law International, 1995).

FURDSON, E., *The European Defence Community: A History* (London: Macmillan, 1980).

GABRIEL, J.M., "The Integration of European Security: A Functionalist Analysis" (1995) 50 *Aussenwirtschaft* 135.

GAJA, G., "How Flexible Is Flexibility under the Amsterdam Treaty?" (1998) 35 *CMLRev.* 855.

GIATAGANAS, X.A., *The Member States of the European Union Facing the Community Legality. Contribution to the Theory of European Integration* (in Greek) (Athens: A.N.Sakkoulas, 1996).

GILSDORF, P., "Portée et Délimitation des Compétences Communautaires en Matière de Politique Commerciale" [1989] *RMC* 195.

—— "Les réserves de sécurité du traité CEE, à la lumière du traité sur l'union européenne" [1994] *Revue du Marché Commun et de l'Union Européenne* 17.

GLAESNER, H.-J., "The European Council" in Curtin, D., and Heukels, T. (eds.), *Institutional Dynamics of European Integration. Essays in Honour of Henry G. Schermers* (Dordrecht, London: Nijhoff, 1994) ii, 101.

GORMLEY, L.W., *Prohibiting Restrictions on Trade within the EEC* (Amsterdam: Elsevier, 1985).

GOVAERE, I., and EECKHOUT, P., "On Dual Use Goods and Dualist Case Law: The *Aimé Richardt* Judgment on Export Controls" (1992) 29 *CMLRev.* 941.

GRUNERT, T., "The Association of the European Parliament: No Longer the Underdog in EPC?" in Regelsberger, E., de Schoutheete de Tervarent, P., and Wessels, W. (eds.), *Foreign Policy of the European Union. From EPC to CFSP and Beyond* (London: Lynne Rienner Publishers, 1996) 109.

GUAY, T.R., *The European Union and Integration Theories: The Case of Europe's Defence Industry* (PhD thesis submitted in the Syracuse University on May 1996).

HARTLEY, K., "The European Defence Market and Industry" in Creasey, P., and May, S. (eds.), *The European Armaments Market and Procurement Cooperation* (London: MacMillan Press, 1988) 31.

HARTLEY, T.C., "The European Court, Judicial Objectivity and the Constitution of the European Union" (1996) 112 *LQR* 95.

HERZOG, P.E., "The Law of the European Community—A Commentary on the EEC Treaty" (New York: Matthew Bender, 1996).

HILF, M., "The ECJ's Opinion 1/94 on the WTO—No Surprise, but Wise?" (1995) 6 *EJIL* 245.

—— "Unwritten EC Authority in Foreign Trade Law" (1997) 2 *EFA Review* 437.

HILL, C., "The Capabilities-Expectations Gap, or Conceptualising the European International Role" (1993) 31 *JCMS* 305.

HOLLAND, M. (ed.), *The Future of European Political Cooperation: Essays on Theory and Practice* (London: Macmillan, 1991).

—— *European Union Foreign Policy: from EPC to CFSP. Joint Action and South Africa* (Basingstoke: MacMillan, 1995).

—— (ed.), *Common Foreign and Security Policy. The Record and Reforms* (London: Pinter, 1997).

HOOPER, N., and COX, N., "The European Union KONVER Programme" (1996) 7 *Defence and Peace Economics* 75.

HUFBAUER, G.C., SCHOTT, J.S., and ELLIOTT, K.A., *Economic Sanctions Reconsidered* (2nd edn., Washington, DC: Institute for International Economics, 1992) i and ii.

HURD, D., "Developing the Common Foreign and Security Policy" (1994) 3 *International Affairs* 421.

HUYSMANS, J., "Security! What do you mean? From Concept to Thick Signifier" (1998) 4 *European Journal of International Relations* 226.

IFESTOS, P., *European Political Cooperation—Towards a Framework of Supranational Diplomacy?* (Aldershot: Avebery, 1987).

JACOBS, F.G., "The Completion of the Internal Market v the Incomplete Common Commercial Policy" in Konstadinidis, S.V. (ed.), *The Legal Regulation of the European Community's External Relations after the Completion of the Internal Market* (Aldershot: Dartmouth, 1996) 3.

JACQUÉ, J.-P., "L'Acte unique européen" (1986) 22 *RTDE* 575.

JOHNSTON, R., "U.S. Export Control Policy in the High Performance Computer Sector" (1998) *The Non-Proliferation Review* 44.

JOPP, M., "The Defence Dimension of the European Union: The Role and Performance of the WEU" in Regelsberger, E., de Schoutheete de Tervarent, Ph., and Wessels, W. (eds.), *Foreign Policy of the European Union. From EPC to CFSP and Beyond* (London: Lynne Rienner Publishers, 1996) 153.

JUSTUS LIPSIUS, "The 1996 Intergovernmental Conference" (1995) 20 *ELRev.* 235.

KALEAGASI, B., "A New European Order, the EC, Foreign Policy and Democracy" in Telò M. (ed.), *Vers une nouvelle Europe?* (Brussels: ULB, 1992) 185.

KAPTEYN, P.J.G., and VERLOREN VAN THEMAAT, P., *Introduction to the Law of the European Communities* (3rd edn., London: Kluwer Law International, 1998).

KHERAD, R., "La Reconnaissance des Etats Issus de la Dissolution de la République Socialiste de Yugoslavie par les Membres de l'Union Européenne" (1997) 101 *RGDIP* 663.

KINTIS, A.G., "The EU's Foreign Policy and the War in Former Yugoslavia" in Holland, M. (ed.), *Common Foreign and Security Policy. The Record and Reforms* (London: Pinter, 1997) 148.

KIRSHNER, J., "The Microfoundations of Economic Sanctions" (1997) 6 *Security Studies* 32.

KLABBERS, J., "Presumptive Personality: The European Union in International Law" in Koskenniemi, M. (ed.), *International Law Aspects of the European Union* (The Hague: Kluwer International, 1998) 231.

KONSTADINIDIS, S.V., "The New Face of the Community's External Relations: Recent Developments on Certain Controversial Issues" in Konstadinidis, S.V. (ed.), *The Legal Regulation of the European Community's External Relations after the Completion of the Internal Market* (Aldershot: Dartmouth, 1996) 19.

KOUTRAKOS, P., "Exports of Dual-use Goods Under the Law of the European Union" (1998) 23 *ELRev.* 235.

—— "EC Law and Equal Treatment in the Armed Forces" (2000) 25 *ELRev.* 433.

KRENZLER, H.-G. and SCHNEIDER, H.C, "The Question of Consistency" in Regelsberger, E., de Schoutheete de Tervarent, P., and Wessels, W. (eds.), *Foreign Policy of the European Union. From EPC to CFSP and Beyond* (London: Lynne Rienner Publishers, 1996) 133.

KUYPER, P.J., "Sanctions against Rhodesia the EEC and the Implementation of General International Legal Rules" (1975) 12 *CMLRev.* 231.

—— "International Legal Aspects of Economic Sanctions" in Sarcevic, P., and Van Houtte, H. (eds.), *Legal Issues in International Trade* (London: Kluwer Law International, 1990) 145.

—— "European Economic Community" in Meessen, K.M. (ed.), *International Law of Export Control: Jurisdictional Issues,* (London: Graham and Trotman, 1992) 57.

—— "Trade Sanctions, Security and Human Rights and Commercial Policy" in Maresceau, M. (ed.), *The European Community's Commercial Policy after 1992: The Legal Dimension* (Deventer: Kluwer Law International, 1993) 387.

LACHMANN, P., "International Legal Personality of the EC: Capacity and Competence" (1984) 1 *LIEI* 3.

LANGRISH, S., "The Treaty of Amsterdam: Selected Highlights" (1998) 23 *ELRev.* 3.

LATHAM, A,. and BOW, B., "Multilateral Export Control Regimes" (1998) 53 *International Journal* 465.

LAWRENCE, P., "European security: A new era of crisis?" in Bideleux, R., and Taylor, R. (eds.), *European Integration and Disintegration. East and West* (London: Routledge, 1996) 46.

LHOEST, O., "La production et le commerce des armes, et l'article 223 du Traité instituant la Communauté Européenne" (1993) 26 *RBDI* 176.

LOUIS, J.-V., "L'efficacité des Moyens de Pressions" [1984–85] XVIII *RBDI* 122 at 129.

—— "Les relations extérieures de l'Union européenne: unité ou complémentarité" (1994) 4 *Revue du Marché Unique Européen* 5.

MACLEOD, I., HENDRY, I.D., and HYETT, S., *The External Relations of the European Communities* (Oxford: Clarendon Press, 1996).

MARTIN, J.M.F., *The Public Procurement Rules: A Critical Analysis* (Oxford: Clarendon Press, 1996).

MATTERA, A., "La politique communautaire des marchés publics: necessité ou souci de perfectionnisme?" (1996) 4 *Revue du Marché de l'Union Européenne* 9.

MCCUTCHEON, J.P., "The Irish Supreme Court, European Political Co-operation and the Single European Act" (1988) 2 *LIEI* 93.

MCDONAGH, B., *Original Sin in a Brave New World: The Paradox of Europe* (Dublin: Institute of European Affairs, 1998).

MCGEE, R., "Trade Embargoes, Sanctions and Blockades. Some Overlooked Human Rights Issues" (1998) 32 *JWT* 139.

MCGOLDRICK, D., "Yugoslavia—The Responses of the International Community and of International Law" (1996) 49 *Current Legal Problems* 375.

—— *International Relations Law of the European Union* (London: Longman, 1997).

MENGOZZI, P., "Trade in Services and Commercial Policy" in Maresceau, M. (ed.), *The European Community's Commercial Policy after 1992: The Legal Dimension* (Deventer: Kluwer, 1993) 223.

MISCHO, J., "Les efforts en vue d'organiser sur le plan juridique la coopération des Etats membres de la Communauté en matière de politique étrangère" in Capotorti (ed.), *Du droit international de l'intégration: liber amicorum Pierre Pescatore* (Baden-Baden: Nomos, 1987) 441.

MONAR, J., "The European Union's Foreign Affairs System after the Treaty of Amsterdam: A 'Strengthened Capacity for External Action'?" (1997) 2 *EFA Review* 413.

——"The Finances of the Union's Intergovernmental Pillars: Tortuous Experiments with the Community Budget" (1997) 35 *JCMS* 57.

——"Mostar: Three Lessons for the European Union" (1997) 2 *EFA Review* 1.

——"The Financial Dimension of the CFSP" in Holland, M. (ed.), *Common Foreign and Security Policy. The Record and Reforms* (London: Pinter, 1997).

MUELLER, H., and VAN DASSEN, L., "From Cacophony to Joint Action: Successes and Shortcomings of the European Nuclear Non-Proliferation Policy" in Holland, M. (ed.), *Common Foreign and Security Policy. The Record and Reforms* (London: Pinter, 1997) 52.

MUELLERSON, R., "NATO Enlargement and the NATO-Russian Founding Act: the Interplay of Law and Politics" (1998) 47 *ICLQ* 192.

MURPHY, D.T., "The European Union's Common Foreign and Security Policy: It is Not Far From Maastricht to Amsterdam" (1998) 31 *Vanderbilt Journal of Transnational Law* 871.

MURPHY, F,. and GRAS, A., "L'Affaire *Crotty*: La Cour Supreme d'Irlande Rejette l'Acte Unique Européen" (1988) 24 *CDE* 276.

NENTWICH, M., and FALKNER, G., "The Treaty of Amsterdam: Towards a New Institutional Balance" (1997) 1 *EIoP* No 15.

NEUNREITHER, K.-H., "The European Parliament: An Emerging Political Role?" in Edwards, G., and Regelsberger, E. (eds.), *Europe's Global Links. The European Community and Inter-Regional Cooperation* (London: St. Martin's, 1990) 169.

NUTTALL, S., "European Political Co-operation and the Single European Act" (1985) 5 *YEL* 203.

——*European Political Cooperation* (Oxford: Clarendon Press, 1992).

——"The Institutional Network and the Instruments of Actions" in Rummel, R. (ed.), *Toward Political Union: Planning a Common Foreign and Security Policy in the European Community* (Baden-Baden: Nomos, 1992) 55.

——"The EC and Yugoslavia—Deus ex Machina or Machina sine Deo" (1994) 32 *JCMS* 25.

——"The Commission and Foreign Policy-making" in Edwards, G., and Spence, D. (eds.), *The European Commission* (London: Cartermill, 1995) 287.

O'KEEFFE, D., and SCHERMERS, H.G. (eds.), *Mixed Agreements* (Deventer: Kluwer Law Inetrnational, 1983).

OBRADOVIC, D., "Repatriation of Powers in the European Community" (1997) 34 *CMLRev.* 59.

OLIVEIRA, A., annotation on Case C–170/96, *Commission v. Council (Airport transit visas)* (1999) 36 *CMLRev.* 149.

OLIVER, P., *Free Movement of Goods in the European Community* (3rd edn., London: European Law Centre, 1996).

OUCHTERLONY, T., "The European Communities and the Council of Europe" (1984) 1 *LIEI* 59.

PASSAS, A., "On the Ratification of the Single European Act: A Dialogue which Did Not Take Place" (1988) 23–24 *Theseis* 99 (in Greek).

PEERS, S., "National Security and European Law" (1996) 16 *YEL* 363.

PERRAKIS, S., "L'incidence de l'Acte Unique Européen sur la Coopération des Douze en Matière de Politique Etrangère" (1988) XXXIV *AFDI* 807.

PERRONI, F., "Le processus de paix au Proche-Orient et l'Union européenne" [1997] *Revue du Marché Commun et de l'Union Européenne* 318.

PETITE, M., "The Treaty of Amsterdam", Harvard Jean Monnet Paper 98/2.

PETRICCIONE, M., "The Common European Export Control Regime and How to Improve It", speech delivered at the University of Muenster/Westfalen, November 1998 (europa.eu.int/comm/dg01/dualuse5.htm).

PIJPERS, A., REGELSBERGER, E., and WESSELS, W., "A Common Foreign Policy for Western Europe?" in Pijpers, A. Regelsberger, E., and Wessels, W. (eds.), *European Political Co-operation in the 1980s: A Common Foreign Policy for Western Europe?* (Dordrecht: Nijhoff, 1988) 259.

PLIAKOS, A.D., "La nature juridique de l'Union européenne" (1993) 29 *RTDE* 187.

PUGH, M., "Combating the Arms Proliferation Problem-Time to Embark on an Integrated Approach" (1994) 42 *NATO Review* 24.

RAMCHARAN, B.G. (ed.), *The International Conference on the Former Yugoslavia* (The Hague: Kluwer Law International, 1997) i and ii.

REGELSBERGER, E., and WESSELS, W., "The CFSP Institutions and Procedures: A Third Way for the Second Pillar" (1996) 1 *EFA Review* 29.

REMACLE, E., *La politique étrangère européenne: de Maastricht à la Yugoslavie* (Brussels: GRIP dossier, 1992).

RÉSEAU, V., *L'Union européenne et les organisations internationales* (Brussels: Bruylant et Editions de l'Université de Bruxelles, 1997).

RICH, R., "Recognition of States: The Collapse of Yugoslavia and the Soviet Union" (1993) 4 *EJIL* 36.

ROGERS, E.S., "Using Economic Sanctions to Control Regional Conflicts" (1996) 5 *Security Studies* 43.

SACK, J., "The European Community's Membership of International Organizations" (1995) 32 *CMLRev.* 1227.

SALMON, T.C., "Testing times for European political cooperation: the Gulf and Yugoslavia, 1990–1992" [1992] *International Affairs* 233.

SCHARF, M.P,. and DOROSIN, J.L., "Interpreting UN Sanctions: the Rulings and Role of the Yugoslavia Sanctions Committee" (1993) 19 *Brooklyn Journal of International Law* 771.

SHAW, J., "The Treaty of Amsterdam: Challenges of Flexibility and Legitimacy" (1998) 4 *ELJ* 63.

SKOENS, E., "Western Europe: Internationalisation of the Arms Industry" in Wulf, H. (ed.), *Arms Industry Limited* (Oxford: OUP, 1993) 160.

SMIT, H., and HERZOG, P.E., *The Law of the European Community—A Commentary on the EEC Treaty* (New York: Matthew Bender, 1996).

SMITH, C.J., "Conflict in the Balkans and the Possibility of a European Union Common Foreign and Security Policy" (1996) XIII/2 *International Relations* 1.

SPEAR, J., "Arms and Arms Control" in White, B. Little, R., and Smith, M. (eds.), *Issues in World Politics* (London: MacMillan, 1997) 111.

SPERLING, J., and KIRCHNER, E., "Economic Security and the Problem of Cooperation in Post-Cold War Europe" (1998) 24 *Review of International Studies* 221.

STANGOS, P.N., "La Communauté et les Etats membres face à la crise yougoslave" in Telò, M. (ed.), *Vers une nouvelle Europe?* (Brussels: ULB, 1992) 177.

STAVRIDIS, S., "The Democratic Control of the CFSP" in Holland, M. (ed.), *Common Foreign and Security Policy. The Record and Reforms* (London: Pinter, 1997).

—— and HILL, C. (eds,), *Domestic Sources of Foreign Policy* (Oxford: Berg Publishers, 1996).

STEFANOU, C., and XANTHAKI, H., *A Legal and Political Interpretation of Articles 224 and 225 of the Treaty of Rome: The Former Yugoslav Republic of Macedonia Cases* (Aldershot: Dartmouth and Ashgate, 1997).

STEIN, R., "European Political Cooperation (EPC) as a Component of the European Foreign Affairs System" (1983) 43 *ZaoRV* 49.

STEPHANOU, C.A., "The Legal Nature of the European Union" in Emiliou, N., and O'Keeffe, D. (eds.), *Legal Aspects of Integration in the European Union* (London: Kluwer Law International, 1997) 171.

STURMA, P., "La participation de la Communauté Européenne à des 'sanctions' internationales" [1993] *RMC* 250.

TAYLOR, T., "Conventional Arms: The Drives to Export" in Taylor, T., and Ryukichi, I. (eds.), *Security Challenges for Japan and Europe in a Post—Cold War. Vol. III: The Defence Trade. Demand, Supply and Control* (London: Royal Institute for International Affairs and Institute for International Relations, 1994) 95.

—— "West European Security and Defence Cooperation: Maastricht and Beyond" (1994) 70 *International Affairs* 1.

—— (ed.), *Reshaping European Defence* (London: Royal Institute of International Affairs, 1994).

TEMPLE LANG, J., "The Irish Court Case which delayed the Single European Act: *Crotty v. An Taoiseach and Others*" (1987) 24 *CMLRev.* 709.

—— "Community Constitutional Law: Article 5 EEC Treaty" (1990) 27 *CMLRev.* 645.

—— "The Core of the Constitutional Law of the Community—Article 5 EC" in Gormley, L. (ed.), *Current and Future Perspectives on EC Competition Law. A Tribute to Professor M.R. Mok* (London: Kluwer Law International, 1997) 41.

TIETJE, C., "The Concept of Coherence in the Treaty on European Union and the Common Foreign and Security Policy" (1997) 2 *EFA Review* 211.

TIMMERMANS, C.W.A., "Communautés européennes et sanctions internationales—Une Réponse à J. Verhoeven" [1984–85] *RBDI* 96.

—— "The Uneasy Relationship Between the Communities and the Second Union Pillar: Back to the 'Plan Fouchet'?" (1996) 1 *LIEI* 61.

—— "General Institutional Questions: the Effectiveness and Simplification of Decision-Making" in Winter, J.A., Curtin, D.M., Kellermann, A.E., and de Witte, B. (eds.), *Reforming the Treaty on European Union—The Legal Debate* (The Hague; London: Kluwer Law International, 1996) 133.

TOXOPEUS, R., "The Greek Embargo and Articles 224 and 225 EEC—A Political Question Looked At From a Juridical Point of View" (1996) 49 *Revue hellenique de droit international* 187.

TRIDIMAS, T., *The General Principles of EC Law* (Oxford: OUP, 1999).

—— and EECKHOUT, P., "The External Competence of the Community and the Case-Law of the Court of Justice: Principle versus Pragmatism" (1994) 14 *YEL* 143.

TRYBUS, M., "European Defence Procurement: Towards a Comprehensive Approach" (1998) 4 *EPL* 11.

—— *European Defence Procurement Law: International and National Procurement Systems as Models for a Liberalised Defence Procurement Market in Europe* (The Hague: Kluwer Law International, 1999).

TSAKALOYANNIS, P. (ed.), *The Reactivation of the WEU: Its effects on the EC and its Institutions* (Maastricht: EIPA, 1985).

—— *The European Union as a Security Community: Problems and Prospects*, (Baden-Baden: Nomos, 1996).

TSOUKALIS, L., "Looking into the Crystal Ball" in Tsoukalis, L. (ed.), *The European Community, Past, Present and Future* (Oxford: Blackwell, 1983) 229.

UETA, T., "The Stability Pact: From the Balladur Initiative to the EU Joint Action" in Holland, M. (ed.), *Common Foreign and Security Policy. The Record and Reforms* (London: Pinter, 1997) 92.

VAN BERGEIJK, P.A.G., *Economic Diplomacy, Trade and Commercial Policy. Positive and Negative Sanctions in a New World Order* (Aldershot: Edward Elgar, 1995).

VAN DEN BROEK, H., "Challenges Facing the European Defence Industry: A Contribution for Action at European Level", speech delivered to the Symposium on One European Defence Industry, The Hague, 17 October 1996.

VAN SCHERPENBERG, J., "Transatlantic Competition and European Defence Industries: A New Look at the Trade–Defence Linkage" (1997) 73 *International Affairs* 99.

VAN STADEN, A., "After Maastricht: Explaining the Movement towards a Common European Defence Policy" in Carlsnaes, W., and Smith, S. (eds), *European Foreign Policy—The EC and Changing Perspectives in Europe* (London: SAGE, 1994) 138.

VEDDER, C., and FOLZ, H.-P., annotation on Case C–124/95, *The Queen, ex parte Centro-Com Srl* v. *HM Treasury and Bank of England* and Case C–177/95 *Ebony Maritime SA and Loten Navigation Co. Ltd.* v *Prefetto della Provinvia di Brindisi and Ministero dell'Interno* (1998) 35 *CMLRev.* 209.

VERHOEVEN, J., "Sanctions internationales et Communautés Européennes—A propos de l'affair des iles Falkland (Malvinas)" [1984] *CDE* 259.

—— "Communautés Européennes et sanctions internationales" (1984–1985) XVIII *RBDI* 79.

VERLOREN VAN THEMAAT, P., "The Internal Powers of the Community and the Union" in Winter, J.A., Curtin, D.M., Kellermann, A.E., and de Witte, B. (eds.), *Reforming the Treaty on European Union—The Legal Debate* (The Hague; London: Kluwer Law International, 1996) 249.

VON BOGDANDY, A., and NETTESHEIM, M., "Ex Pluribus Unum: Fusion of the European Communities into the European Union" (1996) 2 *ELJ* 267.

WALCH, J., "L'européanisation de l'OTAN" [1997] *Revue du Marché commun et de l'Union européenne* 238.

WALLACE, W., and ALLEN, D., "Political Cooperation: Procedure as Substitute for Policy" in Wallace, W., Webb, C., and Wallace, H. (eds.), *Policy Making in the European Communities* (Chichester: John Wiley, 1977) 227.

WEATHERILL, S., *Law and Integration in the European Union*, (Oxford: Clarendon Press, 1995).

WEILER, J.H.H., "The European Parliament and Foreign Affairs: External Relations of the European Economic Community" in Cassese, A. (ed.), *Parliamentary Control over Foreign Policy* (Alphen and Rijn: Sijthoff & Noordhoff, 1980) 151.

—— "Neither Unity Nor Three Pillars—The Trinity Structure of the Treaty on European Union" in Monar, J., Ungerer, W., and Wessels, W. (eds.), *The Maastricht Treaty on European Union. Legal Complexity and Political Dynamics* (Brussels: European Interuniversity Press, 1993) 49.

—— "Editorial: Amsterdam, Amsterdam" (1997) 3 *EJIL* 309.

——and Wessels, W., "EPC and the Challenge of Theory" in Pijpers, A., Regelsberger, E., and Wessels, W. (eds.), *European Political Co-operation in the 1980s: a common foreign policy for Western Europe?* (Dordrecht: Nijhoff, 1988) 229.

WESSEL, R. A., "The International Legal Status of the European Union" (1997) 2 *EFA Review* 109.

WESSELS, W., "EC-Europe: An Actor *Sui Generis* in the International System" in Nelson, B., Roberts, D., and Weit, W. (eds.), *The European Community in the 1990s: Economics, politics, Defence* (Oxford: Berg Publishers, 1992) 161.

——"Rationalizing Maastricht: The Search for an Optimal Strategy of the New Europe" (1994) 70 *International Affairs* 445.

WHEATON, J.B., "Defence Procurement and the European Community: The Legal Provisions" (1992) 1 *Public Procurement Law Review* 432.

WHEELER, N.J., and DUNNE, T., "Good International Citizenship: A Third Way for British Foreign Policy?" (1998) 74 *International Affairs* 847.

WILLAERT, P., "Les sanctions économiques contre la Rhodésie (1965–1979)" (1984–1985) XVIII *RBDI* 216.

——and MARQUÉS-RUIZ, C., "Vers une politique étrangère et de securité commune: état des lieux" (1995) 3 *Révue du Marché Unique Européen* 35.

WINN, N., "The Proof of the Pudding Is In the Eating: The European Union 'Joint Action' As an Effective Foreign Policy Instrument?" (1997) XIII/6 *International Relations* 19.

WOODLIFFE, J., "The Evolution of a New NATO for a New Europe" (1998) 47 *ICLQ* 174.

WULF, H., "Arms Industry Limited: The Turning Point in the 1990s" in Wulf, H. (ed.), *Arms Industry Limited* (Oxford: OUP, 1993) 3.

Index